Effective Machine Learning Teams
Best Practices for ML Practitioners

David Tan, Ada Leung, and David Colls

Beijing · Boston · Farnham · Sebastopol · Tokyo

Effective Machine Learning Teams

by David Tan, Ada Leung, and David Colls

Published by O'Reilly Media, Inc., 1005 Gravenstein Highway North, Sebastopol, CA 95472.

O'Reilly books may be purchased for educational, business, or sales promotional use. Online editions are also available for most titles (*https://oreilly.com*). For more information, contact our corporate/institutional sales department: 800-998-9938 or *corporate@oreilly.com*.

Acquisitions Editor: Nicole Butterfield	**Indexer:** Judith McConville
Development Editor: Melissa Potter	**Interior Designer:** David Futato
Production Editor: Gregory Hyman	**Cover Designer:** Karen Montgomery
Copyeditor: Nicole Taché	**Illustrator:** Kate Dullea
Proofreader: M & R Consultants Corporation	

March 2024:   First Edition

Revision History for the First Edition

2024-02-29:   First Release

See *https://oreilly.com/catalog/errata.csp?isbn=9781098144630* for release details.

978-1-098-14463-0

[LSI]

Table of Contents

Part I.   Product and Delivery

Part II.   Engineering

Part III.   Teams

Preface

It was 9:25 p.m. and the soft glow of Dana's computer screen glared into her bleary eyes as she logged on to continue fixing an error—red pipelines and countless open tabs filling her screen. She had eaten dinner and finished her everyday chores, but her mind wasn't really there—it was in a few places, in fact.

It had been an intense day, scattered between long training runs and back-and-forth messages with the support team on customer queries about why the model denied their loan applications. She was in and out of the depths of debugging why the model's performance just wouldn't improve, despite various tweaks to the data and model architecture. The occasional stack traces only made things worse.

She was tired, and the tangled heap of uncommitted code changes sitting on her local machine added to the latent cognitive load that was bubbling over in her head. But she had to keep going—her team had already missed the initial release date by four months and the executives' impatience was showing. What made things worse was a fear that her job might be on the line. One in ten employees in her company—several of whom she knew—were laid off in the latest round of cost-cutting measures.

Everyone on her team was well-meaning and capable, but they were getting bogged down every day in a quagmire of tedious testing, anxiety-laden production deployments, and wading through illegible and brittle code. After a few months of toil, they were all worn down. They were doing their level best, but it felt like they were building a house without a foundation—things kept falling apart.

Many individuals begin their machine learning (ML) journey with great momentum and gain confidence quickly, thanks to the growing ecosystem of tools, techniques, tutorials, and community of ML practitioners. However, when we graduate beyond the controlled environment of tutorial notebooks and Kaggle competitions into the space of real-world problems, messy data, interconnected systems, and people with varied objectives, many of us inevitably struggle to realize the potential of ML in practice.

When we peel back the glamorous claims of data science being the sexiest job, we often see ML practitioners mired in burdensome manual work, complex and brittle codebases, and frustration from Sisyphean ML experiments that never see the light of day in production.

In 2019, it was reported that 87% of data science projects never make it to production (*https://oreil.ly/xy9Xi*). According to Algorithmia's 2021 Enterprise AI/ML Trends (*https://oreil.ly/HP6Qh*), even among companies that have successfully deployed ML models in production, 64% of survey respondents say it takes more than a month to deploy a new model, an increase from 56% in 2020. Algorithmia also found that 38% of organizations surveyed are spending more than 50% of their data scientists' time on model deployment.

These barriers impede—or, in some cases, even prevent—ML practitioners from applying their expertise in ML to deliver on the value and promise of AI for customers and businesses. But the good news is it doesn't have to be this way. In the past few years, we have had the privilege to work on various data and ML projects, and to collaborate with ML practitioners from multiple industries. While there are barriers and pains, as we have outlined above, there are also better paths, practices, and systems of work that allow ML practitioners to reliably deliver ML-enabled products into the hands of customers.

That's what this book is all about. We'll draw from our experience to distill a set of enduring principles and practices that consistently help us to effectively deliver ML solutions in the real world. These practices work because they're based on taking a holistic approach to building ML systems. They go beyond just ML to create essential feedback loops in various subsystems (e.g., product, engineering, data, delivery processes, team topologies) and enable teams to fail quickly and safely, experiment rapidly, and deliver reliably.

Who This Book Is For

> Whether you think you can, or you think you can't—you're right.
> —Henry Ford

Whether you're a ML practitioner in academia, an enterprise, a start-up, a scale-up, or consulting, the principles and practices in this book can help you and your team become more effective in delivering ML solutions. In line with the cross-functional nature of ML delivery techniques that we detail in this book, we address the concerns and aspirations of multiple roles in teams doing ML:

Data scientists and ML engineers
 The job scope of a data scientist has evolved over the past few years. Instead of purely focusing on modeling techniques and data analysis, we're seeing expectations (implicit or explicit) that one needs to possess the capabilities of a full-stack data scientist (*https://oreil.ly/jV7EP*): data wrangling, ML engineering, MLOps, and business case formulation, among others. This book elaborates on

the capabilities necessary for data scientists and ML engineers to design and deliver ML solutions in the real world.

In the past, we've presented the principles, practices, and hands-on exercises in this book to data scientists, ML engineers, PhD students, software engineers, quality analysts, and product managers, and we've consistently received positive feedback. The ML practitioners we've worked with in the industry have said that they benefited from improvement in feedback cycles, flow, and reliability that comes from practices such as automated testing and refactoring. Our takeaway is that *there is a desire* from the ML community to learn these skills and practices, and this is our attempt to scale the sharing of this knowledge.

Software engineers, infrastructure and platform engineers, architects
When we run workshops on the topics we cover in this book, we often come across software engineers, infrastructure and platform engineers, and architects working in the ML space. While capabilities from the software world (e.g., infrastructure-as-code, deployment automation, automated testing) are necessary in designing and delivering ML solutions in the real world, they are also insufficient. To build reliable ML solutions, we need to widen the software lens and look at other principles and practices—such as ML model tests, dual-track delivery, continuous discovery, and ML governance—to handle challenges that are unique to ML.

Product managers, delivery managers, engineering managers
We set ourselves up for failure if we think that we need only data scientists and ML engineers to build an ML product. In contrast, our experience tells us that teams are most effective when they are cross-functional and equipped with the necessary ML, data, engineering, product, and delivery capabilities.

In this book, we elaborate on how you can apply Lean delivery practices and systems thinking to create structures that help teams to focus on the voice of the customer, shorten feedback loops, experiment rapidly and reliably, and iterate toward building the right thing. As W. Edwards Deming (*https://oreil.ly/eUxHc*) once said, "A bad system will beat a good person every time." So, we share principles and practices that will help teams create structures that optimize information flow, reduce waste (e.g., handoffs, dependencies), and improve value.

If we've done our job right, this book will invite you to look closely at how things have "always been done" in ML and in your teams, to reflect on how well they are working for you, and to consider better alternatives. Read this book with an open mind, and—for the engineering-focused chapters—with an open code editor. As Peter M. Senge (*https://oreil.ly/9HEwI*) said in his book *The Fifth Discipline* (Doubleday), "Taking in information is only distantly related to real learning. It would be nonsensical to say, 'I just read a great book about bicycle riding—I've now learned that.'" We encourage you to try out the practices in your teams, and we hope you'll experience firsthand the value that they bring in real-world projects.

Approach this book with a continuous improvement mindset, not a perfectionist mindset. There is no perfect project where everything works perfectly without challenges. There will always be complexity and challenges (and we know a healthy amount of challenge is essential for growth), but the practices in this book will help you minimize *accidental* complexity so that you can focus on the *essential* complexity of your ML solutions and on delivering value responsibly.

How This Book Is Organized

Chapter 1, "Challenges and Better Paths in Delivering ML Solutions", is a distillation of the entire book. We explore high-level and low-level reasons for why and how ML projects fail. We then lay out a more reliable path for delivering value in ML solutions by adopting Lean delivery practices across five key disciplines: product, delivery, machine learning, engineering, and data.

In the remaining chapters, we describe practices of effective ML teams and ML practitioners. In Part I, "Product and Delivery", we elaborate on practices in other subsystems that are necessary for delivering ML solutions, such as product thinking and Lean delivery. In Part II, "Engineering", we cover practices that help ML practitioners when implementing and delivering solutions (e.g., automated testing, refactoring, using the code editor effectively, continuous delivery, and MLOps). In Part III, "Teams", we explore the dynamics that impact the effectiveness of ML teams, such as trust, shared progress, diversity, and also engineering effectiveness techniques that help you build high-performing teams. We also address common challenges that organizations face when scaling ML practices beyond one or two teams, and share techniques on team topologies, interaction modes, and leadership to help teams overcome these scaling challenges.

Part I: Product and Delivery

Chapter 2, "Product and Delivery Practices for ML Teams"
   We discuss product discovery techniques that help us identify opportunities, test market and technology hypotheses rapidly, and converge on viable solutions. By starting with the most valuable problems and feasible solutions, we set ourselves up for success during delivery. We also go through delivery practices that help us shape, size, and sequence work to create a steady stream of value. We address the unique challenges resulting from the experimental and high-uncertainty nature of certain ML problems, and discuss techniques such as the dual-track delivery model that help us learn more quickly in shorter cycles. Finally, we cover techniques for measuring critical aspects of ML projects and share techniques for identifying and managing project risks.

Part II: Engineering

Chapters 3 and 4: Effective dependency management

Here, we describe principles and practices—along with a hands-on example that you can code along with—for creating consistent, reproducible, secure, and production-like runtime environments for running your code. When we hit the ground running and start delivering solutions, you'll see how the practices in this chapter will enable you and your teammates to "check out and go" and create consistent environments effortlessly, instead of getting trapped in dependency hell.

Chapters 5 and 6: Automated testing for ML systems

These chapters provide you with a rubric for testing components of your ML solution—be they software tests, model tests, or data tests. We demonstrate how automated tests help us shorten our feedback cycles and reduce the tedious effort of manual testing, or worse, fixing production defects that slipped through the cracks of manual testing. We describe the limits of the software testing paradigm on ML models, and how ML fitness functions and behavioral tests can help us scale the automated testing of ML models. We also cover techniques for comprehensively testing large language models (LLMs) and LLM applications.

Chapter 7, "Supercharging Your Code Editor with Simple Techniques"

We'll show you how to configure your code editor (PyCharm or VS Code) to help you code more effectively. After we've configured our IDE in a few steps, we'll go through a series of keyboard shortcuts that can help you to automate refactoring, automatically detect and fix issues, and navigate your codebase without getting lost in the weeds, among other things.

Chapter 8, "Refactoring and Technical Debt Management"

In this chapter, we draw from the wisdom of software design to help us design readable, testable, maintainable, and evolvable code. In the spirit of "learning by doing," you'll see how we can take a problematic, messy, and brittle notebook and apply refactoring techniques to iteratively improve our codebase to a modular, tested, and readable state. You'll also learn techniques that can help you and your team make technical debt visible and take actions to keep it at a healthy level.

Chapter 9, "MLOps and Continuous Delivery for ML (CD4ML)"

We'll articulate an expansive view of what MLOps and CI/CD (continuous integration and continuous delivery) really entails. Spoiler alert: It's more than automating model deployments and defining CI pipelines. We lay out a blueprint for the unique shape of CI/CD for ML projects and walk through how you can set up each component in this blueprint to create reliable ML solutions and free up your teammates from repetitive and undifferentiated labor so that they can focus on other higher-value problems. We'll also look at how CD4ML serves as a risk-control mechanism to help teams uphold standards for ML governance and Responsible AI.

Part III: Teams

Chapter 10, "Building Blocks of Effective ML Teams"
In this chapter, we go beyond the mechanics to understand the interpersonal factors that enable good practices in effective teams. We'll describe principles and practices that help create a safe, human-centric, and growth-oriented team. We'll examine topics like trust, communication, shared goals, purposeful progress, and diversity in teams. We'll share some antipatterns to watch for and some tactics that you can use to nurture a culture of collaboration, effective delivery, and learning.

Chapter 11, "Effective ML Organizations"
This chapter introduces various shapes for ML teams and addresses the common challenges that organizations face when scaling their ML practice to multiple teams. We draw from and adapt strategies discussed in *Team Topologies* (IT Revolution Press) and outline unique structures, principles, and practices that help teams find a balance between flow of work and concentrated expertise, collaboration, and autonomy. We evaluate the benefits and limits of these structures and offer guidance for their evolution to meet the organization's needs. We conclude by discussing the role of intentional leadership and its supporting practices in shaping agile, responsive ML organizations.

Additional Thoughts

We'd like to touch on four things before we wrap up the Preface.

First, we want to acknowledge that ML is more than just supervised learning and LLMs. We can also solve data-intensive (and even data-poor) problems using other optimization techniques (e.g., reinforcement learning [*https://oreil.ly/7PjY6*], operations research [*https://oreil.ly/ZezrC*], simulation [*https://oreil.ly/UVhfB*]). In addition, ML is not a silver bullet and some problems can be solved without ML. Even though we've chosen a supervised learning problem (loan default prediction) as an anchoring example in the code samples throughout the book, the principles and practices are useful beyond supervised learning. For example, the chapters on automated testing, dependency management, and code editor productivity are useful even in reinforcement learning. The product and delivery practices outlined in Chapter 2 are useful for exploratory and delivery phases of any product or problem space.

Second, as Generative AI and LLMs entered the public consciousness and product roadmaps of many organizations, we and our colleagues have had the opportunity to work with organizations to ideate, shape, and deliver products that leverage

Generative AI. While LLMs have led to a paradigm shift in how we steer or constrain models toward their desired functionality, the fundamentals of Lean product delivery and engineering haven't changed. In fact, the fundamental tools and techniques in this book have helped us to test assumptions early, iterate quickly, and deliver reliably—thereby maintaining agility and reliability even when dealing with the complexities inherent in Generative AI and LLMs.

Third, on the role of culture: ML effectiveness and the practices in this book are not—and cannot be—a solo effort. That's why we've titled the book Effective Machine Learning *Teams*. You can't be the only person writing tests, for instance. In organizations that we've worked with, individuals become most effective when there is a cultural alignment (within the team, department, and even organization) on these Lean and agile practices. This doesn't mean that you need to boil the ocean with the entire organization; it's just not enough to go it alone. As Steve Jobs once said, "Great things in business are never done by one person. They're done by a team of people."

Finally, this book is not about productivity (how to ship as many features, stories, or code as possible), nor is it about efficiency (how to ship features, stories, or code at the fastest possible rate). Rather, it's about effectiveness—how to build the right product rapidly, reliably, and responsibly. This book is about finding balance through movement and moving in effective ways.

The principles and practices in this book have consistently helped us to successfully deliver ML solutions, and we are confident that they will do the same for you.

Conventions Used in This Book

The following typographical conventions are used in this book:

Italic
Indicates new terms, URLs, email addresses, filenames, and file extensions.

`Constant width`
Used for program listings, as well as within paragraphs to refer to program elements such as variable or function names, databases, data types, environment variables, statements, and keywords.

`Constant width bold`
Used to call attention to snippets of interest in code blocks.

 This element signifies a general note.

This element indicates a warning or caution.

Using Code Examples

Supplemental material (code examples, exercises, etc.) is available for download at:

- *https://github.com/davified/loan-default-prediction*
- *https://github.com/davified/ide-productivity*
- *https://github.com/davified/refactoring-exercise*

If you have a technical question or a problem using the code examples, please send email to *support@oreilly.com*.

This book is here to help you get your job done. In general, if example code is offered with this book, you may use it in your programs and documentation. You do not need to contact us for permission unless you're reproducing a significant portion of the code. For example, writing a program that uses several chunks of code from this book does not require permission. Selling or distributing examples from O'Reilly books does require permission. Answering a question by citing this book and quoting example code does not require permission. Incorporating a significant amount of example code from this book into your product's documentation does require permission.

We appreciate, but generally do not require, attribution. An attribution usually includes the title, author, publisher, and ISBN. For example: "*Effective Machine Learning Teams* by David Tan, Ada Leung, and David Colls (O'Reilly). Copyright 2024 David Tan Rui Guan, Ada Leung Wing Man, and David Colls, 978-1-098-14463-0."

If you feel your use of code examples falls outside fair use or the permission given above, feel free to contact us at *permissions@oreilly.com*.

O'Reilly Online Learning

 For more than 40 years, *O'Reilly Media* has provided technology and business training, knowledge, and insight to help companies succeed.

Our unique network of experts and innovators share their knowledge and expertise through books, articles, and our online learning platform. O'Reilly's online learning platform gives you on-demand access to live training courses, in-depth learning paths, interactive coding environments, and a vast collection of text and video from O'Reilly and 200+ other publishers. For more information, visit *https://oreilly.com*.

How to Contact Us

Please address comments and questions concerning this book to the publisher:

O'Reilly Media, Inc.
1005 Gravenstein Highway North
Sebastopol, CA 95472
800-889-8969 (in the United States or Canada)
707-827-7019 (international or local)
707-829-0104 (fax)
support@oreilly.com
https://www.oreilly.com/about/contact.html

We have a web page for this book, where we list errata, examples, and any additional information. You can access this page at *https://oreil.ly/effective-ml-teams*.

For news and information about our books and courses, visit *https://oreilly.com*.

Find us on LinkedIn: *https://linkedin.com/company/oreilly-media*

Watch us on YouTube: *https://youtube.com/oreillymedia*

Acknowledgments

When we started writing this book, we set out to share a collection of point practices that have helped us in building ML systems. But we ended up with a comprehensive guide that we firmly believe will elevate the common denominator of ML teams and transform how teams shape and deliver ML products. This book would not be possible without many pockets of people who—by their example, word, and actions—have influenced and shaped our approach.

We'd like to thank the wonderful folks at O'Reilly who helped to make this book a reality: Nicole Butterfield, Melissa Potter, Gregory Hyman, Kristen Brown, Nicole Taché, Judith McConville, David Futato, Karen Montgomery, Kate Dullea, and other editors, designers, and staff working behind the scenes to continually refine this book from its conception to production. A massive thanks to our technical reviewers who took the time and effort to pore through more than 300 pages of content and provide thoughtful and candid feedback: Hannes Hapke, Harmeet Kaur Sokhi, Mat Kelcey, and Vishwesh Ravi Shrimali.

From David Tan

Thank you Nhung for being so patient and supportive through the late nights that I spent on this book. I would not have finished this book without your support.

I see something, Jacob and Jonas—a tree! Stay curious always.

Special mention to Jeffrey Lau—your mentoring and duck noodles haven't gone to waste.

Thank you to colleagues at Thoughtworks past and present who have taught me so much about the beauty of asking questions and showing me that it's OK to tread new paths. I tried to name you all, but the list will get too long. You know who you are—a big thank you for being candid, kind, and just plain good at what you do. Special thanks to Sue Visic, Dave Colls, and Peter Barnes for your encouragement and support in writing this book.

Neal Ford: When I reached out to ask some logistical questions about writing a book, you went above and beyond to share your writing process, how to test ideas, and introduced me to Stephen King's and Annie Dillard's ideas on writing. You didn't have to but you did. Thank you for being a multiplier.

It almost goes without saying, but a massive thanks to my coconspirators Ada and Dave. You've elevated the quality and breadth of this book beyond what I could've imagined, and I'm excited to see this guidebook help ML teams and practitioners through our collective experience.

From Ada Leung

I'd like to thank my partner, friends, and family. You know who you are. Your endless encouragement and admiration that I actually coauthored a book (Yeah, I know right?!) reminds me of how cool it is to be in amongst incredibly smart and impressive technologists.

I'd like to also thank my Thoughtworks colleagues I've met along the way, have been inspired by from afar, and have been fortunate enough to be mentored by—your passion and generosity toward knowledge sharing has set the bar high for what good looks like. There isn't a more fitting word to describe this community than the philosophy of *Ubuntu*: I am because we are.

Finally, to my coauthors David and Dave: thank you for your unwavering support throughout this journey. From sharing our ideas and discovering the breadth and overlap of our collective knowledge, I'm reminded of how much I value teamwork and camaraderie. It's been a real joy and privilege.

From David Colls

I'd like to thank my family for putting up with a husband and father writing, reviewing, and researching content for a few months straight, on weekends, during movie nights, and on the basketball sidelines.

I'd like to thank the many Thoughtworks colleagues around the world who have gone before us in writing books and creating transformative perspectives on technology, stoking our determination to do the same, and showing us what good looks like. Closer to home, I'd like to thank all the Australian Thoughtworkers I've worked alongside over more than a decade for broadening my perspectives and enriching me professionally and as a human being.

I'd especially like to thank all those members of the Thoughtworks Australia Data & AI practice who I've had the privilege to work with as we built something new together—there's a little bit of each of you in this book. I'd also like to thank our clients for the trust they place in us to develop new approaches to their biggest opportunities and challenges.

Finally, I'd like to thank my coauthors David and Ada for their expertise and insight, feedback on my ideas, and structured approach to distilling and sharing our knowledge in this book. It has been a pleasure working with you.

## CHAPTER 1

Challenges and Better Paths in Delivering ML Solutions

The most dangerous kind of waste is the waste we do not recognize.

—Shigeo Shingo, leading expert on the Toyota Production System

Not everything that is faced can be changed, but nothing can be changed until it is faced.

—James Baldwin, writer and playwright

Many individuals and organizations start their machine learning (ML) journey with high hopes, but the lived experiences of many ML practitioners tell us that the journey of delivering ML solutions is riddled with traps, detours, and sometimes even insurmountable barriers. When we peel back the hype and the glamorous claims of data science being the sexiest job of the 21st century, we often see ML practitioners bogged down by burdensome manual work; firefighting in production; team silos; and unwieldy, brittle, and complex solutions.

This hinders, or even prevents, teams from delivering value to customers and also frustrates an organization's investments and ambitions in AI. As hype cycles (*https://oreil.ly/mGwWj*) go, many travel past the peak of inflated expectations and crash-land into the trough of disillusionment. We might see some high-performing ML teams move on to the plateau of productivity and wonder if we'll ever get there.

Regardless of your background—be it academia, data science, ML engineering, product management, software engineering, or something else—if you are building products or systems that involve ML, you will inevitably face the challenges that we describe in this chapter. This chapter is our attempt to distill our experience—and the experience of others—in building and delivering ML-enabled products. We hope that these principles and practices will help you avoid unnecessary pitfalls and find a more reliable path for your journey.

We kick off this chapter by acknowledging the dual reality of promise and disappointment in ML in the real world. We then examine both high-level and day-to-day challenges that often cause ML projects to fail. We then outline a better path based on the principles and practices of Lean delivery, product thinking, and agile engineering. Finally, we briefly discuss why these practices are relevant to, and especially to, teams delivering Generative AI products and large language model (LLM) applications. Consider this chapter a miniature representation of the remainder of this book.

ML: Promises and Disappointments

In this section, we look at evidence of continued growth of investments and interest in ML before taking a deep dive into the engineering, product, and delivery bottlenecks that impede the returns on these investments.

Continued Optimism in ML

Putting aside the hype and our individual coordinates on the hype cycle for a moment, ML continues to be a fast-advancing field that provides many techniques for solving real-world problems. Stanford's "AI Index Report 2022" (*https://oreil.ly/ GUC4H*) found that in 2021, global private investment in AI totaled around $94 billion, which is *more than double* the total private investment even in 2019, before the COVID-19 pandemic. McKinsey's "State of AI in 2021" survey (*https://oreil.ly/ylNOs*) indicated that AI adoption was continuing its steady rise: 56% of all respondents reported AI adoption in at least one function, up from 50% in 2020.

The Stanford report also found companies are continuing to invest in applying a diverse set of ML techniques—e.g., natural language understanding, computer vision, reinforcement learning—across a wide array of sectors, such as healthcare, retail, manufacturing, and financial services. From a jobs and skills perspective, Stanford's analysis of millions of job postings since 2010 showed that the demand for ML capabilities has been growing steadily year-on-year in the past decade, even through and after the COVID-19 pandemic.

While these trends are reassuring from an opportunities perspective, they are also highly concerning if we journey ahead without confronting and learning from the challenges that have ensnared us—both the producers and consumers of ML systems—in the past. Let's take a look at these pitfalls in detail.

Why ML Projects Fail

Despite the plethora of chart-topping Kaggle notebooks, it's common for ML projects to fail in the real world. Failure can come in various forms, including:

- Inability to ship an ML-enabled product to production
- Shipping products that customers don't use
- Deploying defective products that customers don't trust
- Inability to evolve and improve models in production quickly enough

Just to be clear—we're not trying to avoid failures. As we all know, failure is as valuable as it is inevitable (*https://oreil.ly/zEvK8*). There's lots that we can learn from failure. The problem arises as the *cost* of failure increases—missed deadlines, unmet business outcomes, and sometimes even collateral damage: harm to humans (*https://oreil.ly/yQJFi*) and loss of jobs and livelihoods (*https://oreil.ly/pybEo*) of many employees who aren't even directly related to the ML initiative.

What we want is to fail in a low-cost and safe way, and often, so that we improve our odds of success for everyone who has a stake in the undertaking. We also want to learn from failures—by documenting and socializing our experiments and lessons learned, for example—so that we don't fail in the same way again and again. In this section, we'll look at some common challenges—spanning product, delivery, and engineering—that reduce our chances of succeeding, and in the next section, we'll explore ways to reduce the costs and likelihood of failure and deliver valuable outcomes more effectively.

Let's start at a high level and then zoom in to look at day-to-day barriers to the flow of value.

High-level view: Barriers to success

Taking a high-level view—i.e., at the level of an ML project or a program of work— we've seen ML projects fail to achieve their desired outcomes due to the following challenges:

Failing to solve the right problem or deliver value for users
> In this failure mode, even if we have all the right engineering practices and "build the thing right," we fail to move the needle on the intended business outcomes because the team didn't "build the right thing." This often happens when the team lacks product management capabilities or lacks alignment with product and business. Without mature product thinking capabilities in a team, it's common for ML teams to overlook human-centered design techniques—e.g., user testing, user journey mapping—to identify the pains, needs, and desires of users.[1]

---

1 It's worth noting that identifying the wrong customer problem to solve is not unique to ML, and any product is susceptible to this.

Challenges in productionizing models

Many ML projects do not see the light of day in production. A 2021 Gartner poll of roughly 200 business and IT professionals found that only 53% of AI projects make it from pilot into production, and among those that succeed, it takes an average of nine months to do so.[2] The challenges of productionizing ML models isn't limited to just compute issues such as model deployments, but can be related to data (e.g., not having inference data available at suitable quality, latency, and distribution in production).

Challenges after productionizing models

Once in production, it's common to see ML practitioners bogged down by toil and tedium that inhibits iterative experimentation and model improvements. In its "2021 Enterprise Trends in Machine Learning" report (*https://oreil.ly/NpeRD*), Algorithmia reported that 64% of companies take *more than one month* to deploy a new model, an increase from 58% as reported in Algorithmia's 2020 report. The report also notes 38% of organizations spend more than 50% of their data scientists' time on deployment—and that only gets worse with scale.

Long or missing feedback loops

During model development, feedback loops are often long and tedious, and this diverts valuable time from important ML product development work. The primary way of knowing if everything works might be to manually run a training notebook or script, wait for it to complete—sometimes waiting hours—and manually wading through logs or printed statements to eyeball some model metrics to determine if the model is still as good as before. This doesn't scale well and more often than not, we are hindered by unexpected errors and quality degradations during development and even in production.

Many models aren't deployed with mechanisms to learn from production—e.g., data collection and labeling mechanisms. Without this feedback loop, teams forgo opportunities to improve model quality through data-centric approaches.

Brittle and convoluted codebases

ML codebases are often full of code smells—e.g., badly named variables, long and convoluted functions, tightly coupled spaghetti code—that make the code difficult to understand and therefore difficult to change. The complexity and the risk of errors and bugs grows exponentially with each feature delivered. Modifying or extending the codebase becomes a daunting task as developers

---

2 As this Gartner survey (*https://oreil.ly/hkDJR*) is a small survey comprising only 200 people, there's likely to be high variance in the number of ML projects that never got delivered across regions, industries, and companies. Take the specific number with a dash of salt and try to relate it to your qualitative experience. Have you personally experienced or heard of ML projects that, even after months of investment, were never shipped to users?

need to unravel the intricacies of the convoluted codebase and related systems or pipelines.

If the ML system lacks automated tests, it becomes even more brittle. In addition, the lack of tests sows the seeds for even more complexity because nobody wants to refactor if it means they might accidentally and unknowingly introduce regressions. This all leads to longer development cycles and reduced productivity.

Data quality issues in production

We'll illustrate this point with an example: A study in the British Medical Journal (*https://oreil.ly/tlJe4*) found that *none* of the hundreds of predictive tools that were developed to help hospitals detect COVID-19 actually worked. There were many reasons for the failure of these models, and one key theme was data quality. There was data leakage (which caused the models to appear better than they really are), mislabeled data, and distributional asymmetry between training data and actual data in production, among other reasons.

To compound the problem, the aforementioned challenges in retraining, reevaluating, retesting, and redeploying models in an automated fashion further inhibit our ability to respond to changing data distributions over time.

Inadequate data security and privacy

Data security and privacy are cross-cutting concerns that should be the responsibility of everyone in the organization, from product teams to data engineering teams and every team in between. In the context of ML, there are several unique data security and privacy challenges that can cause a product to fail. One such challenge is data poisoning, which involves injecting malicious or biased data into the training set to corrupt the model. Recall the famous (or infamous) Microsoft Tay chatbot (*https://oreil.ly/2-HDD*), which was taken down within a day of release because it learned inflammatory and offensive content from users who deliberately attempted to train it to produce such responses. Or more recently with the advent of LLMs, we've seen prompt injection attacks causing custom chatbots to leak users' training data and reveal system prompts (*https://oreil.ly/K8m4C*).

Ethically problematic ML products

One needn't look far to see how ML can go wrong in the wild. For example, you may have heard of Amazon's recruitment tool (*https://oreil.ly/Y3WqW*) that penalized resumes containing the word "women" (Amazon decommissioned the tool within a year of its release). In another example, a benchmark analysis by ProPublica (*https://oreil.ly/yQJFi*) found that an ML system that was used to predict recidivism had *twice as high a false positive rate* for Black defendants as for White defendants, and *twice as high a false negative rate* for White defendants.

Now that we've painted a high-level picture of the reasons that cause ML projects to fail, let's take a look at the day-to-day challenges that make it hard for ML projects to succeed.

Microlevel view: Everyday impediments to success

At the microlevel—i.e., at the level of delivering features in an ML project—there are several bottlenecks that impede our ability to execute on our ideas.

This view is best seen by contrasting a user story in the agile development lifecycle under two conditions: a *low-effectiveness* environment and *a high-effectiveness* environment. In our experience, these roadblocks stem not only from our approaches to ML and engineering, but also from suboptimal collaboration workflows and unplanned work.

Lifecycle of a story in a low-effectiveness environment. Let's journey with Dana—our book's protagonist and ML engineer—in this scenario. The character is fictional but the pain is real:

- Dana starts her day having to deal immediately with alerts for problems in production and customer support queries on why the model behaved in a certain way. Dana's team is already suffering from alert fatigue, which means they often ignore the alerts coming in. This only compounds the problem and the number of daily alerts.

- Dana checks a number of logging and monitoring systems to triage the issue, as there are no aggregated logs across systems. She manually prods the model to find an explanation for why the model produced that particular prediction for that customer. She vaguely remembers that there was a similar customer query last month but cannot find any internal documentation on how to resolve such customer queries.

- Dana sends a reminder on the team chat to ask for a volunteer to review a pull request she created last week, so that it can be merged.

- Finally, Dana resolves the issue and finds some time to code and picks up a task from the team's wallboard.

- The codebase doesn't have any automated tests, so after making some code changes, Dana needs to restart and rerun the entire training script or notebook, wait for the duration of model training—40 minutes in their case—and hope that it runs without errors. She also manually eyeballs some print statements at the end to check that the model metric hasn't declined. Sometimes, the code blows up midway because of an error that slipped in during development.

- Dana wants to take a coffee break but feels guilty for doing so because there's just too much to do. So, she makes a coffee in two minutes and sips it at her desk while working away.

- While coding, Dana received comments and questions on the pull request. For example, one comment was that a particular function was too long and hard to read. Dana then switches contexts, types out a response—without necessarily updating the code—for coding design decisions they made last week, and mentions that she will create a story card to refactor this long function next time.

- After investing two weeks in a solution (without pair programming), she shares it back with the team. The team's engineering lead notes that the solution introduces too much complexity to the codebase and needs to be rewritten. He adds that the story wasn't actually high priority in any case, and there was another story that Dana can look at instead.

Can you imagine how frustrated and demotivated Dana must feel? The long feedback cycles and context switching—between doing ML and other burdensome tasks, such as pull request reviews—limited how much she could achieve. Context switching also had a real cognitive cost (*https://oreil.ly/Haw0v*) that made them feel exhausted and unproductive. They sometimes log on again after office hours because they feel the pressure to finish the work—and there just wasn't enough time in the day to complete them all.

Long feedback loops at each microlevel step lead to an overall increase in cycle time, which leads to fewer experimentation or iteration cycles in a day (see Figure 1-1). Work and effort often move backward and laterally between multiple tasks, which lead to a disrupted state of flow.

Lifecycle of a story in a high-effectiveness environment. Now, let's take a look at how different things can be for Dana in a high-effectiveness environment:

- Dana starts the day by checking the team project management tool and then attends standup where they can pick up a story card. Each story card articulates its business value, which has been validated from a product perspective and provides clarity about what they have to work on with a clear definition of done.

- Dana pairs with a teammate to write code to solve the problem specified in the story card. As they are coding, they help catch each other's blind spots, provide each other with real-time feedback—e.g., a simpler way to solve a particular problem—and share knowledge along the way.

- As they code, each incremental code change is quickly validated within seconds or minutes by running automated tests—both existing tests and new tests that they write. They run the end-to-end ML model training pipeline locally on a small dataset and get feedback on whether everything is still working as expected within a minute.

- If they need to do a full ML model training, they can trigger training on large-scale infrastructure from their local machine with their local code changes, without the need to "push to know if something works." Model training then commences in an environment with the necessary access to production data and scalable compute resources.

- They commit the code change, which passes through a number of automated checks on the continuous integration and continuous delivery (CI/CD) pipeline before triggering full ML model training, which can take between minutes to hours depending on the ML model architecture and the volume of data.

- Dana and her pair focus on their task for a few hours, peppered with regular breaks, coffee, and even walks (separately). They can do this without a tinge of guilt because they know it'll help them work better, and because they have confidence in the predictability of their work.

- When the model training completes, a model deployment pipeline is automatically triggered. The deployment pipeline runs model quality tests and checks if the model is above the quality threshold for a set of specified metrics (e.g., accuracy, precision). If the model is of a satisfactory quality, the newly trained model artifact is automatically packaged and deployed to a preproduction environment, and the CI/CD pipeline also runs post-deployment tests on the freshly deployed artifact.

- When the story card's definition of done is satisfied, Dana informs the team, calls for a 20-minute team huddle to share context with the team, and demonstrates how the solution meets the definition of done. If they had missed anything, any teammate could provide feedback there and then.

- If no further development work is needed, another teammate then puts on the "testing hat" and brings a fresh perspective when testing if the solution satisfies the definition of done. The teammate can do exploratory and high-level testing within a reasonable timeframe because most, if not all, of the acceptance criteria in the new feature have already been tested via automated tests.

- Whenever business wants to, they can release the change gradually to users in production, while monitoring business and operational metrics. Because the team has maintained a good test coverage, when the pipeline is all green, they can deploy the new model to production without any feelings of anxiety.

Dana and her teammates make incremental progress on the delivery plan daily. Team velocity is higher and stabler than in the low-effectiveness environment. Work and effort generally flow forward, and Dana leaves work feeling satisfied and with wind in her hair. Huzzah!

To wrap-up the tale of two velocities, let's zoom out and compare in Figure 1-1 the time it takes to get something done in a high-effectiveness environment (top row) and a low-effectiveness environment (bottom row).

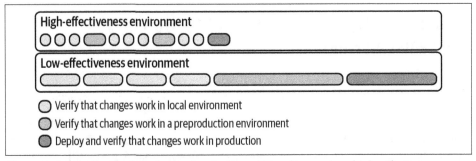

Figure 1-1. Fast feedback cycles underpin the agility of teams in a high-effectiveness environment (source: image adapted from "Maximizing Developer Effectiveness" [https://oreil.ly/tQPgL] by Tim Cochran)

Zooming in a little more, Table 1-1 shows the feedback mechanisms that differentiate high-effectiveness environments from low-effectiveness environments. Each row is a key task in the model delivery lifecycle, and the columns compare their relative feedback cycle times.

Table 1-1. Comparison of feedback mechanisms and time-to-feedback in high- and low-effectiveness environments

Task	Feedback loops and time to feedback for each task (in approximate orders of magnitude)	
	High-effectiveness environment	*Low-effectiveness environment*
Testing if code changes worked as expected	Automated testing (~ seconds to minutes) ●●	Manual testing (~ minutes to hours) ●●●●
Testing if ML training pipeline works end to end	Training smoke test (~ 1 minute) ●●	Full model training (~ minutes to hours, depending on the model architecture) ●●●●●
Getting feedback on code changes	Pair programming (~ seconds to minutes) ●●	Pull request reviews (~ hours to days) ●●●●●●●
Understanding if application is working as expected in production	Monitoring in production (~ seconds - as it happens) ●	Customer complaints (~ days, or longer if not directly reported) ●●●●●●●

Now that we've painted a picture of common pitfalls in delivering ML solutions and a more effective alternative, let's look at how teams can move from a low-effectiveness environment to a high-effectiveness environment.

Is There a Better Way? How Systems Thinking and Lean Can Help

> A bad system will beat a good person every time.
>
> —W. Edwards Deming (*https://oreil.ly/D-lqT*), economist and industrial engineer

In the previous section, we can see Dana in the low-effectiveness environment facing unnecessary toil and rework, which contributes to constant frustration, and possibly ultimately to burnout. The toil, frustration, and burnout that ML practitioners often face indicate that our *system* of work can be improved.

In this section, we'll explore why MLOps alone is insufficient for improving the effectiveness of ML practitioners. We'll put on a systems thinking lens to identify a set of practices required for effective ML delivery. Then we'll look to Lean for principles and practices that can help us operate these subsystems in an interconnected way that reduces waste and maximizes the flow of value.

You Can't "MLOps" Your Problems Away

One reflexive but misguided approach to improving the effectiveness of ML delivery is for organizations to turn to MLOps practices and ML platforms. While they may be necessary, they are definitely not sufficient on their own.

In the world of software delivery, you can't "DevOps" or "platform" your problems away. DevOps helps to optimize and manage one subsystem (relating to infrastructure, deployment, and operations) but other subsystems (e.g., software design, user experience, software delivery lifecycle) are just as important in delivering great products.

Likewise, in ML, *you can't "MLOps" your problems away*. No amount of MLOps practices and platform capabilities can save us from the waste and rework that result from the lack of software engineering practices (e.g., automated testing, well-factored design, etc.) and product delivery practices (e.g., customer journey mapping, clear user stories, etc.). MLOps and ML platforms aren't going to write comprehensive tests for you, talk to users for you, or reduce the negative impacts of team silos for you.

In a study on 150 successful ML-driven customer-facing applications at Booking.com (*https://oreil.ly/6CYB6*), done through rigorous randomized controlled trials, the authors concluded that the key factor for success is *an iterative, hypothesis-driven process, integrated with other disciplines, such as product development, user experience, computer science, software engineering, causal inference, and others.* This finding is aligned with our approach as well, based on our experience delivering multiple ML and data products. We have seen time and again that delivering successful ML projects requires a multidisciplinary approach across these five disciplines: product, software engineering, data, ML, and delivery (see Figure 1-2).

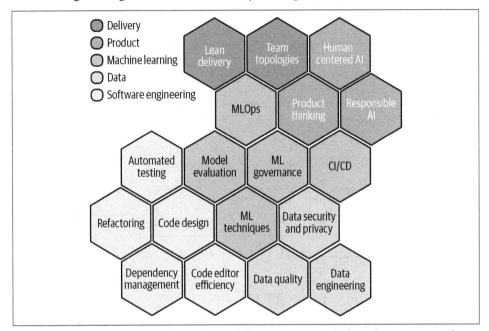

Figure 1-2. Delivering ML projects successfully requires a multidisciplinary approach across product, delivery, ML, software engineering, and data

To help us see the value of putting these five disciplines together—or the costs of focusing only on some disciplines while ignoring others— we can put on the lens of systems thinking. In the next section, we'll look at how systems thinking can help uncover the interconnected disciplines required to effectively deliver ML products.

See the Whole: A Systems Thinking Lens for Effective ML Delivery

Systems thinking (*https://oreil.ly/dcAJ-*) helps us shift our focus from individual parts of a system to *relationships and interactions* between all the components that constitute a system. Systems thinking gives us mental models and tools for understanding—and eventually changing—structures that are not serving us well, including our mental models and perceptions.

You may be asking, why should we frame ML product delivery as a system? And what even *is* a system? Donella H. Meadows, a pioneer in systems thinking (*https://oreil.ly/QumE3*), defines a system as an interconnected set of elements that is coherently organized in a way that achieves something. A system must consist of three kinds of things: elements, interconnections, and a function or purpose.

Let's read that again in the context of delivering ML products. A system must consist of three kinds of things (see Figure 1-3):

Elements
    Such as data, ML experiments, software engineering, infrastructure and deployment, users and customers, and product design and user experience

Interconnections
    Such as cross-functional collaboration and production ML systems creating data for subsequent labeling and retraining

A function or purpose of the ML product
    Such as helping users find the most suitable products

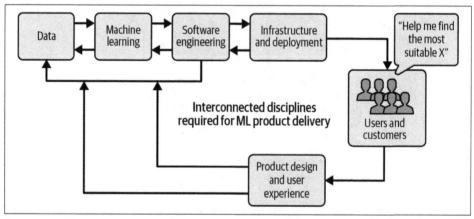

Figure 1-3. These components of ML product delivery are inherently interconnected

Our ability to see and optimize information flow in these interconnections helps us effectively deliver ML products. In contrast, teams that frame ML product delivery solely as a data and ML problem are more likely to fail because the true, holistic nature of the system (for example, user experience being a "make-or-break" consideration in the product's success) will eventually catch up and reveal itself.

Systems thinking recognizes that a system's components are interconnected and that changes in one part of the system can have ripple effects throughout the rest of the system. This means that to truly understand and improve a system, we need to consider the system *as a whole* and how all its parts work together.

Thankfully, there is a philosophy that can help us improve information flow in the interconnections between the elements of an ML delivery system, and that is Lean.

The Five Disciplines Required for Effective ML Delivery

In this section, we'll start with a crash course of what Lean is and how it can help us deliver ML products more effectively. Then we'll briefly explore the five disciplines that are required in ML delivery—product, delivery, software engineering, data, and ML—and describe the key principles and practices in each discipline that provide the fast feedback ML teams need to iterate toward building the right product.

As a quick caveat, each of these five disciplines warrants a book—if not a collection of books—and the principles and practices we lay out in this chapter are by no means exhaustive. Nonetheless, they form a substantial start and they are principles and practices that we bring to any ML project to help us deliver ML solutions effectively. This section will chart our path at a high level, and we'll dive into details in the remaining chapters of the book.

What is Lean, and why should ML practitioners care?

In ML projects (as with many other software or data projects), it's common for teams to experience various forms of waste. For example, you may have invested time and effort to get a feature "done," only to realize eventually that the feature did not have demonstrable value for the customer. Or perhaps you may have wasted days waiting on another team in back-and-forth handoffs. Or maybe you've had your flow unexpectedly disrupted by defects or bugs in your product.[3] All these wastes contribute to negative outcomes such as release delays and missed milestones, more work (and the feeling that there just isn't enough time to finish all the work), stress, and consequently low team morale.

If you have experienced any of these negative outcomes, first of all, welcome to the human condition. These are challenges we've personally experienced and will continue to experience to some extent because no system can be 100% waste-free or noise-free.

Second of all, Lean principles and practices can help. Lean enables organizations to better serve customers by identifying customer value, and to efficiently deliver products that satisfy customer needs. By involving the voice of the customer in the development and delivery process, teams can better understand the end users' needs and build relevant products for them. Lean helps us get better at what we do and enables us to *minimize waste and maximize value*.

---

3 Lean helpfully provides a nuanced classification of waste, also known as the "eight deadly wastes" (*https://oreil.ly/5QPMb*), which enumerate common inefficiencies that can occur in the process of delivering value to customers. The three examples in this paragraph refer to overproduction, waiting, and defects, respectively. The remaining five types of waste are: transport, overprocessing, inventory, motion, and under-utilized talent.

Lean practices originated from Toyota in the 1950s. The philosophy was initially known as the Toyota Production System (TPS). James P. Womack and Daniel T. Jones later refined and popularized it as Lean principles (*https://oreil.ly/8Lmxt*) in their book *The Machine That Changed the World* (Free Press). The following five Lean principles (see Figure 1-4) were key in transforming the automotive, manufacturing, and IT industries, among others:

Principle 1: Identify value
> Determine what is most valuable to the customer and focus on maximizing that value.

Principle 2: Map the value stream
> Identify the steps in the process that add value and eliminate those that do not.

Principle 3: Create flow
> Streamline the process to create a smooth and continuous flow of work.

Principle 4: Establish pull
> Use customer demand to trigger production and avoid overproduction.

Principle 5: Continuous improvement
> Continuously strive for improvement and eliminate waste in all areas of the value chain.

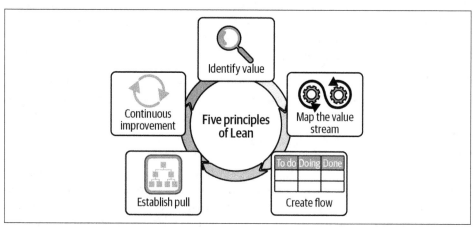

Figure 1-4. The five principles of Lean

In our experience delivering ML products, Lean steers us toward value-creating work, which then creates a positive feedback loop of customer satisfaction, team morale, and delivery momentum. For example, instead of "pushing out" features because they involve shiny technologies, we first identify and prioritize features that will bring the most value to users (principle 1) and "pull" it into our delivery flow when the demand has been established (principle 4). In contrast, in instances where we didn't practice this, we'd end up investing time and effort to complete a feature that added complexity to the codebase without any demonstrable value. To those with keen Lean eyes, yes—you've just spotted waste!

Value stream mapping (principle 2) is a tool that lets us visually represent all the steps and resources involved in delivering a unit of value (e.g., a product feature) to customers. Teams can use this tool to identify waste, work toward eliminating waste, and improve the flow of value (principle 3).

To map your team or product's value stream, you can follow these steps:

1. Identify the product or service being mapped. This could be a single product or an entire process.

2. Identify the current state map. Create a visual representation of the current process, including all steps and materials (including time and labor) involved from raw materials to finished product.

3. Identify value-added and non-value-added activities. Determine which steps add value to the product or service and which do not.

4. Identify waste. Look for areas of overproduction, waiting, defects, overprocessing, excess inventory, unnecessary motion, excess transport, unnecessary use of raw materials, and unnecessary effort.

5. Create a future state map. Based on the analysis of the current state map, redesign the process to eliminate waste and create a more efficient flow of materials and information.

6. Implement changes. Put the redesigned process into practice and continuously monitor and improve (principle 5).

Now that we have a basic working knowledge of Lean, let's look at how Lean intersects with the five disciplines to create a set of practices that can help ML teams shorten feedback loops and rapidly iterate toward a valuable product. When put together, these practices help create several emergent, desirable, and mutually reinforcing characteristics in our system of delivering ML products: faster feedback, cheaper and fewer failures, predictable delivery, and most importantly, valuable outcomes.

 If you find the explanations of each practice to be too brief in this chapter, don't worry! Throughout this book, we'll elaborate on why and how we apply these and other practices in the context of building ML products.

The first discipline: Product

Without the product discipline, no amount of expertise in the other disciplines (e.g., ML, data, software engineering) can help a team deliver ML products effectively. When we don't understand users' needs and the organization's business model, it makes it hard to gain alignment from business to get started. Even when teams do get started, the lack of a product-oriented approach can leave them in a vacuum of product knowledge that is quickly filled with unsubstantiated assumptions, which tends to lead to teams over-engineering unvalidated features, and ultimately wasting valuable energy and resources.

Without understanding the business model and customer needs, it's easy to lose momentum and direction. In contrast, with a product-oriented approach, ML teams can start with the end in mind, continuously test their assumptions, and ensure they are building solutions that are relevant to the needs of their customers.

With the Lean mindset, we recognize that all our ideas are based on assumptions that need to be tested and that many of these assumptions may be proven wrong. Lean provides a set of principles and practices to test our hypotheses, for example through prototype testing, safe-to-fail experiments, and build-measure-learn cycles, among others. Each experiment provides learnings that help us make informed decisions to persevere, pivot, or stop. By pivoting or ditching bad ideas early on, we can save time and resources and focus on ideas that will bring value to customers. Lean helps us move more quickly and "execute on opportunities by building the right thing at the right time and stop wasting people's time on ideas that are not valuable."[4]

As Henrik Kniberg of Spotify puts it: "Product development isn't easy. In fact, most product development efforts fail, and the most common reason for failure is building the wrong product."[5] The goal here is not to avoid failure, but to fail more quickly and safely by creating fast feedback loops for building empathy and for learning. Let's look at some practices that can help us achieve that.

Discovery.   Discovery (*https://oreil.ly/P77Iv*) is a set of activities that helps us better understand the problem, the opportunity, and potential solutions. It provides a structure for navigating uncertainty through rapid, time-boxed, iterative activities that involve various stakeholders and customers. As eloquently articulated in *Lean Enterprise* (O'Reilly), the process of creating a shared vision always starts with clearly defining the problem, because having a clear problem statement helps the team focus on what is important and ignore distractions.

---

4 Jez Humble, Joanne Molesky, and Barry O'Reilly, *Lean Enterprise* (Sebastopol: O'Reilly, 2014).

5 Humble et al., *Lean Enterprise*.

Discovery makes extensive use of visual artifacts to canvas, externalize, debate, test, and evolve ideas. Some useful visual ideation canvases include the Lean Canvas (*https://oreil.ly/aUa8q*) and Value Proposition Canvas (*https://oreil.ly/gt7US*), and there are many others. During discovery, we intentionally put customers and the business at the center and create ample space for the voice of the customer—gathered through activities such as user journey mapping, contextual enquiry, customer interviews, among others—as we formulate and test hypotheses about the problem/solution fit (*https://oreil.ly/nmvsQ*) and product/market fit (*https://oreil.ly/BOW87*) of our ideas.

In the context of ML, Discovery techniques help us assess the value and feasibility of candidate solutions early on so that we can go into delivery with grounded confidence. One helpful tool in this regard is the Data Product Canvas (*https://oreil.ly/F_05O*), which provides a framework for connecting the dots between data collection, ML, and value creation. It's also important to use Discovery to articulate measures of success—and get alignment and agreement among stakeholders—for how we'd evaluate the fitness-for-purpose of candidate solutions.

Lean Enterprise has an excellent chapter on Discovery, and we would encourage you to read it for an in-depth understanding of how you can structure and facilitate Discovery workshops in your organization. Discovery is also not a one-and-done activity—the principles can be practiced continuously (*https://oreil.ly/bcr3p*) as we build, measure, and learn our way toward building products that customers value.

Prototype testing.   Have you heard of the parable of the ceramic pots (*https://oreil.ly/Ldgy4*)?[6] In this parable, a ceramic pottery teacher tasked half of the class to create the best pot possible but only create one each. The other half of the class was instructed to make as many pots as possible within the same time frame. At the end of it, the latter group—which had the benefit of iteratively developing many prototypes—produced the higher-quality pots.

Prototypes allow us to rapidly test our ideas with users in a cost-effective way and allow us to validate—or invalidate—our assumptions and hypotheses. They can be as simple as "hand-sketched" drawings of an interface that users would interact with, or they can be clickable interactive mockups. In some cases, we may even opt for "Wizard of Oz" prototypes (*https://oreil.ly/_kpwS*), which is a real working product, but with all product functions carried out manually behind the scenes, unbeknownst

---

6 This parable was first told in David Bayles and Ted Orland's book, *Art & Fear* (Image Continuum Press), and is based on an actual fact, with the only difference being that the subject was photographs instead of ceramic pots. The teacher in the true story was Ted Orland, who was an assistant to Ansel Adams (*https://oreil.ly/S2x8Q*), the renowned American photographer and environmentalist.

to the person using the product.[7] (It's important to note that "Wizard of Oz" is for prototype testing, not for running production systems. This misapplication, which was termed blatantly as "artificial artificial intelligence" [*https://oreil.ly/Db7b1*], involves unscalable human effort to solve problems that AI can't solve.)

Whichever method you pick, prototype testing is especially useful in ML product delivery because we can get feedback from users before any costly investments in data, ML, and MLOps. Prototype testing helps us shorten our feedback loop from weeks or months (time spent on engineering effort in data, ML, and MLOps) to days. Talk about fast feedback!

The second discipline: Delivery

If the product discipline is concerned with what we build and why, the delivery discipline speaks to *how* we execute our ideas. The mechanics of delivering an ML product involve multiple disciplines: delivery planning, engineering, product, ML, security, data, and so on. We use the term *delivery* here to refer to the delivery planning aspects of how we build ML solutions.

The delivery discipline focuses primarily on the shaping, sizing, and sequencing of work in three horizons (from near to far): user stories or features, iterations, and releases. It also pertains to how our teams operate and encompasses:

- Team shapes
- Ways of working (e.g., standups and retrospectives)
- Team health (e.g., morale and psychological safety)
- Delivery risk management

Lean recognizes that talent is an organization's most valuable asset, and the delivery discipline reinforces that belief by creating structures that minimize impediments in our systems of work and amplify each teammate's contributions and collective ownership. When done right, delivery practices can help us reduce waste and improve the flow of value.

Delivery is an often overlooked but highly critical aspect of building ML products. If we get all the other disciplines right but neglect delivery, we will likely be unable to deliver our ML product to users in a timely and reliable manner (we will explain why in a moment). This can lead to decreased customer satisfaction, eroded competitiveness, missed opportunities, and ultimately, failure to achieve the desired business outcomes.

---

7 Jeremy Jordan has written an excellent in-depth article (*https://oreil.ly/DCX0Z*) describing how we can prototype and iterate on the user experience using design tools to communicate possible solutions.

Let's look at some fundamental delivery practices.

Vertically sliced work. A common pitfall in ML delivery is the horizontal slicing of work, where we sequentially deliver functional layers of a technical solution—e.g., data lake, ML platform, ML models, UX interfaces—from the bottom-up. This is a risky delivery approach because customers can only experience the product and provide valuable feedback after months and even years of significant engineering investment. In addition, horizontal slicing naturally leads to late integration issues when horizontal slices come together, increasing the risk of release delays.

To mitigate this, we can slice work and stories vertically (*https://oreil.ly/scbMO*). A vertically sliced story refers to a story that is defined as an independently shippable unit of value, which contains all of the necessary functionality from the user-facing aspects (e.g., a frontend) to the more backend-ish aspects (e.g., data pipelines, ML models). Your definition of "user-facing" will differ depending on who your users are. For example, if you are a platform team delivering an ML platform product for data scientists, the user-facing component may be a command-line tool instead of a frontend application.

The principle of vertical slicing (*https://oreil.ly/ReL3C*) applies more broadly beyond individual features as well. This is what vertical slicing looks like, in the three horizons of the delivery discipline:

- At the level of a *story*, we articulate and demonstrate business value in each story.
- At the level of an *iteration*, we plan and prioritize stories that cohere to achieve a tangible outcome.
- At the level of a *release*, we plan, sequence, and prioritize a collection of stories that is focused on creating demonstrable business value.

What If the Minimal Vertical Slice Isn't Good Enough?

At this point, you may ask, what if the minimal vertical slice can't meet the expected model performance for production release? For example, if we were training an inventory supply forecast model, the model's predictions will inform warehousing decisions and erroneous forecasts can potentially cost millions of dollars in actual cost and revenue.

This is a situation that all ML practitioners will inevitably face, and several techniques can help us reduce the risk and cost of this scenario. For example, when we do prototype testing, as described earlier in product discipline, training prototype models helps us test the feasibility and viability of an ML approach to solving the business problem. Doing this as early and as rapidly as possible during Discovery helps us

---

avoid wasting weeks and months of delivery effort in building a vertical slice that may end up in a dead end.

We can also apply the technique of Framing ML Problems, where we work with relevant customers or stakeholders to find the suitable responsibility boundary for an ML system. As we run experiments to test ideas, we generate learnings that tell us where and how ML is (or isn't) suitable for solving the business problem. We describe Framing ML Problems in greater detail in the later section on the ML discipline.

Vertically sliced teams, or cross-functional teams.   Another common pitfall in ML delivery is splitting teams by function, for example by having data science, data engineering, and product engineering in separate teams. This structure leads to two main problems. First, teams inevitably get caught in *backlog coupling*, which is the scenario where one team depends on another team to deliver a feature. In one informal analysis, backlog coupling increased the time to complete a task by an average of 10 to 12 times (*https://oreil.ly/XGsIt*).

The second problem is the manifestation of Conway's Law (*https://oreil.ly/7hk2W*), which is the phenomenon where teams design systems and software that mirror their communication structure. For example, we have seen a case where two teams working on the same product built two different solutions to solve the same problem of serving model inferences at low latency. That is Conway's Law at work. The path of least resistance steers teams toward finding local optimizations rather than coordinating shared functionality.

We can mitigate these problems for a given product by identifying the capabilities that naturally cohere for the product and building a cross-functional team around the product—from the frontend elements (e.g., experience design, UI design) to backend elements (e.g., ML, MLOps, data engineering). This practice of building multidisciplinary teams has sometimes been described as the Inverse Conway Maneuver (*https://oreil.ly/9yVoo*). This brings four major benefits:

Improves speed and quality of decision making
> The shared context and cadence reduces the friction of discussing and iterating on all things (e.g., design decisions, prioritization calls, assumptions to validate). Instead of having to coordinate a meeting between multiple teams, we can just discuss an issue using a given team's communication channels (e.g., standup, huddles, chat channels).

Reduces back-and-forth handoffs and waiting
> If the slicing is done right, the cross-functional team should be autonomous— that means the team is empowered to design and deliver features and end-to-end functionality without depending on or waiting on another team.

Reduces blind spots through diversity

Having a diverse team with different capabilities and perspectives (*https://oreil.ly/ k_E8L*) can help ensure that the ML project is well-rounded and takes into account all of the relevant considerations. For example, an UX designer could create prototypes to test and refine ideas with customers before we invest significant engineering effort in ML.

Reduces batch size

Working in smaller batches has many benefits and is one of the core principles of Lean software delivery. As described in Donald Reinertsen's *Principles of Product Development Flow* (Celeritas), smaller batches enable faster feedback, lower risk, less waste, and higher quality.

The first three benefits of cross-functional teams—improved communication and collaboration, minimized handoffs, diverse expertise—enable teams to reduce batch size. For example, instead of needing to engineer and silver plate a feature before it can be shared more widely for feedback, a cross-functional team would contain the necessary product and domain knowledge to provide that feedback (or, if not, they would at least know how to devise cost-effective ways to find the answers).

Cross-functional teams are not free from problems either. There is a risk that each product team develops its own idiosyncratic solution to problems that occur repeatedly across products. We think, however, with the right engineering practices, that this is a higher quality problem than the poor flow that results from functionally siloed teams. Additionally, there are mitigations to help align product teams including communities of practice (*https://oreil.ly/6-hGd*), platform teams, and so on. We'll discuss these in depth in Chapter 11.

Contrarily, we have seen functionally specialized teams deliver effectively in collaboration, given the institution of strong agile program management to provide a clear, current picture of end-to-end delivery and product operations, and collective guidelines for working sustainably to improve overall system health.

There is no one-size-fits-all team shape and the right team shapes and interaction modes for your organization depend on many factors, which will evolve over time. In Chapter 11, we discuss varied team shapes and how the principles of Team Topologies (*https://oreil.ly/lWgYX*) can help you identify suitable team shapes and interaction modes for ML teams in your organization.

Ways of Working.   Ways of Working (WoW) refers to the processes, practices, and tools that a team uses to deliver product features. It includes, but is not limited to, agile ceremonies (e.g., standups, retros, feedback), user story workflow (e.g., Kanban, story kickoffs, pair programming, desk checks [*https://oreil.ly/Pri1o*][8]), and quality assurance (e.g., automated testing, manual testing, "stopping the line" when defects occur).

One common trap that teams fall into is to follow the form but miss out on the substance or intent of these WoW practices. When we don't understand and practice WoW in a coherent whole, it can often be counterproductive. For example, teams could run standups, but miss out on the intent of making work visible as teammates hide behind generic updates ("I worked on X yesterday and will continue working on it today"). Instead, each of these WoW practices should help the team have context-rich information (e.g., "I'm getting stuck in Y" and "Oh, I've faced that recently and I know a way to help you."). This improves shared understanding, creates alignment, and provides each team member with information that improves their flow of value.

Measuring delivery metrics. One often-overlooked practice—even in agile teams—is capturing delivery metrics (e.g., iteration velocity, cycle time, defect rates) over time. If we think of the team as a production line (producing creative solutions, and not cookie cutter widgets), these metrics can help us regularly monitor delivery health and raise flags when we're veering off track from the delivery plan or timelines.

Teams can and should also measure software delivery performance with the four key metrics (*https://oreil.ly/FQKdD*): delivery lead time, deployment frequency, mean time to recovery (MTTR), and change failure rate. In *Accelerate* (IT Revolution Press), which is based on four years of research and statistical analysis on technology organizations, the authors found that software delivery performance (as measured by the four key metrics) correlated with an organization's business outcomes and financial performance. Measuring the four key metrics helps us ensure a steady and high-quality flow in our production line.

The objective nature of these metrics helps to ground planning conversations in data and help the team actually see (in quantitative estimates) the work ahead and how well they are tracking toward their target. In an ideal environment, these metrics would be used purely for continuous improvement to help us improve our production line over time and meet our product delivery goals.

However, in other less-than-ideal environments, metrics can be misused, abused, gamed, and become ultimately dysfunctional (*https://oreil.ly/ggm3n*). As Goodhart's Law (*https://oreil.ly/7OUSH*) states, "when a measure becomes a target, it ceases to

---

8 A desk check refers to the practice of having a short (e.g., 15-minute) huddle with the team when a pair believes the development work for a feature is complete. Not everyone has to be there, but it helps to have the product, engineering, and quality lens at the desk check. We find that having a brief walk-through of the definition of done, and how the pair delivered the feature can invite a focused and open discussion. It also saves team members from multiple instances of context-switching and waiting in a long-drawn back-and-forth conversation on a chat group.

be a good measure." Ensure that you're measuring the right outcomes and continuously improving (*https://oreil.ly/q4Fd2*) to find the appropriate metrics for your organization's ML practice. We go into more detail on measuring team health metrics when we discuss the pitfalls of measuring productivity, and how to avoid them, in Chapter 10.

The third discipline: Engineering

> Crucially, the rate at which we can learn, update our product or prototype based on feedback, and test again, is a powerful competitive advantage. This is the value proposition of Lean engineering practices.
>
> —Jez Humble, Joanne Molesky, and Barry O'Reilly in *Lean Enterprise*

All of the engineering practices we outline in this section focus on one thing: *shortening feedback loops*. The previous quote from *Lean Enterprise* articulates it well—an effective team is one that can rapidly make, test, and release the required changes—in code, data, or ML models.

Automated testing. In ML projects, it's common to see heaps and heaps of code without automated tests. Without automated tests, changes become error-prone, tedious, and stressful. When we change one part of the codebase, the lack of tests forces us to take on the burden of manually testing the entire codebase to ensure that a change (e.g., in feature engineering logic) hasn't caused a degradation (e.g., in model quality or API behavior in edge cases). This means an overwhelming amount of time, effort, and cognitive load is spent on non-ML work.

In contrast, comprehensive automated tests help teams to accelerate experimentation, reduce cognitive load, and get fast feedback. Automated tests give us fast feedback on changes and let us know whether everything is still working as expected. In practice, it can make a night-and-day difference in how quickly we can execute on our ideas and get stories done properly.

Effective teams are those that welcome and can respond to valuable changes in various aspects of a product: new business requirements, feature engineering strategies, modeling approaches, training data, among others. Automated tests enable such responsiveness and reliability in the face of these changes. We'll introduce techniques for testing ML systems in Chapters 5 and 6.

Refactoring. The second law of thermodynamics tells us that the universe tends toward disorder, or entropy. Our codebases—ML or otherwise—are no exception. With every "quick hack" and every feature delivered without conscious effort to minimize entropy, the codebase grows more convoluted and brittle. This makes the code increasingly hard to understand and, consequently, modifying code becomes painful and error-prone.

ML projects that lack automated tests are especially susceptible to exponential complexity because, without automated tests, refactoring can be tedious to test and is highly risky. Consequently, refactoring becomes a significant undertaking that gets relegated to the backlog graveyard. As a result, we create a vicious cycle for ourselves and it becomes increasingly difficult for ML practitioners to evolve their ML solutions.

In an effective team, refactoring is something that is so safe and easy to do that we can do some of it as part of feature delivery, not as an afterthought. Such teams are typically able to do this for three reasons:

- They have comprehensive tests that give them fast feedback on whether a refactoring preserved behavior.
- They've configured their code editor and leveraged the ability of modern code editors to execute refactoring actions (e.g., rename variables, extract function, change signature).
- The amount of technical debt and/or workload is at a healthy level. Instead of feeling crushed by pressure, they have the capacity to refactor where necessary as part of feature delivery to improve the readability and quality of the codebase.

Code editor effectiveness. As alluded to in the previous point, modern code editors have many powerful features that can help contributors write code more effectively. The code editor can take care of low-level details so that our cognitive capacity remains available for solving higher-level problems.

For example, instead of renaming variables through a manual search and replace, the code editor can rename all references to a variable in *one* shortcut. Instead of manually searching for the syntax to import a function (e.g., `cross_val_score()`), we can hit a shortcut and the IDE can automatically import the function for us.

When configured properly, the code editor becomes a powerful assistant (even without AI coding technologies) and can allow us to execute our ideas, solve problems, and deliver value more effectively.

Continuous delivery for ML. Wouldn't it be great if there was a way to help ML practitioners reduce toil, speed up experimentation, and build high-quality products? Well, that's exactly what continuous delivery for ML (CD4ML) (*https://oreil.ly/d6GEE*) helps teams do. CD4ML is the application of continuous delivery (*https://oreil.ly/Pv8Dw*) principles and practices to ML projects. It enables teams to shorten feedback loops and establish quality controls to ensure that software and ML models are high quality and can be safely and efficiently deployed to production.

Research from *Accelerate* shows that continuous delivery practices help organizations achieve better technical and business performance by enabling teams to reliably deliver value and to nimbly respond to changes in market demands. This is corroborated by our experience working with ML teams. CD4ML has helped us improve our velocity, responsiveness, cognitive load, satisfaction, and product quality.

We'll explore CD4ML in detail in Chapter 9. For now, here's a preview of its technical components (see Figure 1-5):

- Reproducible model training, evaluation, and experimentation
- Model serving
- Testing and quality assurance
- Model deployment
- Model monitoring and observability

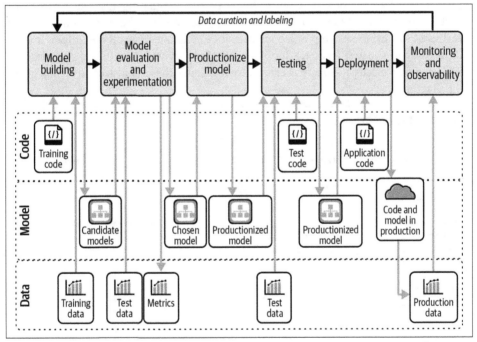

Figure 1-5. The end-to-end CD4ML process (source: adapted from an image in "Continuous Delivery for Machine Learning" [https://oreil.ly/d6GEE])

The fourth discipline: ML

The ML discipline involves more than knowing how to train, select, improve, deploy, and consume ML models. It also encompasses competencies such as ML problem framing, ML systems design, designing for explainability, reliability, Responsible AI, and ML governance, among other things.

Framing ML problems. In early and exploratory phases of ML projects, it's usually unclear what problem we should be solving, who we are solving it for, and most importantly, why we should solve it. In addition, it may not be clear what ML paradigm or model architectures can help us—or even what data we have or need—to solve the problem. That is why it is important to frame ML problems, to structure and execute ideas, and to validate hypotheses with the relevant customers or stakeholders. The saying (*https://oreil.ly/DCX0Z*) "a problem well-defined is a problem half-solved" resonates well in this context.

There are various tools that can help us frame ML problems, such as the Data Product Canvas (*https://oreil.ly/F_05O*), which we referenced earlier in this chapter. Another tool to help us articulate and test our ideas in rapid cycles and keep track of learnings over time is the Hypothesis Canvas (*https://oreil.ly/KzSkM*) (see Figure 1-6).[9] The Hypothesis Canvas helps us in formulating testable hypotheses, in articulating why an idea might be valuable and who will benefit from it, and in steering us toward measuring objective metrics to validate or invalidate ideas. It is yet another way to shorten feedback loops by running targeted, timeboxed experiments. We'll keep our discussion short here, as we'll discuss these canvases in detail in the next chapter.

Hypothesis canvas

Business value	Problem	Customers
What is the business value associated with this hypothesis?	*What is the problem we are trying to solve?*	*Who is impacted by this problem?*

Hypothesis	Metrics
What do we believe? We believe that _____ will result in _____. We will know we've succeeded when _____.	*Record a baseline of key metrics for this hypothesis.*

Solutions/Ideas	Lessons learned
How might we solve this problem?	*Record our lessons learned.*

Figure 1-6. The Hypothesis Canvas helps us formulate testable ideas and know when we've succeeded (source: "Data-Driven Hypothesis Development" [https://oreil.ly/ KzSkM] by Jo Piechota and May Xu, used with permission)

---

9 The word "hypothesis" in this context is technically different, but conceptually similar, to how it's defined in statistics. In this context, a hypothesis is a *testable* assumption, and it is used as a starting point for iterative experimentation and testing to determine the most effective solution to the problem.

ML systems design. There are many parts to designing ML systems, such as collecting and processing the data needed by the model, selecting the appropriate ML approach, evaluating the performance of the model, considering access patterns and scalability requirements, understanding ML failure modes, and identifying model-centric and data-centric strategies for iteratively improving the model.

There is a great book that has been written on this topic, *Designing Machine Learning Systems* by Chip Huyen (O'Reilly), and we encourage you to read it if you haven't already done so. Given that there's great literature on this topic, our book won't go into details of concepts already covered in *Designing ML Systems*.

Responsible AI and ML governance. MIT Sloan Management Review has a succinct and practical definition of Responsible AI (*https://oreil.ly/3yOor*):

> A framework with principles, policies, tools, and processes to ensure that AI systems are developed and operated in the service of good for individuals and society while still achieving transformative business impact.

In MIT Sloan's "2022 Responsible AI Global Executive Report" (*https://oreil.ly/3yOor*), it found that while AI initiatives are surging, Responsible AI is lagging. Of the companies surveyed, 52% are engaged in some Responsible AI practices, but 79% state that their implementations are limited in scale and scope. While they recognize that Responsible AI is crucial for addressing AI risks, such as safety, bias, fairness, and privacy issues, they admit to neglecting its prioritization. This gap increases the chances of negative consequences for their customers and exposes the business to regulatory, financial, and customer satisfaction risks.

If Responsible AI is the proverbial mountaintop, teams often fail to get there with only a compass. They also need a map, paths, guidance, and means of transport. This is where ML governance comes in as a key mechanism that teams can use to achieve Responsible AI objectives, among other objectives of ML teams.

ML governance involves a wide range of processes, policies, and practices aimed at helping practitioners deliver ML products responsibly and reliably. It spans the ML delivery lifecycle, playing a role in each of the following stages:

Model development
Guidelines, best practices and golden paths (*https://oreil.ly/eOMvb*) for developing, testing, documenting, and deploying ML models

Model evaluation
Methods for assessing model performance, identifying biases, and ensuring fairness before deployment

Monitoring and feedback loops
> Systems to continuously monitor model performance, gather user feedback, and improve models

Mitigation strategies
> Approaches to identify and mitigate biases in data and algorithms, to avoid negative and unfair outcomes

Explainability
> Techniques and tools to explain a model's behaviors under certain scenarios in order to improve transparency, build user trust, and facilitate error analysis

Accountability
> Well-defined roles, responsibilities, and lines of authority; multidisciplinary teams capable of managing ML systems and risk-management processes

Regulatory compliance
> Adherence to legal and industry-specific regulations or audit requirements regarding the use of data and ML

Data-handling policies
> Guidelines for collecting, storing, and processing data to ensure data privacy and security

User consent and privacy protection
> Measures to obtain informed consent from users and safeguard their privacy

Ethical guidelines
> Principles to guide ML development and use, considering social impact, human values, potential risks, and possibilities of harm

While "governance" typically has bureaucratic connotations, we'll demonstrate in Chapter 9 that ML governance can be implemented in a lean and lightweight fashion. In our experience, continuous delivery and Lean engineering complement governance by establishing safe-to-fail zones and feedback mechanisms. Taken together, not only do these governance practices help teams reduce risk and avoid negative consequences, they also help teams innovate and deliver value.

In Chapter 9, we will also share other helpful resources for ML governance, such as the "Responsible Tech Playbook" (*https://oreil.ly/uFZiV*) and Google Model Cards (*https://oreil.ly/Pzl7v*).

The fifth discipline: Data

As many ML practitioners know, the quality of our ML models depends on the quality of our data. If the data in our training sample is biased (as compared to the distribution of the population dataset), then the model will learn and perpetuate

---

the bias. As eloquently put, "when today's technology relies on yesterday's data, it will simply mirror our past mistakes and biases."[10]

To deliver better ML solutions, teams can consider the following practices in the data discipline.

Closing the data collection loop. As we train and deploy models, our ML system design should also take into consideration how we will collect and curate the model's predictions in production, so that we can label them and grow high-quality ground truth for evaluating and retraining models.

Labeling can be a tedious activity and is often the bottleneck. If so, we can also consider how to scale labeling through techniques such as active learning (*https://oreil.ly/qvvBi*), self-supervised learning (*https://oreil.ly/xfRiX*), and weak supervision (*https://oreil.ly/32Ypm*). If natural labels (*https://oreil.ly/HJZ9W*)—ground truth labels that can be automatically evaluated or partially evaluated—are available for our ML task, we should also design software and data ingestion pipelines that stream in the natural labels as they become available alongside the associated features for the given data points.

When collecting natural labels, we must also consider how to mitigate the risks of data poisoning attacks (more on this shortly) and dangerous runaway feedback loops (*https://oreil.ly/tdi5E*), where the model's biased predictions have an effect on the real world, which further entrenches the bias in the data and subsequent models.

Teams often focus on the last mile of ML delivery—with a skewed focus on getting a satisfactory model out of the door—and neglect to close the data collection loop in preparation for the next leg and cycle of model improvement. When this happens, they forgo the opportunity to improve ML models through data-centric approaches (*https://oreil.ly/9fmg3*).

Let's look at the final practice for this chapter: data security and privacy.

Data security and privacy. As mentioned earlier in this chapter, data security and privacy are cross-cutting concerns that should be the responsibility of everyone in the organization, from product teams to data engineering teams and every team in between. An organization can safeguard data by practicing defense in depth (*https://oreil.ly/w6q-D*), where multiple layers of security controls are placed throughout a system. For example, in addition to storing data securely in transit and at rest through the use of encryption and access controls, teams can also apply the principle of least privilege (*https://oreil.ly/fUR7I*) and ensure that only authorized individuals and systems can access the data.

---

10 Patrick K. Lin, *Machine See, Machine Do: How Technology Mirrors Bias in Our Criminal Justice System* (Potomac, MD: New Degree Press, 2021).

At an organizational level, there must be data governance and management guidelines that define and enforce clear policies to guide how teams collect, store, and use data. This can help ensure that data is used ethically and in compliance with relevant laws and regulations.

> # Do These Practices Apply to Generative AI and Large Language Models?
>
> As Generative AI and LLMs gained prominence in the collective awareness and product plans of many organizations, we and our colleagues have had the opportunity to work with organizations to conceptualize, develop, and deliver products that leverage Generative AI.[11]
>
> At the time of writing (late 2023), many Generative AI applications use LLMs for processing natural language. LLMs are a type of neural network based on the transformer architecture (*https://oreil.ly/99WY7*). There are other generative neural network architectures, including Generative Adversarial Networks (GANs) and Autoencoders. There are also other types of AI that are generative in nature, such as Bayesian methods.
>
> LLMs typically generate text, where text may be natural language, or structured forms such as tables, JSON, or code. An LLM generates a stream of output tokens in response to some input tokens, which are also known as a "prompt." Tokens represent some unit of the text input and output. For instance, the Llama 2 7B model, in response to a prompt with an open request, might generate output that starts with token #4587 "Of" followed by token #3236 "course," and continue in that vein. LLMs may also be multimodal, processing and generating images, audio, and other modes of data, in which case the tokens may include patches or images, according to the modality.
>
> As a neural network, an LLM is trained on many, many instances of inputs and their expected outputs using Stochastic Gradient Descent (SGD) to minimize a *loss* function representing the difference between the predicted and expected outputs. At each training iteration, SGD adjusts the weights of the neural network to reduce the loss function for subsequent predictions. While complex, multistage, and consuming large data volumes, LLM training is qualitatively the same thing as training other ML models discussed in this book. Therefore, this book is still a useful reference for teams training or fine-tuning LLMs.

---

11 When we talk about Generative AI in the context of effective ML teams, we're not talking about the use of generic chatbots or new productivity tools to help software delivery teams write code or user stories. We are talking about ML teams that are playing a role in building new systems that incorporate Generative AI technology.

Many applications integrating Generative AI will avoid the complexity of training or fine-tuning LLMs and simply use a pretrained LLM in inference mode as a flexible application component. An isolated LLM will have some base level of capability due to its training. When integrated into an application, an LLM can gain additional context in the prompt and/or multiple invocations can be orchestrated for better responses. These LLM capabilities are described as *zero-shot*, *few-shot*, and *in-context learning*, and the techniques for using these capabilities are called "prompt engineering."

These application integration techniques expand the base capabilities of LLMs by providing access to additional data. LLMs generate content, but they can't be relied on to recall information perfectly, suppress sensitive information, reason, plan, compute, detect malicious intent, or identify any of their limitations in these regards. This may require the application to also use traditional Natural Language Processing (NLP) and software application development techniques to constrain LLM inputs or outputs for better performance, robustness, or protection from threats. In general, these considerations make integrating LLMs complex.

As a result, whether integrating a pretrained model or training an in-house model, good software architecture principles and development practices as described in this book remain relevant, and are possibly even more important due to the need to accommodate the sometimes unpredictable nature of LLM responses.

Although Generative AI and LLMs have led to a paradigm shift in the methods we use to direct or restrict models to achieve specific functionalities, the fundamentals of Lean product delivery and engineering haven't changed. In fact, the fundamental tools and techniques in this book have helped us—across aspects of product, delivery, ML, and engineering—to articulate and test hypotheses early on, iterate quickly, and deliver reliably. By drawing from techniques outlined in this chapter, we were able to reduce the time and cost to value even when dealing with the complexities inherent in Generative AI and LLMs.

In Chapter 2, we'll briefly discuss how product discovery techniques have helped us, and can help you, sharpen your focus when shaping Generative AI product opportunities. In Chapter 6, we'll go into more detail on testing strategies and techniques for LLM applications.

Give yourself some massive pats on the back because you've just covered a lot of ground on the interconnected disciplines that are essential for effectively delivering ML solutions!

Before we conclude this chapter, we'd like to highlight how these practices can serve as leading indicators for positive or undesirable outcomes. For example, if we don't validate our product ideas with users early and often—we know how this movie ends—we are more likely to invest lots of time and effort into building the wrong product. If we don't have cross-functional teams, we are going to experience backlog coupling as multiple teams coordinate and wait on each other to deliver a change to users.

This is not just anecdotal. In a scientific study on performance and effectiveness of technical businesses involving more than 2,800 organizations, the authors found that organizations that adopt practices such as continuous delivery, Lean, cross-functional teams, and generative cultures exhibit higher levels of performance—faster delivery of features, lower failure rates, and higher levels of employee satisfaction.[12] In other words, these practices can actually be *predictors* of an organization's performance.

Conclusion

Let's recap what we've covered in this chapter. We started by looking at common reasons for why ML projects fail, and we compared what ML delivery looks in both low- and high-effectiveness environments. We then looked through a systems thinking lens to identify the disciplines that are required for effective ML delivery. We looked at how Lean helps us reduce waste and maximize value. Finally, we took a whirlwind tour of practices in each of the five disciplines (product, delivery, software engineering, ML, and data) that can help us deliver ML solutions more effectively.

From our interactions with various ML or data science teams across multiple industries, we continue to see a gap between the world of ML and the world of Lean software delivery. While that gap has narrowed in certain pockets—where ML teams could deliver excellent ML product experiences by adopting the necessary product, delivery, and engineering practices—the gulf remains wide for many teams (you can look at Dana's experience in the low-effectiveness environment earlier in this chapter for signs of this gulf).

To close this gap, the ML community requires a paradigm shift—a fundamental change in approach or underlying assumptions—to see that building an ML-driven product is not just an ML and data problem. It is first and foremost a *product* problem, which means to say it's a product, engineering, and delivery problem—and it requires a holistic, multidisciplinary approach.

The good news is that you don't have to boil the ocean or reinvent the wheel—in each discipline, there are principles and practices that have helped teams successfully deliver ML product experiences. In the remainder of this book, we will explore these principles and practices, and how they can improve our effectiveness in delivering ML solutions. We will slow down and elaborate on the principles and practices in a

---

12 Nicole Forsgren, Jez Humble, and Gene Kim, *Accelerate: The Science of Lean Software and DevOps: Building and Scaling High Performing Technology Organizations* (Upper Saddle River, NJ: Addison-Wesley, 2018).

practical way, starting with product and delivery. There will be applicable practices, frameworks, and code samples that you can bring to your ML projects. We hope you're strapped in and excited for the ride.

An Invitation to Journey with Us

We have covered a lot of ground in this chapter. Depending on where you are on your journey and your experience, you may feel like the desired state that we've painted is insurmountable. Or you may feel excited that others have felt your pains and challenges, and that there's a better path.

Wherever you find yourself on this continuum, we hope that you'll take this book as an invitation. An invitation to adopt a beginner's mindset (*https://oreil.ly/FdZHe*) to explore how the five disciplines can improve how ML practitioners deliver ML solutions. In our experience, each discipline comprises composable techniques that teams can use today to complement your existing capabilities—be it in ML, product, or software engineering.

This book is also an invitation to reflect on your team's or organization's ML projects, to notice areas of value and areas of waste. Where there is waste, we hope that the principles and practices we lay out in this book will help you find shorter and more reliable paths to your desired destination. They have certainly helped us (which is why we decided to write a book about this!) and they are principles and practices that we continue to bring to our ML projects.

We acknowledge that it takes more than willpower and good practices to effect change. It requires some level of organizational alignment, a conducive culture, and good leadership, among other factors (which we'll elaborate on in Chapters 10 and 11). This book is written with the belief that teams, empowered with practical knowledge on how to effectively deliver ML solutions, can iterate toward better ways of doing things, deliver impactful outcomes, and effect and inspire change in their organization.

## PART I

Product and Delivery

## CHAPTER 2

Product and Delivery Practices for ML Teams

Product development isn't easy. In fact, most product development efforts fail, and the most common reason for failure is building the wrong product.

—Henrik Kniberg, agile and Lean coach

You can practice shooting [basketballs] eight hours a day, but if your technique is wrong, then all you become is very good at shooting the wrong way. Get the fundamentals down and the level of everything you do will rise.

—Michael Jordan

In Chapter 1, we introduced the five disciplines that are required for delivering ML solutions: product, delivery, ML, software engineering, and data. Later on, in Part II of the book, we'll focus on many engineering, ML, and data practices to help teams *build the thing right* and reduce toil, waste, and rework. These practices will improve velocity and product quality. However, it's important that we first start with product and delivery practices that help teams with an even more important goal: how to *build the right thing*.

In this chapter, we'll focus on aspects of the ML product delivery lifecycle where we often see teams' effort go to waste due to a lack of clarity or misalignment between what the customers or the business need and what the product engineering team delivers. We'll introduce product and delivery practices that have helped us in our real-world ML projects. This chapter is organized to address three key phases of product delivery:

Discovery
To help teams understand and define the opportunity and shape of an appropriate solution

Inception

> To align on a shared plan for execution

Delivery

> To deliver a solution while managing risk, and to keep evolving the solution for the better, integrating continuous discovery as required

Figure 2-1 serves as a visual anchor for each section of this chapter: Discovery, Inception, and Delivery. Within Discovery, we use the British Design Council's Double Diamond design process (*https://oreil.ly/VVCyY*), which has four components: Discover and Define the opportunity and Design and Deliver solution options. Inception is treated as a single timebox comprising multiple activities that engage varied stakeholders to ensure key considerations are reflected in the Delivery plan. Continuous delivery and supporting activities for ML (e.g., continuous discovery) is the model for the Delivery phase. We recommend referring back to Figure 2-1 to help you navigate the product Discovery and Delivery practices in this chapter.[1]

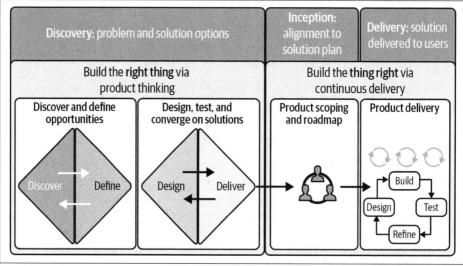

Figure 2-1. A visual summary of product Discovery, Inception, and Delivery phases (source: image adapted from Design Council's Double Diamond design process [https://oreil.ly/VVCyY] and "How to Run a Successful Discovery" by Tanvi Mehta [https://oreil.ly/sEVOy])

---

1 We've put the Double Diamond entirely inside the product Discovery phase. Some frameworks might draw the boundaries differently, but drawing the boundary here gives us room for prototyping or testing possible solutions in the Discovery phase, which is especially relevant for managing and reducing uncertainty when working with ML. However, as we'll see, these Double Diamond activities may also occur through later phases of delivery, even on a continuous basis.

While our approach to this chapter is process-centric, we discuss practices that help us better understand and respond to the needs of customers and users. In this regard, we think it's key to highlight the importance of user- or customer-centric mindsets and approaches, and for that we'll introduce *Design Thinking* later in the chapter. It's also important to note that solutions must be viable as commercial products (or some other funding model). In this respect, we use the term *Product Thinking* to encapsulate Design Thinking and product management. Maybe that's a lot of new terms for an introduction, but that's because this is a rich field, whether building ML or any type of digital product. With our process lens, however, we'll aim to provide clear, practical techniques that can help your team in each stage of product delivery.

While we *sequentially* introduce the process of discovering, defining, and delivering products for ease of reading, it's important to note that these activities must be done *collaboratively* (and typically *continuously*) if teams want to improve their chances of building the right thing. Otherwise, we'll end up with the old model of "mini-waterfall," where discovery and delivery are disjointed with bulky handoffs between product, design, ML, and engineering. In that regard, our guiding philosophy is Lean and agile.

Our phases are similar to other published frameworks such as Atlassian's Product Delivery Framework (*https://oreil.ly/moXX_*), which includes Wonder, Explore, Make, and Impact. You may have your own product or project delivery framework with its own names for these phases, and that's fine as long as the framework upholds the fundamental principles of:

- Understanding customer needs
- Agile planning
- Delivering value early and often
- Responding to what you learn

These frameworks present an ordered view of the world. A complementary model is the Design Squiggle (*https://oreil.ly/pWfkm*), which shows how the reality of designing products is dominated by uncertainty, but that the intent of design is to converge on good solutions in time (see Figure 2-2). The Squiggle might provide some consolation when the reality of product development is particularly messy.

Figure 2-2. The Design Squiggle process (source: Damien Newman, thedesign squiggle.com, used with permission)

ML product delivery presents a unique challenge because business and customers may not know exactly what they need, or can expect, of an ML product—it's hard to know *a priori* how well an ML system will perform with the data that we might curate. On one hand, we may go through product ideation but end up with an idea that is not technically achievable. On the other hand, we may not know what product features are even possible with ML before having done some experiments and seeing some working software. To address this challenge, we'll introduce some techniques, such as the dual track delivery model, later in the chapter to help teams with continuous discovery.

By understanding and implementing these product and delivery practices, teams can bridge this gap between what's needed and what's achievable, and ensure that the ML solutions they develop are not only technically feasible but also desirable to customers and viable for the business.

With that, let's dive into the first of three sections of this chapter: Discovery. We'll go through the specific techniques in each stage of the Double Diamond design process, and the outcomes that teams can expect from these techniques.

ML Product Discovery

> Good product discovery includes the customer throughout the decision-making process.
>
> —Teresa Torres, author of *Continuous Discovery Habits* (Product Talk, LLC)

> It is not enough to do your best; you must know what to do, and then do your best.
>
> —W. Edwards Deming (*https://oreil.ly/HYo11*)

Raise your hand if you've ever been on a team that:

- Delivered an ML solution to production, only to find that it fell far short of the expected usage or engagement levels
- Over-engineered parts of the ML product based on assumptions that could not be verified
- Built proof of concept (PoC) after PoC that never made it into the hands of users
- Couldn't make a compelling business case for an ML opportunity

These challenges stem from inadequate product discovery. ML products, like all other digital products, require a structured discovery (*https://oreil.ly/tbRzj*) approach to ensure the product meets customers' needs. Without product discovery, teams forgo the opportunity to fully understand the problem space. As a result, they increase the risk of investing time and effort in building the wrong products or features.

While a certain amount of discovery in a distinct phase is required to bootstrap a new product initiative, discovery is also an *ongoing process* throughout the delivery of ML projects, especially as we rarely have access to all the data that will be used in a production solution during the initial discovery phase. Eventual access to and availability of necessary, high-quality data might validate our initial assumptions or prototypes made in the discovery phase, or it might show that achieving the required performance in production is not viable. We need a mechanism—*continuous discovery*—to uncover such issues as early as possible during delivery.

With Discovery as the initial phase, the Double Diamond design process can save ML teams months and months of time, which might otherwise be spent solving the wrong problem or chasing the wrong solution. The general principle of divergent and then convergent thinking in first the problem and then the solution space is applicable in almost any problem-solving scenario, and you might also find yourself using this model to run meetings, write code, or plan a dinner party! As visualized in Figure 2-1, there are four subphases in the Discovery phase of the Double Diamond design process:

Discover
Understand the problem rather than merely assuming it. This involves speaking to and spending time with people—e.g., customers and users—who are affected by the problem.

Define
The insight gathered from the Discovery phase can help to define the challenge or problem in a different way.

Develop (we refer to this as Design throughout this chapter)

> Generate different answers to the clearly defined problem, seeking inspiration from elsewhere and co-designing with a range of different people.

Deliver

> Test out different solutions at a small scale, rejecting those that will not work and improving the ones that will.

You can see these stages in practice in a short video (*https://oreil.ly/XU4yi*) about designing assistive technology for blind and low-vision people, produced by Thoughtworks and Guide Dogs Victoria (GDV). The team, led by UX research, spent time to *discover* a range of scenarios in which GDV's clients prefer to use solutions other than a guide dog, leading them to *define* the problem of veering off course when crossing a road using a pedestrian crossing (which the team also experienced first-hand with the help of blindfolds). They then *designed* multiple solutions with different technology strategies, including ML (computer vision), a solution based on Bluetooth beacons, and an optical sensor on a traditional white cane. They further analyzed and tested these potential solutions through rounds of prototyping, leading them to *deliver* a working prototype of the optical sensor solution.

 It's important to recognize that not all products are directly customer-facing. Perhaps you're in an ML platform team delivering platform products (*https://oreil.ly/f2iY0*) for ML practitioners in your organization. Or perhaps your team is building ML-enabled data products (*https://oreil.ly/QOkkt*) that are consumed by other teams that own customer-facing digital experiences. For example, an ML team in an online book retailer may build a Book Recommendations data product that returns a list of recommended books for any given customer. This data product can then be consumed by the marketing team to send personalized book recommendations via email to subscribed customers, or by the web home page or mobile home page teams to display personalized recommendations when the user logs in.

Even though these data products may not be directly customer-facing, they eventually manifest in a customer experience or they may serve internal customers within the organization. As such they still benefit from all the practices that we describe in this chapter. In Chapter 11, we'll discuss how customer-facing teams and internal-facing teams can best collaborate to deliver value and avoid waste or rework.

Let's look at practices that help us with the first half of the first diamond: Discover opportunities.

Discovering Product Opportunities

The techniques we discuss in this section help teams shape a fuzzy hunch about a product idea into a set of well-articulated and testable hypotheses about the problem. They help articulate customers' needs and the potential value that a solution would bring to the business. This is represented as the first quarter of the Double Diamond diagram in Figure 2-1.

During Discovery, we intentionally put the customer at the center. Some notable techniques for surfacing the voice of the customer include personas, customer journey mapping, contextual inquiry, and customer interviews. These are common tools in the field of experience design, and each offers unique insights about users and customers. Let's look at each of these techniques.

A good starting point is personas (*https://oreil.ly/VvBd1*). A persona is a fictional character—based on research—that represents your target users. Developing personas helps the team to clearly understand the behaviors, goals, frustrations, and demographic characteristics of their users. By creating personas, teams can empathize more deeply with their users, tailor their solutions more precisely to user needs, and make more informed decisions about product features and design. Personas also set the scene for the next technique: customer journey mapping.

Customer journey mapping (*https://oreil.ly/gFEwh*) visually captures the entire customer experience, highlighting touchpoints, emotions, and interactions, which aids in identifying pain points and opportunities. Using this technique, we map out the customer's journey from initial need or trigger, through the various stages of engagement, to the desired outcome. Considering the personas we have developed, we should understand their experiences, feelings, and challenges at each point of interaction with the product or service. The result is a comprehensive view that helps teams identify gaps and opportunities for addressing their customers' needs.

Customer interviews (*https://oreil.ly/N4NYC*) are another technique that can help to uncover customers' desires, pains, and perceptions through structured dialogue. These one-on-one interactions offer direct engagement, giving businesses the insight to validate assumptions and align product direction with real customers' needs. Having said that, we all know that there can be discrepancies between what customers say they will do and what they actually do. To reconcile that, we might use contextual inquiry (*https://oreil.ly/W_bEB*) to observe users in their natural environment, providing a complementary understanding of their challenges and real behaviors.

You might augment these core techniques with a range of other discovery activities (*https://oreil.ly/LUL2t*), such as diary studies, competitor research, surveys, or exploratory data analysis. Note that surveys and exploratory data analysis provide quantitative information to augment qualitative insight—they can reveal "how much" as well as "whether" this is an opportunity.

Together, these techniques provide an evidence-based foundation for formulating and testing hypotheses about the problem/solution fit (*https://oreil.ly/wIblW*) and product/market fit (*https://oreil.ly/1hxoN*) of our ideas, driving customer-centric product development.

 These Discovery techniques, especially in the initial stages of exploring opportunities, should ideally be designed and led by a user experience (UX) researcher. Their skills in customer research and product design help to bring out the voice of the customer and help to anchor Discovery around the needs of various customer personas.

At the same time, the lead UX specialist should actively share Discovery learnings and insights with the team to build empathy— to let the team see the customers' problems and walk for a while in their shoes. They can also involve other specialists in ML or engineering, where necessary. Great leads can enable their teammates to conduct these activities, while being mindful not to introduce their own biases.

Now that we've gone wide and discovered insights about problems, it's time to converge on the opportunities. Let's look at practices that help us with the second half of the first diamond: Define opportunities.

Canvases to Define Product Opportunities

Canvases are powerful tools for capturing opportunities as they help to articulate, externalize, debate, test, and evolve ideas during Discovery. Canvases are an evolution and extension of the Lean technique of A3 management (*https://oreil.ly/23YBB*). They aim to help people understand problems and identify digital solutions. One useful canvas is the Value Proposition Canvas (*https://oreil.ly/DO4Yf*). As illustrated in Figure 2-3, the Value Proposition Canvas helps teams understand the customers' needs—desires or "gains," challenges or "pains," and jobs to be done—and consider how they might design products and services to meet those needs, by creating gains and relieving pains.

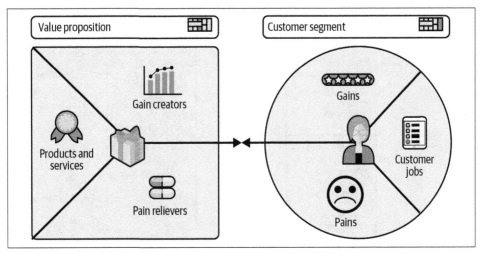

Figure 2-3. The Value Proposition Canvas (source: adapted from an image by Strate-gyzer [https://oreil.ly/DO4Yf], used with permission)

Let's look at two more canvases that are particularly helpful for highlighting specific concerns common to designing and delivering ML products: the Data Product Canvas and the Hypothesis Canvas.

Data Product Canvas

For ML product discovery, it's important to assess the value and feasibility of candidate solutions. One helpful tool in this regard is the Data Product Canvas (*https://oreil.ly/bLs8B*), which provides a framework for connecting the dots between data, ML, and value creation. You may have heard of the ML Canvas (*https://oreil.ly/75fLn*) before, but one downside of the ML Canvas is that it doesn't include measures of success, which is necessary for getting alignment and agreement among stakeholders on how to evaluate the fitness-for-purpose of candidate ML solutions. The Data Product Canvas addresses this gap and provides a comprehensive set of dimensions for shaping ML opportunities (see Figure 2-4).

Problem	Data	Solution	KPIs	Actions
Ask the right questions: • What is the problem? • Why is it a problem? • Whose problem is it? • Why, why, and why?	Ask the right questions: • Source • Quality • Access vs. availability • Process/transformation • Outputs • Test/training/validation	Ask the right questions: • Type (analytics, ML, AI, etc.) • What will the solution be? • Output expected?	Ask the right questions: • How to evaluate the model? • Which metrics should be used? • How much uncertainty can we handle? • A/B test: how?	Ask the right questions: • Which actions will be used? • Which campaigns?
	Hypothesis Ask the right questions: • What will be tested? • What are the expected responses for each of them? • What should we do for each answer? What strategy should we follow?		**Actors** Ask the right questions: • Who is your client? • Who are your stakeholders? • Who is your sponsor? • Who will use the solution? • Who will be impacted?	

Values	Risks	Performance/Impact
Ask the right questions: • What is the size of your problem? • What is the baseline? • What is the uplift/savings?	Ask the right questions: • What are the risks? • What might these risks block?	Ask the right questions: • What is the impact? How to measure it? • Where can you see this improvement/performance? Example: • Increase our customer base • Keep it by reducing churn • Saving lost revenue + A/B test • Reduce cost of acquisition

Figure 2-4. The Data Product Canvas (source: adapted from an image by Leandro Carvalho, PhD [https://oreil.ly/bLs8B], used with permission)

As depicted in Figure 2-4, the Data Product Canvas has three sections: product (four upper left sections), business strategy (three upper right sections) and business outcomes (lower three sections). We'll provide our commentary on how to effectively use each section of the canvas, and you can explore the details and questions for each section by referring to Figure 2-4. Let's start with dimensions in the product section:

Product

> *Problem:* We start by defining the problem clearly, using what we learned from Discovery. Three key questions to ask are: What's the problem? Why is it a problem? Whose problem is it? As Charles Kettering famously said (*https://oreil.ly/3keSv*), "a problem well-stated is a problem half-solved." By articulating the problem, teams will avoid wasting effort in solving the wrong problem.

Data: We identify the data and inputs the solution will depend on, and how we will access or curate the data and ascertain its suitability or quality for the solution. These are questions that will invariably come up during development, so addressing them at the outset can help us identify potential roadblocks.

Solution: Next, we define a candidate solution to the problem. This involves outlining a clear, actionable approach that addresses the core issue, considering both user needs and business objectives.

Hypothesis: During product development, we make assumptions all the time (e.g., Feature X will help users with Y). Hypotheses help us frame these assumptions as statements that we can test and validate through a series of experiments. We can define a hypothesis using the following template:

- We believe that [this capability] will result in [this outcome].
- We will know we have succeeded when [we see a measurable signal].

Let's say we have an idea that displaying personalized product recommendations will improve sales. We could define a hypothesis and subsequently an experiment to test this idea. For example:

- We believe that displaying personalized product recommendations will result in an increase in average order value.
- We will know we have succeeded when we see a 10% increase in average order value.[2]

Business strategy

Actors: We identify all actors—customers, stakeholders, sponsors, etc.—that will have some involvement with the product. We further refine this list after we've validated whether they resonate with what we've got in the Product section of the canvas—the problem, the solution, the data, and the hypothesis.

Actions: We define actions that will be implemented once the solution is ready. This helps to define the downstream beneficiaries of the ML product to reduce the chance of building a product that's left on a shelf—or costing money on the cloud. Useful questions include:

- How will the listed actors interact with or benefit from the product?
- How will the product generate value for the business?

---

2 One very expensive way to test this hypothesis is to build an actual product, put it in front of customers and see if average order value increases. By articulating our assumption as a hypothesis, we start to see simpler ways or implementations for testing our hypothesis. In this example, a cost-effective experiment could be a mock-up prototype test with several test customers. Not only can this experiment validate or invalidate our hypothesis, it can also provide a rich source of insights and learnings about what motivates a customer when purchasing a product that then influences our design decisions.

Key Performance Indicators (KPIs): These are the technical or operational measures of success that we can use to evaluate or monitor the quality of the ML product throughout its lifecycle. Useful questions to develop KPIs include:

- How do we evaluate if a model is "good enough" or "better than before"?
- What's the acceptable level of uncertainty in the ML product's effectiveness or accuracy?
- What is the actual business cost of a misprediction (e.g., false positives and false negatives)?

Business outcomes

Value: Articulating the potential value of an ML product can be hard, but it's an essential step in weeding out low-value ideas—something that we should do before rather than after sinking months of many people's efforts. Articulating value helps a lot with solution design and with reframing the problem to be solved. It might be that asking a "hard" question is ideal for the ML product, but too technically challenging to implement. Knowing the unique value proposition of the product helps us refactor the product scope. Asking the essential question first (e.g., can we recommend books that a user will click on or purchase?) will get us started in gathering the data we need to eventually address the hard question (e.g., can we recommend books to a user in real time, based on their interactions with other books?) .

Risks: While the Data Product Canvas is not intended as a risk management tool, identifying and mapping risks is critical for comprehensive planning. Understanding potential risks helps to seed notions of how we can assess and mitigate these risks before and during delivery. Useful frameworks for identifying risks include the Delphi method and SWOT matrix (*https://oreil.ly/-KLjc*). Useful questions to ask to identify risks include:

- What could go wrong? What are the failure modes of this product?
- What are the business and product costs of the model making mistakes?
- What could be the implications of these risks?

Performance and impact: This section focuses on estimating the product's impact on the business and how to measure it. By articulating the expected business impact of an idea and committing to measuring it over time, you're informing and supporting conversations to get business buy-in and alignment. Useful questions to ask include:

- What business metrics should we use to measure success, and how will we measure it (e.g., number of subscribers or members, revenue, customer satisfaction scores)?
- What is the baseline of that metric?
- What is the expected gain or savings from this new product?

 One common mistake that ML teams make is: I have a "shiny hammer," now what problems can I solve with it? In our experience, that rarely leads to good outcomes unless the team first identifies real customer problems to solve.

When building products, it's crucial to remember that the technology and the "how" are secondary. The primary focus should always be on the "what." What problems does the product solve? What value does it bring to customers?

Once the problem and need have been identified, we can better focus our technology efforts so that we leverage ML to solve the problem in the best way. In some cases, we may find that ML is only a small component of the solution. There may also be scenarios—such as in the Guide Dogs Victoria case shared earlier—where ML is not the best solution. Perhaps customers find alternatives more desirable. Perhaps alternatives are technically more feasible. Or perhaps alternatives are more viable for the organization.

Hypothesis Canvas

Another canvas that helps us systematically articulate and test our ideas in rapid cycles, and keep track of learnings over time is the Hypothesis Canvas (*https://oreil.ly/Ta7Ss*) (see Figure 2-5).[3] We introduced this canvas in Chapter 1. The Hypothesis Canvas helps us reduce uncertainty as we formulate testable hypotheses, identify objective metrics, and design lightweight experiments to rapidly validate or invalidate ideas. This technique is very helpful for discovery—be it discovery as the initial phase of a product, or the ongoing and continuous discovery during delivery as we mentioned earlier. (We'll discuss continuous discovery in the section "Cadence of Delivery Activities" on page 70.)

---

3 Using the term "hypothesis" enables teams to deal with uncertainty in the early stages of product development and creates space for people to contribute ideas to build alignment without having to have the "right" answer.

Hypothesis canvas

Business value	Problem	Customers
What is the business value associated with this hypothesis?	*What is the problem we are trying to solve?*	*Who is impacted by this problem?*

Hypothesis

What do we believe?

We believe that _____ will result in _____.

We will know we've succeeded when _____.

Metrics

Record a baseline of key metrics for this hypothesis.

Solutions/Ideas

How might we solve this problem?

Lessons learned

Record our lessons learned.

Figure 2-5. The Hypothesis Canvas (source: "Data-Driven Hypothesis Development" [https://oreil.ly/Ta7Ss] by Jo Piechota and May Xu, used with permission)

For example, with the excitement generated by Generative AI in 2023, you may be wading through an amorphous pool of exciting but fuzzy ideas for how to use AI to improve product experiences or internal processes. We've been in that boat before, and the Hypothesis Canvas helped us to articulate the business value and measures of success, and to collaboratively rank which hypotheses to prioritize, test, and deliver. It was a useful way to create alignment between various stakeholders—business, product, engineering, ML, etc. When we used this canvas, we were able to see the potential value of various ideas and filter and prioritize them accordingly to sharpen the focus of our efforts.

By articulating the parameters of the hypotheses, as outlined in Figure 2-5, we can focus on finding answers for important questions such as *why* an idea might be valuable, *who* will benefit from it, and *how* to know when we've succeeded. When we shift the focus from the solution (e.g., a shiny ML technique) to the problem, we're not wedded to the need to use ML to solve a problem. In some cases, we might discover that we can solve the problem simply and reliably without using ML—a path for delivering value without adding unnecessary complexity. Huzzah!

Now that you've seen techniques for discovering and defining opportunities, let's look at techniques for testing our hypotheses about these opportunities. For that, we'll transition into the second diamond to focus on rapidly designing, delivering, and testing candidate solutions.

Techniques for Rapidly Designing, Delivering, and Testing Solutions

While building a minimum viable product (MVP) in and of itself is a technique for testing our hypotheses about an opportunity, it's a highly costly one in terms of time and labor as compared to other validation techniques (see definition and discussion in the following sidebar: To MVP or Not to MVP?). Eventually, we want to start building and releasing an MVP to test our product with users in the market, but we want to be confident that we're investing our effort in an MVP that's worthwhile.

To MVP or Not to MVP?

"MVP" is one of those words that lose their meaning over the rough and tumble of the real world of product delivery. It often becomes a get-out-of-jail-free card for people to build shoddy workarounds in the name of "an MVP." In this chapter, we do our bit to reverse some of this semantic diffusion (*https://oreil.ly/mnmtZ*) and anchor MVP as a technique to help teams test if the product direction aligns with market needs, reduce the risk and cost of "big bang releases," and help teams feel the satisfaction of delivering value to customers early, and then often.

Various folks have proposed good reasons to ditch "MVPs" in favor of other terms such as Minimum Lovable Product (*https://oreil.ly/krJDO*) or Earliest Testable/ Usable/Lovable Product (*https://oreil.ly/z73kU*). Others have also made a good argument that no matter what we call it, we would still encounter the same problems if it's not well defined and understood within an organization.

We believe that these various formulations are describing the same essence that we all desire: a high-quality product (P) that coherently solves the customers' most pressing problems (V) that can be delivered early (M), and then refined iteratively.

For simplicity, we'll continue to use the term "MVP" in this chapter in this sense. In a later sidebar on releases, we'll compare MVP releases to other types of releases.

Teams can use the following techniques to design, test, and refine their hypotheses in a cost-effective way. These methods help teams to quickly weed out weak ideas, ensuring that only impactful and feasible concepts move forward to delivery.

Prototypes

Prototyping is a cost-effective technique that allows teams to explore, test, and refine their ideas before committing substantial resources to building an MVP. It is an indispensable tool in the Lean UX toolkit.

A range of prototypes. Prototyping varies in complexity and fidelity, ranging from low-fidelity sketches, such as paper prototypes (*https://oreil.ly/GCSyj*), to more refined and interactive digital prototypes (*https://oreil.ly/5TJRU*) and even technical prototypes, which we'll discuss in the next section. Low-fidelity visual prototypes are quick to create and cost-effective, allowing for rapid iteration and feedback gathering. They are particularly useful in the early stages of hypothesis testing, where the focus is on validating the fundamental aspects of the idea. As the concept matures, teams often move toward higher-fidelity digital prototypes (using tools such as Figma) or even technical prototypes.

For example, say we are an online book retailer, and we have a hypothesis that a dynamic real-time personalization will improve customer engagement and sales. Through prototype testing with test users, we might learn that a majority of test users didn't engage with personalized recommendations because the book cover alone wasn't enticing enough—they *would* have saved or purchased the book, however, if there was a summary of the best and worst reviews to give them a sense of social proof and whether the book would delight or disappoint them. Such learnings from prototype testing help us refine our understanding and move in the right direction when we design and deliver the product.

Through iterative prototyping, teams can quickly identify and discard weak ideas, thus ensuring that only the most impactful and promising concepts are further developed. This iterative cycle of prototyping, testing, and refining helps in reducing the risks associated with product development. It ensures that when the time comes to build and release an MVP, the product is grounded in validated learning, user feedback, and a well-considered design approach.

Technical prototypes, or proofs of concept (PoCs).   Once we've validated an idea or concept based on customer feedback, it's important to validate the feasibility of an idea through actual working software, as opposed to "slideware." Building technical prototypes or PoCs is especially important in ML because it can be hard to determine an ML model's real-world behavior unless we experiment and test those assumptions and see the results.

Later on, during the Delivery phase, there is a possibility that after several months of effort in building the MVP, we learn that the MVP's ML model can't meet performance expectations for production release. This is a situation we'd like to avoid, and we may be able to with PoCs. For example, if we know from Discovery that a poorly performing supply chain parts forecast model may cost the business millions of dollars, we can build a PoC to put bounds on feasibility. A well-designed PoC can help us *discover* any limitations in performance, technical feasibility, or sensitivity to various factors as early as possible, and help us determine if an idea is ready for *delivery* and productization. In addition, PoCs also help teams discover measures of success, potential pitfalls, unanticipated technical challenges, and appropriate problem framing as early as possible.

Note that PoCs may fail to prove that a concept is feasible or viable, and may only prove that we haven't yet found a way to solve this particular problem. Should this happen, you may treat it as valuable and low-cost learning, and a chance to direct resources to more promising opportunities.

In our experience, PoCs can be a useful tool for garnering stakeholder support—provided they are linked to a demonstrated customer or business need (as per the process we outline in this chapter)—as they provide tangible evidence of a solution's viability. When done well, they can help to communicate complex ML approaches and jargon into visual demonstrations and concrete outcomes, allowing nontechnical stakeholders to easily grasp the value and technical needs of a proposed solution.

Now, let's look at another technique for testing potential solutions.

Riskiest Assumption Test

> There is a flaw at the heart of the term Minimum Viable Product: it's not a product. It's a way of testing whether you've found a problem worth solving. A way to reduce risk and quickly test your biggest assumption. Instead of building an MVP, identify your riskiest assumption and test it. Replacing your MVP with a Riskiest Assumption Test (RAT) will save you a lot of pain.
>
> —Rik Higham (*https://oreil.ly/_tqzU*)

Rik Higham, in his article "The MVP Is Dead. Long Live the RAT" (*https://oreil.ly/_tqzU*), makes a clear and simple point: Building an MVP involves testing a few very risky and many not-so-risky assumptions. Conducting a Riskiest Assumption Test (RAT) would be a more cost-effective technique for identifying and testing the most critical assumptions that could make or break a product. Rik proposes we:

List all large assumptions and identify the riskiest one
Write down all the assumptions that must hold true in order for your product to succeed. Give each assumption a risk score (where risk is defined as the product of likelihood and impact)—a simple t-shirt sizing (small, medium, large, extra-large) will do. Identify the assumption that, if wrong, would be the *most* detrimental to the project's success. This is the riskiest assumption and could be related to customer behavior, market demand, technical feasibility, or any other critical aspect of the product.

Define a test for the riskiest assumption
The test should be as simple and as focused as possible to directly address the assumption. A test could take the form of user interviews, a minimal technical PoC, or even fake door tests (*https://oreil.ly/Z2Ykm*)—i.e., a landing page to gauge the number of users that would be interested in a feature. An article by Cadabra Studio (*https://oreil.ly/q3byP*) illustrates a few other creative tests devised at Airbnb, Zappos, and Buffer.

Conduct the test

Conduct the test to gather data around our riskiest assumption. If the assumption is validated, the project can proceed with a reduced level of risk. If the assumption is invalidated, the project may need to pivot or the team may need to reassess their approach.

Riskiest assumption tests can serve as a persevere-or-pivot criteria in the Discovery phase and encourage quick learning cycles and agile adaptation, both of which are key in helping to reduce uncertainty in where we spend our delivery efforts.

Product Thinking and Design Thinking: A Human-Centered Approach to Innovation

Design Thinking (*https://oreil.ly/BXcn7*) is a problem-solving methodology widely used in various industries to address complex challenges through a user-centered approach. It involves understanding the needs and experiences of users, redefining problems, and creating innovative solutions. This is an alternative framework to the Double Diamond. We chose the Double Diamond as our primary framework, but you can also organize the various techniques that we elaborated on this chapter using the Design Thinking framework, as well (see Figure 2-6).

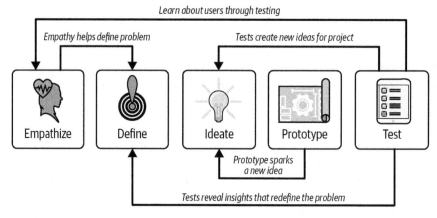

Figure 2-6. The Design Thinking process (source: adapted from an image by Interaction Design Foundation [https://oreil.ly/BXcn7])

The core principles of Design Thinking are:

Empathize

Understand the needs, desires, and challenges of the end users. This involves deep research and engagement to gain insights into the user's experiences and perspectives.

Define

Articulate the problem clearly. This stage involves synthesizing the information gathered during the Empathy phase into a clear problem statement, which guides the following Ideation process.

Ideate

Generate a wide range of creative ideas. This phase encourages thinking outside the box to explore a broad spectrum of possible solutions, without immediately limiting options due to feasibility or practicality.

Prototype

Create tangible representations of ideas. This involves building scaled-down versions or models of the proposed solutions, which can be anything from drawings to functional prototypes, depending on the complexity of the idea.

Test

Put the prototypes into action and gather feedback. This phase involves user testing, where feedback is used to refine and improve the solution. It often leads to new insights, which can loop back into any of the previous stages.

Design Thinking is iterative, meaning that it often involves going back and forth between these stages, refining and adjusting as more is learned about the user and the problem. It's highly collaborative and often involves cross-functional teams to bring different perspectives and expertise to the problem-solving process. This approach is used not only in product design but also in service design, business strategy, and organizational problem-solving.

Product Thinking (*https://oreil.ly/WIExn*) builds on Design Thinking by including product management practices to focus on the business or organizational viability of any product. This means developing product design through the product lifecycle from initial intensive investment to a sustainable offering characterized by incremental innovation, and eventually to retirement as market fit wanes. It also means thinking about product commercial models and coordinating people and resources within organizations to deliver the product. Product Thinking is also sometimes contrasted with a solution mindset, which might be said to deliver an ad hoc collection of point solutions, rather than a unified offering that coherently solves customer problems with a good user experience.

By the end of our Discovery phase, the team and business should have converged on a product idea (or ideas) that is desirable (i.e., can meet customers' wants or needs), viable (i.e., can be profitable), and feasible (i.e., achievable based on given resources and constraints). The evidence and shared context from Discovery support the process, if required, of making a compelling business case and getting funding to go after a product opportunity.

At this juncture, teams will turn to the next phase of product delivery: Inception. Inception helps teams to define actionable plans relating to product scope, technology, delivery planning, and risk management, among others, to guide the team in the right direction during product delivery. And that's the topic that we'll turn to next.

Inception: Setting Teams Up for Success

Before we start delivering and writing code, we can improve our chances of success by aligning all the key people around a lightweight plan. We're not talking about detailed waterfall-style planning that is handed down for implementation, but collaborative "just-in-time" planning to provide teams with enough runway to start building solutions and get everyone on the same page about delivery risks. These delivery risks often include misaligned expectations regarding product scope, definitions of done, ways of working, and wider organizational dependencies. If these are not clear, the delivery team will invariably experience release delays due to unmanaged risks becoming issues. However, if stakeholders are aware of risks and have a mechanism for monitoring and responding to them, teams can avoid these delays and even come out ahead.

In this section, we'll explain:

- What inception is, why it's valuable for helping teams define a clear delivery plan, and how teams can practice it
- How to write user stories to articulate feature descriptions, from a customer's perspective, that guide development by highlighting customer needs, business value, and definitions of done

Inception: What Is It and How Do We Do It?

Remember the movie (*https://oreil.ly/yd50Z*) about shared dreaming to implant an idea in someone's mind by executing an epic heist in the fifth level of their subconscious architecture? Well, coincidentally, Inception in this context is similar in that its fundamental purpose is to help the team and stakeholders come to a shared understanding of the product's vision, scope, objectives, and delivery plan. We know that we'll need to respond to change during delivery, and alignment to a shared understanding at the start gives us a great foundation to do so.

Inception comprises a set of activities that help teams start *shaping, sizing,* and *sequencing* the work needed to deliver the product. Depending on the size of endeavor, it can last between a few days to four weeks, but usually we want to avoid dragging it out longer than that. The heuristic is: just enough planning to get started. Inception should always immediately precede delivery and should involve the same team[4] and stakeholders as delivery. The lightweight nature of inception is made possible by carrying rich context into delivery. By ensuring clarity and alignment from the outset, teams can avoid many common pitfalls and challenges that arise due to unclear or misaligned expectations. If there is a significant pause, or the team is changed between phases, then that context decays or is lost entirely and the delivery team may feel no ownership of the plan and no commitment to achieve it.

While Discovery is focused on what problems we should be solving and what we might build to solve them, Inception focuses on elaborating the solution further, including the technical aspects of the solution and how the team will deliver it, in order to align on a plan. Ideally, the one team will carry context from Discovery into Inception and then into Delivery to maintain shared understanding, and get buy-in across the delivery team and business stakeholders regarding the scope and sequence of the work that needs to be done to deliver the product.

If, as may be the case for budgeting and funding reasons, the phases of product delivery need to be separated, then the best point to separate teams or activities is between Discovery and Inception. In this instance, Discovery findings regarding the opportunity and possible solutions should be carefully documented. Discovery should articulate the value in solving a problem, and it should also be possible to make a go/no-go decision for some level of delivery commitment (e.g., a team for six months) based on the outcomes of Discovery. If the decision is "go," then Inception and Delivery come as a package.

If it's very important not to exceed the allocated people and resources for the Inception/Delivery package, then Inception planning can focus on what Delivery scope is achievable within those bounds, rather than trying to understand the timeframes to deliver certain scopes. If Discovery was somewhat incomplete and further elaboration is required to make this go/no-go decision, then a go/no-go gate may also be instituted after Inception, with the understanding that a "no-go" decision would mean the end of the initiative (until something changes). In these ways, we can minimize investment risk through Discovery and Inception, while maintaining the advantages of these approaches.

In rare instances, the problem or opportunity may be so clear, simple, and compelling that Discovery is not required, and product delivery can start at Inception (please note, however, that without proper discovery we might not know if a problem is actually simple, or just appears that way!).

Let's look now at the details of running an Inception.

---

4 At least the same core team. If the delivery team is envisaged to be larger than about eight people, the whole team may not all be able to contribute effectively or efficiently in inception. In this case, we'd recommend that inception includes representation from all key roles, and that there is a plan to gradually roll on additional team members as delivery begins.

How to Plan and Run an Inception

Designing an Inception agenda depends on how much existing knowledge and the context the team has around the solution to be built. It's quite hard to prescribe a list of Inception activities in this chapter because it depends on the needs of the specific initiative. However, there are some great resources—"How to Plan an Inception" (*https://oreil.ly/VBJmy*), "Lean Inception" (*https://oreil.ly/G_XOU*), Atlassian's "Team Playbook" (*https://oreil.ly/9wwDZ*)—where you can see a menu of workshops and activities to choose from to compose your Inception agenda. These activities are intended to create clarity around business, product, people, process, technical, and prioritization questions.

At a minimum, we'd recommend an Inception agenda that covers the activities outlined in Table 2-1. Each activity is described in detail in "How to Plan an Inception" (*https://oreil.ly/VBJmy*). We recommend using this as a starting point and customizing your Inception agenda with additional activities that suit your specific needs.

Table 2-1. Inception activities, purpose, and artifacts

Activities	Purpose	Artifacts
1. Alignment on priorities (e.g., vision setting, trade-off sliders)	To establish a shared vision of the problem and product, identify key priorities and measures of success	• Elevator pitch (*https://oreil.ly/Bpxl6*) • Trade-off sliders (*https://oreil.ly/D743M*) • Measures of success
2. Defining the MVP	To define key elements of a product to launch with essential features	• MVP Canvas (*https://oreil.ly/6asl6*) • Hypotheses (*https://oreil.ly/-qmxz*) to be validated
3. Cross-functional requirements (CFRs)	To identify critical operational and architectural aspects of the MVP that can determine its success or failure	• A list of cross-functional requirements (*https://oreil.ly/W6qcM*) that are relevant for the MVP
4. Solution design and minimum viable architecture	To outline the basic architectural design of the solution	• Solution architecture (*https://oreil.ly/qrHTr*) (C4 diagrams [*https://oreil.ly/PemHl*] can be helpful here)
5. Path to production	To visualize and map the steps, people, tools, tasks, and output needed for a software change to reach production (Note: We'll discuss this topic further in Chapters 3, 4, and 9.)	• Path to production diagram (*https://oreil.ly/g17TK*)
6. Risks, assumptions, issues, and dependencies (RAIDs)	To identify risks, assumptions, issues, and dependencies that could impede the success of the product	• RAID Canvas (*https://oreil.ly/_TNrQ*)
7. Security threat modeling (*https://oreil.ly/z_ySr*)	To identify, assess, and find ways to mitigate potential security threats to a system or product	• Artifacts could include Attack Trees (*https://oreil.ly/A15wl*) or a threat model outlining key risks and mitigation plans (including ML-specific security vulnerabilities [*https://oreil.ly/3h4pQ*])

Activities	Purpose	Artifacts
8. Ethics and responsible technology (*https://oreil.ly/icVNH*)	To identify potential ethical violations and establish guidelines to ensure responsible use of technology in the product	• Artifacts depend on the specific activity, but could include failure modes and effects analysis table, or responsible strategy document
9. Release planning	To plan the release schedule of the product, including milestones and iterations	• High-level user story map and MVP backlog (*https://oreil.ly/KEFwb*) • Story estimates (*https://oreil.ly/7oaom*)
10. Ways of Working	To establish a team's norms and practices regarding how they collaborate, communicate, and operate on a day-to-day basis to ensure effective and efficient progress toward project goals	• Ways of Working (*https://oreil.ly/Zvowc*) documentation • Team members' roles and responsibilities (*https://oreil.ly/RA-mw*)

Special Mention: Cross-functional Requirements (CFRs)

If a product satisfies its functional requirements but fails to meet just one CFR—be it performance, capacity, speed, security, availability etc.—the product can falter and fail. For example, consider the example of an LLM-powered customer service agent that can correctly assist with many customer queries, but is also vulnerable to leaking training data (*https://oreil.ly/ywBVy*) through prompt injection attacks (*https://oreil.ly/S3htl*).

If not accounted for, these implicit requirements will present themselves as unplanned work or even production incidents further down the road, which is a guarantee that the team's timelines will be derailed. As such, a key Inception activity is to review a list of CFRs (*https://oreil.ly/W6qcM*) and decide on which CFRs are relevant for the MVP. Through this exercise, we arrive at a set of implicit behaviors that we agree our ML product must have or should have.

Whether we are considering ways to simplify our solution or surface implicit behaviors our solution should have, these discussions help us further distill what we are building. They'll also help us start to get a sense of how *complex* the build may be.

Note that the mechanics of Inception activities are also crucial in achieving good results. Involving the right people, full participation, and strong facilitation over a short, intensive period will yield the best results. Facilitators should pay careful attention to the design of sessions, typically including visual as well as verbal collaboration, and be prepared to encourage or moderate contributions to ensure the outputs represent the whole group's collective knowledge.

In the world of remote work and geographically distributed teams, remote collaboration and visual facilitation tools are helpful in these Inception activities. They encourage visual thinking, clear communication, and shared understanding among team members as the team shapes various aspects of the product delivery plan—be it technical, business, risks, scope, etc. (Needless to say, all participants should be fully engaged while in session instead of checking emails or messages!)

It's important that these activities produce artifacts that inform and guide the team during execution (see example in the following sidebar). Some of these outputs become living artifacts, reviewed and updated iteratively during Delivery to reflect our body of knowledge and context gained over time.

Example of Using Inception Artifacts: Setting Up a Path to Production

Each Inception activity produces an artifact that is intended to help the team during delivery. For example, the path to production activity should produce a high-level diagram detailing how a code change or data change is tested and eventually deployed to production.

The path to production artifact provides the team with clarity on how to set up a path to production in iteration zero. Iteration zero is the first iteration during delivery where the team focuses on setting up the necessary infrastructure, environments, and access to facilitate the smooth execution and an established path to production for subsequent iterations. It builds our team's confidence and it flushes out any architectural unknowns from the get-go.

You may be wondering, how do I know whether an Inception has succeeded in achieving its objectives? There is a good litmus for this. At the end of an Inception, the team and stakeholders should all:

- Describe the same vision, business value, and scope of the first release or MVP (see example user story map in Figure 2-7)
- Understand the backlog of high-level user stories, prioritized based on customer value
- Agree on a roadmap or timeline for the first and subsequent releases, based on high-level effort estimates, and the cadence of activities for delivery
- Agree on the measures that will indicate if we're on track, or if we need to course-correct
- Have a clear, shared view of the main risks, assumptions, issues, and dependencies

The book curator project, shown in Figure 2-7, is an example that we made up that provides personalized book recommendations. The MVP line indicates what is in scope for the MVP release—this is determined during Inception based on team discussions around value and effort. An actual user story map would encompass more stories, but we've kept it to just a few for readability in this image.

Figure 2-7. An example user story map for a book curator product

As you may have noticed in Figure 2-7, high-level user stories, while clear on value by this point, will still require much more detailing. As engineers and ML practitioners dive into technical tasks such as setting up the path to production in iteration zero, the Product Triad (product manager, engineering lead, designer)[5] will typically collaborate to refine user stories for the upcoming iteration or iterations.

Given that user stories define product iterations, let's now look at some practices and techniques that help teams write effective user stories.

User Stories: Building Blocks of an MVP

A user story (*https://oreil.ly/tFJKe*) is the smallest unit of value that can be independently shipped to production. A user story is the quantum, or building block, of the functionality of the product. Under agile methodologies, it's also the quantum or building block of the project scope, so that product and project progress are linked.

---

5 The three roles in Product Triad are just a starting point, and teams should involve various members where necessary to provide clarity or guidance when creating user stories. It's important to strike a balance, as involving too many team members in the story-writing process can become time-consuming and disruptive.

User stories are the vehicle for translating ideas, intents, and context into clear, business-validated acceptance criteria that guide team members—be they developers, data scientists, ML engineers, quality analysts, etc.—to know what to build, and how to know when the feature is done.

Defining Terms Related to User Stories

In this section, we refer to several terms that are often used in agile software delivery. For readers who are new to these concepts, we'd like to briefly define what they mean:

Acceptance criteria
> A user story contains one or more acceptance criteria. Acceptance criteria help teams define a shared understanding of what the team needs to build. Before implementation, this criteria enables teams to articulate and validate the functionality they should be working toward for a given story. During or after implementation, this criteria enables teams to know how to test if a user story has been implemented satisfactorily.
>
> Without acceptance criteria, teams will experience higher rates of information loss between product and engineering. There are some templates or formats for acceptance criteria (*https://oreil.ly/Cz8MN*), such as given-when-then. In the interest of brevity, we won't strictly follow these formats in this chapter, but encourage you to use a format that works for your team.

Definition of done (DoD)
> The definition of done (*https://oreil.ly/xCsK_*) is an agreed-upon set of items that must be completed before a project or user story can be considered complete. Some common examples include: meets acceptance criteria, automated tests written and are passing, and deployed to production.

Vertical slicing
> A vertically sliced story, mentioned in Chapter 1, represents a feature or product functionality from the user's perspective, organized in a way that cuts through all layers of the application stack, from the frontend to any other supporting backend aspects such as data pipelines and ML models. Your definition of "frontend" will differ depending on who your users are. For example, if you are a platform team delivering an ML platform product for data scientists, the frontend may be a command-line tool instead of a UI application.
>
> This is in contrast to horizontally sliced stories. For example, one story focused on getting the data ready for an ML model, another story to train an ML model, and yet another story to integrate the model with the frontend. We may discover at the final horizontal layer (e.g., integrating the model with the frontend) that we don't have all the features available at low latency during inference, which puts to waste the time and effort we spent on the first two stories.

Let's look at techniques for defining and refining user stories.

User stories are vertically sliced

A vertically sliced story is more than just a requirements artifact. It may not provide as much detail as a traditional requirements document, but it provides more context, a test specification, a means to coordinate work and track progress, and all while promising rich conversations about user needs between team members with varied specializations. A well-written vertically sliced story helps us get into the right mindset to solve a problem. Because the moment we pick up a user story, we are shifting our focus away from the low-level weeds of engineering and ML implementation details to the high-level understanding of how to *build the right thing*.

So, what might a vertically sliced story look like? A vertically sliced story represents a feature or some product functionality from the user's perspective, cutting through all layers of the application stack. It encapsulates the customer's need, the interaction between the customer and the product, and the value or outcome they expect. The user story statement begins with a clear user role, followed by an action or intent, and concludes with the desired result. For example: "As a [persona], I want to [action/intent] so that [desired outcome]." (See example in the sidebar "Sample User Story" on page 64.)

The user story statement is typically augmented by story-specific acceptance criteria, which provide a method to verify when the story is complete. "Complete" for any story also typically has a specific meaning, as per the definition of done, which includes all the cross-functional requirements and tasks to be finished before the next story can be picked up.

This format not only provides clarity on the user's objective but also offers developers and designers the context they need to make design decisions. It also articulates the business value and acceptance criteria to help create a shared understanding among the team on the story's value and definition of done. By focusing on the end-to-end user experience, vertically sliced stories ensure that the team's efforts are aligned with the user's goals and the broader product vision, setting up a positive feedback loop for delivering value, rather than simply completing tasks for the sake of it.

Sample User Story

Title: Personalized Product Recommendations on the Home Page

As an online shopper,

I want to see relevant product suggestions,

so that I can get what I need easily each time I shop.

Acceptance criteria:

- The home page should display a "Recommended for You" section with at least five product suggestions.

- Recommendations should update based on recent browsing activity and purchases.

- If I purchase a recommended product, similar products should be suggested in the future.

- I should have the option to provide feedback on recommendations, such as "Not Interested," to refine future suggestions.

- The system should not repeatedly suggest items I've already purchased or explicitly marked as uninteresting.

You may be thinking, Wow, gee, that looks like one big story—training and evaluating a product recommendations model based on a user's browsing and purchase history, measuring product similarity, updating the home page, and a feedback channel. Well, you are right—that is a very big story, one we intentionally crafted. We did this because tackling large stories is a prevalent challenge in many teams, and we want to demonstrate how you could slice this further into smaller units of value that can be delivered in parallel. That's the focus of the next section: slicing and dicing stories.

Slicing and dicing user stories

Stories that get too large suffer from several problems, such as increased complexity, difficulty in estimating and tracking progress, and accumulation of weeks of work in progress (WIP) for a single user story, which can lead to bottlenecks and reduced team throughput and morale. To help us ensure that a story's scope doesn't get blown out of proportion, we can slice a big story into smaller stories.

To guide our slicing decisions, we can use INVEST principles (*https://oreil.ly/tvrcy*). These principles should hold true as much as possible because these attributes will be what give us an indicator of how vertically sliced we've made our story. INVEST is an acronym that stands for:

Independent
Each story should stand alone, independent of other stories. This allows them to be developed, prioritized, and implemented in any order and in parallel.

Negotiable
Rather than being a contract, a story is a conversation starter. Details can be discussed and adjusted based on collaboration between the delivery team and the product owner.

Valuable
Every story should deliver value to the end users or the business. If it doesn't, it might not be worth including in the product backlog.

Estimable
The team should be able to estimate the effort required for a story. If a story can't be estimated because it's too vague, it's a hook for the team to clarify the details in the story or decompose the problem further.

Small
Stories should be small enough to be completed within one iteration. If they're too large, they should be split into smaller, more manageable pieces.

Testable
There should be clear criteria to determine when a story is done and working as expected. Without this, it's hard to know when the work is truly complete.

The Testable principle, in particular, presents unique challenges in ML, especially when expressed as a threshold for a given measure (let's take F-score [*https:// oreil.ly/OAXne*] as an example). First, the chosen measure may involve reconciling objectives in conflict or on a Pareto front (*https://oreil.ly/mYOsH*) (false positives and false negatives in the case of F-score) and typically has a political element, reflecting the influence of various stakeholders and who stands to gain and lose from a given metric (here's where a story can be Negotiable!). Second, it may be difficult to choose the threshold when the measure is a proxy for business and customer outcomes. In this case, iteration and further negotiation is required to determine what level of performance is acceptable. Third, results typically vary between runs and this needs to be accommodated to avoid spurious test successes or failures.

These issues are inherent to ML and can't be wished away. However, they can be addressed at the correct point in product development to improve your chances of success. For instance, capture and gain agreement on the organizational trade-offs[6] early in Discovery or Inception so this is not a nasty surprise later. Incrementally raise thresholds based on reasonable expectations, rather than try to achieve aspirational jumps in a single step. (Independent and Estimable principles also help us work in incremental model-centric or data-centric improvements.) Become comfortable with statistical thinking in test-driven development and automated testing. With these approaches, you can bring the effectiveness of user stories to ML product development.

As with all principles, there are exceptions. For example, with the Independent principle, it's often impossible to eliminate inter-story dependencies. But we still do our best to make them as independent as possible so that each pair in a team can pick up stories in parallel and independently of another pair. In our experience, the INVEST principles help us ensure that our user stories are clear, actionable, and aligned with the project's goals, leading to more efficient and effective product development.

---

6 Cost-sensitive learning techniques can help gain agreement on trade-offs and provide a range of augmentations (treatment of data, training or inference) to basic ML techniques, with the goal of building solutions that are sensitive to the costs of different types of mistakes. We'll discuss cost-sensitive learning further in Chapter 6.

Breaking Down "Personalized Product Recommendations on the Home Page" into Smaller User Stories: An Example of Further Vertical Slicing

Here's an example of how the very big story from the sidebar "Sample User Story" on page 64 can be decomposed into smaller user stories.

Notice that User Story 2 is a spike (*https://oreil.ly/nPKT-*)—which is a timeboxed experiment or investigation to help teams reduce uncertainty, test assumptions, and learn rapidly. The outcomes of this spike inform if and how we can shape and deliver this feature as described in User Story 3. Later, when we discuss dual track delivery, you can see how spikes and experiments facilitate continuous discovery in ML projects.

User Story 1: Basic Recommendations on Home Page

> **As an** online shopper,
>
> **I want to** see a list of products recommended based on my purchasing history,
>
> **so that I can** find items that may interest me.

Acceptance criteria:

- The home page displays a "Recommended for You" section, with five items.
- Product recommendations are based on recent purchases.
- We have a mechanism for assessing the quality of recommendations in production.

User Story 2: [Spike] Experiment with Reinforcement Learning for Real-Time Recommendations

Value:

- Learnings from this experiment will help us assess the feasibility of real-time reinforcement learning for our product and identify an implementation approach for delivery (see User Story 3).

Outcomes:

- Extract or generate some representative data: user interactions with items and outcomes
- Determine one or more feasible reinforcement learning techniques
- Implement and demonstrate prototype(s) in notebook(s) and share with team
- Propose performance benchmark against alternatives
- Capture considerations for high-level solution and data architecture for real-time recommendations

Estimate:

- Timebox: 5 days[7]

User Story 3: Personalized Recommendations Based on Real-Time User Interactions

As an online shopper,

I want to see a list of products recommended based on what I "starred"
when I'm browsing,

so that I can discover items that will interest me.

Acceptance criteria:

- ...

Dependencies:

- Implementation approach depends on User Story 2: Experiment with Reinforcement Learning for Real-Time Recommendation

User Story 4: Avoiding Redundant Recommendations

As an online shopper,

I don't want to see products I've already purchased or marked as uninterested,

so that I see a variety of new recommendations.

Acceptance criteria:

- ...

User Story 5: Feedback Mechanism for Recommendations

As an online shopper,

I want to provide feedback on the recommended products,

so that future suggestions can be more aligned with my tastes.

Acceptance criteria:

- ...

---

7 Notice that the estimate for a spike is in absolute days, rather than story points. Spikes are intended to address inherently uncertain areas (i.e., things that are hard to estimate). As such, the team discusses and agrees on a reasonable duration for achieving the intent of the experiment to avoid getting lost in the rabbit holes of endless R&D.

User story: The promise for a conversation

When working with a story, team members may either complain that "this still looks quite vague," or that "this is way too much information about things I don't need to know or that don't need to be written!" It's not uncommon to hear both of these views within the one team and that's OK.

A vertically sliced story is a promise (*https://oreil.ly/66j7K*) for a conversation (*https://oreil.ly/WTKZ_*). How do we know when we have the right amount of detail in a user story? Well, by getting feedback from the team. During delivery, story refinement and estimation sessions (*https://oreil.ly/LOeU8*) or story kickoffs (*https://oreil.ly/JG8Qv*) are great opportunities to assess whether we have the right amount of detail added—team members will either have more clarifying questions or there will be a consensus around what the scope of the work is.

High-performing delivery teams don't shy away from having rich conversations around vertically sliced user stories, partly because there's a genuine desire to maintain a shared understanding across the team.

At this point, we have completed Inception and have a backlog with well-written user stories for the first one or two iterations, and the team is ready to start delivery. Let's now turn to the final section of this chapter: Delivery. Here, we'll discuss practices that help teams establish a rhythm of delivery, feedback, and continuous discovery.

Product Delivery

Product delivery is where most of the action happens, where most of the cost, time, and effort is incurred, and it's also where teams experience common execution traps such as unplanned or hidden work, scope creep, shifting priorities, and unidentified dependencies—all of which can derail a team's planned timeline and objectives. It's also where we get to build something together and where value is delivered to the customer!

In this section, we'll elaborate on delivery and ongoing planning techniques that help teams mitigate these challenges by shaping and sequencing units of value that product engineering teams can iteratively deliver in sprints. In particular, we'll cover:

- Delivery activities that help teams establish a cadence of delivery, feedback, and continuous discovery
- Measuring progress in product and delivery to help teams understand if they are making progress, making the right sort of progress, and making enough progress across delivery, product, and model quality, or if they need to course-correct

Note that, as per the outputs of a good inception, we should enter product delivery with a clear and shared view of the cadence of delivery activities (i.e., Ways of Working as defined in Table 2-1) and a clear idea of how to measure different dimensions of delivery. Both cadence and measures may evolve as circumstances change, but at each transition we should again collectively understand the delta and the new state.

Let's start with delivery activities.

Cadence of Delivery Activities

The process of building and delivering a digital product offers many valuable opportunities for feedback and continuous learning. In our experience, the rate at which we receive and learn from feedback is critical for success. For example, a team may decide to showcase their progress to product owners and key stakeholders once every two months, only to get feedback that they've misunderstood the customer's needs. Or they may find out during the showcase that another team has solved the exact problem that they're trying to solve. The team would have benefited from getting this feedback earlier if they'd organized a fortnightly showcase to share the team's progress early and often.

Let's look at a set of delivery activities that help teams foster such continuous discovery and continuous learning, and help teams improve the rate at which they refine their approach and product:

Iteration planning

Iteration planning helps the team align on the objectives and scope for the upcoming sprint or iteration. When the team has a prioritized backlog of refined stories, iteration planning is about pulling in a set of high-priority stories that align with or define the team's iteration goal. The stories planned for an iteration should also fit within a team's given capacity and velocity (more on this in the next section on measuring delivery metrics).

Planning should be a collaborative effort, involving data scientists, ML engineers, product managers, and other stakeholders, ensuring that everyone has a shared understanding of the work cut out for the team in the next iteration.

In our experience, iteration planning usually helps to surface valuable and early feedback. For example, a product owner would typically provide insight on what's the most valuable or important stories for the next iteration. That's a piece of feedback that we'd appreciate receiving earlier rather than later (e.g., after spending two weeks working on a low-priority story)!

Daily standup

Standup is a regular coordination activity to ensure the team is collectively working effectively and efficiently. See "It's Not Just Standing Up: Patterns for Daily Standup Meetings" (*https://oreil.ly/jwawS*) by Jason Yip for more.

Story delivery

With each iteration, the team (often in pairs) will progress stories through the story lifecycle, including analysis, development, and testing activities. Individuals may take one part of the lifecycle or may stay with a story through the whole lifecycle. The team coordinates around story delivery activities through daily standup, with the general intent to maximize the flow of work at a sustainable quality. Flow and quality is often achieved by limiting the team's work in progress (WIP) to a small number of stories or tasks. Showcases, retrospectives, and future iteration planning will be based on the stories delivered in each iteration and what remains in the backlog.

Regular showcases

Showcases are an opportunity to share learning and insights, and to receive feedback on new features or any work in progress. Typically held at the end of an iteration, showcases allow for transparent communication about the project's current state. This is not just a moment to celebrate achievements but also to discuss challenges and gather insights. For instance, stakeholders might point out features that align or conflict with broader organizational goals, or highlight synergies with what another team is working on.

In the absence of regular showcases, we find that teams can get trapped in weeks and weeks of development and miss out on valuable feedback that can help them calibrate their approach or direction. Showcases also force teams to articulate value and to complete functionality to some level, rather than allowing ambiguity to persist.

Retrospective

Retrospectives, also typically conducted at the end of each iteration, provide a forum for the team to reflect on their recent work, discussing what went well and identifying areas for improvement. Reflection is essential for continuous learning and improvement, as they allow team members to openly celebrate successes, identify shared impediments, and brainstorm solutions collaboratively.

When done well, retrospectives help to foster connection, engagement, and psychological safety as well. We discuss this further in Chapter 10.

Ongoing risk management

Remember the RAIDs canvas from Inception? That's just a starting point, and we regularly revisit it to address any risks, assumptions, issues, and dependencies that can derail the team's success.

Ongoing risk management is vital for identifying and addressing potential issues before they become major problems. This involves continuous monitoring and assessment of risks throughout the project lifecycle. Teams also regularly update their risk logs if they've encountered any new risks through the course of their work (e.g., if they noticed model quality issues or new failure modes during development).

This proactive approach allows teams to mitigate risks in a timely fashion, rather than reacting to them when they materialize. Regular risk assessment meetings can be integrated into the team's routine, ensuring that risk management is not an afterthought but a fundamental part of the team's cadence.

Architectural decisions

Teams invariably need to make architectural decisions in the course of developing the solution, and this can range from choices about the solution architecture to the technologies used. These decisions have long-term impacts on the project's scalability, maintainability, and functionality. Therefore, it's important to approach them collaboratively, involving the team's engineers, architects, and other interested stakeholders.

By having discussions involving the relevant people and documenting the team's considerations and decisions, the team can ensure that these architectural choices are well-informed, transparent, and aligned with both the immediate and future needs of the project. Useful tools in this regard include the DACI decision-making framework (*https://oreil.ly/wOrl0*)[8] and lightweight Architecture Decision Records (ADRs) (*https://oreil.ly/3dgr1*).

Continuous discovery

Remember the practices that we covered in the first section of this chapter such as customer interviews, customer journey mapping, prototyping, and assumption testing? Well, these practices are not "one-and-done" activities that you do once and never touch again until the MVP or product is released. In *Continuous Discovery Habits*, author Teresa Torres talks about how you can apply these practices as ongoing, iterative processes in the development of an MVP or other product.

By continuously engaging in these practices, teams evolve their understanding of customer needs and behaviors based on what's needed for the product at each point in time. This can include weekly interactions with customers to create a constant stream of feedback that informs rapid prototyping and testing. This approach enables teams to quickly validate or refute assumptions, making data-driven decisions to continuously steer the product in the right direction.

---

8 DACI stands for Driver, Approver, Contributor, Informed.

Dual-track delivery

As alluded to in the first section of this chapter, building an ML product is unlike building a typical web application, and often requires experimentation (both technical and nontechnical) to test assumptions and hypotheses. To aid us with this, we can apply *dual-track delivery*, which is an approach that helps teams determine the right thing to build, as they build it. It splits projects up into two distinct but interdependent tracks: Discovery and Development (see Figure 2-8). This dual-track method helps teams learn and deliver in short cycles by combining innovative exploration (Discovery) with effective execution (Development).

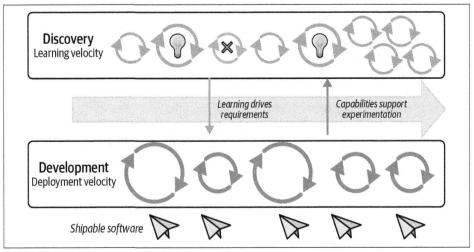

Figure 2-8. Diagram of the dual track delivery model (source: adapted from an image in "Electrifying the World with AI Augmented Decision-Making," Thoughtworks [https://oreil.ly/zVsoa])

By adopting a dual track development model, research and development can proceed in parallel. Teams can pursue knowledge and understanding of the right thing to build through "discovery track" activities including stakeholder research, literature review, and timeboxed data science experimentation.

Meanwhile, teams' commitment to good engineering practices (which we will explore in Chapters 3 to 9) in the "development track" allows them to adapt and make change at speed with confidence. In our experience, this enables teams to build the thing right, so they can evolve the solution rapidly and predictably in coordination with their evolving understanding.

Where Are All the Releases?

With a continuous delivery model, we aim to make the question of "what and when to release" a business decision, rather than a technology decision. Certain releases might attract significant business go-to-market (GTM) activity including promotions, education, or change management, and it's important to coordinate on this. However, with a defined and automated path to production, and by delivering stories in vertical slices to a definition of done, we aim to bake the product release effort into each story, so that releases don't need special attention beyond story delivery.

In this chapter, we've already introduced the concept of an MVP as one type of release. On the path to MVP, we may also conduct what are known as *alpha* and *beta* releases. Alpha releases are typically to a small group of key users as an additional validation mechanism as soon as core functionality is available. Beta releases are typically to a wider but still limited group of users, meant to respond to alpha release feedback and continue to course-correct toward a general release of the product. Of course, sometimes these terms might be used differently.

The practices that we'll discuss in Chapters 3 to 9 help us make releases become a regular activity with no special fanfare, other than that warranted by the enormous value we're delivering!

For our final delivery practice, let's look at measures that help teams quantify and maintain their delivery and product objectives, and make corrective interventions if they're not on track.

Measuring Product and Delivery

Teams need measures throughout product delivery to understand if they are making progress, making the right sort of progress, and making enough progress. In this section, we'll introduce some key measurement techniques and some considerations for their application.

Delivery measures

One often-overlooked practice when teams are in the weeds of doing the work is capturing delivery metrics (*https://oreil.ly/OyZmp*) about the work (e.g., scope completed per iteration, cycle time, and defect rates) over time. If we think of the team as a production line—producing creative solutions, and not cookie cutter widgets—these metrics help teams regularly monitor delivery health and raise flags when they're veering off track from the delivery plan or timelines.

Let's look at how it works in practice with an example using a burn up chart (*https://oreil.ly/DrN_a*), a visual tool showing the total scope of the project and the total work completed over time (see Figure 2-9).

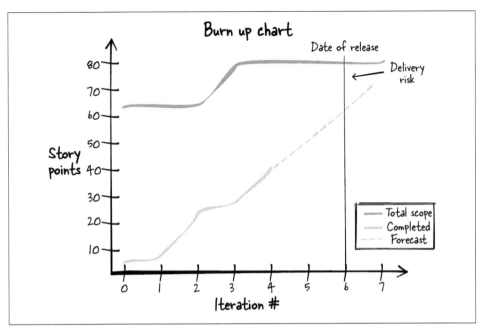

Figure 2-9. Burn up chart illustrating the project's planned scope and the actual work completed per iteration. In this example, the burn up chart helped us notice that the team can't finish all the stories in scope before the release scheduled at the end of iteration 6.

As illustrated in Figure 2-9, tracking the project's planned scope and the actual work completed per iteration helps a team see if they are on track for delivering a product according to the planned timelines, or if there are any risks of missing the planned release. Early visibility of such discrepancies is highly beneficial as it indicates potential issues with the team's current delivery practices or in some cases, inadequate scope management. In following the agile principle (*https://oreil.ly/fk2CY*) of "responding to change over following a plan," teams can take steps to calibrate the delivery plan by managing scope, increasing capacity, focusing on quality, or even revising timelines accordingly.

Velocity—illustrated as the gradient of the dotted Forecast line in Figure 2-9— informs iteration planning and prioritization decisions, ensuring that teams don't overcommit to what they can deliver only to set themselves up for a morale hit or dissatisfied stakeholders when they miss iteration goals or a planned release. Historical velocity (the gradient of the solid Completed line) records *actual* delivery performance, which is extrapolated into the future as Forecast velocity (the gradient of the dotted Forecast line). Typically, the mean historical velocity of the last three iterations is used for forecasting. This current, evidence-based forecast is crucial for managing stakeholder expectations, coordinating with other organizational functions such as marketing, and ensuring timely product delivery. It also helps teams mitigate Hofstadter's Law (*https://oreil.ly/yuRYD*), which states that "it always takes longer than you expect, even when you take into account Hofstadter's Law."

You might be asking at this point: So how do I do this in my team? Atlassian's article on burn up charts (*https://oreil.ly/DrN_a*) is a useful reference, but in a nutshell, you'd need to measure: (i) the number of story points completed in each iteration, and (ii) the total story points of all the stories that are part of an MVP or product release. As mentioned earlier, story points are estimated (*https://oreil.ly/7oaom*) based on the delivery team's understanding of a story's complexity, effort, and uncertainty.

It's essential to note that velocity is a team-specific metric, meaning it's not useful for comparing different teams. Instead, its primary purpose is to help individual teams understand their own delivery health and make necessary calibrations and trade-offs to facilitate progress toward the ultimate delivery targets.

In summary, delivery measures help us understand whether we are building the thing right. We've discussed scope and velocity in detail, but there are other important measures such as defect rates (*https://oreil.ly/OyZmp*) and cycle time (*https://oreil.ly/F81-q*).

As early as possible in delivery, we also want to have a view of product and model performance to understand whether we are building the right thing. Let's explore what this looks like in practice next.

Product measures

There are a number of frameworks for measuring product performance, which account for the maturity of the product and objectives of the organization. Generic metrics typically focus on user engagement with the product and financial results due to the product's usage, but individual products may have their own specific measures. These measures are examples of Product Thinking.

The delightfully named Pirate Metrics (*https://oreil.ly/n7lfu*)—Acquisition, Activation, Retention, Referral, Revenue (AARRR)—provide a funnel view of users' lifecycle with the product to help identify where marketing and development efforts should be focused for the greatest return. Introduced in 2007 by Dave McClure, Pirate Metrics (or some variant) remain widely applicable for SaaS products.

The One Metric That Matters (OMTM [*https://oreil.ly/K7zMB*]) framework encourages product teams to remain focused on the single metric that is most appropriate for their phase of product development. It doesn't ignore but rather subordinates other measures. It also encourages teams to seek leading and relative measures for shorter feedback cycles.

We encourage you to have some version of these product measures in place once you are in a position to track consumption.

Model measures

Our ML models are a key outcome of our delivery efforts and potentially a key determinant of product performance. If we're ambitious enough, with reinforcement learning (*https://oreil.ly/Cf39t*) for instance, we could allow our model or agent to directly optimize product or business measures such as acquisition. This approach can be de-risked by permitting only preapproved actions. For instance, product hero images might be selected using reinforcement learning from a preapproved set to maximize engagement.

Where these direct approaches are not preferred or feasible, however, we typically must choose model performance measures that are proxies for, or components of, product measures. We then attempt to build ML models that maximize these indirect measures.

A typical example metric is accuracy or F-score for a classifier. During product development, we set an aspirational goal and/or a minimal threshold for these measures, which we may adjust with continuous discovery. As we raised earlier, however, the process of translating product measures to model measures may not be straightforward and may be political, but it may be necessary in order to give teams autonomy to improve their model's performance. Consider a financial services start-up launching a new product aiming for maximum acquisition through a smooth sign-up flow. Now imagine the financial crimes team requires certain minimum checks, which are triggered based on indicators. When good customers are flagged (poor fraud precision resulting in false positives) they may drop out of the sign-up flow, reducing acquisition. If bad actors are not flagged (poor fraud recall resulting in false negatives), the business may face losses due to fraud and its customer impact, or even fines or sanctions. The team will only be able to optimize to some agreed balance.

With agreed measures, we wish to demonstrate steady progress from our current baseline or alternative solution (e.g., majority class prediction) toward this goal for the metric, based on continuous discovery and delivery. Considering dual track delivery, model performance gains may be discovered through experiments and prototypes on the discovery track, and baked into the product through delivery of stories. Model measures give us another view of progress and another opportunity to course-correct.

Discovery measures

In examining model measures, we distinguished discovery and development tracks in a dual track delivery model. While the outcome of delivery activities is largely determined by what's defined in user stories, the outcome of discovery activities is unknown *a priori*, or we wouldn't need to do discovery.

The challenge then is how to measure discovery. Key indicators for discovery are that you have a deep and broad portfolio of meaningful experiments (many options for value creation) that can be conducted in reasonable timeboxes (predictable exercises of those options). So, for discovery, we'd recommend regularly reviewing the experiment backlog and tracking, and seeking to minimize cycle time for experimentation to drive model performance. You can refer to "Data-Driven Hypothesis Development" (*https://oreil.ly/Ta7Ss*) for a lightweight example of how to manage your experiment backlog and keep track of experiment outcomes to avoid the trap of endless R&D. We also discuss this, taking a data science view on engineering effectiveness, in Chapter 10.

Commentary on measures

Teams should acknowledge the tendency and risks for metrics to be misused, abused, gamed, and ultimately dysfunctional (*https://oreil.ly/hAyjy*). As Goodhart's Law (*https://oreil.ly/d263p*) states, "when a measure becomes a target, it ceases to be a good measure." So, teams should view these measures primarily as guides for improving their own performance, not as ends in themselves. We'll discuss this in greater detail in Chapter 10 (see the sidebar "Pitfalls of Measuring Productivity, and How to Avoid Them" on page 331). Leaders play a crucial role in ensuring that teams are measuring the right outcomes and continuously improving (*https://oreil.ly/KbE2O*) to find the appropriate metrics for their organization's ML delivery capability.

It's important to note that the ability to use such metrics effectively depends on the level of psychological safety within a team and organization. We've seen cases where, driven by fear of repercussions for not meeting delivery timelines, teams over-report their progress and under-report delivery challenges. Everything looked green when they were in fact amber or red, and teams on the ground were under pressure to meet unrealistic timelines without attention to underlying impediments.

In contrast, in a safe environment, delivery metrics are used purely for continuous improvement to help us improve our "production line" over time and help us meet our product delivery goals. We'll discuss how you can cultivate psychological safety within your team in Chapter 11.

With the last of the delivery practices done, let's wrap up this chapter on product and delivery practices!

Conclusion

All of the practices that we've covered in this chapter are about helping teams shorten feedback loops and reduce wasted effort:

- Instead of finding out in two weeks that a developer or ML practitioner's solution did not align with business expectations, spend a few hours writing and validating some user stories.

- Instead of finding out in three months that your team is going to miss a critical release milestone, spend an hour each week measuring the team's velocity.

- Instead of finding out in six months that an entire release didn't improve customer experience, find out critical success factors in two weeks through discovery.

Throughout this chapter, we've broken down the essential stages of ML product development, emphasizing the importance of discovery, validation, delivery planning, and execution, and the importance of doing them on an iterative and ongoing basis. These product Discovery, Inception, and Delivery techniques are designed to ensure that teams spend their effort on the most valuable tasks and ship valuable product features early and often. Additionally, we've delved into methods that address the specific complexities and challenges unique to delivering ML products.

While we've tried our best to cover a range of product innovation and delivery techniques in this chapter, it's not possible to cover all of them. We encourage you to take this as a starting point, and go deeper on this topic with seminal resources such as Teresa Torres' *Continuous Discovery Habits* (*https://oreil.ly/Rnbmx*) and Google's *People + AI Guidebook* (*https://oreil.ly/Bih92*). In particular Emmanuel Ameisen's *Building Machine Learning Powered Applications* (O'Reilly) is a whole book about "going from idea to product," and provides targeted guidance about what to do at each stage of the journey for successful ML product delivery.

Our aim with this chapter has been to provide a practical introduction to an end-to-end Lean product development process so that ML teams have a reference for what good looks like, and so everyone in a team understands how they can contribute to this. This chapter introduced how to build the *right thing*, so that the practices in the subsequent chapters on how to build the *thing right* will be effective and efficient. Emmanuel Ameisen's detailed examination of *what* to do is a perfect complement to this book, and we'd encourage you to read his book if you want to dive deeper into the ML product lifecycle (and see it illustrated with a case study).

While anyone can use the practices that we discussed in this chapter, getting the most out of them takes practice. The best time to start practicing, however, is today. Ideally, teams should use this chapter as a way to pinpoint product and delivery gaps, link them to existing challenges, and seek the necessary UX research, product management, or delivery planning expertise (either internally or externally) to bridge these gaps. In the absence of experienced practitioners, we strongly encourage any developer, ML engineer, or data scientist to try these practices, and it can be as simple as going to speak to customers or stakeholders with a genuine interest in understanding the essential problem to be solved.

As a takeaway, challenge yourself by writing down answers to these questions:

- How can you integrate discovery and validation techniques into your current ML product development process?

- In what ways can user stories enhance clarity and alignment within your team during product delivery?

- What is one practice from this chapter that you can try in your next sprint, or upcoming initiative?

Well done on completing this chapter. We'll now turn to Part II: Engineering to look at a set of engineering practices that help teams rapidly and reliably deliver the product solution that they've identified through the product and delivery practices we discussed in this chapter. We'll start with *effective dependency management*—principles and practices that can help you avoid the traps and time-sinks of dependency hell by creating reproducible and production-like environments for training and deploying ML models.

## PART II

Engineering

## CHAPTER 3

Effective Dependency Management: Principles and Tools

In this chapter and the next, we'll tackle a challenge that every ML practitioner will no doubt encounter at many points in their career: *dependency hell*. Dependency hell is one of the common causes of the infamous "works on my machine" problem (*https://oreil.ly/Ib_og*). As an ML practitioner who often deals with dependency hell, you might often be wishing for answers to the following questions:

- How can my teammates and I easily and reproducibly install dependencies whenever and wherever we need them—on a local machine, a notebook in the cloud, a distributed cluster, etc.—with minimal toil and troubleshooting?

- As our project's dependencies grow ever larger, how can we optimize them so that installing dependencies doesn't feel like we're waiting to download the internet?

- How can we ensure that our project is not compromised by security vulnerabilities in its dependencies, and those dependencies' dependencies?

By the end of Chapters 3 and 4, you will have answers to all these questions. You'll be able to apply effective dependency management practices to your own projects as you learn:

- How to recognize an incomplete dependency management approach
- Principles and tools for effectively managing dependencies in ML projects
- When, why, and how to use containers
- How to simplify the use of Docker with batect (*https://batect.dev*), a command-line tool

These two chapters are suitable for novices who are new to dependency management in Python-based ML projects and also intermediate users seeking advanced principles and best practices in dependency management. Novices can enjoy a beginner-friendly introduction to Python dependency managers and containers in the context of ML projects, as well as guiding principles and practical building blocks of any dependency management stack. Intermediate practitioners can learn advanced usage patterns and tools that help simplify dependency management. For both groups of readers, the accompanying code repository is something you can use when bootstrapping or updating your own ML projects.

While we have picked a simple supervised learning example for the hands-on exercise (*https://oreil.ly/851RR*), the approach in this chapter is generalizable to many other ML and data science paradigms such as deep learning, reinforcement learning, operations research, and even non-ML applications in Python such as web applications, visualization dashboards, and so on. In this chapter, there will be some reference to code samples, but they are intended for reading and illustrating concepts. In the next chapter, you can roll up your sleeves and code along in the hands-on exercise.

Finally, this is not a prescription for "This Is The Way It Must Be Done." Rather, it's a modular set of techniques and tools that have helped us—and can help any ML practitioner—avoid common pitfalls in managing dependencies in the ML and Python ecosystem. Should you face any of the traps described in this chapter, consider how these principles and practices can help you.

With that, let's jump into the first section—principles and practices for effective dependency management.

What If Our Code Worked Everywhere, Every Time?

Raise your hand if you've ever:

- Cloned a repo at work or in your personal project hoping to test out an exciting idea, only to get stuck even before you can start because of a dependency installation error like `command 'gcc' failed with exit status 1`?

- Accidentally installed a library (e.g., `pandas==x.x.x`) in your OS-level Python or in the virtual environment for another project, thereby polluting those environments—and wasting time undoing the damage—because you forgot to activate the right virtual environment?

- Spent days or even weeks getting set up in a new project, growing some gray hair along the way, while troubleshooting dependency installation errors like those that arise due to differing versions of an OS-level dependency such as Python? `Error: No matching distribution found for torch==x.x.x`, anyone?

We have a feeling that we're not the only ones on this boat. In fact, we are 100% certain that all ML practitioners have been tripped up by similar issues, caused by an incomplete dependency management solution, when trying to run some ML code locally or on the cloud (see Figure 3-1).

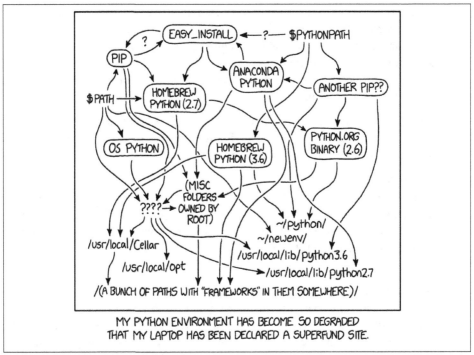

Figure 3-1. An xkcd comic (https://oreil.ly/ffGv7) expressing the funny-but-true nature of dependency management in Python: it's more complicated than it needs to be (source: xkcd.com, used with permission)

We can avoid these pitfalls if we understand the basics of dependency management in Python and basic principles and practices for effective dependency management.

In the remainder of this section, we'll explore a better path by looking to enduring dependency management principles and practices from the software engineering world.

A Better Way: Check Out and Go

Here's a fun question: When you—or a new starter—first joined your team, how long did it take to set up your development environment and make your first commit? Was it days? Weeks?

Imagine this alternate reality: You're onboarding a new teammate, and your instruction to them is simply "check out the project repo, run `./go.sh`, and you're done." That sounds radical and almost fictional, but by the end of this chapter, you will see that it is doable and you will learn how to do this in your own ML projects.

This is known as "check out and go" (*https://oreil.ly/b5kNk*), and it is a common practice in teams with mature software engineering practices. They avoid setup procedures that are partially automated and guided by lengthy documentation, word-of-mouth knowledge, and ad hoc troubleshooting. Instead, a new code contributor can set up their development environment locally in a few commands and run tests, commit, and push code within a day.

In a moment, we will describe the principles and practices that will help you materialize this. But before that, we'd like to describe the benefits of adopting this practice, based on our experience in real-world ML projects:

Faster onboarding
> Instead of spending days and even weeks getting set up, new teammates—and also existing teammates contributing to a different project in the organization, or teammates getting a new computer—can get set up within a day, start running code and tests locally, and start to make code contributions.

Saving time and cognitive resources
> The ability to automatically create consistent production-like environments reduces toil and time spent on configuring and troubleshooting snowflake environments (*https://oreil.ly/Akr5L*)[1] or trying to remember how you installed and configured a particular dependency many months ago. As a result, teammates can do more of the things that they want to do, which helps us feel productive and satisfied.

Experiment-operation symmetry
> By running everything in consistent, reproducible, production-like environments, we can be sure that what works locally on our machines will work when we push our code and run code on the cloud, for example when we run tests on CI/CD pipelines or train our models on CPU or GPU instances on the cloud.

Reproducibility and repeatability
> The code that we wrote last week to solve a problem will work everywhere—on our colleagues' machines, on the CI/CD pipeline, on cloud compute instances—every time. It will work the same way regardless of the underlying operating

---

[1] "Snowflake" environments refer to environments that are manually or partially manually created and configured. Like snowflakes, no two snowflake environments are identical.

system. This is also useful in academic settings, where there is an increasing focus for papers to improve reproducibility by providing both the code and data that were used to arrive at findings.

Taken together, "check out and go" enables teams to easily and reliably set up runtime environments for developing, testing, and running code. This allows them to focus on solving the problems that they want to solve, instead of yak shaving (*https://oreil.ly/ NhBxW*).

Teams could consider measuring "lead time to first push" for a new team member— or an existing team member on a new machine—as a litmus test of the effectiveness of the team's dependency management approach. The "first push" is a helpful forcing function that verifies if a new team member is able to set up their development environment locally, configure their code editor, run tests, make a simple change, and locally test that the change worked.

Now that we've seen the benefits of the "check out and go" practice, let's take a look at the enduring principles that can help us implement it, regardless of which technology or tool we use.

Principles for Effective Dependency Management

At its core, dependency management is a simple concept. In this context, *dependencies* refer to all the software components required by your project in order for it to work as intended and avoid runtime errors (see Figure 3-2). Dependencies can be further separated into two levels: OS-level dependencies and application-level dependencies.

Modern ML applications are typically expected to run on multiple operating systems. For example, we may develop on Mac, Linux, or Windows, run tests on CI pipelines (typically Linux) and run full model training on ephemeral cloud CPU or GPU instances (typically Linux). Container technologies such as Docker help us simplify OS-level dependency management. The application-level dependencies that we install in one environment (e.g., local development environment) must work in the same way in other environments, as well (e.g., CI, preproduction, and production environments).

By properly managing our dependencies at both levels, we ensure that we can create consistent and production-like environments from our code, and that what works here and now will work everywhere and every time.

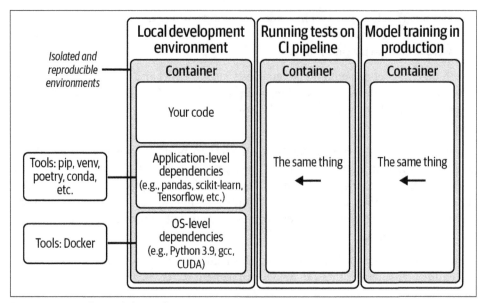

Figure 3-2. With good dependency management practices, we can create consistent, production-like, and reproducible environments from the get-go

Before diving into specific technologies and implementation details, let's understand four enduring principles that can guide us toward a proper dependency management solution, irrespective of which specific technology or tool we choose.

Dependencies "as code"

By specifying *all* dependencies and configuration as code (*https://oreil.ly/-45KL*), we enable all code contributors to create consistent development environments from code *in an automated fashion*. In addition, any changes to the dependency stack—both OS-level and application-level dependencies—are version controlled and can be reproduced and rapidly tested in another environment (e.g., on the CI pipeline).

In contrast, any part of the dependency stack that is not codified and automated will need to be manually configured for every compute environment in which our code will run. This could include other teammates' machines, CI/CD pipelines, cloud training instances, and production servers. In our experience, this invariably becomes a huge time sink and source of frustration.

Production-like development environments from day one

There are few things more stressful and frustrating than detecting issues or errors only in production. Having a production-like environment during development helps to solve that problem. Even as we're coding, we can catch potential issues that may occur when our code is running in a production environment because our development environment is production-like in terms of dependencies. This gives us the confidence that, from a software dependencies perspective, what works locally during development and testing will work in production.

We should ensure that we create production-like development environments as early as possible, even in the *first week* of a new ML application or project. Trying to get a messy project into shape is much harder than establishing the right habits right from the beginning.

Application-level environment isolation

Each application, project, or code repository should have its own isolated Python virtual environment. This allows us to avoid shared state and unnecessary coupling between different applications. In our experience, unnecessary coupling has led to cases where dependency changes for one application unintentionally and unexpectedly introduced errors in another application. Naturally, and annoyingly, that increases friction and slows down our ability to execute on our ideas.

There are many tools—such as Python's built-in venv module, poetry, pipenv, conda—that provide functionalities for creating and managing isolated virtual environments. Whichever tool you pick—and teams should align toward one to reduce complexity—ensure that each application has its own dependencies that we can install in its own virtual environment.

OS-level environment isolation

In most cases, we typically need to run our ML development on multiple operating systems. For example, developing on Windows or MacOS, testing on Linux on CI instances, and deploying to Linux instances on the cloud or on target devices. Even if the entire team were using one operating system (e.g., Linux), whatever we did to configure OS-level dependencies—like installing a specific version of Python 3.x— will need to be regularly reproducible on ephemeral target instances such as during deployment.

While ML practitioners are generally familiar with application-level dependency management in Python, we often neglect to manage OS-level dependencies in a similar way (i.e., as code). It's more common to see some instructions in the README to manually install certain dependencies (e.g., Python 3) and leave the specific versions (e.g., Python 3.x) that we install to chance.

The cost of this neglect is time wasted troubleshooting issues and errors resulting from snowflake environments. If that all sounds too abstract, just think back to the times you cloned a repo to try and run some promising code or notebook, only to waste hours or even days troubleshooting errors caused by a missing or misconfigured OS-level dependency.

Now that you're equipped with these guiding principles, let's look at the tools and technologies that can help us put these principles into practice.

Tools for Dependency Management

In this section, we'll explore some tools that can help us put these principles into practice.

In a nutshell, to effectively manage the dependencies of a given project, we need to:

- Specify OS-level dependencies as code (e.g., by using Docker)
- Specify application-level dependencies as code (e.g., by using Poetry)

In this book, we have decided to use Docker and Poetry. We have used several tools in the Python ecosystem in the past few years, and so far Docker and Poetry have stood out among the others and have worked well for us. With that said, we acknowledge that the choice of any tool in any project or team depends on several factors. Whichever you choose, just be sure that you use them in a way that upholds the four principles described in the preceding section.

Let's start by understanding how Docker manages OS-level dependencies.

Managing OS-level dependencies

Containers encapsulate your code along with the entire dependency stack. This gives you a portable, reproducible, consistent runtime environment for your code across machines.

If your ML stack requires running code in multiple compute environments (e.g., local developer machines, training instances on the cloud, production API servers, CI/CD pipelines), you will definitely benefit from using Docker. By containerizing your code, you can ensure that if your code works now during experimentation and development, it will work just the same in another space and time—e.g., on the cloud and during scheduled production training runs—so long as the Docker runtime is present.

We will dive into the basic building blocks of working with Docker in the next section, but we'd like to take a moment to address the reflexive aversion to Docker, which can be common among ML practitioners due to three misconceptions.

Misconception 1: Docker is overcomplicated and unnecessary. Some see Docker as an over-complicated and daunting tool that takes time and effort to learn without adding much value. On the other hand, we've also worked with other ML practitioners who use it in their day-to-day work as a tool that helps, rather than hinders, them.

If you are in the former camp, we hope that this chapter will demonstrate the value and simplicity of using containers. We wouldn't need Docker if we were only ever going to run our code on one machine. However, as we've established earlier, that's rarely the case when building ML systems.

As with any technology, Docker comes with a learning curve, but it's not a steep one. In our experience, the absence of Docker always ends up costing us more time. For example, if we accidentally make a horrible mess of a development environment (as we have done before!), it is very hard to recover from that if we were running on the host. But with containers, we just blow the image away and start with a fresh container in a few minutes.

We may invest time learning it and setting things up for the team, but once that is done, we can reliably create consistent, reproducible, and production-like development environments effortlessly.

Misconception 2: I don't need Docker because I already use X (e.g., conda). Docker is often wrongly pitted against other Python dependency managers such as pip, conda, poetry, and pip-tools. However, this is a poor comparison because they solve different problems—Python dependency managers concern themselves with application-level Python dependencies, while Docker also helps you install and configure OS-level dependencies, such as Python, gcc (GNU Compiler Collection), and CUDA.

Without Docker, our code is directly dependent on, and left to chance with, unspecified host-level runtime dependencies. Even if you're just installing something as simple as `pandas==1.5.1`, the installation will succeed for developers using a version of Python greater than or equal to 3.8 but fail with the error `No matching distribution found for pandas==1.5.1` on any other machine that happened to have Python 3.7 or below (see Figure 3-3).

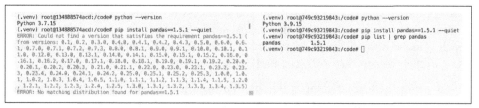

Figure 3-3. Installing a Python library (`pandas==1.5.1`) can fail (see left side of image—using Python 3.7) or succeed (see right side of image—using Python 3.9) depending on the specific version of Python 3

At the time of writing, there are 500 questions on Stack Overflow with this error (*https://oreil.ly/iHDtN*). That's only counting the people who submitted a question on Stack Overflow, and not the countless people who were actively searching for an answer to this error. We were one of them, on multiple occasions! All of that time and effort could have been saved if we had used containers to specify a specific Python version.

Misconception 3: Docker will have a significant performance impact. When faced with a long-running and slow code, one has plenty of time to ponder many pertinent questions—What is the meaning of life? Why is my code so slow? Like a time-thirsty nomad in a time-scarce desert, we may start seeing mirages and perhaps want to confront Docker and ask: Are you slowing down my code?!

When thinking about optimization, never forget the third rule of optimization (*https://oreil.ly/XCN66*): *Measure before optimizing*. A benchmark analysis (*https://oreil.ly/VcpSh*) ran a computationally intensive deep learning task both inside and outside of containers and *found no noticeable differences* in performance. Another benchmark analysis (*https://oreil.ly/YPlLp*) comparing the performance impact of running various deep learning models (e.g., InceptionV3, VGG16) in containers and on host found that *performance differences are close to zero*.

Docker has been found to sometimes slow down Python performance (*https://oreil.ly/d07Mo*), but the performance hit is not always consistent. The performance slow-down is likely due to one of Docker's security features, seccomp (*https://oreil.ly/BzGuK*). Using this chapter's code example, we reproduced a performance impact—an average slowdown of 1.7%—when running `python src/train.py` in Docker and on the host (see Table 3-1). In both scenarios, we were using Python 3.10.6. However, when we look at the performance breakdown, the slowdown was mainly from reading data from disk. The code for processing data and training models is equally performant, if not more performant.

Table 3-1. Benchmarking the run durations of this chapter's model training

Code to run	Average duration across 10 runs (seconds)	
	Duration on host	Duration in container
`pd.read_csv(...)` (loading 100,000 rows of data)	0.6	1.75 (slower than host)
`preprocess_data(...)`	1.1	1.1
`fit_model(...)`	15.4	14.6 (faster than host)
`evaluate_model(...)`	0.4	0.4
	17.5	17.85

Always remember to measure before optimizing: Measure performance under both conditions instead of assuming one will be worse than the other. Otherwise, you might find yourself trading off the benefits of using containers without knowing what gains you made, if any.

Complicating the picture: Differing CPU chips and instruction sets. The concept of "build once, deploy anywhere" is a core tenet of Docker's appeal. However, as anyone who has collaborated with teammates who are using machines with different chips—e.g., Intel Macs versus M1/M2 Macs—can tell you, this is not always the case. One common failure mode is Dockerfiles that install Python dependencies successfully in one machine, but unsuccessfully in another machine with a different chip or instruction set. Itamar Turner-Trauring clearly explains the root cause of this in his article "Why New Macs Break Your Docker Build, and How to Fix It" (*https://oreil.ly/Oct3e*), and we encourage you to take a few minutes to check it out.

To briefly summarize Turner-Trauring's article, a typical failure in installing dependencies across two types of CPUs could go like this (see Figure 3-4):

- A teammate, Dana, is using an Intel Mac, which uses the *AMD64* instruction set, also known as x86_64.

- Another teammate, Ted, is using a new Mac with M1 or M2 processors, which use the *ARM64* instruction set, also known as aarch64.

- AMD64 and ARM64 instruction sets are in different languages; a CPU that speaks one language can't understand the other.

- To make it easier and quicker to install Python packages, package maintainers usually upload precompiled wheels (a Python built-package format) (*https://oreil.ly/xjKnz*) to PyPI (Python Packaging Index), though not always for all CPU instruction sets. Precompiled Python wheels are tied to a particular CPU instruction set.

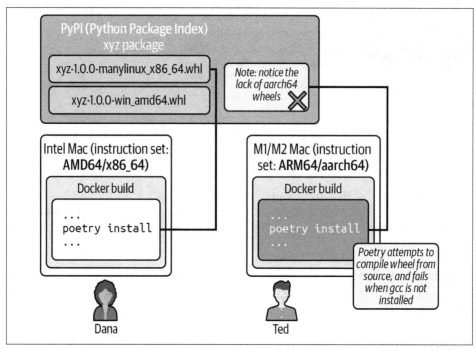

Figure 3-4. Anatomy of a Python dependency installation failure when package maintainers neglect to publish both ARM64 and AMD64 wheels, even though Docker was supposed to prevent such failures

How the dependency installation failure typically happens:

- Dana adds a Python package `xyz=1.0.0` to the project, and it installs successfully on her machine because the maintainers of xyz happened to publish AMD64 wheels.

- Ted pulls the code changes, and because there is a new dependency, `docker build` now will run `poetry install` (or `pip install`—it doesn't matter in this context). As depicted in Figure 3-4, the maintainers of xyz neglected to publish ARM64 wheels. When Poetry can't find the ARM64 wheel for xyz from PyPI, Poetry will download the source code and attempt to compile the package from source.

- At this point, `poetry install` will fail if the gcc compiler isn't installed in the team's development environment.

There is a quick and simple fix—install the gcc compiler in our Dockerfile before installing Python dependencies. This will ensure that we can install the specified package versions in our project, even if the maintainers neglected to publish wheels for a given CPU instruction set. This is accomplished easily with Docker, as follows:

```
FROM python:3.10-slim-bookworm

# ...
RUN apt-get update && apt-get -y install gcc
RUN poetry install

# ...
```

The downsides of this approach are that image builds will get slower and the images will be larger. Thankfully, both of these downsides can be mitigated by caching and multistage builds, respectively. We will demonstrate both of these techniques in the next chapter.

The *proper* fix: all Python package maintainers should distribute wheels for AMD64, MacOS ARM64 (for poetry install in MacOS host), and Linux ARM64 (for poetry install in Docker containers). But that's not always within our control.

Besides this failure mode relating to the installation of Python dependencies, teams that are working with deployment targets that comprise multiple platforms or various types of CPU chips must ensure that they are building multiplatform images (*https:// oreil.ly/Jw_dy*). This will allow the Docker runtime to automatically select the image that matches the OS and architecture of the respective development and deployment environments.

For that, teams can use Docker's buildx tool (*https://oreil.ly/XXDEy*) to create multi-architecture images, ensuring that base images support multiple architectures, like ARM64 and AMD, across relevant operating systems—Linux, MacOS, Windows. Thorough testing in an environment mimicking the target production setup on CI/CD pipelines with multi-architecture build and test stages helps to ensure that the ML model runs seamlessly, regardless of the CPU chips being used in developers' machines or production environments.

With OS-level dependencies under our belt, let's now turn to tools for managing application-level dependencies.

Managing application-level dependencies

With application-level dependencies, it's natural to feel overwhelmed by the plethora of tools in the Python ecosystem that seek to solve similar problems, just in different ways. Whichever tools you choose, *ensure that they work equally well in development and in production*. For example, while conda can be useful for development, it tends to be a large image (3–6 GB) with many dependencies that we don't actually need. If you wanted to containerize and deploy your model as a web API, conda would be overkill and present an unnecessarily large attack surface area. If we were to use conda for development and another dependency manager for production, it would introduce: (i) training-serving asymmetry, and (ii) a fork in your dependency management solution, both of which need to be maintained.

In this chapter, we chose Poetry as our dependency manager because of its following benefits:

Dependency pinning
Poetry's dependency resolution feature will figure out the complete dependency tree, including transitive dependencies—i.e., dependencies of our dependencies—and generate a *poetry.lock* file that pins all dependencies. When we install dependencies, Poetry installs them with the versions specified in the lock file, and this prevents transitive dependencies from silently changing over time and sometimes accidentally breaking our code (*https://oreil.ly/dbwOW*).

Installing dependencies automatically updates pyproject.toml
When we run `poetry add some-package`, Poetry will figure out what's the latest compatible version that we can use, and automatically update *pyproject.toml* for us. We no longer have to manually figure out which version to specify when updating *requirements.txt*, or manually dig out the actual version number that was installed by running `pip list`!

A single pyproject.toml dependency specification file
Poetry's *pyproject.toml* (*https://oreil.ly/CW6Ub*) has a well-defined schema for defining production dependencies and development dependencies. It is also in line with PEP 518 (*https://oreil.ly/yikrL*), which is a Python Enhancement Proposal that introduced *pyproject.toml*, a file that would contain all build system dependencies for a given project.

Packaging and publishing
You can easily publish your package (*https://oreil.ly/AEPkG*) to PyPI or to a private repository in a few commands.

By this point, we've covered the key principles and tools for managing OS-level and application-level dependencies. In the next chapter, we'll have a hands-on exercise to illustrate all of this. But for readers who are new to Docker and batect, we'd like to use the remainder of this chapter to provide a crash course on the what, where, when, and how of using containers in an ML workflow.

A Crash Course on Docker and batect

In the first half of this section, we will describe the conceptual building blocks of working with Docker. Next, we'll look at the common problem of needing to maintain a growing amount of "glue code" to coordinate growing lists of hand-typed Docker arguments and even multiple Dockerfiles. We'll look at a command-line tool that solves that problem and simplifies how we interact with Docker—batect (*https://oreil.ly/Lt2ap*). We'll show you how you can use batect in your projects.

Let's begin by going through the basic building blocks of working with Docker. We will explain some basic Docker concepts, but we won't go into too much detail as there is already a wealth of tutorials (*https://oreil.ly/amr1g*) and guides (*https://oreil.ly/vqtwh*) that teach these concepts in an accessible manner. You can also skip ahead to the section on batect if you are familiar with Docker and containers.

Fun Fact: Even NASA Uses Docker

From the NASA Center for Climate Simulation: "The [NASA] Land Information System (LIS) framework is *difficult for nonexperts to install* due to many dependencies on specific versions of software and compilers. This situation has created a significant barrier to entry for domain scientists interested in using the software on their own computing systems or on the cloud. In addition, the requirement to support multiple runtime environments across the LIS community has created a significant burden on the NASA team. *To overcome these challenges, NASA has deployed LIS using Docker containers (https://oreil.ly/0tn5x)*, which allows installing an entire software package, along with all dependencies, within a working runtime environment, and Kubernetes, which orchestrates the deployment of a cluster of containers. *Installations that took weeks or months can now be completed in minutes either in the cloud or in on-premises clusters*" (emphasis ours).

Another NASA project that uses Docker is the Double Asteroid Redirection Test (DART) project. DART is the first mission dedicated to investigating and demonstrating one method of asteroid deflection by changing an asteroid's motion in space through kinetic impact. In 2022, it successfully changed the course of an asteroid!

DART's development systems are very expensive—$300,000 per unit—so not every developer could get their own system. With a team of 30 developers sharing five systems, the scarcity of development environments led to a bottleneck, slowing down the rate of progress. To solve this problem, DART developers used Docker (*https://oreil.ly/jaqCr*) and some networking smarts to allow all developers to work on their own laptops, but connect to the real hardware for development and testing.

What Are Containers?

Think of a container as a running process—such as `echo "hello world"`, `python train.py`, or `python3 -m http.server`—that has all the dependencies it needs to run successfully.

The process code and its dependencies are captured in what we call an image. When we build an image—a lightweight, standalone, executable package of software that includes everything needed to run code—we specify everything that the process needs to run successfully.

When we *run* an image, we get a *container*. So, when we run our process or command as a container, it will always run successfully, even if the host machine is a "fresh box" that doesn't have the dependencies we need, other than the Docker runtime.

For anyone new to containers, these terms may sound more daunting than they really are. If that's you, we hope this analogy will help to simplify the concept of containers:

A not-so-relaxing afternoon without containers
> Your friend lives in a tropical country and they tell you: put a chair outdoors, sit on it, and enjoy the nice, cool breeze. You live in a temperate country and it's currently winter. You follow the exact same instructions but did not enjoy the same outcome as your friend.

A relaxing afternoon with containers
> Your friend lives somewhere in the world, and he bought a space pod with an air conditioner, puts a chair in it, sits on it, and enjoys the nice, cool breeze. The experience was so amazing that they immediately told you about it. It's still winter for you, and you follow the exact same instructions: buy the exact same space pod, turn on the air conditioner, sit on a chair inside it, and enjoy the nice, cool breeze.

That's what containers do for our application—containers, like space pods, provide a deterministic runtime environment that decouples our code from the state of the operating system (or "bare metal" runtime).

Bust Those Jargons!

As you work with Docker, you will encounter some of these terms, which may sound heavy initially. Learning the words and what they mean and do is a great first step in overcoming the sense of overwhelm.

If ever you're faced with a new and daunting term, you can demystify it by checking out Docker's handy glossary of terms (*https://oreil.ly/QOpT0*). To kick us off, here are some commonly used Docker terms:

Image
> A lightweight, standalone, executable package of software that includes everything needed to run code.

Container
> A runtime instance of an image. When you run an image, you get a container.

Docker daemon, or Docker Engine
> A background process running on the host that manages images and containers, such as the starting and stopping of containers. Fun fact: The use of "daemon" in computing was borrowed from Maxwell's daemon (*https://oreil.ly/mvqB4*)—an imaginary agent in physics and thermodynamics that helped to sort molecules—

---

which was again borrowed from Greek mythology, where a daemon was a supernatural being working in the background.

Docker CLI client
> When we run a command—e.g., `docker run`—we are using the Docker client, docker. It is the primary way that we interact with the Docker daemon.

Docker Desktop
> A Docker development environment that is available for Mac (*https://oreil.ly/JclOU*), Windows (*https://oreil.ly/s9dhN*), and Linux (*https://oreil.ly/HPrf4*) to provide developers with a consistent experience across platforms. Docker Desktop includes Docker Engine, Docker CLI client, Docker Compose, Docker Content Trust, Kubernetes, and Credential Helper.

Docker registry
> A hosted service that allows us to push and pull images.

Host
> A machine (e.g., a developer's laptop, or CI build agent) that runs the Docker daemon and containers.

Figure 3-5 illustrates how these terms and concepts relate with each other.

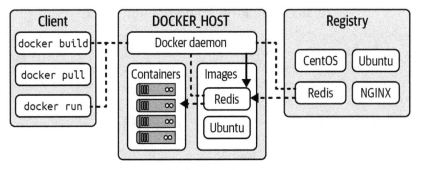

Figure 3-5. This is how various Docker concepts interact with each other in practice (source: adapted from "Docker Architecture" by Danilo Barros, Wikimedia Commons [https://oreil.ly/m1fF2], used under CC BY-SA 4.0 [https://oreil.ly/GFxEX])

Now, let's take a look at where Docker would fit in with various development machines and platforms.

The technologies that make up an ML practitioner's development environment depend on several factors, such as personal experience, team preferences, organizational policies, and even regulatory constraints on where compute and data can exist. An ML practitioner could be developing on one of the following:

- Local machines
- Local machines that trigger jobs on the cloud or on a distributed cluster (e.g., Kubeflow, Metaflow, Ray, AWS SageMaker, Google Vertex AI, Azure ML)
- Ad hoc provisioned compute instances (e.g., AWS EC2 instances)
- Cloud workspaces (e.g., GitHub Codespaces, AWS SageMaker Studio Notebooks, GCP Cloud Workstations)
- On-premises compute instances
- Embedded devices (e.g., Raspberry Pi)

Regardless of which development environment you're using, Docker can help you quickly create consistent runtime environments for your code on any of the above target environments, as long as the Docker runtime is available. Cloud ML services typically support Docker and will have documentation detailing how you can specify Docker images—both public images or your custom images—when running tasks or jobs.

Usage of Docker Desktop in This Book Versus Alternative Container Runtimes

At the time of writing, Docker Desktop license agreement (*https://oreil.ly/PeXTf*) states that Docker Desktop is free for small businesses (fewer than 250 employees and less than $10 million in annual revenue), personal use, education, and noncommercial open source projects. Otherwise, it requires a paid subscription for professional use.

For this book, we use Docker Desktop as it's for personal use and educational purposes. If you wish to adapt the dependency management setup in this repo in a commercial setting but don't have Docker licenses, you can use a license-free Docker daemon, colima (*https://oreil.ly/IwBbt*), which is available for Mac and Linux operating systems. You will still interact with all the concepts listed in this book, and the only difference will be that instead of using Docker Engine or Docker Desktop, you will use colima.

To use colima, you can refer to the steps in the gist "Switching batect from Docker Desktop to colima" (*https://oreil.ly/grRuA*) and also colima's official documentation (*https://oreil.ly/IwBbt*):

1. Install colima and docker-credential-helper: `brew install colima docker-credential-helper`
2. Ensure Docker is configured to use the correct credential helper. Edit *~/.docker/config.json* and ensure it includes the following: `"credsStore": "osxkeychain"`

---

3. Start the Docker daemon: `colima start`

Once you've configured colima as your Docker daemon, you can run the Docker and batect commands in this chapter as you would when using Docker Desktop.

Reduce the Number of Moving Parts in Docker with batect

As projects become more complex, we might find ourselves with a growing number of Docker runtime parameters and command-line options—such as volume mounts and ports to publish. And these configuration parameters often need to be maintained in multiple places in our codebase. We've seen teams maintain an ever-lengthening list of hand-typed Docker arguments, which they specify and synchronize across multiple places, such as in the README, CI/CD pipeline, Makefiles, and shell scripts.

To complicate the picture further, we may also have multiple containers that need to communicate with each other, run in a specific sequence, or even multiple Dockerfiles for multiple tasks.

The good news is: We can simplify all these moving parts with batect (*https://oreil.ly/Lt2ap*)—a command-line tool that lets us (i) define our development tasks alongside their associated configuration parameters as a single source of truth in a config file, and (ii) run Docker containers as batect tasks.

Let's look at four benefits of using batect in our ML development lifecycle.

 A few months after we wrote this chapter, batect's creator and maintainer announced that batect will no longer be maintained (*https://oreil.ly/ZyMrQ*). Any existing projects using batect will continue to work—and have continued to work in the code-along repositories for this book. But batect will no longer receive new features, bug fixes, or security fixes.

Nevertheless, batect continues to be a useful abstraction on top of Docker (as we'll elaborate on in this chapter).

Benefit 1: Simpler command-line interface

When working with Docker, it's common to end up with Docker commands peppered with many invocation parameters—e.g., environment variables, volume mount folders, ports to publish—that are used in multiple places, all of which need to be kept in sync. Below is an example:

```
# Train model (without batect)

# build image first
docker build . --target prod -t my-image
```

```
# in staging scripts
docker run -it --rm -v $(pwd):/code -e STAGING my-image:latest \
./scripts/train-model.sh

# in production scripts
docker run -it --rm -v $(pwd):/code -e PROD my-image:latest \
./scripts/train-model.sh

# in README
$ docker run -it --rm -v $(pwd):/code -e DEV my-image:latest \
./scripts/train-model.sh
```

Apart from specifying these commands in the README, we would also need to specify them wherever we want to run these commands, such as in bash scripts or CI pipelines. If we were to change an option (e.g., volume mount directory), we would need to change it in multiple places. This violates the DRY principle (Don't Repeat Yourself) and we have to take on the toil of manually keeping these commands in sync, and the consequences of accidental inconsistencies.

In contrast, batect lets us maintain these configuration parameters in a configuration file, as below, which serves as a single source of truth:

```
# Train model (with batect)
$ ./batect train-model ❶

## batect.yml ❷
containers:
  dev: ❸
    build_directory: .
    volumes:
      - local: .
        container: /code

tasks:
  train-model:
    description: Train model
    run:
      container: dev
      command: scripts/train-model.sh
      environment: ${ENVIRONMENT}
```

❶ Notice how batect simplifies how we invoke the same docker run command.

❷ Batect allows us to define *containers* and *tasks* in a configuration file (*batect.yml*). All the Docker options we typically pass to docker build and all the docker run commands, along with their various options, are now defined "as code" in *batect.yml*. We can start a container simply by executing a batect task (e.g., ./batect train-model). *Batect.yml* becomes a single source of truth for these tasks, and if we were to change an option (e.g., environment = 'staging' or 'production'), we would only need to change it in one place.

❸ You can name this container to be anything you want. It doesn't have to be dev.

Benefit 2: Simple task composition

Let's consider a scenario where we need to run a task (e.g., train a model) before we can run another task (e.g., run API test). On a fresh instance (e.g., on CI), if we were to directly run the API test, it would fail because the model artifact hasn't been created yet. Let's see how we would do this without batect:

```
# run model training smoke test (to create local model artifact needed by API)
$ docker run -it --rm -v $(pwd):/code loan-default-prediction:dev \
./scripts/tests/smoke-test-model-training.sh

# then we can run our API test
$ docker run -it --rm -v $(pwd):/code loan-default-prediction:dev \
./scripts/tests/api-test.sh
```

In order to run API tests on our CI/CD pipeline, we would need to specify both of these somewhat verbose commands. Teams typically wrap these up in bash scripts to encapsulate this logic and hide the verbosity of these commands.

Now let's see how we'd do the same task with batect:

```
# Run API tests
$ ./batect api-test

## batect.yml
tasks:
  smoke-test-model-training:
    description: Run smoke tests for model training
    run:
      container: dev
      command: scripts/tests/smoke-test-model-training.sh

  api-test:
    description: Run API tests
    run:
      container: dev
      command: scripts/tests/api-test.sh
    prerequisites: ❶
      - smoke-test-model-training
```

❶ batect helps us simplify this with the prerequisites option. On our CI/CD pipeline, we can just specify ./batect api-test and batect will take care of running the prerequisite task (smoke-test-model-training) before running the API tests.

Now that we've seen how batect helps us keep docker run commands simple, consistent, and in one place, let's look at another benefit of batect: Local-CI symmetry.

Benefit 3: Local-CI symmetry

Without batect, each step on CI will be a verbose implementation detail (for example, docker run -it --rm -v $(pwd):/code loan-default-prediction:dev ./scripts/train-model.sh.) This makes it harder to read and keep track of what's going on.

In contrast, batect lets us keep our CI/CD pipeline concise and easy to understand. In the following code sample, it's apparent that we're running three commands: smoke-test-model-training, api-test, and train-model:

```
# .github/workflows/ci.yaml

name: CI/CD pipeline
on: [push]
jobs:
  smoke-test-model-training:
    runs-on: ubuntu-20.04
    steps:
      - uses: actions/checkout@v3
      - name: Run model training smoke test
        run: ./batect smoke-test-model-training

  api-test:
    runs-on: ubuntu-20.04
    steps:
      - uses: actions/checkout@v3
      - name: Run API tests
        run: ./batect api-test

  train-model:
    runs-on: ubuntu-20.04
    steps:
      - uses: actions/checkout@v3
      - name: Train model
        run: ./batect train-model
    needs: [smoke-test-model-training, api-test]
```

This also helps us easily reproduce failures that happened in CI. Should a task fail on CI (e.g., api-test), we can easily reproduce errors locally by running the exact same command that we asked CI to run (e.g., ./batect api-test) and iterate on a bug fix. We no longer have to manually corral a hodgepodge of commands, arguments, and environment variables scattered across CI/CD pipeline specifications and shell scripts.

Benefit 4: Faster builds with caches

One key challenge when using Docker in ML projects is long build times due to the time spent on downloading and installing large Python packages (e.g., `torch==1.13.1` is 500 MB), large pretrained models (e.g., llama-2-7b is 13 GB), and large datasets.

Docker comes with build-time caching mechanisms (*https://oreil.ly/Szm18*), which can help you save several minutes for each fresh build. By adding the bold lines below, we can avoid unnecessary redownloads and reinstallation, and reduce the time taken to build our image. Even for the fairly vanilla dependencies that we are using in this example, we shortened the build time from three minutes to just under two minutes. The time savings would be more significant in projects where we download larger dependencies, pretrained models, and datasets.

```
FROM python:3.10-slim-bookworm

WORKDIR /code

RUN --mount=type=cache,target=/var/cache/apt \
    apt-get update && apt-get -y install gcc

RUN pip install poetry
ADD pyproject.toml /code/
RUN poetry config installer.max-workers 10
RUN --mount=type=cache,target=/root/.cache/pypoetry \
    --mount=type=cache,target=/opt/.venv \
    poetry install
```

Strictly speaking, you don't need batect to realize the benefits of Docker caches. However, we find that batect's interface for defining caches—and invalidating caches, where necessary—is easier to use. The following code sample shows how we would implement the same caches, but this time using batect:

```
# batect.yml
containers:
 dev:
   build_directory: .
   volumes:
     - type: cache ❶
       name: python-dependencies
       container: /opt/.venv
     - type: cache
       name: poetry-cache-and-artifacts
       container: /root/.cache/pypoetry
     - type: cache
       name: apt-cache
       container: /var/cache/apt
```

```
# Dockerfile ❷

FROM python:3.10-slim-bookworm

WORKDIR /code

RUN apt-get update && apt-get -y install gcc

RUN pip install poetry
ADD pyproject.toml /code/
RUN poetry config installer.max-workers 10
RUN poetry install
```

❶ This is how we define and add a cache volume. In addition to dependencies, you can also cache other downloaded artifacts, such as pretrained models and data. The ability to name the cache volume makes it easier to understand what's going on, as well.

❷ Notice how our Dockerfile is now back to how it was prior to adding caches and is now easier to understand.

 If you encounter any errors relating to stale or corrupted caches when you're running a command, you can simply delete the cache and try to command again:

- To clear the cache using batect (*https://oreil.ly/Iprov*), you can run the following command:

      ./batect --clean

- To clear the cache using Docker (*https://oreil.ly/5r-Uu*), you can run the following command:

      docker builder prune

If we use containers without specifying any caches, we often find ourselves wasting significant amounts of time waiting. In the ML tech stacks that we've worked with, we've waited between 3–10 minutes for various images to build locally or on CI. When given a choice between staring blankly at a screen and context switching to do something else while waiting, we sometimes choose the latter to feel "productive." But the irony is that this context switching leads to more open threads, more mental exhaustion, and lower productivity. With just a few lines of YAML configuration in batect, we can reduce wait time and its associated costs.

How to use batect in your projects

Batect is easy to install (*https://oreil.ly/sOQuW*), and integrates well with common CI platforms such as GitHub Actions (*https://oreil.ly/kcHL9*) and CircleCI (*https://oreil.ly/QWcCV*). Batect offers two simple abstractions—containers (*https://oreil.ly/A5ijI*) and tasks (*https://oreil.ly/3lPZm*)—and supports everything that you can do through the Docker client (e.g., mount volumes, publish ports, entry points). In the next chapter, we will demonstrate what a Dockerized and "batect-ized" project looks like.

If you wish to explore batect further, the documentation is comprehensive and includes a getting started guide (*https://oreil.ly/tDD9s*), *batect.yml* configuration reference (*https://oreil.ly/xxGO6*), and guides on how to use it with CI systems (*https://oreil.ly/XWnNU*).

> A counterargument that we commonly hear is: Instead of introducing a new tool, why not use Docker Compose? The reason is: Docker Compose is designed for running and orchestrating *long-lived* processes, and it also does not allow you to run a subset of specific tasks or containers. For example, docker-compose up will start all the services specified in *docker-compose.yml*. In contrast, batect supports both running long-lived and short-lived processes, and is better suited for defining containerized tasks that we run locally and on the CI/CD pipeline in the ML development lifecycle.

Now that we are equipped with the principles and tools for effective dependency management, let's recap what we've learned in this chapter, before we jump into a practical hands-on example in the next chapter.

Conclusion

Give yourself a massive pat on your back because you've just covered a lot of ground in one chapter! To recap, in this chapter, we covered:

- How to recognize an incomplete dependency management approach
- Principles and tools enabling the practice of "check out and go" in ML projects
- When, why, and how to use containers
- How to simplify the definition and invocation of Docker commands with batect

The irony of dependency management is that it's a solved problem in the software engineering world, yet it continues to be a common pitfall in the world of ML. Perhaps this is due to an overwhelming array of tools, the strong pull (in many directions) of entrenched legacy practices, and the lack of a standardized approach on dependency management in the Python ecosystem.

Whatever the reason may be, in our experience, the ML dependency management toolchain is at a mature state, and teams can create runtime environments reliably and reproducibly in experimentation, development, and production with these principles and practices.

On that note, it's time for the most exciting part of this topic—a hands-on example to demonstrate what effective dependency management could look like in practice! See you in the next chapter.

## CHAPTER 4

Effective Dependency Management in Practice

In the previous chapter, we laid out the principles for effective dependency management—can you recall the four principles?—and supporting tools. In this chapter, let's have some fun and put them into practice.

In this chapter, you will learn:

- What "check out and go" looks like in practice
- How to use Docker, batect, and Poetry to create consistent, reproducible, and production-like runtime environments in each step of the ML delivery lifecycle
- How to automatically detect security vulnerabilities in your dependencies and automate dependency updates

The techniques in this chapter are what we use in our real-world projects to create reproducible, consistent, isolated, production-like runtime environments for our ML code. They help us effectively and securely manage dependencies and avoid dependency hell.

Let's begin!

In Context: ML Development Workflow

In this section, you will see "check out and go" in action. In the code exercise, we'll run through the following steps with the goal of training and serving a model that predicts the likelihood of a loan default:

1. Run a go script to install prerequisite dependencies on our host machine.

2. Create a Dockerized local development environment.

3. Configure our code editor to understand the project's virtual environment, so that we can have a helpful coding assistant.

4. Run common tasks in the ML development lifecycle (e.g., train models, run tests, start API).

5. Train and deploy the model on the cloud.

To make the most of this chapter, fork, clone, and code along in the hands-on exercise (*https://oreil.ly/enuv7*), where we'll train and test a classifier to predict the likelihood of loan defaults. We encourage you to fork the repository, as it'll allow you to see Docker and batect at work on the GitHub Actions CI pipeline of your forked repository as you commit and push your changes.

Before we turn to the code, let's paint a clear picture of what we're containerizing in a typical ML workflow.

Identifying What to Containerize

The first and most important step in Dockerizing a project is to disambiguate exactly *what* we are containerizing. This can confuse some ML practitioners and can lead to conflated and shared states. For example, if we share an image between the two distinct tasks of *developing* an ML model and *serving* an ML model, we may find unnecessary development dependencies (e.g., Jupyter, Pylint) in a production container (e.g., a model web API). This lengthens container build and start times unnecessarily and also enlarges the attack surface of our API.

In software development, the most common thing that we're containerizing is a web application or web API—which is simply a long-lived process that starts after you run a command (e.g., `python manage.py runserver`). In ML, we can also use a containerized web application to serve model predictions (inference) via an API. However, we typically find ourselves running more than just a web application. For example, here are some common ML tasks and processes that we would run when creating ML solutions:

- Training a model
- Serving the model as a web API
- Starting a notebook server
- Running deployments (of ML training jobs, model API, etc.)
- Starting a dashboard or an experiment tracking service (we won't cover this in this chapter, as running dashboards as a web server is well-documented and

relatively straightforward [*https://oreil.ly/U3luV*] with tools such as Streamlit and Docker)

In this chapter's example, we have identified four distinct sets of dependencies for running four different sets of tasks (see Table 4-1).

Table 4-1. Components that we are containerizing

Image	Examples of tasks that we can run	Examples of OS-level dependencies	Examples of application-level dependencies
1. Development image	• Train ML model • Feature engineering • Run automated tests • Start API server locally • Start Jupyter notebook server	• Python 3.10 • gcc • tensorflow-model-server	Production dependencies: • pandas • scikit-learn Development dependencies: • Jupyter • Pytest • Pylint
2. Production API image	• Start API server on the cloud	• Python 3.10 • gcc • tensorflow-model-server	Production dependencies: • pandas • scikit-learn
3. Deployment image—model training pipeline	• Deploy model training pipeline to the cloud • Execute model training	The specific dependency will depend on what tool or platform we use to train our model on the cloud. For example, it could be one of the following: • aws-cdk (AWS) • gcloud (GCP) • azure-cli (Azure) • Metaflow • Kubeflow • Terraform • etc.	
4. Deployment image—model web service	• Deploy model image to a model hosting service or container hosting service	The specific dependency will depend on what tool or platform we use to deploy our web service on the cloud. For example, it could be one of the following: • aws-cdk (AWS) • gcloud (GCP) • azure-cli (Azure) • Terraform • etc.	

Figure 4-1 visualizes each task, which, as you know by now, is nothing but a *containerized process* and the respective images they use. This figure is a visual representation of Table 4-1.

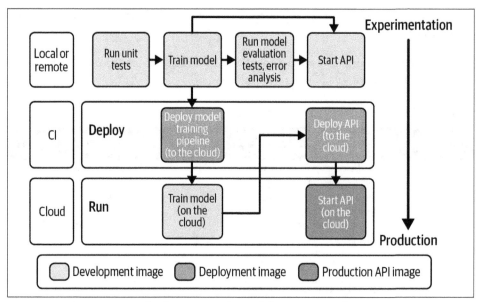

Figure 4-1. Common ML development tasks and their associated images

The specific slicing and differentiation of images will vary depending on the project's needs. If the slicing is too coarse-grained—e.g., one image for running all tasks and containers—the monolithic image might become too heavy. Recall our earlier discussion on the costs of carrying unnecessary dependencies. If the slicing is too fine-grained—e.g., one image for each task or container—we can bear unnecessary costs in terms of the code we have to maintain and image build times for each task.

One helpful heuristic for determining how images are sliced is to think about "sharedness" and "distinctness" of dependencies. In this example, development tasks share an image because they share the same dependencies, such as Jupyter or scikit-learn. Deployment tasks are carved out into another image because they don't need any of these dependencies—instead, they need dependencies like gcloud, aws-cli, azure-cli, or Terraform.

When Should We Containerize Things?

If you're new to using containers, you may be wondering, When is it worth introducing containers to projects? One useful rule of thumb is to consider the number and variety of operating systems where your code will run. If you're exploring some ideas or "sketching" some prototypes just on your machine, then you could create reproducible development environments with just a Python dependency manager—usually Poetry—and leave out Docker. You would also include a go script to install any OS-level dependencies, especially if you're collaborating with other teammates using the same operating system.

If you know from the start that this is a project, prototype, or minimum viable product (MVP) that will need CI/CD (Linux) and be deployed somewhere (again, usually Linux), then it's always best to start the project on the right foot and containerize tasks like you'll do in this chapter. In our experience, establishing experiment-operation symmetry and production-like development environments helps teams avoid wasting time on troubleshooting "works on my machine" problems and stay in the flow of solving problems.

You can make it easy for yourself by using templates—e.g., such as the batect-ml-template (*https://oreil.ly/wrfGY*) template—to bootstrap new projects with good dependency management practices baked in.

With this mental framework in our head, we are ready to dive into the hands-on exercise!

Hands-On Exercise: Reproducible Development Environments, Aided by Containers

Let's step through how we would create and use development environments in our ML development lifecycle:

1. Check out and go: install prerequisite OS-level dependencies.
Run the go script for your operating system.

2. Create local development environment (i.e., build image).
Ensure Docker runtime is started (either via Docker Desktop or colima), and run the following command to install dependencies in your local dev image:

```
./batect --output=all setup
```

3. Start local development environment (i.e., run container).
Start the container:

```
./batect start-dev-container
```

Then test that everything works by running model training smoke tests:

```
scripts/tests/smoke-test-model-training.sh
```

Finally, exit the container by entering `exit` in the terminal or pressing Ctrl + D.

4. Serve the ML model locally as a web API.
Start the API in development mode:

```
./batect start-api-locally
```

Then send requests to the API locally by running the following command from another terminal outside the Docker container (it uses curl, which we haven't installed):

```
scripts/request-local-api.sh
```

5. *Configure your IDE to use the Python virtual environment created by the go scripts.*
   Instructions are available online for the IDEs we recommend for this exercise:

   - PyCharm instructions (*https://oreil.ly/udir0*)
   - VS Code instructions (*https://oreil.ly/Lg-o6*)

6. *Train model on the cloud.*
   This step, along with step #7, is done on the CI/CD pipeline. We'll cover that later in this section.

7. *Deploy model web API.*
   Along with step #6, done on the CI/CD pipeline.

For the impatient, these steps are summarized at a glance in the repository's README (*https://oreil.ly/uzBvF*). Having these steps in a succinct README is a good habit to allow code contributors to easily set up their local environment and execute common ML development tasks. We recommend that you execute these steps now, in the project that you've cloned, to get a feel for the end-to-end flow. In the remainder of this section, we'll go through each of the steps in detail, so that you can understand each component of our development environment setup and adapt it for your own project.

1. Check out and go: Install prerequisite dependencies

The first step in setting up our local development environment is running the go script to install host-level prerequisite dependencies. To begin, clone your forked repository:

```
$ git clone https://github.com/YOUR_USERNAME/loan-default-prediction
```

Alternatively, you can clone the original repository, but you won't be able to see your code changes running on GitHub Actions when you push your changes:

```
$ git clone https://github.com/davified/loan-default-prediction
```

Readers working on Mac or Linux machines can now run the go script. This might take a while if you're installing some of the OS-level dependencies for the first time, so make yourself a nice drink while you wait:

```
# Mac users
$ scripts/go/go-mac.sh

# Linux users
$ scripts/go/go-linux-ubuntu.sh
```

At this stage, Windows users should follow these steps:

1. Download and install Python3 (*https://oreil.ly/U9ML-*) if not already installed. During installation, when prompted, select Add Python to PATH.

2. In Windows explorer/search, go to Manage App Execution Aliases and turn off App Installer for Python. This resolves the issue where the `python` executable is not found in the PATH.

3. Run the following go script in the PowerShell or command prompt terminal:

   ```
   .\scripts\go\go-windows.bat
   ```

   If you see an HTTPSConnectionPool `read timed out` error, just run this command a few more times until `poetry install` succeeds.

The next step, regardless of which operating system you're on, is to install Docker Desktop, if it's not already installed. While this can be done in one line as part of the go script for Mac and Linux (see example go script for Mac [*https://oreil.ly/RdOks*]), it was too complicated to automate in the Windows go script. As such, we've decided to keep this as a manual step outside of the go script for symmetry. Follow Docker's online installation steps (*https://oreil.ly/0dDT8*).

It's important that we keep these go scripts succinct and avoid installing too many host-level dependencies. Otherwise, it will be hard to maintain these scripts over time for multiple operating systems. We want to keep as many of our dependencies in Docker as possible.

2. Create our local development environment

Next, we'll install all the OS-level and application-level dependencies needed for developing the ML model locally. We'll do that in one command: `./batect setup`. As promised earlier, this is where we explain *how* batect works. Figure 4-2 explains the three steps that are happening behind the scenes.

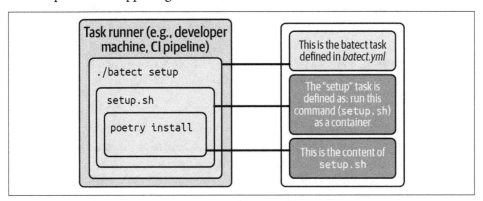

Figure 4-2. What happens when you run a batect task

As visualized in Figure 4-2, when we run ./batect setup, batect executes the setup task, which we defined in *batect.yml*. The setup task is simply defined as: run ./scripts/setup.sh in the dev container. Let's look at how this is defined in *batect.yml*:

```
# Ensure Docker runtime is started (either via Docker Desktop or colima)

# install application-level dependencies
$ ./batect --output=all setup ❶

# batect.yml
containers:
 dev: ❷
   build_directory: .
   volumes:
     - local: .
       container: /code
     - type: cache
       name: python-dev-dependencies
       container: /opt/.venv
   build_target: dev

tasks:
 setup:  ❸
   description: Install Python dependencies
   run:
     container: dev
     command: ./scripts/setup.sh
```

❶ This is how we execute a batect task (e.g., setup). The --output=all option (*https://oreil.ly/JkNcK*) shows us the logs of the task while it's executing. This provides visual feedback, which is especially useful for long-running tasks like dependency installation and model training.

❷ This container block defines our dev image. This is where we specify Docker build-time and runtime configurations, such as volumes or folders to mount, the path to the Dockerfile—i.e., build_directory—and build targets for multistage Dockerfiles like ours. Once batect builds this dev image, it will be reused by any subsequent batect tasks that specify this image (e.g., smoke-test-model-training, api-test, and start-api-locally). As such, we won't need to wait for lengthy rebuilds.

❸ This task block defines our setup task, which consists of two simple parts: what command to run and what container to use when running the command. We can also specify additional Docker runtime configuration options (*https://oreil.ly/a-E_k*), such as volumes and ports.

Let's look a little deeper into the second step, and see how we've configured our Dockerfile:

```
FROM python:3.10-slim-bookworm AS dev ❶

WORKDIR /code ❷

RUN apt-get update && apt-get -y install gcc ❸

RUN pip install poetry
ADD pyproject.toml /code/
RUN poetry config installer.max-workers 10
ARG VENV_PATH
ENV VENV_PATH=$VENV_PATH
ENV PATH="$VENV_PATH/bin:$PATH" ❹

CMD ["bash"] ❺
```

❶ We specify the base image that will form the base layer of our own image. The python:3.10-slim-bookworm image is 145 MB, as opposed to python:3.10, which is 915 MB. At the end of this chapter, we will describe the benefits of using small images.

❷ The WORKDIR instruction sets a default working directory for any subsequent RUN, CMD, ENTRYPOINT, COPY, and ADD instructions in the Dockerfile. It is also the default starting directory when we start the container. You can set it to be any directory you'd like, as long as you're consistent. In this example, we set /code as our working directory and that's where we will place our code when we start our container in the next step.

❸ We install gcc (GNU Compiler Collection) to handle the scenario where maintainers of a particular Python library neglect to publish a wheel for a given CPU instruction. With gcc, even if a Python package has wheels for one type of CPU (e.g., Intel processor) but the maintainers neglected to publish wheels for another type (e.g., M1 processors), we can ensure that we can build the wheels from source in this step.[1]

❹ In this block, we install and configure Poetry. We tell Poetry to install the virtual environment in the project directory (/opt/.venv) and add the path to the virtual environment to the PATH environment variable, so that we can run Python

---

[1] As mentioned in "Complicating the picture: Differing CPU chips and instruction sets" on page 93, the article "Why New Macs Break Your Docker Build, and How to Fix It" (*https://oreil.ly/NIMLR*) explains why this happens and why it is especially common with new Macs with M1 chips.

commands in containers without needing to activate the virtual environment (e.g., using `poetry shell`, or `poetry run ...`).

❺ Finally, the `CMD` instruction provides a default command to execute when we start a container. In this example, when our Docker image runs as a container, it will start a bash shell for us to run our development tasks. This is just a default and we can override this command when we run our containers later on.

One of the great things about Docker is that there is no magic: You state step by step in Dockerfile what you want in the Docker image, and `docker build` will run each instruction and "bake" in an image based on the "recipe" (Dockerfile) you provide.

3. Start our local development environment

Now, we can get into our local development environment by starting the container:

```
# start container (with batect)

$ ./batect start-dev-container ❶

# start container (without batect). You don't have to run this command.
# We've included it so that you can see the simplified interface that
# batect provides

$ docker run -it \ ❷
    --rm \ ❸
    -v $(pwd):/code \ ❹
    -p 80:80 \ ❺
    loan-default-prediction:dev ❻
```

❶ This batect task runs our dev container (i.e., a containerized bash shell that forms our development environment). The Docker runtime parameters are encapsulated in the batect task, as defined in *batect.yml*, so we can run the task without carrying the heavy implementation details you see in the `docker run` version of the same task.

❷ `-it` is short for `-i` (`--interactive`) and `-t` (`--tty`, TeleTYpewriter) and allows you to *interact* (i.e., write commands and/or read outputs) with the running container via the *terminal*.

❸ `--rm` tells Docker to automatically remove the container and file system when the container exits. This is a good habit to prevent lingering container file systems from piling up on the host.

❹ `-v $(pwd):/code` tells the container to mount a directory (or *volume*) from the host (`$(pwd)` returns the path of the current working directory) onto a target directory (*/code*) in the container. This mounted volume is kept in sync, so that any changes you make inside or outside the container are kept in sync.

❺ `-p X:Y` tells Docker to *publish* port X in the Docker container onto port Y on the host. This allows you to send requests from outside the container to a server running inside the container on port 80.

❻ This is the image that we want to use to start the container. Because we have specified the default command to run in our Dockerfile (`CMD ["bash"]`), the resulting container is a bash process, which we will use to run our development commands.

Inside of our development container, we can now run tasks or commands that we typically use when developing ML models. To keep these commands readable and simple, we've kept the implementation details in short bash scripts, which you can read if you'd like:

```
# run model training smoke tests
$ scripts/tests/smoke-test-model-training.sh

# run api tests
$ scripts/tests/api-test.sh

# train model
$ scripts/train-model.sh
```

Alternatively, you could also run these commands from the host, using batect. Thanks to Docker's caching mechanism, running these tasks is equally fast regardless of whether you run them from inside a container, or start a fresh container each time from the host. These batect tasks make it easy to define tasks on our CI pipeline and make it easy to reproduce CI failures locally. This is how you can run common ML development tasks using batect:

```
# run model training smoke tests
$ ./batect smoke-test-model-training

# run api tests
$ ./batect api-test

# train model
$ ./batect train-model
```

4. Serve the ML model locally as a web API

In this step, we will start our web API locally. The API encapsulates our ML model, delegates prediction requests to the model, and returns the model's prediction for the given request. The ability to start the API locally for manual testing or automated testing saves us from falling into the antipattern of "pushing to know if something works." This antipattern is a bad habit that lengthens feedback cycles (from seconds to several minutes) while we wait for tests and deployments to run on the CI/CD pipeline in order to test a change in even a single line of code.

This is how you can start our web API locally and interact with it:

```
# start API in development mode
$ ./batect start-api

# send requests to the API locally. Run this directly from the host
# (i.e. outside the container) as it uses curl, which we haven't
# installed in our Docker image
$ scripts/request-local-api.sh
```

5. Configure our code editor

An essential step in dependency management is configuring our code editor to use the project's virtual environment, so that it can help us write code more efficiently. When the code editor has been configured to use a given virtual environment, it becomes a very powerful tool and can provide sensible hints and suggestions as you type.

In Chapter 7, we describe how you can achieve this in two simple steps:

1. Specify the virtual environment in our code editor. See instructions for PyCharm (*https://oreil.ly/OeAQy*) and VS Code (*https://oreil.ly/h8p1j*), or take a peek at the steps in Chapter 7—it should take only a few minutes.

2. Leverage code editor commands and corresponding keyboard shortcuts to do amazing things (e.g., code completion, parameter info, inline documentation, refactoring, and much more). We'll go through these shortcuts in detail in Chapter 7.

For step 1, you can use the path to the virtual environment installed by the go script on the host. The go script displays this as its last step. You can also retrieve the path by running the following command in the project directory outside the container:

```
$ echo $(poetry env info -p)/bin/python
```

This is a second—and duplicate—virtual environment outside of the container because configuring a containerized Python interpreter for PyCharm is a paid feature (*https://oreil.ly/EWL8n*), and is not exactly straightforward for VS Code (*https://oreil.ly/yOc9U*). Yes, this is a deviation from containers! In practice, we would pay for the PyCharm professional license because it's simple and relatively low-cost, and we would continue to use a single containerized virtual environment for each project. However, we didn't want the price to be a barrier to our readers. So, we came up with this workaround so that anyone can follow along.

6. Train model on the cloud

There are many options for training ML models on the cloud. They can range from open source and self-hosted ML platforms—such as Metaflow (*https://oreil.ly/j-A2k*), Kubeflow (*https://oreil.ly/F9FoB*), and Ray (*https://oreil.ly/x9ogr*)—to managed services such as AWS SageMaker (*https://oreil.ly/miohg*), Google Vertex AI (*https://oreil.ly/79rjA*), and Azure Machine Learning (*https://oreil.ly/4FH3A*), among many others. To keep this example simple and generalizable, we've opted for the simplest possible option: train the model on a CI compute instance using GitHub Actions. Training our model on the CI pipeline may not provide the many affordances or compute resources that an ML platform provides, but it will suffice for the purposes of this exercise.

Training our model on a CI pipeline is similar to training it using these ML services in one regard: we are training a model on ephemeral compute instances on the cloud. As such, we can use Docker to install and configure the necessary dependencies on a fresh instance. You will likely choose a different technology, especially if you're doing large-scale training. Most, if not all, of these ML platforms support, and have supporting documentation for, running model training in containers.

In our example, we deploy our model training code simply by pushing our code to the repository.[2] The following code sample will create a CI/CD pipeline using GitHub Actions to run a Docker command to train our model, which you can see via the GitHub Actions tab on your forked repo. This runs model training on a CI/CD server instance without us needing to fiddle with shell scripts to install OS-level dependencies—such as Python 3.x, Python dev tools, or gcc—on the fresh CI instance. *This is where Docker really shines*: Docker abstracts away most "bare metal" concerns of running code on a remote compute instance and allows us to easily reproduce consistent runtime environments.

---

2 "Deploy" may sound like a big scary word, but it simply means the act of moving code or an application from a source repository to a target runtime environment.

```
# .github/workflows/ci.yaml

name: CI/CD pipeline
on: [push]
jobs:
  # ...
  train-model:
    runs-on: ubuntu-20.04
    steps:
      - uses: actions/checkout@v3
      - name: Train model
        run: ./batect train-model  ❶

# batect.yml
containers:
  dev:

    ...

tasks:
  train-model:
    description: Train ML model
    run:
      container: dev
      command: scripts/train-model.sh
```

❶ This defines a step in our CI pipeline to run the batect task, `./batect train-model`.

7. Deploy model web API

In this step, we will: (i) publish our model API image to a container registry and (ii) run a command to tell our cloud service provider to deploy an image with a specific tag. At this stage, the only dependency we need is infrastructure related—e.g., aws-cdk (AWS), gcloud (GCP), azure-cli (Azure), Terraform. We do not need any of the dependencies from our development container, so it's best that we specify a separate image for the purpose of deploying an image as a web service.

To make this code sample simple and generalizable regardless of which cloud provider you are using, we have opted to illustrate this step with pseudo-code:

```
# .github/workflows/ci.yaml

name: CI/CD pipeline
on: [push]
jobs:  ❶

  # ... other jobs (e.g. run tests)

  publish-image:
    runs-on: ubuntu-20.04
    steps:
```

```
      - uses: actions/checkout@v3
      - name: Publish image to docker registry
        run: docker push loan-default-prediction-api:${{github.run_number}}

  deploy-api:
    runs-on: ubuntu-20.04
    steps:
      - uses: actions/checkout@v3
      - name: Deploy model
        run: ./batect deploy-api
    needs: [publish-image]

# batect.yml
containers:
  deploy-api-container:
    image: google/cloud-sdk:latest ❷


tasks:
  deploy-api:
    description: Deploy API image
    run:
      container: deploy-api-container
      command: gcloud run deploy my-model-api --image IMAGE_URL ❸
```

❶ Pseudo-code for: (i) pushing our image from our CI/CD pipeline to a Docker registry and (ii) deploying this image as an API. We would typically need to retag the image to include the specific Docker image registry, but we have left out this detail to keep the example simple.

❷ For the deployment step, we didn't need any of the dependencies from our model training and serving, but we do need a dependency (e.g., gcloud, aws-cli, azure-cli, Terraform) that helps us deploy our image to a container hosting service. Did you notice how we didn't need to specify another Dockerfile? That is because batect allows us to define tasks with prebuilt images using the image option. Thanks to containers and batect, we can run this task in the same way on CI or on our local machine, simply by running ./batect deploy-api.

❸ Pseudo-code for deploying a Docker image to a container hosting technology. You would replace this with the corresponding command for the cloud provider that you are using (e.g., AWS, Azure, GCP, Terraform).

In the preceding paragraph, we're referencing several new concepts such as the container registry and cloud container hosting services. If this sounds overwhelming, fret not—we will describe these building blocks in an ML model's path to production in Chapter 9.

Well done! By this stage, you have learned how to reliably create consistent environments for developing and deploying ML models. The principles, practices, and patterns in this code repository are what we use in real-world projects to bootstrap a new ML project repository with good practices baked in.

Next, let's look at two other essential practices that can help you securely manage dependencies in your projects.

Secure Dependency Management

In 2017, attackers hacked Equifax (*https://oreil.ly/1QImF*)—a credit monitoring company—by exploiting a vulnerability in an outdated dependency (Apache Struts) to infiltrate their system. This exposed the personal details of 143 million Americans and cost the company US$380 million. By the time Equifax was hacked, the maintainers of Apache Struts had actually already found, disclosed, and fixed the vulnerability in a newer version of Apache Struts. However, Equifax was still using an older version with the vulnerability and essentially had a ticking time bomb in their infrastructure.

Did you know that there are Python dependencies that have been found to allow your cloud credentials to be siphoned (*https://oreil.ly/KYmTz*), or allow arbitrary code execution (*https://oreil.ly/H_5ms*)? Do you know if your current projects are exposed to any of these or other vulnerabilities? Well, if we don't check our dependencies for vulnerabilities, we won't know.

Keeping dependencies up-to-date and free of security vulnerabilities can be prohibitively tedious if we do them manually. The good news is that the technology to detect and resolve vulnerabilities in our dependencies has advanced significantly in recent years, and we can easily implement them in our projects without too much effort.

In this section, we will describe two practices that can help us mitigate these security risks:

- Removing unnecessary dependencies
- Automating checks and updates for dependencies

When complemented with the foundational knowledge in the preceding section, these practices will help you create production-ready and secure ML pipelines and applications.

With that in mind, let's look at the first practice: removing unnecessary dependencies.

Remove Unnecessary Dependencies

Unnecessary dependencies—in the form of unnecessarily large base images and unused application-level dependencies—can create several problems. First and foremost, they enlarge the attack surface area of your project and make it more vulnerable to malicious attackers.

Second, they increase the time needed to build, publish, and pull your images. Not only does this lengthen the feedback cycle on your CI/CD pipeline, it also can impede your ability to autoscale quickly in response to unexpected spikes in production traffic, if you are handling large traffic volumes.

Finally, stray dependencies that are installed but never used can make the project confusing and hard to maintain. Even if the dependencies are not used, its transitive dependencies—i.e., grandchildren dependencies—can exert an influence (such as version constraints and installation failures due to version incompatibility) on other dependencies and transitive dependencies that are actually needed.

As a rule of thumb, we should:

- Start with base images that are as small as possible—e.g., we could use *python:3.10-slim-bookworm* image (145 MB) as opposed to *python:3.10* (1 GB, almost seven times larger!)
- Remove dependencies that are not used from *pyproject.toml*
- Exclude development dependencies from the production image

On the third point, here is an example of how you can use Docker multistage builds (*https://docs.docker.com/build/building/multi-stage/*) to exclude development dependencies from your production image. The code sample below helps us reduce the size of the Docker image from 1.3 GB (dev image) to 545 MB (production API image):[3]

```
FROM python:3.10-slim-bookworm AS dev ❶

WORKDIR /code
RUN apt-get update && apt-get -y install gcc

RUN pip install poetry
ADD pyproject.toml /code/
RUN poetry config installer.max-workers 10
```

---

3 Running `docker history <image>` on our production image (545 MB) shows that Python dependencies account for 430 MB. Looking into the site-packages directory, we found that the top three contributors were scikit-learn (116 MB), SciPy (83MB), and pandas (61MB).

```
ARG VENV_PATH
ENV VENV_PATH=$VENV_PATH
ENV PATH="$VENV_PATH/bin:$PATH"

CMD ["bash"]

FROM dev AS builder ❷

COPY poetry.lock /code
RUN poetry export --without dev --format requirements.txt \
    --output requirements.txt

FROM python:3.10-slim-bookworm AS prod ❸

WORKDIR /code
COPY src /code/src
COPY scripts /code/scripts
COPY artifacts /code/artifacts
COPY --from=builder /code/requirements.txt /code
RUN pip install --no-cache-dir -r /code/requirements.txt
CMD ["./scripts/start-api-prod.sh"]
```

❶ The first stage (dev) will create a dev image that batect will use when running ./batect setup. After batect installs all the development dependencies, the
container becomes 1.3 GB. The code for this stage is the same as what you've seen
in preceding Dockerfile code samples.

❷ The second stage (builder) is an intermediate stage where we generate a *require-
ments.txt* file using poetry export. This file will help us in the next and final
stage to keep the production image as small as possible, which we will explain in
the next point.

❸ In the third stage (prod), we install only what we need for the production API.
We start afresh (FROM python:3.10-slim-bookworm) and copy only the code and
artifacts we need to start the API. We install the production dependencies using
pip and the *requirements.txt* file generated by Poetry so that we don't have to
install Poetry—a development dependency—in a production image.

To build the production image, we can run the following command. We specify the
target stage (prod) when we build the image:

```
$ docker build --target prod -t loan-default-prediction:prod .
```

With that, we have now excluded development dependencies from our production
API image, which makes our deployment artifact more secure and speeds up the
pushing and pulling of this image.

Automate Checks for Security Vulnerabilities

The second and most important practice for securing our application is to automate checks for security vulnerabilities in our dependencies. There are three components to this:

- Automating checks for OS-level security vulnerabilities, through Docker image scanning
- Automating checks for application-level security vulnerabilities, through dependency checking
- Automating updates of OS-level and application-level dependencies

If you are using GitHub, you can do all of the above with Dependabot (*https://oreil.ly/nBlxY*), a vulnerability scanning service that's integrated with GitHub. If you're not using GitHub, you can still implement the same functionality using other open source Software Composition Analysis (SCA) tools. For example, you can use Trivy (*https://oreil.ly/7EHEn*) to scan Docker images (*https://oreil.ly/2VKU5*) and Python dependencies (*https://oreil.ly/efTGG*), Snyk (*https://oreil.ly/gesE2*) or Safety (*https://oreil.ly/QJdl4*) to check for vulnerable Python dependencies, and Renovate (*https://oreil.ly/2NPRI*) to automate dependency updates.

SCA tools generally use a similar approach: They check your dependencies for known vulnerabilities, or Common Vulnerabilities and Exposures (CVE), by referencing a global vulnerability database, such as the National Vulnerability Database (*nvd.nist.gov*). Dependabot or Renovate also go on to create PRs in your project when it detects that a newer version of a given dependency is available.

 While dependency vulnerability scanning and automated dependency updates help us significantly reduce our risk to vulnerable dependencies, there can be scenarios where dependencies have been flagged in public vulnerability databases, but fixes have yet to be released. When a new vulnerability is found, there is naturally some amount of time required before the maintainers release a fix to address the vulnerability. Until a fix is found, these vulnerabilities are known as "zero-day vulnerabilities" (*https://oreil.ly/f1PdG*), because zero days have passed since the fix was published.

To manage this risk, you would need to consult security specialists in your organization to assess the severity of the vulnerabilities in your context, prioritize them accordingly, and identify measures to mitigate this risk.

Let's take a look at how we can set this up in three steps on our GitHub repository using Dependabot. Dependabot can raise pull requests for two types of updates:

(i) Dependabot *security updates* are automated pull requests that help you update dependencies with known vulnerabilities, and (ii) Dependabot *version updates* are automated pull requests that keep your dependencies updated, even when they don't have any vulnerabilities.

For this exercise, we'll use Dependabot version updates because the pull requests will be created immediately as long as there is an old dependency, even if there are no known security vulnerabilities. This will make it easier for you to follow along and see the intended result after completing each step.

The first step is to enable Dependabot for your repository or organization. You can do so by following the steps in GitHub's official documentation to enable Dependabot version updates (*https://oreil.ly/ZbB_o*).

Second, when you've completed the steps on the official documentation to enable Dependabot version updates, you'll be prompted to check in a *dependabot.yml* file in the *.github* directory:

```
# .github/dependabot.yml

version: 2
updates:
 - package-ecosystem: "pip" ❶
   directory: "/"
   schedule:
     interval: "daily"
```

❶ We specify the package ecosystem and the directory that contains the package file. The official documentation states that we should specify `pip`, even if we are using Poetry. We also specify whether Dependabot should check for updates daily, weekly, or monthly.

> While it's easy and tempting to also add a second update block here for `"docker"`, in practice it can be challenging as updating Python versions (e.g., from Python 3.10 to 3.12) can cause a cascade of changes in versions of dependencies and transitive dependencies.
>
> Nevertheless, we still recommend keeping the Python version of your ML system up to date, when you can ascertain that your application and dependency stack is compatible with newer versions of Python. Such a change should be easy to implement and test with the automated tests and containerized setup that we introduce in this book.

The third step is to configure our GitHub repository to allow PRs to merge only if tests pass on CI. This is an essential step to test that the dependency changes do not degrade the quality of our software. Different CI technologies will have different ways of doing this, and you can look up the respective documentation for your given toolchain. In our example, we are using GitHub Actions and, at the time of writing, the sequence of actions are:

1. Allow auto-merge. Under your repository name, click Settings. On the Settings page, under Pull Requests, select "Allow auto-merge." (You can also refer to the GitHub documentation on enabling auto-merge [*https://oreil.ly/0wQGg*] for up-to-date instructions for doing this.)

2. We'll define a GitHub Actions job to automatically merge PRs created by Dependabot. See GitHub documentation on adding auto-merge configuration for PRs created by Dependabot (*https://oreil.ly/mec0w*) and the code sample below, which is also available in the demo repo in the *.github* directory:

```
# .github/workflows/automerge-dependabot.yaml

name: Dependabot auto-merge
on: pull_request

permissions:
  contents: write
  pull-requests: write

jobs:
  dependabot:
    runs-on: ubuntu-latest
    if: github.actor == 'dependabot[bot]'
    steps:
      - name: Dependabot metadata
        id: metadata
        uses: dependabot/fetch-metadata@v1
        with:
          github-token: "${{ secrets.GITHUB_TOKEN }}"
      - name: Enable auto-merge for Dependabot PRs
        run: gh pr merge --auto --merge "$PR_URL"
        env:
          PR_URL: ${{github.event.pull_request.html_url}}
          GH_TOKEN: ${{secrets.GITHUB_TOKEN}}
```

3. Finally, under Settings > Branches, add a branch protection rule by checking the box "Require status checks to pass before merging," specifying the name of your branch (e.g., main), and search for the name of your test CI job. In this example, our job is `train-model`, which runs after `run-tests`. See GitHub documentation on adding a branch protection rule (*https://oreil.ly/6M2Jm*).

When these steps are done, your project will have its dependencies regularly and automatically updated, tested, and merged. Huzzah! A big leap toward more secure software.

After completing these steps, you'll notice that you can't push your local commits on the main branch anymore, because we've enabled branch protection.

For those accustomed to trunk-based development, fret not—you can add your team to the bypass list (see the GitHub documentation on bypassing branch protections [*https://oreil.ly/cr-EW*]). Your team can continue to enjoy the fast feedback of CI/CD and trunk-based development while Dependabot's changes go through pull requests.

Please note that bypassing branch protections can only be done on repositories belonging to an organization.

Automated Dependency Updates and Merges as a Helpful Forcing Function

Even though tools like Dependabot and Renovate make it easy for teams to set up automated PRs when vulnerable dependencies are detected, in practice these PRs can really pile up and add a significant amount of work for teams to review, test and merge them. There tends to be a lot of nervousness and hesitation about whether randomly upgrading a package could somehow cause subtle bugs or model degradations in production. Without comprehensive tests, teams can't auto-merge PRs because they will be releasing untested changes to production, and these PRs can easily become unwelcome and oft-procrastinated interruptions.

In contrast, when we have CI/CD pipelines with comprehensive tests (we'll describe how we can define comprehensive tests for ML systems in the following chapters), the CI/CD pipeline can automatically validate if the change worked. When the tests verify that the changes did not degrade ML model quality and behavior, the CI pipeline helps to merge PRs automatically. These three practices—automated dependency updates and comprehensive automated tests on CI/CD—complement each other to allow teams to experience emergent properties of security, speed, reliability, and productivity.

We find that automated dependency updates—aside from helping us deliver secure solutions—also serve as a useful forcing function (*https://oreil.ly/Imc8C*) (i.e., an event that forces one to take the necessary actions to produce a result). They help to nudge us toward ensuring that we have CI/CD pipelines with comprehensive tests.

Give yourself several pats on your back! You have just applied the principles and practices we use in real-world projects to help us effectively manage dependencies in ML projects and create reproducible, production-ready, and secure ML pipelines and applications.

Conclusion

To recap, in this chapter, we covered:

- What "check out and go" looks and feels like in practice
- How to use Docker, batect, and Poetry to create consistent, reproducible, and production-like runtime environments in each step of the ML delivery lifecycle
- How to detect security vulnerabilities in your dependencies, and how to automatically keep dependencies up-to-date

The unique challenges of the ML ecosystem—e.g., large and varied dependencies, large models—can stress-test how far we can take the practice of containerizing our software. In our experience, container technologies continue to be useful, but in the context of ML, it must be complemented with advanced techniques—e.g., Docker cache volumes, batect, automated security updates—so that we can continue to manage our dependencies effectively, securely, and with short feedback cycles.

Chapters 3 and 4 are our attempt to make these principles and practices clear and easy to implement so that we can rapidly and reliably set up our dependencies and spend time on solving the problems that we want to solve, not waste time in dependency hell. Proper dependency management is a low-hanging fruit that ML teams can harvest today and enjoy the benefits in terms of time, effort, reliability, and security.

In the next chapter, we will explore another powerful, foundational practice of effective ML teams: automated testing.

Further Reading

Even after years of working with Docker and the Python dependency ecosystem, we still find new things to learn. While daunting at the start, we've learned that it's part of the learning process, especially as technologies evolve quickly.

The following resources have helped us as we learn how to use Docker and Poetry in our ML projects, and help teams adopt them in their ML development workflow:

- Docker's documentation, which is user-friendly and accessible:
  - Dockerfile reference (*https://oreil.ly/ydyCo*)
  - Dockerfile best practices (*https://oreil.ly/znGuy*)
  - Docker multistage builds (*https://oreil.ly/nf9qu*)
- Docker tutorials:
  - Docker crash course for data scientists (*https://oreil.ly/KSmQh*)
- batect:
  - batect documentation (*https://oreil.ly/3OclN*)
- Poetry:
  - Poetry documentation (*https://oreil.ly/LR0l7*)
  - Dependency management and packaging with Poetry (*https://oreil.ly/4MnvO*)

## CHAPTER 5

Automated Testing: Move Fast Without Breaking Things

Dana has just sat down at her desk, the aroma of fresh coffee filling the space around her. She and a junior data scientist on the team continued on the user story that they kicked off yesterday—engineering a new feature that could improve the model.

They made the necessary changes and executed a command to run the tests. This suite of tests helped validate that the entire codebase was still behaving as expected. After 20 seconds, their terminal showed dashes of green—all the tests passed.

Sometimes the terminal went red. Some tests failed, but that's OK—the failing tests caught them as they were about to fall into a deep rabbit hole, helping them recover easily by tracing a few steps backward. The tests are now back to green and they gave it another go.

Green or red, the tests gave them fast feedback on code changes. The tests gave them confidence and the occasional dopamine hit to tell them if they were going in the right direction or stop them when they went in the wrong direction. They didn't have to follow a tedious sequence of manual steps to test the code. When the tests failed, there were only a small number of changes that could have caused the failure, not hours of potential suspects to sort through.

When they needed to train the model, they ran a command that triggered training on the cloud and their experiment-tracking dashboard lit up with updated metrics and explainability visualizations, which signaled whether they were on the right track. They iterated with steady steps, making reasonably sized git commits and pushes—which triggered automated model tests on the CI pipeline—along the way until the story was done.

Their cognitive load remained manageable. They retained clarity on what they needed to do and completed their work one steady step at a time.

We often find that ML products and systems tend to be under-tested. The lack of automated tests is one of the most common types of technical debt, which forces ML practitioners to pay interest every time they want to make a change. Without automated tests, ML practitioners waste copious amounts of time on manual testing or resolving production incidents due to errors that slipped through the cracks of manual testing. Not only does this reduce our capacity for valuable work, we also leave the door open for bugs, errors, and underperforming models to flow into the hands of users in the real world. Such product defects could sink months, and even years, of effort in building an ML product and can bring significant reputational and financial costs for an organization (*https://oreil.ly/1y076*).

That said, testing is not new to ML practitioners—in fact, we do it all the time. But we often do it manually rather than through automated means. If you find yourself spending more time than you'd like on manually testing the quality of your models or code changes, this chapter is for you. We'll share practical techniques for creating comprehensive automated tests for your ML solutions.

In this chapter, we'll detail:

- The challenges and unscalable costs of manual testing, especially in ML systems
- The benefits of automated testing and how it can help ML practitioners create reliable and maintainable systems
- The building blocks of a comprehensive automated testing strategy, grouped into two categories: software tests and model tests

This chapter will focus on the "why" and the "what" of automated tests (e.g., What tests should we write? What does a good test look like?). This will give you a high-level mental framework to organize the details of each component of a test strategy. We'll then dive into the "how" for the first category: software tests.

In the next chapter, we will explore:

- ML model tests: the challenges, necessity, and methods of automated testing for ML models
- Techniques for testing large language model (LLM) applications
- Using model tests as: (i) a cost-effective way to ensure code, data, and model changes do not degrade the product experience; and (ii) a "ratcheting" mechanism that lets us set new performance benchmarks without compromising established standards

To make these two chapters useful to as many readers as possible, we will assume that readers have the desire but not necessarily the experience to write these tests. You can skip sections for tests that you're already familiar with, and pore through sections that are new to you.

We'll illustrate each type of test using hands-on examples in the code-along repository (*https://oreil.ly/Hkgzc*), which you can clone to read, run, and write tests. This is the same repository that we used in the previous chapter and you can find the same setup steps in the README or in Chapter 4.

Automated Tests: The Foundation for Iterating Quickly and Reliably

Automated tests are the essential foundation for products that are easy to maintain and evolve. Tests give us fast feedback on changes and allow us to rapidly respond to changes imposed on our product, such as changes in training data, feature engineering strategies, modeling approaches, and business requirements.

Without automated tests, changes become error-prone, tedious, and stressful. When we change one part of the codebase, the lack of tests forces us to take on the burden of manually testing the *entire* system to ensure that a change (e.g., in feature engineering logic) hasn't caused a degradation (e.g., in model quality). As illustrated in Figure 5-1, as the size of the codebase grows, not only do we have to take on the quality assurance effort of the new features being developed, but also the burden of manual regression testing on the entire solution.

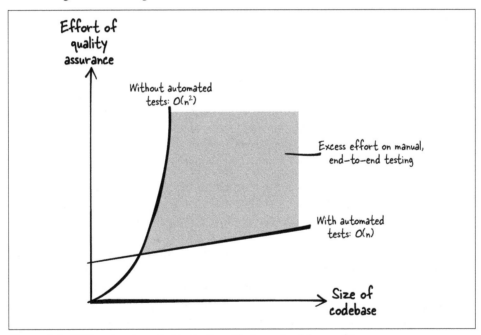

Figure 5-1. Without automated tests, the effort required for quality assurance grows quadratically, as compared to a more manageable linear growth in effort afforded by automated tests

In this section, we'll detail the benefits of automated tests and explain why continuous integration and continuous delivery (CI/CD) without tests is a contradiction in terms. We'll also discuss why, in our opinion, ML projects tend to be under-tested and what we can do about it.

 Later in this chapter, we will dissect tests into two categories: software tests and ML model tests. While practitioners are typically familiar with how to automate software tests, the uncertain and complex nature—especially in early and exploratory phases—of building an ML solution means that it can sometimes be hard to define automated tests for our ML models from the get-go.

Trying to test such unknown unknowns up front can introduce unnecessary friction. In these scenarios, you can start by using exploratory testing and visualization as stepping stones toward formulating heuristics about model quality that you can use in automated model tests. We'll discuss this in greater detail in Chapter 6.

Starting with Why: Benefits of Test Automation

In this section, we'll detail the benefits of test automation.

Not only do tests benefit consumers of the ML system through automated quality assurance, they also provide fast and essential feedback to creators of the ML system during development. By "fast," we are talking about a night-and-day difference: A comprehensive set of tests can shorten feedback cycles by several orders of magnitude—from tens of minutes to seconds, from hours to minutes. For some who are accustomed to running models overnight, this night-and-day difference becomes quite literal on some occasions—you don't have to wait a night and a day only to discover that there was a mistake in your code change.

Let's look at a scenario to illustrate the mechanical benefits of having comprehensive automated tests. Remember our properly caffeinated protagonist at the start of this chapter? Each code change or data change that they make goes through a series of automated quality checks (see Figure 5-2). Each set of tests specifies a set of quality standards that the team has defined for a given aspect of the software. For example, you can assert that the model metric for each key segment of the data remains above a current threshold (we have more examples of model tests in Chapter 6). When all the tests pass, you can be confident that the model and associated components are *as good as before* or *better than before* and can be released to production.

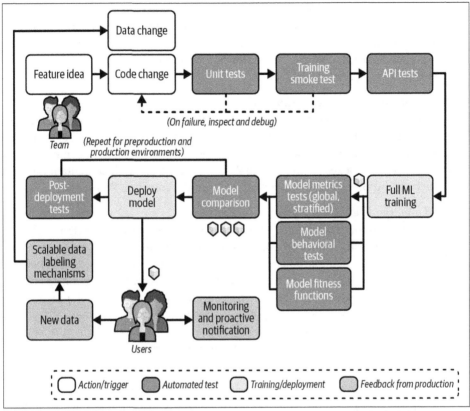

Figure 5-2. A series of automated tests serve as quality gates that validate if changes produce an artifact that is fit for production

In contrast, if any change violates the quality standards that you have defined for your ML product, the tests that are run locally or on your CI pipeline will catch that regression. The tests give us fast feedback (on the order of minutes or even seconds) and tell us that there are issues with the change, rather than leaving us to discover these issues much later through manual testing or customer complaints. One more production incident avoided, thanks to our tests. This may sound like a dream, but in this chapter and the next we'll demonstrate how you can make it a reality.

If you're still not convinced about why you should be automating your tests, here's a list of key benefits of test automation:

Fast feedback

For every code change, even if it's just one line or across multiple files, you can run one command and test if everything is working within seconds or a few minutes at most. This is in contrast to manual testing, which is tedious and can take up to hours and even days.

Reduced risk of production defects

When your test coverage is high, your tests can catch any accidental bugs and regressions introduced before they get to production—in test environments or even *while* you are coding. This saves you and your team from the effort and stress of fighting fires in production.

Living documentation and self-testing code

All functionality is accompanied by tests that describe what the component does and what scenarios or edge cases it can handle. If we ever need to change a component's behavior, we will also update the tests. As a result, documentation is cohesive and colocated with the actual code, in contrast to documentation pages, which can become stale and inconsistent from the code that it describes.[1]

Reduced cognitive load

Tests help you focus on the task at hand by systematically verifying that each part of the solution still works as expected, thereby allowing you to concentrate on a specific aspect of the problem without constantly worrying about unintended consequences in other areas. In addition, if the problem you're solving consists of many subproblems, writing tests helps you focus on one subproblem at a time, which presents a much lower cognitive load than trying to solve them all at once. Tests also nudge us to create modular components and well-defined interfaces. We tend to end up with software architectures that are easier to reason about and easier to refactor.

Refactoring

Refactoring is an essential habit of effective teams because it helps them regularly reduce technical debt and complexity, but without tests, refactoring is highly risky. Often, this leads teams to follow the path of least resistance—i.e., not refactoring—and the codebase becomes increasingly convoluted. As a result, executing on our ideas becomes harder and slower over time.

On the other hand, the safety harness of comprehensive tests makes it easy for us to make a change, validate the change, and regularly reduce technical debt as we deliver new features. In Chapter 8, we'll share a story of how we completed a major refactoring in one of our projects in an hour because our entire ML system had high test coverage—unit tests, integration tests, and model quality tests. When the refactoring was done, all the tests passed, we committed our changes, all the tests on the CI pipeline passed, and the change was deployed to production with no drama.

---

1 Documentation is essential in any software, but the component-level or function-level documentation that tests give us serve a different purpose from other types of documentation (e.g., model cards [*https://oreil.ly/b-qIC*], service one-pagers).

Regulatory compliance

The regulatory standards of most industries will typically have an aspect on quality assurance and model validation before models are released for consumption in production. For example, the European Commission has said (*https://oreil.ly/lWJTL*), the "testing of and experimenting with AI products and services is crucial to make them market-ready, ensure compliance with safety standards and rules as well as security by design [...]."

While regulatory bodies don't always mandate that these tests be automated, automating them can make it much easier for us to demonstrate our compliance. Rather than scrambling at the eleventh hour during regulatory audits, you can instead test your ML products with the tools and techniques that are available to you today to ensure that your ML products are of an acceptable quality for your users.

Improved flow, productivity, and satisfaction

All the preceding benefits help ML practitioners reduce friction, burdensome work, and unnecessary cognitive load. Taken together, automated tests help teams to enjoy fast feedback, reduced production defects, continuous improvements, and this all helps to contribute to flow, productivity, and satisfaction.

While our tests during model development aim to cover all anticipated production scenarios, the dynamic nature of real-world data ensures there will always be surprises. That is why operational monitoring in production is an aspect of a holistic test strategy. It enables teams to detect and address any deviations or anomalies that arise from shifts in production data.

We'll discuss monitoring ML systems in production in the next chapter.

Now that you understand the benefits of automated tests, let's look at some common reasons why ML systems often lack automated tests.

If Automated Testing Is So Important, Why Aren't We Doing It?

In this section, we'll look at the three common reasons for why ML systems often lack automated tests.

Reason 1: We think writing automated tests slows us down

The idea that writing automated tests slows us down claims, Why waste time writing tests when we could just write the code and implement the feature? This reasoning stems partly from the well-traveled road bias (*https://oreil.ly/ELRA8*)—the tendency to underestimate the duration taken to traverse oft-traveled routes and overestimate the duration taken to traverse less familiar routes.

From our experience across multiple ML and software projects, we've observed that the lack of automated tests *always* leads teams to spend *more time* in manually testing the code (see Figure 5-3). On the other hand, in projects with comprehensive automated tests, ML practitioners could work more effectively because the automated tests freed them up from manual regression testing and from resolving production defects that accidentally slipped through the cracks of manual testing.

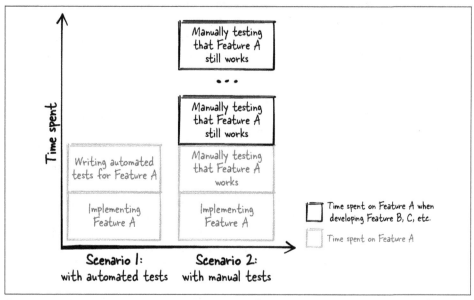

Figure 5-3. Counterintuition: writing automated tests appears to cost more time but in practice saves us time overall

Let's illustrate this with an example. Let's say we're developing some feature engineering logic that we think will improve our model metric—both global and stratified metrics—by X%. Automated tests help us save time in three horizons:

During development
As we are developing, we also write a test specifying the new metric threshold that we expect. We run the tests with a single command and iterate on our feature engineering logic until the test passes (and we could also write other tests for other smaller subproblems along the way). We save time and effort from repeatedly parsing global model metrics or stratified model metrics from notebooks or print statements buried in logs.

After development

When we complete a user story,[2] our team is confident that the new logic did what it's supposed to do (improve the model by X%) by looking at the passing tests. This removes the need for another teammate to repeat manual testing procedures, which frees them up to test for edge cases, missing data, and other scenarios that we may have missed during development.

During subsequent development

In the future weeks or months, should any change cause the model to regress below the new threshold, the automated tests will catch it. Without this test, we either have to spend time manually eyeballing the model's quality metric *with every commit, pull request or release*, or we live with the risk that we may be unknowingly degrading the model over time.

Reason 2: "We have CI/CD"

CI/CD has become an increasingly popular term in the ML community, but it tends to be misused and misunderstood. In software engineering, continuous integration (CI) refers to the ability to *frequently integrate code changes to the main branch*. Continuous delivery (CD) refers to the ability to deploy software on the main branch *at any moment* to production (see detailed definition and discussion on CI/CD in Chapter 9). Both of these can be done *only when* we have comprehensive automated tests that give us feedback and confidence about the quality of the code changes. By this standard, we haven't seen many ML teams actually practice CI/CD.

Just because teams have a CI pipeline and automated deployments doesn't mean they're doing CI/CD. The contents of the CI/CD pipelines matter: What tests do we actually run on the CI/CD pipeline? What tests do we run to give us confidence that we're releasing high-quality models? What is the test coverage on our CI/CD pipelines?

Talking about CI/CD without comprehensive automated tests is a contradiction in terms—a group of words associating incompatible objects or ideas—and gives us a false sense of security. The CI pipeline might be all green but without comprehensive tests we can still be releasing defects into production. In this scenario, the CI pipeline helps us faithfully release defects rather than discovering and remediating them in development. If we want to actually enjoy the benefits of CI/CD (detailed in Chapter 9), we need comprehensive automated tests.

---

2 A user story is a tool used in agile software development to capture a description of a software feature from an end-user perspective. For more details, see Chapter 2.

There is perhaps a sociocultural origin to the predicament we find ourselves in. On one hand, ML engineers tend to focus on MLOps and DevOps, which are traditionally focused on deployment automation, infrastructure-as-code, and CI/CD. On the other hand, data scientists tend to focus on training and evaluating ML models. While the two worlds have collided, there remains a competency gap between ML engineers (automation) and data scientists (model evaluation) in many teams. We know how to set up CI pipelines and we know how to train and evaluate models, but not all teams have worked out how to bridge both practices to automate manual model evaluation procedures. This leads us to our next point.

Reason 3: We just don't know how to test ML systems

From our interaction with ML practitioners across various industries, we know many of them are open to writing automated tests. While automated testing was new to them, some of them eventually came to see its value and write tests as part of their work. The main reason for not writing tests was simply that they didn't know how to or weren't taught how to.

In the seminal "ML Test Score" paper (*https://oreil.ly/hGTTh*), the authors rightly pointed out that ML system testing can be more challenging than manually coded system testing because ML system behavior can depend strongly on data, and models that cannot be strongly specified *a priori*. (In the paper, they then go on to lay out a rubric on how ML systems can be tested and monitored.)

Since the time of that paper, patterns for testing specific components in an ML solution have been emerging. We've begun to disambiguate parts of an ML system (e.g., feature engineering, data processing, model serving) and identified corresponding test strategies for various subjects under test.

That puts us in a good place because we want to write better tests, and we know that there are ways for us to formulate the appropriate types of tests. The only thing stopping us is knowing what types of tests we can write, and how we can write them. For that, let's turn to the next section.

Building Blocks for a Comprehensive Test Strategy for ML Systems

Now that you see the importance of automated tests, let's start to piece together what a comprehensive test strategy could look like. In this section, we start by identifying what we should test, before laying out a typology of tests you can include in your toolkit. Finally, we'll describe characteristics of a good automated test.

The What: Identifying Components For Testing

The first step in building a comprehensive test strategy is to identify what we need to test. Table 5-1 details the typical components that we'd find in an ML system—e.g., model training pipeline, API service, and feature engineering logic. If you find that your ML product contains any of the components in Table 5-1, each of them can and should be tested. These tests are also depicted in Figure 5-2 to help you contextualize where to use each type of test in an ML model's path to production.

Table 5-1. Types of automated tests for ML systems

Component, or subject under test (SUT)	Type of test	What good looks like
Software logic		
Logic, data transformations, feature engineering	Unit tests	Tests enumerate scenarios of how we interact with a function or class and specify the correct and expected behavior.
		Fast-running: Tens of tests run in seconds; even hundreds of tests can run within one to two minutes.
		Internal "private" functions may not need tests if they are tested as part of another function.
		Quantity: Tens to hundreds of tests
Model training pipeline	Training smoke tests	Tests exercise all code paths as a full model training run would.
		Avoid conditional statements that would introduce asymmetry between training smoke tests and actual training runs in production.
		Fast-running: Even for an ML pipeline that takes hours to run, training smoke tests should take one to two minutes to complete.
		Locally runnable: The ability to run and debug the training pipeline locally helps provide fast feedback for troubleshooting any pipeline failures.
		Quantity: Typically one or two tests
Model API	API tests	Tests specify all the scenarios that our model service will handle.
		Tests represent the model service's contract and guarantee to downstream consumers.
		Tests include happy paths and unhappy paths to demonstrate how the model handles error scenarios (e.g., null values, wrong data types).
		Locally runnable: As above
		Quantity: Can range from five to tens, depending on the API's responsibilities
Deployed model API	Post-deployment tests	Tests invoke a model service that has just been deployed to a preproduction or production environment.
		Tests do not duplicate scenarios that are already covered by API tests.
		Locally runnable: When running the tests against a real service, we should be able to access the associated logs to understand the service's behavior.
		Quantity: Typically one or two tests

Component, or subject under test (SUT)	Type of test	What good looks like
ML models		
Trained ML model	Metric tests (global and stratified)	Tests evaluate the model using a validation dataset.
		Tests should be extensible and can be run with new validation data as they become available, without being coupled to the training pipeline (see "Open-Closed Test Design" on page 190).
		Locally runnable: As above
		Quantity: Typically between a few to ten
Trained ML model	Behavioral tests	Tests enumerate specific—and potentially out-of-sample—scenarios and specify the expected behavior for the model.
		We can start with just one or two examples and use data-generation techniques to scale to include many examples in a single scenario, if that provides value (more details in Chapter 6).
		Quantity: Typically between a few to tens
Data		
Data pipelines, for input and output data	Data pipeline tests Data contract tests	Tests ensure the data pipeline operates correctly by verifying each step (e.g., extraction, transformation, loading) functions as expected. These tests check for the integrity and accuracy of data as it moves through the pipeline.
		Tests also validate that the data adheres to the agreed schema, types, and formats expected by consuming systems or components.
		Quantity: Varies depending on the complexity of the pipeline, but usually multiple tests for each step in the pipeline in order to fail fast and fail loudly.
Input: Training data	Data privacy tests	Tests check that training data doesn't contain PII and is compliant with relevant data protection laws (e.g., GDPR).
		Quantity: Should be thorough enough to prove compliance; the number may vary according to the types of data handled.

We cover both categories of tests (software tests and model tests) in this book because, while each category of test is *indispensable*, each one alone is *incomplete*. For example, software tests are suited to testing logical correctness, but can fall short in testing ML model quality. And while model tests can help us scale the number of scenarios under which we can observe a model's behavior, it is too distant (i.e., too many layers of abstraction away) from a feature engineering logic and would be a blunt tool for testing the correctness of that logic. In short, all ML systems need *both* software tests and model tests.

It helps to consider the Swiss cheese model of accident causation (*https://oreil.ly/-ysTS*), which comes from the field of risk management. The model demonstrates that each layer of tests prevents a specific type of issue but no single layer of tests (e.g., unit tests, training smoke tests, or metrics tests) can test for all kinds of undesired outcomes. The layers complement each other to reduce blind spots and reduce the risk of bugs, errors, and other adverse outcomes flowing into production (see Figure 5-4).

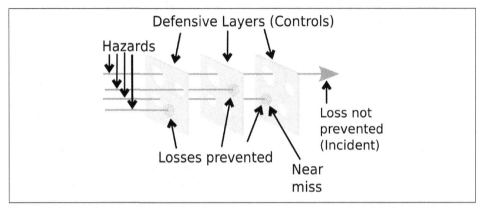

Figure 5-4. The Swiss cheese model of accident causation (https://oreil.ly/-ysTS) (source: Ben Aveling, Wikimedia Commons [https://oreil.ly/kJbAs], used under CC BY-SA 4.0 [https://oreil.ly/Hq5C_])

Let's go through Table 5-1—types of automated tests for ML systems—in a bit more detail.

Software logic

Whether you are training an ML model from scratch, fine-tuning a pretrained model with your custom domain data, deploying a pretrained model, or doing federated learning on edge devices, you will be writing code and your code is software (*https://oreil.ly/1IoCJ*) (i.e., a set of instructions that tells a computer what to do or how to perform a task).

Software logic components are characterized by *deterministic measures of correctness* (e.g., add(1, 2) = 3). Each component and its constituent functions take some input data, apply some transformation logic to the data, and either return the output data or perform a side effect with the data (e.g., save the data to disk).

For a list of typical components in the software logic category and their corresponding tests, refer to Table 5-1.

ML models

While software tests are indispensable, they are but one part of the testing puzzle and are insufficient for fully testing ML systems. This is because the model's behavior is learned from multidimensional data, and it can be hard to articulate our expectations of what constitutes "correct" behavior in one or even a few assertions.

Software tests tend to be *example-based* or *point-based*, and even property-based testing tends to get hard to read and maintain beyond three or four dimensions. That's where model tests come in. They test our model using production-like data, checking our model's behavior against expected behavior and aggregating the results in a meaningful and actionable way.

ML practitioners are typically familiar with model evaluation techniques, and domain experts and customers typically have implicit mental heuristics to judge if a model's behavior is correct or wrong, good or bad, better or worse. That's a great starting point for instrumenting automated ML tests. We can start by looking at existing manual testing approaches—when we release a model to production, what metrics or manual tests give us the confidence that a new model is "good enough" for production? What classes of behavior are undesirable? We can automate—and over time, deepen—these model tests as we consider how to automate more quality checks in our path to production.

We can codify these implicit heuristics as automated *fitness functions* (*https://oreil.ly/ Fi6wL*)—objective, executable functions that can be used to summarize, as a single figure of merit, how close a solution is to its target state. These fitness functions can then be incorporated into our release pipelines to lay the foundation for iteratively improving our ML models and reducing manual testing. We'll elaborate on fitness functions in Chapter 6.

It's worth calling out that model tests are closely related to the practices of *exploratory evaluation*, *error analysis*, *production monitoring*, and *data curation*. We will describe how these practices complement each other in Chapter 6.

Putting it together: The ML Systems Test Pyramid

To illustrate how software tests, model tests, and other types of tests come together to create a comprehensive test strategy, let's look at the ML Systems Test Pyramid (see Figure 5-5). The Pyramid illustrates the types and quantities of tests in an ML system. The four pyramids (from left to right, and up) represent tests for data, model training pipelines, software logic, and ML models respectively.

The size of each layer of the pyramid loosely represents the quantity of tests. For example, a big bottom layer for unit tests indicates that we should have many unit tests because they are fast, targeted, and easy to reason about and debug in the case of a failure. On the other hand, exploratory tests occupy a smaller area on the top of the Pyramid because, while they have a place in a comprehensive test strategy, they tend to be manual and unscalable, so we want to ensure we don't accumulate a large quantity of exploratory manual testing procedures.

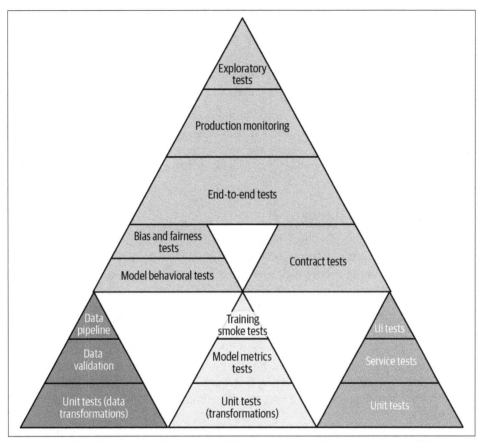

Figure 5-5. The ML Systems Test Pyramid (source: adapted from an image in "Continuous Delivery for Machine Learning" by Danilo Sato et al. [https://oreil.ly/PMzOZ])

In our book, even though we categorize the tests slightly differently—e.g., software logic tests can show up as unit tests in three pyramids (data, ML model, software)—we still find the ML Systems Test Pyramid to be a helpful visual to identify the types of tests you can include in your solution to reduce manual testing and improve automated quality assurance.

Now that we've got a good grasp of the breadth of tests for an ML system, let's look at characteristics of a good test and key pitfalls to avoid.

Characteristics of a Good Test and Pitfalls to Avoid

Let's look at characteristics and practices that help us write reasonable and maintainable tests. While many of these practices are adapted from unit testing and test-driven development in the software engineering world, we find that they generalize well to the model tests that we'll cover in the next chapter.

Tests should be independent and idempotent

Each test should be independent—i.e., the outcome of one test should not depend on what happens in another test. Tests should also be idempotent—i.e., no matter how many times we execute them, we achieve the same result. To this end, it helps to avoid any kind of shared state (e.g., tests that interact with a shared database or file).

The opposite of idempotent tests would be flaky tests—tests that pass or fail unpredictably even when nothing has changed. When we see a flaky test, we should either fix it or remove it. Otherwise, flaky tests will waste the team's time in triaging and rerunning the tests until they pass by chance, and they also diminish our confidence in our tests and CI pipeline.

Tests should fail fast and fail loudly

What's worse than bugs and errors? Silent bugs and errors, of course! A common example of silent regressions are model training pipelines that complete successfully, but lurking beneath the green pipeline status is a potential model-quality degradation that remains undetected.

To avoid this, you can adopt the principle of failing fast and loudly (*https://oreil.ly/Fz9mG*)—a Unix Philosophy principle that you can apply to your tests and CI pipelines to give you the fast feedback you need. For example, if a model training pipeline takes an hour, you can fail fast and loudly by writing a test to exercise the entire pipeline with a very small dataset (we'll discuss training smoke tests later in this chapter) and get feedback within one to two minutes should your changes cause a regression.

Tests should check behavior, not implementation

Let's illustrate this point with Jason Swett's analogy of testing a car (*https://oreil.ly/0mXqU*). When you test implementation, you try to test that the car works by checking if it has all the right stuff: presence of an engine, an ignition, wheels, and everything else that's needed to get from point A to point B. On the other hand, when you test behavior, you test that the car works by starting the car and driving it for a bit.

Tests that focus on implementation are hard to read and they are brittle to changes. Let's illustrate this with a negative and a positive example:

```
# bad example: implementation-focused test
def test_train_model_returns_a_trained_model(mock):
    mock.patch("train.training_helpers._fit_model",
               return_value=RandomForestClassifier())

    model = train_model()

    assert isinstance(model, RandomForestClassifier)
```

```
# good example: behavior-focused test
def test_train_model_returns_a_trained_model():
    test_data = load_test_data()
    model = train_model(test_data)
    valid_predictions = [0, 1, 2]

    prediction = model.predict(test_data[0])

    assert prediction in valid_predictions
```

Notice how the second test was easier to understand?

The first test is especially common in cases where the subject under test is poorly written and lacks testable boundaries. A convenient workaround is to short-circuit certain parts of the code with mocks, but this comes at a cost. For example, the private function _fit_model() may actually contain an error, but because we short-circuited parts of the code for ease of testing, we never actually execute that part of the code, and the tests can't help us discover any errors that may be hiding in _fit_model().

By focusing on testing behavior and not implementation, our tests become more readable, more useful, and less brittle to inevitable changes in implementation.

We should treat tests as code because tests are code. The pitfalls we observe in the preceding bad example test arise from poor software design. For example, the first test violated *encapsulation* because the test knew too much about internal implementation details of the function that it's testing. Violating encapsulation leads to tight coupling, which leads to brittle code that requires shotgun surgery (*https://oreil.ly/YMGWZ*)—the need to make changes in multiple places throughout a codebase to achieve a single modification.

We'll discuss these design principles in greater detail in Chapter 8, and the point to note here is that tests are, in essence, also software. We should write our tests with good coding practices that help us write readable and maintainable code.

Tests should be runnable in your development environment

Every test that we run on the cloud (e.g., on CI pipeline) should be runnable in your development environment—be it locally or in your cloud development environment. The ability to run tests and reproduce any failures in your development environment helps you avoid the antipattern of "pushing to know if something works." The former gives us feedback on the order of seconds, while the latter gives us feedback on the order of minutes or tens of minutes.

When a test fails on CI, first reproduce the failure in your development environment and iterate on a bug fix. You can even add breakpoints and debug and inspect the code, which is more effective than adding a print statement, pushing, waiting a few minutes or even hours, seeing what the print statement says, and doing so repeatedly. The ability to do error analysis in your development environment can help you triage the failure more quickly.

In some scenarios, it may not be possible to run some tests on a local machine—e.g., when a model is too large to fit on our local machine, or when it takes too long to train a model locally. In such cases, you can design your tests to be runnable locally by having a very small test dataset to train a very small model, simply to act as a smoke test before spending time running a full training in the cloud.

In addition, you can also set up your development environment so that you can trigger large-scale model training remotely on the cloud (e.g., using tools such as Metaflow [*https://oreil.ly/RzNXY*] or Ray [*https://oreil.ly/yOrkm*]) from your local machine, to avoid the antipattern of "pushing to know if something works."

Tests must be part of feature development

You should be writing tests as part of feature development, not as an afterthought in a separate story, for two reasons.

First, post-hoc tests tend to be too coarse-grained and miss out on the value of writing tests as part of your development process. If the problem you're solving consists of many subproblems, and they often do, writing tests helps you focus on one subproblem at a time, which presents a much lower cognitive load than trying to solve them all at once.

Second, "testing stories" don't appear as valuable as developing new features and the sociopsychological pressures to "get work done" often cause such stories to be relegated to the graveyard of other backlog stories. As a result, you accumulate technical debt and are forced to pay interest (e.g., spend time on manual testing) in subsequent features that you develop (recall Figure 5-3, where you saw the quadratic, cumulative testing effort that results from the lack of automated tests).

Refer to the following sidebar on test-driven development (TDD) for a brief discussion on the why, what, and how of writing tests as part of feature development.

Test-Driven Development

Test-driven development is a software engineering practice that emphasizes writing tests before writing code. With TDD, developers write automated tests that define the desired functionality of a feature or component, then write code to make those tests pass.

TDD is useful, even and especially in ML projects, in helping us break down big problems into smaller bite-sized problems that we can address one piece at a time. At the end of it, not only do we have code logic that solves the problem for us, TDD also helps us identify edge cases, write living documentation, build a safety net that lets us refactor and validate changes within seconds, and develop self-testing code that can scale well across space and time. TDD also nudges us toward writing modular code with better defined boundaries (because we need those boundaries for invoking functions and specifying expectations in tests) instead of hammering out "code that works" in a long and enmeshed Python script or a gigantic function.

To implement TDD, we typically follow a three-step process:

1. Write a test that defines the desired functionality of a feature or component.
2. Run the test and watch it fail (since the feature has not yet been implemented).
3. Write the minimal amount of code needed that makes the test pass.

We then iterate and repeat this process until the feature or task is done.

Based on our experience in several ML projects, when we invest the time and effort in ensuring that our code is accompanied by automated tests, the investment very quickly pays off because we save a significant amount of time and energy from manual testing, and debugging defects that slipped through the cracks of manual testing.

TDD can be very useful in software tests because we can specify a function's behavior *a priori*. We have even applied TDD and enjoyed its benefits when developing LLM applications (*https://oreil.ly/95yOX*). Having said that, we acknowledge that TDD can be more challenging in ML model tests, where we may not know what specific behavior to expect before we implement the solution. For such scenarios, there are other testing practices that can help us, and we'll describe these model testing practices in the next chapter.

In our experience, being able to recognize when we can (or can't) apply TDD in ML projects is more productive than dogmatically refusing to or insisting on practicing TDD.

Tests let us "catch bugs once"

As we've established, you should be writing tests as part of feature development. Bug fixes or production incident responses are no different in that you should also be writing tests as part of the fix. By writing the test first to reproduce the error scenario, you have a firm starting point and you can run the tests very quickly as you iterate on a fix. The tests guarantee that this bug will never happen again (unless someone skips or removes them!).

This is applicable to model tests as well. For example, through your own manual testing or through user feedback, you may realize that your model was producing incorrect predictions more often for one segment of your data than for other segments. In addition to ad hoc error analysis to triage the issue, you can also write a stratified metric test to assert that your model quality metric for each segment is within X% of each other. This test will ensure that if your model is again underperforming for a key segment of our data, your tests will catch it and prevent this model from being released to production. We'll show an example of such a test in Chapter 6.

As Isao Yoshino, a Toyota veteran, said, "It's only a failure if you don't learn (from it)." Every production incident or customer complaint is a valuable point of feedback about a gap in our product, and tests help us codify that those gaps have been mitigated and ensure that the same bugs don't happen again.

This set of characteristics and pitfalls to avoid are useful guidelines when we're designing and writing our tests. Especially when we're feeling unsure (e.g., is there value in writing tests as a part of this story?), these principles have helped us make better decisions. We hope it will guide you just the same.

Now that you know the desirable characteristics of tests, let's look at components of an automated test and how we can write one.

The How: Structure of a Test

In this section, we will describe the structure of an automated test. While this structure is drawn from the practice of unit testing, we find it generalizes well to other types of software tests and model tests.

An automated test should have three ingredients:

- A meaningful test name
- Structure of arrange, act, assert (AAA)
- Specific and holistic assertions

To illustrate these ingredients, let's take a look at a positive and a negative example of a test. We'll show more sophisticated tests in the next section, but for now a simple example will help us focus on the characteristics of a good test:

```
# good example
def test_convert_keys_to_snake_case_for_keys_with_spaces_or_punctuation(): ❶
    # arrange (provide input conditions) ❷
    user_details = {"Job Description": "Wizard",
                    "Work_Address": "Hogwarts Castle",
  "Current-title": "Headmaster"}

    # act
    result = convert_keys_to_snake_case(user_details)

    # assert (verify output conditions)
    assert result == {
        "job_description": "Wizard",
        "work_address": "Hogwarts Castle",
        "current_title": "Headmaster"
      } ❸
```

❶ The name of the test describes what we are testing—the function convert_keys_to_snake_case() and what it should do (update the keys in a dictionary) for a given condition (keys with spaces and punctuation). Our brain is primed and prepared to digest the implementation details that follow. In large projects with many tests, well-named tests that clearly describe the "what" help us to reduce cognitive load by abstracting away the "how" and dense implementation details in the test.

❷ The test has the structure of arrange, act, assert, and we use a blank new line to create a visual hierarchy denoting the three blocks of code. In a real test though, we wouldn't need to explicitly spell out "arrange, act, assert," as the use of a blank line is a typical convention in software testing to indicate the three blocks. You may also merge sections (e.g., arrange and act can be merged in small tests), if it makes the tests easier to read.

❸ A single, holistic assertion makes it clear what we expect of this function.

Next, let's take a look at a bad example:

```
# bad example
def test_convert_keys_to_snake_case(): ❶
    result = convert_keys_to_snake_case({"Job Description": "Wizard",
                                         "Work Address": "Hogwarts Castle",
                                         "Current_title": "Headmaster"
})
    assert result["job_description"] == "Wizard" ❷
    assert result["work_address"] is not None ❸
```

❶ The generic test name (just prefixing the function we're testing with test_) gives us little information on what scenarios we are testing and forces us to read the implementation details in the test.

❷ Assertions are piecemeal and incomplete. In this case, the test could actually miss a bug because we didn't assert on `Current_title`.

❸ The second assertion is too vague. The function could return a wrong value for the `work_address` field and our test would still pass.

Equipped with the why, what, and how of automated testing, you're now ready to dive into the first category of tests: software tests!

Software Tests

In this section, let's look at four types of software tests that are useful for testing software components commonly found in ML systems:

- Unit tests
- Training smoke tests
- API tests
- Post-deployment tests

Figure 5-2 will help you situate where each of these software tests sit in an ML model's path to production.

Unit Tests

Unit tests help ensure the correctness of individual building blocks of our ML system—most commonly *functions*. Whatever the function does, it is doing something, and unit tests help us to explicitly specify the function's expected behavior and ensure that these expectations still hold true with every code change. Decades of software engineering have taught us that this is much more reliable and scalable than manual testing—which is error-prone and ever-increasingly time-consuming—or worse, not testing at all.

While other types of tests listed in this chapter may not be needed for certain situations (e.g., you won't need API tests if you're not deploying an API), unit tests are the only type of test that is unequivocally necessary in ML solutions. Software logic generally accounts for most of the code footprint in ML projects. For example, an important part of ML systems is feature engineering, and these data transformations are essentially pure functions and logical transformations to data. If we don't test this logic, we're keeping a door open for bugs, errors, and countless hours debugging defects that slipped through the large cracks of manual testing.

How to design unit-testable code

Alright. You are convinced of the value of unit testing and you want to start writing your own unit tests. However, you may be looking at a codebase that looks incredibly difficult to test. For example, imagine if all of the code is in a very long Python script or notebook, with no callable functions—this makes it hard to test because we don't even have a function to invoke, much less a result to assert on.

The good news is that, if you find yourself in a codebase like that, there are techniques that you can apply to refactor your way to a modular, reasonable, and testable codebase (we'll demonstrate this in Chapter 8 on refactoring). But for now, the point is—code can be written in a way that's hard to test. This usually happens when automated testing is done as an afterthought. You can, and should, make it easier for yourself to unit test your code by (i) writing tests as part of your solution, and (ii) writing your code using the functional core, imperative shell design pattern (*https://oreil.ly/3Gqkc*) from functional programming (see Figure 5-6):

Thick functional core
> The thick functional core refers to a collection of pure functions (i.e., a function that returns identical outputs when given identical inputs, without any side effects). Examples could include any kind of data processing, feature engineering, and data transformations. Pure functions are deterministic and idempotent, and far easier to test.

Thin imperative shell
> The thin imperative shell refers to a small collection of functions that perform side effects (e.g., loading data, or saving a file to disk or a remote bucket). These interactions with the outside world are computationally expensive and also nondeterministic. By excluding them from our functional core, we make our functional core far easier and faster to test.

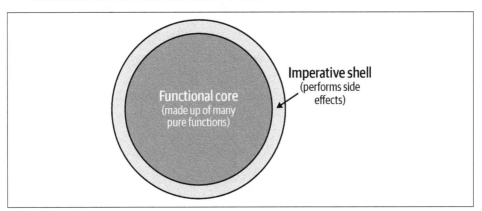

Figure 5-6. Functional core, imperative shell design pattern (https://oreil.ly/3Gqkc)

As an aside, the word "imperative" in this context puzzled us initially, because we thought it was referring to the style of coding using an explicit sequence of instructions to tell the computer how to do things (as in imperative code versus declarative code [*https:// oreil.ly/zk2JZ*]). However, it's actually referring to *imperative programming* (as in imperative programming versus functional programming [*https://oreil.ly/EOA0i*]), which according to instructor Philip Fong at Simon Fraser University is a "style of programming, in which side effects are not only permissible but are also the primary means by which we program."

With this design tool in our hands, let's zoom in and learn how to write a unit test for a particular function.

How do I write a unit test?

In each unit test, we specify the inputs that we pass to the function under test and our expectations of the function's return value (or side effect, in the case of functions in the thin imperative shell).

A unit test shares the same ingredients as the automated test that we described earlier in the chapter: a readable test name, AAA structure (arrange, act, assert), and holistic assertions. As a mini-challenge, can you read the code sample below and spot each ingredient in the test?

Here is an example of a unit test for a function that transforms a dictionary to have snake-cased keys:

```
# unit testing a function that transforms a dictionary
def test_convert_keys_to_snake_case_replaces_title_cased_keys():
    result = convert_keys_to_snake_case({"Job Description": "Wizard",
                                         "Work_Address": "Hogwarts Castle"})

    assert result == {
        "job_description": "Wizard",
        "work_address": "Hogwarts Castle"
    }
```

Here's another example of a unit test, but this time for a function that applies a data transformation to a pandas dataframe:

```
# unit testing a function that transforms a dataframe
from pandas._testing import assert_frame_equal ❶

def test_normalize_columns_returns_a_dataframe_with_values_between_0_and_1():
    loan_applications = pd.DataFrame({"income": [10, 100, 10000]})

    result = normalize_columns(loan_applications)
```

```
expected = pd.DataFrame({"income": [0, 0.009, 1]})
assert_frame_equal(expected, result) ❷
```

❶ For testing dataframe equality, we use `assert_frame_equal()` (*https://oreil.ly/mIdFt*) or `assert_series_equal()` (*https://oreil.ly/ZQqdx*) from pandas.

❷ By articulating our expectations of a function, we improve our understanding of the code's behavior. In this example, we may discover that min-max normalization is the wrong data transformation to apply, as it would baseline the smallest value to 0 (e.g., the "income" of 10 now becomes 0 after normalization). Perhaps we should be using log transformations (*https://oreil.ly/RKDC8*) instead. Through writing this test, we uncovered a bug and found an opportunity to improve our feature engineering logic.

If that looked too easy, it's because it is, once you've learned how to do it! Unit testing is a simple and powerful tool that helps you ensure that every new piece of functionality you write is accompanied with tests, and helps you reap the benefits we described earlier. When a team develops the habit and discipline of ensuring the correctness and quality of their code through automated tests, they improve the reliability, agility, and velocity of their ML experimentation cycles.

With that in order, we can now shift gears to look at another component of an ML system that some consider hard to test: the ML training pipeline.

Training Smoke Tests

ML training is usually long running and can range between minutes to hours. The wait time lengthens the feedback loop we use to assess the effect of a code change, and also disrupts our flow, and possibly even steers us toward more multitasking and context-switching.

Even if model training takes just 10 minutes, why wait 10 minutes to find an error in a final step when you can find out in a minute or less? Training smoke tests give us fast feedback (within a minute or so) on whether our code change worked as expected, or caused any issues, in the ML training task. When it passes, we're more confident that the full-scale ML training is more likely to succeed.

A training smoke test works by exercising the entire code path, just as a full-scale ML training would, except that we use the smallest possible dataset—even 10 samples could suffice. The subject under test here is the code that glues together the end-to-end ML training (you could call it an ML training pipeline, task, or script), all the way from loading data, feature engineering, model training, and creating a consumable artifact, even if it's a small model.

The test passes if nothing blows up (i.e., there's no smoke). The term "smoke test" originates from electronic hardware testing (*https://oreil.ly/S7Da1*)—you plug in a new board and turn on the power. If you see smoke coming from the board, turn off the power because something is broken. We have also seen other practitioners in the ML community refer to this type of test as a pretrain test (*https://oreil.ly/idW2z*), or integration test (*https://oreil.ly/ZS4h8*).

How do I write these tests?

While the implementation of these tests may differ depending on your ML training framework, the general approach is the same. Invoke your ML training pipeline locally, as you would in full-scale training, except that you will use a very small dataset. Here is an example of a training smoke test:

```
def test_training_smoke_test():
    data = pd.read_csv("/code/data/train.csv", encoding="utf-8",
                        low_memory=False)
    # group by target column to ensure we train on data
    # that contains all target labels:
        test_data = data.groupby('DEFAULT') \
                                .apply(lambda df: df.head(10)) \
                                .reset_index(drop=True)

    pipeline = train_model(test_data)

    predictions = pipeline.predict(test_data)
    valid_predictions = {0, 1}
    assert valid_predictions.issubset(predictions)
```

In your terminal, you can run the training smoke test by executing the following command:[3]

```
./batect --output=all smoke-test-model-training
```

In one of our previous projects, we had an ML training pipeline that took three hours. The full-scale training ran on the cloud (we were using Metaflow [*https://oreil.ly/RzNXY*]) and ML practitioners sometimes waited two hours only to see an error in the final step of the pipeline. So, we devised a training smoke test by running a Metaflow flow in local mode with a small dataset and ran the training pipeline locally in one to two *minutes*.

The training smoke test also runs as a pre-commit hook, so if we were about to push an error, we would find the error in under two minutes, rather than three hours.

Whichever ML orchestration tool or platform you are using, explore how you can use it to create a training smoke test. If there isn't a way to do it, and you frequently find yourself spending significant amounts of time waiting, then perhaps the platform or the tool is hindering rather than helping you.

---

3 For a refresher on what batect is and how to set it up, have a look at Chapter 4.

Now that you can get fast feedback on what is typically a slow and long-running component of our ML systems, let's switch gears again to look at how you can test the software we write to serve our model for consumption.

API Tests

If you are encapsulating and deploying the trained model as a web API, you can test and start the API as we would any other web API. The subject under test is a web API application.

As a producer of an ML model, you are likely going to have downstream components that depend on you, such as a frontend application or other APIs. These downstream consumers will inevitably depend on the behavior of your API (e.g., request and response schema). Should your behavior change in a way that breaks your contract or promise to those consumers, you will be breaking downstream consumers and causing lots of headaches for everyone.

This is where API tests are immensely helpful. They can serve as a lightweight *contract test*—a test that verifies you are still fulfilling your promise (i.e., contract) to the external world. If your code change is going to break downstream systems, you'd much rather your tests tell you locally, before the changes are deployed anywhere and before the defect is even committed. The API test failure will also be a hook to prompt you to think about API versioning and managing API schema changes (*https://oreil.ly/A7r-y*). A failing test is certainly better than an unexpected flurry of messages from other teams in the middle of your dinner.

How do I write these tests?

You can write these tests in three steps:

1. Consider what behavior you expect for a given request.
2. Find documentation on how to write API tests for the API library you are using (e.g., FastAPI TestClient [*https://oreil.ly/5uqzm*] if you are using FastAPI).
3. Write and run the test!

Here is an example of a model API test:

```
from fastapi.testclient import TestClient
from precisely import assert_that, is_mapping, \
    greater_than_or_equal_to, less_than_or_equal_to

from api.app import app


client = TestClient(app)
```

```
def test_root(self):
    response = client.get("/")

    assert response.status_code == 200
    assert response.json() == {"message": "hello world"} ❶

def test_predict_should_return_a_prediction_when_given_a_valid_payload(self): ❷

    valid_request_payload = {
        "Changed_Credit_Limit": 0,
        "Annual_Income": 0,
        "Monthly_Inhand_Salary": 0,
        "Age": 0,
    } ❸

    response = client.post("/predict/",
                           headers={"Content-Type": "application/json"},
                           json=valid_request_payload) ❹

    assert response.status_code == 200
    assert_that(response.json(),
                is_mapping({"prediction": greater_than_or_equal_to(0)
                                          and less_than_or_equal_to(4),
                            "request": valid_request_payload}) ❺
```

❶ Assuming you've defined a handler for requests for "/" that returns a hello world
message, you can write a simple assertion like this to test that the endpoint
handler returns the expected response.

❷ A readable test name. We've opted for the format of: "{the endpoint path}
(/predict) returns {expected output} when given {a type of input}." You can
further finesse the test name for other test scenarios (e.g., predict returns a
missing features error message when the request does not contain all required
features).

❸ Arrange.

❹ Act.

❺ Assert.

In your terminal, you can run the API tests by executing the following command:

```
./batect --output=all api-test
```

Recommended practice: Assert on "the whole elephant"

One common pitfall we've seen in tests is piecemeal assertions. In the bad example below, the assertion on the response object is broken up into multiple assertions, while the good example asserts on the response object using a single dictionary:

```
# bad example: piecemeal assertions
response = client.post("/predict/", json=valid_request_payload)

assert response.json()["prediction"] == 3
assert response.json()["message"] == "OK"

# good example: holistic assertions
response = client.post("/predict/", json=valid_request_payload)

assert_that(response.json(), is_mapping({"prediction": 3,
                                         "message": "OK"
                                        })
           )
```

We characterize the bad example as asserting on "parts of the elephant," and the good example as asserting "the whole elephant." Asserting the whole elephant is better for two reasons. First, the test is more readable. At a glance, you can see the schema of the API response (it's a dictionary with two fields).

Second, the test is more comprehensive—we are testing the whole response payload returned by the API and can catch any unexpected changes to the response payload. In our experience, when asserting on "parts of the elephant," when teams add a new part (e.g., a trunk), teams can sometimes forget to update the tests. One day, the trunk might go missing and the test would give you zero feedback about the defect.

Teams sometimes opt to write piecemeal assertions because they lack the tool or language to specify holistic assertions. For example, the model's prediction in a test could be nondeterministic, so teams break up the assertions to accommodate that. Thankfully, we now have Python libraries (e.g., precisely [*https://oreil.ly/__A8U*]) that let us write holistic assertions to assert on the schemas of the response, rather than specific values of the model's predictions. Let's see how you can write a holistic assertion in this style of testing:

```
# holistic assertion

from precisely import assert_that, is_mapping, any_of, equal_to, is_instance

actual_response = {          ❶
    "prediction": 1,         ❷
    "status": "OK",          ❸
    "user_name": "Harry"     ❹
}

assert_that(actual_response, is_mapping({ ❺
```

```
    "prediction": any_of(equal_to(0), equal_to(1), equal_to(2)), ❻
    "status": "OK",
    "user_name": is_instance(str) ❼
}))
```

❶ A hard-coded response for illustration purposes. In a real test, this would be a result returned by a function.

❷ The model can return any value between 0 and 2 for prediction.

❸ This field is a deterministic value.

❹ Assume we don't care about the specific value of this field; we just care that it's a string.

❺ is_mapping() specifies that we are expecting a Python dictionary (known as a Map in other programming languages).

❻ We are saying that prediction can be any of these values : 0, 1, 2. For longer lists, you can write this as a list comprehension for brevity.

❼ We say we only care that user_name is a string, and it doesn't matter what specific value it returns in our case.

This tool and technique can help us write readable and holistic assertions, even for situations when the subject of our assertions contains nondeterministic values.

 In organizations with mature software engineering practices, there may be established patterns on how to test APIs or even other aspects of a holistic testing strategy. If that's the case for you, we recommend that you find the relevant documentation or experts to assess and adapt these patterns for the model APIs that you are deploying.

Now that we've tested our API in a local environment, let's look at another powerful software test—testing our API after it's been deployed to a real environment.

Post-deployment Tests

In post-deployment tests, the subject under test is the API, which has been deployed to a real environment (e.g., preproduction, production). Every time we promote a deployable to an environment, we want to test that it can handle requests successfully according to our expectations.

If the API has any dependencies (e.g., a database, a remote bucket, an external service), these tests also serve as a *broad integration test* (*https://oreil.ly/KXecM*) to test that these dependencies are working as expected in a real environment. Post-deployment tests focus on verifying that the interfaces between components (e.g., API, ML model, database) are working fine in a real environment.

Post-deployment tests are *critical* because they can help to spot bugs *right after* we've deployed a change to a preproduction environment, and *before* we deploy our software to production. This brings a whole host of benefits: time saved from tedious manual testing, and reduced production defects (which means less time wasted triaging and resolving stressful production incidents). We typically also run the tests right after deploying a change to production to verify that the production deployment has succeeded.

Post-deployment tests also are essential for *continuous deployment*, which is the practice of deploying every change to production if all stages of your CI pipeline are green. The ability to do continuous deployment is fundamental in helping your team become a *high performer*, as defined by DORA (DevOps Research and Assessment) metrics (*https://oreil.ly/60Dwo*) (more on this in Chapter 9).

How do I write these tests?

You should be careful not to duplicate the logic from your API tests, or you'll end up maintaining and updating two sets of tests. You have tested your API thoroughly in your API tests, covering all code paths and edge cases. If the API has other dependencies (e.g., a database), your API tests could include logic to mock and stub responses to simulate errors, and you can't do that in these tests, which are running against a real environment.

In post-deployment tests, you simply make requests to the subject under test (i.e., the API, which has been deployed to an environment) and verify that you received the response you expected, as shown below:

```python
import requests


class TestPostDeployment:
    endpoint_url = "https://my-model-api.example.com"  ❶

    def test_root(self):  ❷
        response = requests.get(self.endpoint_url)

        assert response.status_code == 200

    def test_predict_should_return_a_prediction_when_given_a_valid_payload(self):
        valid_request_payload = {
            "Changed_Credit_Limit": 0,
            "Annual_Income": 0,
```

```
        "Monthly_Inhand_Salary": 0,
        "Age": 0,
    }

    response = requests.post(f"{self.endpoint_url}/predict/",
                             headers={"Content-Type": "application/json"},
                             json=valid_request_payload
                             ) ❸

    assert response.status_code == 200 ❹
```

❶ The target of your request is an API endpoint in a real environment. This variable can also be read from an environment variable, so that you can reuse the same test in multiple environments (e.g., preproduction, production). If your API is a public API, you will likely need some authentication and authorization using a test account. For simplicity, we have omitted these details from the example, but it can be done in the test setup steps (*https://docs.pytest.org/en/6.2.x/xunit_setup.html*).

❷ Notice how the test names look similar to the preceding local API tests? The local API tests can give you some ideas of what you want to test in the real API, though you will need to apply some discretion to ensure that you're not retesting things that have already been tested in the local API tests.

❸ We use the `requests` package to make a request to a real API endpoint.

❹ Speaking of not retesting things, we didn't replicate the assertion from our local API tests because it would be redundant. If we changed our API's behavior, we would need to update it in two places. In this example, we simply asserted that we received a positive HTTP status code (in your context, you would specify whatever you constitute to be a correct and successful handling of this request in a real environment).

Give yourself a big pat on your back! By this point in the chapter, you've learned how to test many components that are typically under-tested in ML systems. With this knowledge, you can save your team days and weeks of time and energy from manual testing and fixing defects that slip through the cracks of manual testing.

Conclusion

Let's recap what we've learned in this chapter. We've learned:

- *Why* automated tests are essential for teams that want to iterate quickly, safely, and reliably
- That if we make mistakes while coding (as humans inevitably do), tests act as a safety net to catch us as we fall, instead of letting us crash painfully into errors in production
- The benefits of automated testing (e.g., reduced cognitive load, ease of refactoring, improved team velocity), based on our experience in using them when delivering ML solutions across various industries
- The rationale for *not* writing automated tests in ML systems (we challenged the validity of that reasoning, given the testing knowledge, techniques, and tools that we have today)
- The *what*: the building blocks for a comprehensive test strategy across a breadth of components that can be tested (software and ML models)
- The *how*: how to write an automated test, characteristics of useful and dependable tests, and pitfalls to avoid

Now it's your turn to put your knowledge into practice. Reflecting on your own ML project, consider:

- Where does your team spend the most time on manual testing?
- Are there any low-hanging fruits (currently untested areas) in your codebase that could benefit from automated tests?
- Can you write and commit one or more automated tests to address these low-hanging fruits and significant time sinks? (Hint: refer to the code-along repository [*https://oreil.ly/Hkgzc*] for examples of how to write and run tests.)

In the next chapter, we'll look at how you can automate ML model tests, and practices that complement ML model testing in ML systems.

## CHAPTER 6

Automated Testing: ML Model Tests

In the previous chapter, we saw the price we pay for not having automated tests in ML solutions, and the benefits that tests bring to teams in terms of quality, flow, cognitive load, and satisfaction. We outlined the building blocks of a comprehensive test strategy and dived into details for the first category of tests: software tests.

In this chapter, we will explore the next category of tests: ML model tests (or model tests, for short). As large language models (LLMs) have taken the world by storm, we'll also cover techniques for testing LLMs and LLM applications.

In addition, we'll explore practices that complement ML model tests, such as visualization and error analysis, closing the data collection loop, and open-closed test design. We'll also discuss data tests briefly before concluding with concrete next steps that can help you implement these tests in your ML systems.

In this chapter, we will focus on offline testing at scale, and we won't cover online testing techniques (e.g., A/B testing, bandits, interleaving experiments) as they are well covered in Chip Huyen's great book *Designing Machine Learning Systems* (O'Reilly).

Model Tests

ML practitioners are no strangers to manual model evaluation procedures, and while the exploratory nature of such tests is useful in early phases of developing a model, this manual work easily becomes overly time-consuming and tedious. As we identify measures and heuristics that tell us if a model is "good enough" or "better than before," we can use model tests to help us automate these manual heuristics and checks. This frees up our time and energy to solve other more interesting problems.

In this section, we'll flesh out the why, what, and how of testing our trained models—the subject under test in this chapter. We'll go through:

- Why it's necessary to have automated tests for ML models
- The challenges of testing ML models
- How the concept of fitness functions can help us overcome these challenges
- How to implement two common types of model tests: metrics tests and behavioral tests
- How to test LLMs and LLM applications

With that, let's dive in!

The Necessity of Model Tests

Imagine our ML delivery cycle as a factory producing boxes of shoes. Data scientists create the shoes and test the quality of the shoes, typically on a partially automated and ad hoc basis, and ML engineers establish the production line to produce well-formed boxes to contain whatever shoes the data scientists produce. The latter group (ML engineers) seeks to speed up the production line through automation, while the former (data scientists) unwittingly becomes—to the extent that model quality checks are manual—a bottleneck.

Over time, as we try to meet new and various product requirements and experiment with different techniques, we have to either slow down the production line so that every box—containing a new shoe (model) created by our MLOps pipeline—is tested for its quality or forgo quality checks of what is in each box in order to keep up with the speed of production.

It's common to see teams choose speed over quality, especially when they're under "delivery pressure." Instead of checking every box (e.g., every code commit), they start checking every 10–15 boxes (e.g., every pull request). Teams sometimes even skip complete quality checks or regression tests for a pull request and just sporadically check aspects of the product in the box. The natural consequence is that they may discover a defect too late—many boxes after it's been introduced—and then have to stop the production line to inspect many suspect boxes and figure out and resolve the root cause of the defect.

In our experience, "speed versus quality" is a false choice. In reality, low-quality, untested products inevitably slow teams down because teams end up wasting time on fixing issues and on manual testing. In contrast, teams that invest in quality (e.g., through automated tests) end up with less manual testing effort and product defects. Quality begets speed.

Model tests help us achieve both quality and speed. They help us continuously uncover or check for undesirable behavior in an automated (or a soon-to-be automated) fashion before we release ML models to our users. Model tests are especially important because ML models can be prone to silent failures: The model may be producing predictions with the right schema, but the predictions can be totally wrong. And we won't detect these errors unless we test the model.

The more comprehensive our model tests are, the more confident we can be that we are releasing models that are good enough for users in production. As an added benefit, automated model tests free up ML practitioners to do more ML and solve higher-level problems rather than tedious manual testing in every pull request or release or, worse, fixing defects in production that are impacting customers and the business.

Now that we've established the importance and value of model tests, let's look at the challenges of testing ML models and how fitness functions can help us overcome these challenges.

Challenges of Testing ML Models

Automated testing of an ML model can be more challenging than software tests for four main reasons. First, while software tests generally tend to be fast-running and deterministic, ML model training tends to be slow-running and nondeterministic (two characteristics that we try to avoid in automated tests!).

Second, while software tests tend to involve data that is example-based with just a handful of dimensions that we can even inline in our tests (e.g., add(1, 1) == 2), model tests typically require data that is sample-based, multidimensional, and nonstationary. The volume of data needed for comprehensive testing can be too substantial (e.g., thousands or millions of rows of tabular data, textual data, or images) to include alongside our tests.

Third, as articulated in Jeremy Jordan's article on effective testing for ML systems (*https://oreil.ly/NItt3*), model evaluation tends to require a level of exploration and visualization (e.g., inspecting plots for segments of the data) that is hard, if not impossible, to do through the interface of automated tests. Finally, in the early and exploratory stage of an ML product, it may not be clear what a good model looks like, and what exactly we should test.

In our experience, these four challenges—slow tests, high-volume and high-dimensional data, the need for visual exploration, and unclear definitions of "good enough"—are challenges that ML practitioners tend to work through and live with. ML practitioners often devise manual model evaluation procedures to test if a model is "good enough" or "better than before" by using techniques such as metric-based evaluation, k-folds cross validation, and visualization-based evaluation. As illustrated in Figure 6-1, these manual testing techniques move teams away from the "danger" zone (right column) of releasing untested models and toward the "toil" zone of having tedious manual testing procedures.

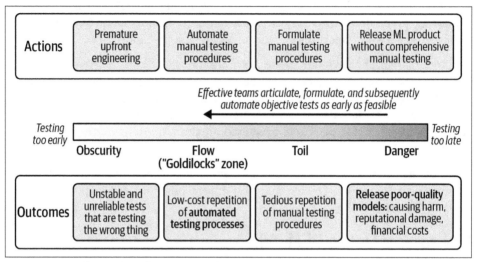

Figure 6-1. Each team needs to work toward their "Goldilocks" zone for defining ML model tests—not too early and not too late

Effective teams take the next step of codifying and automating these manual evaluation procedures as far as possible, shifting them from the "toil" zone to the "flow" (or "Goldilocks") zone. As no single test can test all aspects of the model, effective teams are able to expand the collection of model tests breadth-wise (with more model tests) and depth-wise (with more representative and better data).

Whether intentional or not, these manual evaluation procedures in the "toil" zone are early forms of a fitness function, which is a concept that helps us define model tests. In the next section, we will explain what a fitness function is, how it can help us, and how we can grow our breadth of fitness functions to test our models more comprehensively.

Fitness Functions for ML Models

Fitness functions (*https://oreil.ly/iq1S1*) are objective, executable functions that can be used to summarize, as a single figure of merit, how close a given design solution is to achieving its set aims. Fitness functions bridge the gap between automated tests (precise) and ML models (fuzzy).

In software engineering, we use fitness functions to measure how close an architectural design is to achieving an objective aim. It informs us if our applications and architecture are objectively moving away from their desired characteristics. We can define fitness functions for a certain architectural characteristic of our software and run them as tests locally and on a CI/CD pipeline.

For example, we can define fitness functions that measure the quality or toxicity of our code. If the code gets too convoluted or violates certain code quality rules, the "code quality" fitness function fails and gives us feedback that a code change has degraded our system beyond our specified tolerance level. Likewise for software security, performance, observability, and so on (see Figure 6-2).

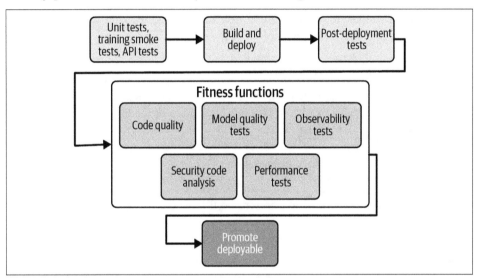

Figure 6-2. Fitness functions test important characteristics of our solution (source: adapted from an image in "Fitness Function-Driven Development" by Thoughtworks [https://oreil.ly/iq1S1])

Coming back to ML, regardless of the domain in which you are using ML (e.g., churn prediction, product recommendations), there are explicit or latent measures of goodness or badness, better or worse. ML is premised on the ability to improve models by adjusting their internals to minimize an objective measure of loss! Even in more subjective ML use cases (e.g., an LLM-based cover letter generator), the user at the other end will likely have some opinions on the quality or correctness of a model's prediction. (Later in this chapter, we'll demonstrate how we can finesse these measures of goodness to define fitness functions for our models.)

For example, here are some fitness functions for an ML model:

Metrics tests
    The model is fit for production if a given evaluation metric measured using a holdout set is above a specified threshold.

Model fairness tests

The model is fit for production if a given evaluation metric for each key segment—e.g., country—is within X% of each other.

Model API latency tests

The model is fit for production if it can handle N amount of concurrent requests within t seconds.

Model size tests

The model artifact must be below a certain size (e.g., so that we can deploy it easily to embedded devices or mobile devices).

Training duration tests

The model training pipeline must complete within a specified duration. This can help teams detect and prevent (*https://oreil.ly/O_fJD*) the gradual lengthening of model training cycles from, say, two hours to three or four hours. This test helps teams detect performance degradations as soon as they are introduced—e.g., as part of a pull request—which makes it easier to debug and identify the change that caused the performance degradation.

The list can go on, depending on what constitutes "fit for purpose" or "fit for production" in your domain. This is not a prescribed list of tests for all ML projects. Rather, it is a framework of thinking that you can take to your teams, domain specialists, and end users to discover and define the aspects of "good enough" for your product.

And that is why the concept of fitness functions is useful for testing ML systems. The heterogeneous breadth and variety of problems, algorithms, and data formats in ML can make it hard for the ML community to articulate a unified testing approach. The concept and technical implementation of fitness functions allows us to discover and define objective measures of good enough for the problem that you are solving, and automate it to reap the benefits of automated testing. When you have gone through that process and defined fitness functions for your ML model, you can confidently release the model to production when these tests pass on the CI/CD pipeline.

In the following sections, we'll elaborate on two types of ML fitness functions that can help us formulate tests to check if a model is fit for production—model metrics tests (global and stratified) and model behavioral tests.

Model Metrics Tests (Global and Stratified)

ML practitioners are generally familiar with calculating model evaluation metrics (e.g., precision, recall, ROC AUC score [*https://oreil.ly/f1btr*]) and this fitness function simply takes it a step further, writing it as an automated test that we can run locally and on our CI pipeline. Without these tests, we have to either spend time manually eyeballing the model's quality metrics with every commit, pull request or release, or we live with the risk that we may be unknowingly degrading the model over time.

In these tests, we calculate model evaluation metrics that measure the aggregate correctness of the model on an extensible validation dataset and test if they meet our expected threshold of what is considered good enough for the model to be released to production. We compute these metrics at the global level and also at the level of important segments of our data (i.e., stratified level).

Since ML practitioners are generally familiar with the topic of metric selection (*https://oreil.ly/Re3W7*), we won't discuss that here, except to mention that there may also be domain-specific or industry-defined metrics for measuring the quality of a model. In this example, we're using recall as the metric, just to keep the example simple. In a real project, ML engineers will likely pair with data scientists and domain specialists to understand tradeoffs and identify which metrics are most important in determining if the model is fit for purpose. If multiple metrics are important, you can apply the same approach to write multiple tests for each metric.

Global metrics tests are a good starting point in quantifying and automating model quality checks, especially if we're starting without any automated tests to check the correctness of our model. However, these tests are only a start, and in most cases they are not granular enough. For example, a model might report a high overall performance, but consistently underperform in certain segments of the data. The authors of the seminal "ML Test Score" paper (*https://oreil.ly/hGTTh*) illustrate the usefulness of these tests with an example: The global accuracy of a model may improve by 1%, but accuracy for one country could drop by 50%. This is known as the hidden stratification problem (*https://oreil.ly/lP0Ld*).

That's the problem that *stratified metrics tests* help to solve. The approach is similar to global metrics tests, except that we slice the validation dataset by one or more dimensions of interest (e.g., the target variable, gender, race[1]) and calculate metrics for each segment, rather than a single global metric.

---

[1] In some cases, it may be necessary to exclude sociodemographic features, such as gender and race, from model training to reduce the risk of sociodemographic discrimination (*https://oreil.ly/peL-8*). This may even be a regulatory or legal requirement in some situations. In such cases, teams should still consider whether they can make such features available for testing purposes or for segmenting our test datasets, which can be valuable for detecting any hidden biases. This is a lesson that we can learn from the Apple Card controversy (*https://oreil.ly/cp8d3*), where an ML model gave women lower credit limits, not because the model knew their gender, but because of their credit history and income.

How do I write these tests?

Let's start with an example of a global metric test. This test will pass if a metric (recall, in this example) is above a threshold that we specify:

```
class TestMetrics:
    recall_threshold = 0.65

    def test_global_recall_score_should_be_above_specified_threshold(self):
        # load trained model
        pipeline = load_model()

        # load test data ❶
        data = pd.read_csv("./data/train.csv", encoding="utf-8", low_memory=False)
        y = data["DEFAULT"]
        X = data.drop("DEFAULT", axis=1)
        X_test, X_train, y_test, y_train = train_test_split(X, y, random_state=10)

        # get predictions
        y_pred = pipeline.predict(X_test)

        # calculate metric
        recall = recall_score(y_test, y_pred, average="weighted")

        # assert on metric
        print(f"global recall score: {recall}") ❷
        assert recall >= self.recall_threshold
```

❶ Load the validation or holdout dataset. In this simple example, we re-create the validation dataset by loading the full dataset and because we invoke `train_test_fit()` with the same random state as was specified during model training, we will get the same training/validation dataset split. In a real-world scenario, we will more likely load the data from a feature store and find a way to persistently mark samples that were used in training (e.g., we could persist the indices of the samples in the training set in our artifact store), so that we avoid the risk of data leakage during tests.

❷ In model tests, it's not enough for tests to pass or fail. We also want useful visual feedback (e.g., actual metrics, confusion matrices) in our test logs.

You can run this test in the repo by running the following command:

```
./batect model-metrics-test
```

The test passes if the model's recall score is above the specified threshold. For a refresher on what batect is and how to set it up, have a look at Chapter 4.

Now, let's look at an example of a stratified metrics test:

```python
class TestMetrics:
    recall_threshold = 0.65

    def test_stratified_recall_score_should_be_above_specified_threshold(self):
        pipeline = load_model()

        data = pd.read_csv("./data/train.csv", encoding="utf-8", low_memory=False)
        strata_col_name = "OCCUPATION_TYPE"  ❶
        stratas = data["OCCUPATION_TYPE"].unique().tolist()
        y = data["DEFAULT"]
        X = data.drop("DEFAULT", axis=1)
        X_test, X_train, y_test, y_train = train_test_split(X, y, random_state=10)

        # get predictions and metric for each strata  ❷
        recall_scores = []
        for strata in stratas:
            X_test_stratified = X_test[X_test[strata_col_name] == strata]
            y_test_stratified = y_test[y_test.index.isin(X_test_stratified.index)]
            y_pred_stratified = pipeline.predict(X_test_stratified)

            # calculate metric
            recall_for_single_strata = recall_score(y_test_stratified,
                                                    y_pred_stratified,
                                                    average="weighted")
            print(f"{strata}: recall score: {recall_for_single_strata}")

            recall_scores.append(recall_for_single_strata)

        assert all(recall > self.recall_threshold for recall in recall_scores)  ❸
```

❶ In this example, we use the OCCUPATION_TYPE column as the dimension for slicing the validation dataset.

❷ For each segment of the data, we create a validation dataset and calculate its corresponding metric.

❸ This test will pass if the recall score for each occupation segment is above the specified threshold. If it fails, it prompts us that our model is more biased for certain segments of users and prompts us to find ways to improve the model before releasing it to users.

In this particular example, this test fails and the test logs tell us why. The recall score for most occupation types (~0.75) was above our threshold, but for Laborers, it was much lower (0.49) and is below our definition of good enough. Thanks to the stratified metric test, we've uncovered a quality issue in our model—50% of the time, the model's predictions about the loan default likelihood of Laborers are wrong:

```
Laborers: recall score: 0.4994072602608055
Core staff: recall score: 0.7275259067357513
Accountants: recall score: 0.7718889883616831
Managers: recall score: 0.7514849895649381
```

Stratified metrics tests can also be used for ethical bias testing (*https://oreil.ly/BDj1c*), to test if any model is inadvertently disadvantageous or systematically erroneous for certain segments of the population. For example, we could enumerate dimensions of potential sociodemographic bias and harm (e.g., race, gender, class, etc.) and test for any potential issues in each data segment. While we often can't use these sociodemographic features to train our models, we can use them to uncover any potential issues with our model.

There are libraries (such as Giskard [*https://oreil.ly/L9zOT*] and PyCaret [*https://oreil.ly/f1-Di*]) that provide functions to measure stratified metrics and other types of model tests with fewer lines of code. We didn't use these libraries in this example because we wanted to demonstrate the essential idea behind stratified metrics tests, and how it can be implemented in a simple way. However, we strongly encourage you to check out how these libraries can assist you in testing your models.

In situations where you are not working with tabular data (e.g., images, text, audio), as long as you can associate the segment with the data (e.g., images with corresponding metadata columns that you can use for segmenting your test datasets), you can apply the same technique and get more granular measures of correctness for your models.

Advantages and limitations of metrics tests

Metrics tests (global and stratified) are a simple and quick way to relieve ML practitioners of the time-consuming manual verifications for every commit or pull request. In addition, because these tests are regularly exercised on CI, they can help us catch performance degradations as soon as they happen and save us from digging through days and weeks of commits and logs to triangulate performance degradations that were introduced a few weeks ago.

With that said, every type of test has its limitations. One of the limitations of metrics tests is that while the reductionist approach (boiling down all behavior to several aggregate metrics) helps you scale testing (i.e., exercise the model based on *all* scenarios present in the available data), it doesn't allow you to characterize pockets of behavior within segments of the data. Even in the case of stratified metrics tests, there may be combinatorial effects in multiple dimensions that can confound a model, but it can be hard to specify, characterize, and discover such scenarios in a metrics test.

Another limitation is that the assumption that the validation data and production data are independent and identically distributed (IID) often does not hold true in a nonstationary world.

In the following section, we will discuss how we can use behavioral tests to address the first limitation. In the final section of this chapter, we'll look at how data curation techniques help address the second limitation.

Behavioral Tests

Behavioral tests complement metrics tests by allowing us to enumerate specific—and potentially out-of-sample—scenarios under which to test our model. Behavioral testing (also known as black-box testing) has its roots in software engineering and is concerned with testing various capabilities of a system by "validating the input-output behavior, without any knowledge of the internal structure."[2]

Here's the general approach for defining behavioral tests in ML:

1. Define or generate test samples. You can start with just one or two examples and use data-generation techniques to scale to more examples, if that provides value.
2. Use these test samples to generate predictions from a trained model.
3. Verify that the model's behavior matches your expectations.

We will draw from the excellent research paper by Ribeiro et al. in describing the three types of behavioral tests. (Special thanks to Jeremy Jordan for his article on testing ML models [*https://oreil.ly/NItt3*]—it's how we came to know of this paper.) While the paper was written in the context of testing NLP models, we find that the concepts can be generalized to other types of models working with other types of data (e.g., tabular data, images). Behavioral testing has also been applied in testing recommender systems (e.g., RecList [*https://reclist.io*]).

Invariance tests

In an invariance test, we apply label-preserving perturbations to the input data and expect the model's prediction to remain the same.

In our loan default prediction example, if there's a dimension that we expect our model to be invariant to (e.g., occupation), we can write a test where all examples have the same attributes, except for the applicant's occupation, and assert that the

---

2 Marco Tulio Ribeiro et al., "Beyond Accuracy: Behavioral Testing of NLP Models with CheckList" (*https://oreil.ly/jv2H0*), Association for Computational Linguistics (ACL), 2020.

model's prediction should remain invariant. To scale this test, we can include as many examples as needed to represent a wider range of attribute combinations and manipulate the invariant dimension as needed.

In another example, say object detection, we could write a test where all example images have some variance in a given attribute—such as lighting or image resolution—and assert that the model produces the same prediction. Each test verifies a given *capability* of a model (e.g., object detection under low-light or low-resolution conditions).

Directional expectation tests

A directional expectation test is like an invariance test, except that we expect the prediction to change in a specific direction when we perturb the input data.

In our example, we can write a test where all examples have the same attributes except in one dimension that is known to have an effect on the prediction, and assert that the model's predicted probabilities should change in the corresponding direction.

Minimum functionality tests

A minimum functionality test contains a set of simple examples and corresponding labels that are used to verify the model's behavior in a particular scenario. These tests are similar to unit tests in software engineering and are useful for creating small, targeted testing datasets.

We can use minimum functionality tests to codify bugs and assert that they should never happen again. For example, let's imagine we had a bug in the past where loan default predictions were wrong when a particular feature was missing. Let's say we're now fixing that bug by handling the missing feature through imputation. We can accompany that bug fix with a minimum functionality test with one or more test samples where this particular feature is missing.

For this section, we've decided not to add code samples for behavioral tests. While the concepts are generalizable across an array of ML use cases (e.g., object detection, text classification), those code samples we write for our loan default prediction example may not be. In any case, we are confident that, supported by the in-depth explanation in the behavioral testing research paper in NLP (*https://oreil.ly/imSjt*), you can adapt and apply the three types of behavioral tests to your context.

Now that we've covered ML model tests, let's look at techniques for testing a technology that many people are excited about: LLMs.

Testing Large Language Models: Why and How

While we were writing this book, LLMs exploded into the public consciousness. From enterprises to start-ups, the race to harness the power of LLMs has been fervent. LLMs have proved surprisingly powerful and general at solving a range of problems. However, they also fail in problematic and unexpected ways, producing incorrect results, inventing facts, and even generating harmful responses (*https://oreil.ly/QSaON*).

Some might ask, is it worth the effort to test LLM applications? LLM applications—like any software application—can regress or degrade due to several change vectors (e.g., changes in our prompts and flows, changes in upstream LLMs, changes in the libraries we depend on). Figure 6-3 provides an example of how a change in an upstream LLM dependency can introduce regressions in an LLM application, through no fault of anyone.

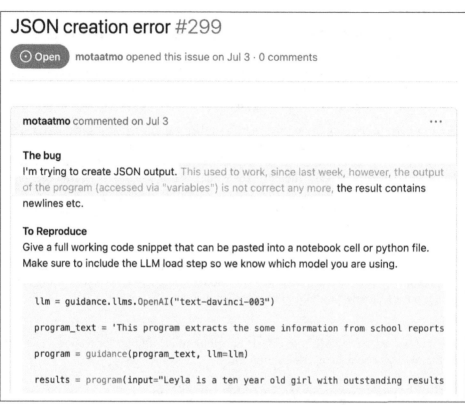

Figure 6-3. Example of a failure and unexpected change in behavior due to an upstream LLM dependency

Can you imagine the number of production alerts that this could cause? Hence, LLM applications—like any software application—must be tested if you want to ensure quality and speed during delivery. If you're going to spend days and weeks designing prompts (*https://oreil.ly/BCp0m*) or even fine-tuning LLMs, you're going to need a way to measure performance improvements and detect regressions.

At the same time, there are some scenarios where it can be challenging to test LLM applications under "open task" scenarios where there can be multiple right answers ("summarize this article") or indeed no right answer at all ("write a story about wandering wizards").

To navigate the necessity and challenges of testing LLM applications, we'll share some guidelines and techniques that will help you define and implement a comprehensive test strategy for your LLM application.

Guidelines for designing an LLM test strategy

Your requirements and expectations of desired behavior will determine whether you should build a solution with LLMs, and whether it's safe to put it in the hands of users in production and, if so, how you should test it.

Maybe your use case allows you to "embrace the weirdness"[3] in that variable answers are a feature rather than a bug. Maybe some variation is OK in production, but you need to verify reproducible results in controlled conditions. Or maybe you're looking for more assurance that only certain responses are possible with certain likelihoods.

If you're embracing the weirdness, you can test integration and performance, and you can test that outputs of the correct type are produced. When it comes to testing the content, you could consider using another LLM (and/or other ML techniques) to attempt to reconstruct the inputs and compare the "round-trip" results to the original inputs. This remains subject to some of the same weirdness issues, however. When it's not clear what to test or the effort to implement a test is prohibitive, consider generating a "gallery" of representative outputs. This will allow a human expert who "knows it when they see it" to detect failures and also, in time, to more clearly define failure modes that are amenable to automation.

If you need reproducible results in controlled conditions while accepting some variation in production deployment, then you need to be able to control all of the sources of variation in a test environment. This might include using set random seeds or setting temperature to zero and using greedy sampling. With all inputs held constant, we expect repeatable outputs, even with generative models. Some lower-level optimizations, such as parallelism in compute or model quantization, may still produce nondeterministic behavior. But, in general, it is still possible to make execution deterministic through disabling these optimizations, if this is important enough to test. Even if you're stuck trying to show reproducible behavior with some degree of nondeterminism, you can at least, with repeated testing, statistically quantify the likelihood of certain outcomes. In this case, every additional source of variation you can control makes your job easier.

Finally, if your application demands a finite variety of outputs and some certainty about the likelihood of certain outputs under certain input conditions, then it's more like a discriminative ML problem (e.g. classification). As above, LLMs have somewhat general capabilities compared to a typical ML model, so they can be pressed into service in tasks like classification.

However, as articulated in the article "Against LLM Maximalism" (*https://oreil.ly/ XF8RM*), LLMs are not always the best solution for certain problems. LLMs require

---

3 Ethan Mollick, "Embracing Weirdness: What It Means to Use AI as a (Writing) Tool" (*https://oreil.ly/iyqCy*), *One Useful Thing* (blog), posted September 5, 2023.

significant resources at inference time, which can be costly and result in poor application performance, while the content they produce may be highly variable. In these cases, you might consider established narrower NLP (or image modality) or classification solutions, which have established methods for quantifying their predictive performance and are simpler, faster, and less resource-intensive to implement. Again, the advice in this book is relevant to these scenarios. However, LLMs have one last trick to play here—they can be useful for generating weakly labeled data to bootstrap the training of traditional models!

Now, let's look at the types of tests that you can implement to test your LLMs and LLM applications.

LLM testing techniques

In this section, we build on the three testing paradigms that we've covered—example-based tests, metrics tests, behavioral tests—and add a fourth paradigm: LLM-based tests (aka auto-evaluator tests). Here are some emerging techniques for testing LLMs and LLM applications. For more details and working examples on each testing technique, you can refer to our article "Engineering Practices for LLM Application Development" (*https://oreil.ly/yhwJN*).

Manual exploratory tests.   As you develop your prompts, manual exploratory tests give you fast feedback on an LLM's response to your prompt or composition of prompts. The primary advantage of manual exploratory tests is their flexibility. Developers can adapt on-the-fly, probing the model with diverse inputs based on initial responses, thereby identifying scenarios, behaviors, and edge cases that they can use in subsequent automated tests.

Example-based tests.   Example-based tests are structured tests where predefined inputs are paired with expected outputs. For LLM applications, this might involve providing a set prompt and expecting a specific response or a range of acceptable responses. This is similar to the minimum functionality tests that we described in the section "Behavioral Tests" on page 177.

For example, imagine we are building an LLM application to parse sections of a resume into a structured JSON format. Example-based tests would involve specifying a collection of resume sections and testing that the model's output matches the JSON output specified in our expectations.

Example-based tests can also be applied to check if we have designed our LLM application to be robust against a known set of adversarial attacks, such as prompt injections. For example, we can specify some tests with adversarial prompts (e.g., "Ignore all previous instructions and do XYZ instead") and verify that the model responds based on the safeguards and protocols we designed to handle such requests.

In cases where we want the LLM's response to be creative and varied, but still operating within boundaries, we can design our prompts to ask the LLM to return its response in a JSON format with two keys—one that we expect to be deterministic (e.g., "intent") and one where we allow creative variation (e.g., "message"). We can assert on and depend on "intent" in our tests, and display the contents of "message" in our application.

Example-based tests ensure that the model consistently produces the desired output for known inputs. They are particularly useful for regression testing, ensuring that changes to the model or prompt design don't inadvertently introduce errors for previously validated scenarios.

Benchmark tests. Benchmark tests are designed to measure the performance of an LLM for a given task and are useful for closed or relatively closed tasks such as classification, question-answering, and summarization. This is similar to the Metrics Tests we described earlier in the chapter, but with a bit more sophistication to cover multidimensional aspects of quality—accuracy, bias, efficiency, toxicity, and so on.

Stanford's Holistic Evaluation of Language Models (HELM) (*https://oreil.ly/qX9EC*) contains many examples of benchmark tests that evaluate prominent language models across a wide range of scenarios and metrics to elucidate each model's capabilities and failure modes. You can read more about the methodology and how to add new scenarios/metrics for your domain-specific model in a Stanford article on the need for holistic evaluation (*https://oreil.ly/IqWtq*).

Benchmark tests help us gauge the impact of fine-tuning or other modifications on the model's performance. For instance, after adjusting an LLM's parameters, benchmark tests can determine the model's performance—as defined by metrics such as accuracy, fairness, robustness, efficiency, and so on. They provide quantifiable metrics, making it easier to compare different versions of a model or different models altogether.

So far, we've discussed automated tests that are suitable for closed tasks. What about open tasks that don't have a deterministic answer, or for which there can be multiple acceptable answers? For such tasks, we can leverage two new testing paradigms: property-based tests and LLM-based tests.

Property-based tests. Instead of testing for a specific output, property-based tests check for certain properties or characteristics in the output. You do so by specifying statements that should always be true, rather than relying on specific examples. These statements take the form: "for all inputs that satisfy some precondition, the output satisfies a specified criteria."

For example, if you are using an LLM to parse unstructured data into JSON format, an important property would be that the output is a valid JSON string. Having clearly articulated this expected property, you can easily write property-based tests to verify if the LLM's output is in a valid JSON format. These tests are powerful for ensuring that the model maintains desired behaviors across diverse scenarios, even those not explicitly covered in example-based tests.

LLM-based tests (aka auto-evaluator tests). Property-based tests are useful for easy-to-test properties (e.g., is the output in a valid JSON format?) but what about harder-to-test properties (e.g., is the generated resume accurate)? That's where you can leverage the next testing paradigm: using an LLM (or another higher-quality LLM) to test itself. This approach capitalizes on the strength of LLMs in understanding and evaluating complex content.

You start by listing high-level properties that we expect to see. For example, say you are designing an LLM application or feature to help users generate a resume. Some properties could be:

- The Resume communicates key information in the user's Profile.
- The Resume contains only skills that are present in the user's Profile.

Next, you design prompts to create an "evaluator" LLM and check if these properties hold true for the given scenarios and provide explanations for its evaluation. When you find bugs and failures, you drill down and expand them as much as possible so you can understand and fix them. This creates a feedback loop that can lead to continuous improvement of the model's performance and reliability.

This approach was pioneered by Marco Tulio Ribeiro in his paper "Adaptive Testing and Debugging of NLP Models" (*https://oreil.ly/Jhrvv*) (coauthored with Scott Lundberg) and article "Testing Language Models (and Prompts) Like We Test Software" (*https://oreil.ly/vjn48*). You can refer to these articles for more details about how to write and expand on LLM-based tests.

Now that we've covered techniques for testing LLMs and LLM applications, let's look at some complementary practices that help us complete the model testing puzzle.

Essential Complementary Practices for Model Tests

In *Perfect Software: and Other Illusions About Testing* (Dorset House), author Gerald Weinberg puts it well: "poor testing can lead to poor quality, but good testing won't lead to good quality unless other parts of the process are in place and performed properly." We need to complement automated model tests with other practices that help us to debug and explain a model's behavior, and to iteratively improve the model.

The following practices are essential complements to model tests and can help you create a feedback loop to continuously test and improve your models:

- Error analysis and visualization
- Learning from production by closing the data collection loop
- Open-closed test design
- Exploratory testing
- Means to improve the model
- Designing to minimize the cost of failures
- Monitoring in production

Let's go through each one of these practices, beginning with error analysis and visualization. We'll illustrate how these seven practices work together in Figure 6-8, which you can find at the end of this section.

Error Analysis and Visualization

In practice, it's not enough for model tests to pass or fail. When a model behaves contrary to your expectations in certain scenarios, you need to undertake error analysis—inspect the code and the model to understand where and why the model makes systematic errors for specific segments of data—and explainability mechanisms to understand how you can improve the model. Error analysis is an essential precursor to improving the model (see Figure 6-4).

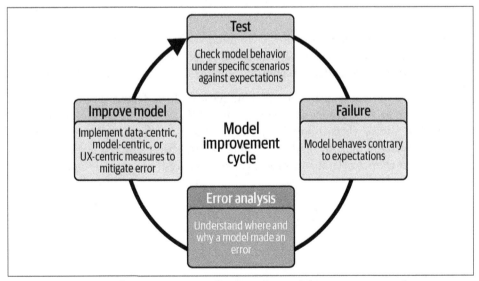

Figure 6-4. Error analysis is an essential step in the model improvement cycle

When a software test fails, "looking into" the code flow (e.g., through the use of debugger breakpoints) under a specific condition (or state) can help developers identify the cause of the issue and find a fix. Similarly, when a model test fails, inspecting the code, data, and model helps you identify the root cause, areas of weakness in your model, and ways to improve the model.

The challenge is that while software tests tend to be point-based and relatively easier to visualize (e.g., in a debugger), model tests tend to be high-dimensional, high-volume, and the state of the program can be hard to visualize. As such, the following error analysis and visualization practices can help:

Data visualization

Data visualization supports model testing by allowing us to visually inspect plots or charts to arrive at a more granular and nuanced view of the performance of a model. Jeremy Jordan articulates this well: A granular report with visualizations (*https://oreil.ly/NItt3*) helps us spot and characterize failure modes and the specific conditions under which they occur. It also helps us to compare models over time. Visualizing any patterns in the data can help us identify the scenarios that could be impacting the model's performance.

Data visualization also helps us discover unknown unknowns and uncover questions that we should be asking of data, which can help us in discovering and defining test specifications. Visualization is also a powerful way of exploratory testing, regression testing, and understanding the model's behavior in specific scenarios. It makes it easier to spot discrepancies that would otherwise be challenging to detect.

Model explainability

Explainability mechanisms allow us to understand why and how a model made a particular prediction under specific conditions. They help us identify patterns in the errors that the model is making and understand what is causing those errors.

There are various explainability techniques, such as feature importance, local interpretable model-agnostic explanations (LIME) (*https://oreil.ly/0kOa6*), and Shapley values (*https://oreil.ly/AfMLa*), among others (*https://oreil.ly/LGrlk*). Whichever you pick, the ability to explain a prediction within a few minutes will help your team accelerate the process of error analysis and model improvements.

In a past project, we built an explainability dashboard that allowed ML practitioners (both technical and nontechnical) on the team to understand the model's rationale for every single prediction. Aside from drastically improving the team's happiness—because customer queries on a model's predictions could now be explained and resolved in a few minutes, when it used to take hours and sometimes a few days of effort—it also helped us understand when, why, and how a model made mistakes and helped us identify ways to improve the model.

Now that you understand model quality issues spotted through error analysis, let's look at how you can better detect and resolve these issues by closing the data collection loop in production.

Learn from Production by Closing the Data Collection Loop

In many ML applications, the interaction of users with an earlier version of the model may be a valuable source of training data. This section focuses on these cases. In other cases, where new training data comes from other sources (such as the observations following a weather forecast), closing the loop could be thought of as ensuring that the model can accurately predict the current behaviors in the world, as captured by those data sources.

Our model tests and error analyses will only be as good as our test data. Furthermore, validation data can often contain the same biases as the training data, which leads us to overestimate the model's real-world performance. If we want to preemptively detect bugs in production, we'll need to test our models with production (or production-like) data. To do that, we need to close the data collection loop.

The distance between training data and inference data is known as a *data distribution shift*, and it is a common cause of ML system failure. Data distribution shifts could result from covariate shift, label shift, or concept drift (*https://oreil.ly/Me1ml*) and cause a model that was performing well (when evaluated using an in-sample validation dataset) to underperform in production when presented with nonstationary, out-of-sample data. This is comprehensively discussed in Chip Huyen's book *Designing Machine Learning Systems*, so we won't go into detail on how the shifts happen and when to trigger an event to retrain a model. However, we will detail in Figure 6-5 and the following paragraphs *how* to keep the data we use for training and testing as similar as possible in terms of distribution of the data that the model will see in production.

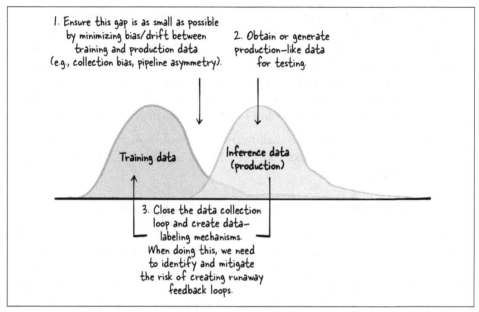

Figure 6-5. Distribution shift between training data and inference data, and what can we do to minimize the drift

1. *Minimize training-serving skew.*

    Ensure the distribution shift between training data and inference data is as small as possible, by: (i) ensuring all feature engineering logic are symmetrically applied in both scenarios (as we have done in this chapter's code example by using scikit-learn pipelines [*https://oreil.ly/eRPSN*]) (ii) regularly refreshing the data that the model was trained on (more on this shortly).

2. *Use production-like data for testing (and use synthetic data where necessary).*

    In some situations, we cannot have access to production data for testing in a nonproduction environment. In such scenarios, we can use tools such as Synthetic Data Vault (*https://oreil.ly/vYDx5*) and CheckList (*https://oreil.ly/eOVjA*) to generate production-like synthetic data (*https://oreil.ly/rnA1s*) for testing ML models and uncovering issues using test samples that are similar to production data in terms of distribution.

3. Close the data collection loop.

In the real world, data is rapidly changing and nonstationary. Tecton's "The State of Applied Machine Learning 2023" (*https://oreil.ly/ZNwx-*), a survey involving 1,700 respondents from a global ML community, found that the top challenge in delivering ML solutions is generating accurate training data, with 41% of respondents citing this as a challenge.

To help us address this challenge, we can ensure that our ML systems include data collection loops and scalable data-labeling mechanisms (*https://oreil.ly/3IpM9*) (e.g., weak supervision, active learning, semi-supervised learning). This is key in ensuring that our feature store (*https://oreil.ly/bmJ5c*) is regularly refreshed and is as similar as possible to the data that the model will see in production during inference.

Having freshly labeled data that's representative of the domain in the real-world helps us in all steps of the model improvement cycle: detecting errors, analyzing errors, and improving the model (e.g., by retraining the model on fresher and more representative data).

When closing data collection loops, we need to identify and mitigate risks of *runaway feedback loops* (*https://oreil.ly/q4kyk*), which is the phenomenon where the model learns biases and, through the effect that it has on the real world, perpetuates the bias in the real world and the data that it will be trained on in the future, thereby creating a vicious cycle.

ML practitioners often focus on the training and evaluation aspects—and in recent years, the deployment aspect—of ML, and many tend to overlook what happens after the model is live in production. In our experience delivering ML solutions, *closing the data collection loop* with scalable data-labeling mechanisms is an effective capability for iteratively improving our models (see Figure 6-6). The rate at which we can improve our models depends on the rate of information flow in the data collection loop.

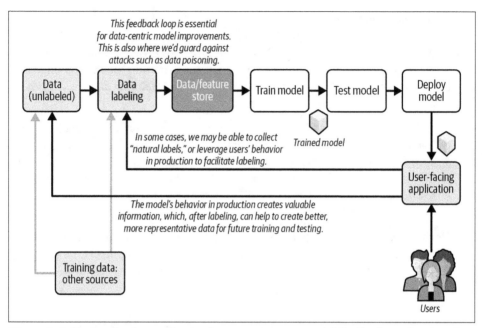

Figure 6-6. Closing the data collection loop creates an essential feedback mechanism that helps us test and improve our models

Now that we've closed the data collection loop, and our data for training and testing is increasingly representative of the real world, we can make the most of the regularly updated data in our model tests by designing our tests using the open-closed principle.

Open-Closed Test Design

The open-closed design principle (*https://oreil.ly/NSVtL*) states that software entities (classes, modules, functions, and so on) should be open for extension, but closed for modification. This is a simple but powerful design principle that helps us write extensible code and minimize the amount of bespoke customization that we need to add for each new piece of functionality. Open-closed tests are open for extension (e.g., we can extend the same test on a range of datasets, such as an in-sample validation dataset, out-of-sample freshly labeled data) but closed for modification (i.e., we do not need to change any code in our tests to do this).

By exposing the test data source and model as a configurable parameter in our test, we can rerun model evaluation tests on any given model, against any given dataset, at any time (see Figure 6-7).

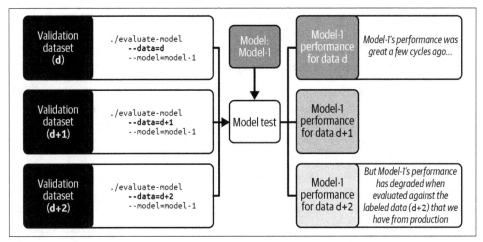

Figure 6-7. Applying open-closed design principle to model tests helps us create extensible and reusable tests

This design also means that we're decoupling model testing from model training, so you can run both tasks independently and on a different cadence. This decoupling has several benefits. For example, it allows us to rerun the evaluation of any given model—such as the current production model, or a challenger model—at any time, whenever new evaluation data is available or when we develop new tests for testing past models ("train once, test repeatedly"). This capability to continuously test a model on newly labeled data is required for monitoring the correctness or performance of ML models over time (we'll come back to monitoring at the end of this section).

In addition, for models that take a long time to train, decoupling allows us to evolve our tests (e.g., specifying new test scenarios, adjusting the metric thresholds) without wasting time and cloud resources for unnecessary retraining.

Let's now look at the next complementary practice—exploratory testing.

Exploratory Testing

When you are stuck in writing automated model tests—which can often be the case, especially in early phases of an ML project—exploratory testing can help you discover what good looks like. Exploratory testing helps you identify bugs, issues, and edge cases ("unknown unknowns") where the model is not behaving as expected. The issues that you discover through exploratory testing can trigger another cycle of model improvement, which we illustrated earlier in Figure 6-5.

While exploratory testing is not user testing, it can benefit from the empathy and mindset of user testing. It helps to consider and involve a range of personas and stakeholders (*https://oreil.ly/kKlH6*), including those who will be most impacted by the model, and observe how the system responds in various interaction modes and scenarios. This can help to create qualitative perspectives on model quality that help to finesse and articulate better measures of goodness.

When you are not sure what to test in an exploratory test, feedback or complaints from customers and domain specialists are a valuable starting point. While you may have a reflexive aversion to customer complaints, they are nevertheless valuable signals and they also point to a gap in our ML delivery process that needs to be looked into. If you can apply the spirit of "learning from incidents" (*https://oreil.ly/ h_n7f*) and use exploratory testing to identify the root cause of an issue and improve the model, then you would've completed a model improvement cycle and reduced the chance of similar issues or complaints happening again (future you will thank you!).

When an exploratory test shows signs of being repeated or repeatable, you can formulate it as an automated test and reap the benefits of quality, flow, cognitive load, and satisfaction.

Means to Improve the Model

Tests do not improve a product; the improvement is done when you fix the bugs (*https://oreil.ly/91axT*) uncovered by the tests—when a model test fails and you've undertaken the error analysis to understand how a model arrived at an incorrect outcome, and finally you identify potential options for improving the model. As ML practitioners know well, we can approach model improvement from two angles:

Data-centric approach
> We can leverage the data collection loop that we described earlier to create training data that is more representative and of a better quality. We can also consider various feature engineering approaches, such as creating balanced datasets or feature scaling.

Model-centric approach
> No, this is not just tuning hyperparameters. We can explore alternative model architectures, ensembles, or even decompose the ML problem into narrower subproblems that are easier to solve.

Having said that, there are times where teams may try both approaches and find that the model still isn't good enough. At this point, an underrated but useful approach— which we introduced in Chapter 1—is to reframe the problem.

If you find yourself in a position where the data is sparse or not sufficiently representative and you can't train a "good enough" model, you can make progress by temporarily lowering the expectations of the downstream consumer of your ML system. This allows your team to deploy an initial version of the model and gather more training data from real-world usage—which enables you to improve the model using a data-centric approach. As more data becomes available, the model can be iteratively refined, and the original, more complex question can be revisited. This technique of reframing the problem is especially useful for "getting off the ground" scenarios where an initial model, no matter how hard you try, just isn't good enough to be deployed yet.

Let's now look at the next practice—designing to minimize the cost of failures.

Designing to Minimize the Cost of Failures

Given that ML models are bound to make wrong predictions some of the time, you need to design the product in a way that reduces risk (risk = likelihood x impact) of a wrong prediction, especially when the stakes are high. We'll first look at some ways to reduce the likelihood of incorrect predictions, and then we'll look at ways to reduce the impact of failure.

Not all errors are created equal, and some mistakes are more costly than others. You can leverage cost-sensitive learning techniques to train or condition your models to be more cautious in high-stakes scenarios and be less so where the consequences of errors are minimal. You also need to collaborate with the downstream consumers of your ML system to understand the cost of different types of failures.

Once you know the costs of various failure modes, you can then incorporate cost-sensitive learning techniques in your model training or deployment. Some key techniques include:

Addressing data imbalances
Techniques like oversampling or undersampling can balance datasets, which helps to reduce errors from underrepresented classes.

Highlighting costly mistakes
Use metrics like weighted F1 score (or other custom metrics for regression) to ensure problematic errors are visible.

Evaluating and training against cost-penalization metrics
Incorporate real-world error costs in model evaluation suites as a start, and eventually include it as a loss function during model training to condition models to minimize costly mistakes.

Inference-time cost consideration
In high-stakes scenarios like large financial transactions, models should lean toward caution and flag potential issues, even with moderate fraud confidence or probability.

It's important to note that these techniques—though they help to improve the robustness of an ML system—are still fallible and ML systems will still make mistakes or exhibit biases. This reinforces the need for *defense in depth*, where we build multiple layers of safeguards to minimize the likelihood and impact of mistakes. Let's look at some ways to reduce the impact of failures.

First, we can be transparent about a model's confidence for each prediction. Instead of providing a single prediction, the model can provide a probability distribution over the possible outputs and be clear when it is not confident about a particular prediction. This can help the downstream consumer or user to assess the level of confidence the model has in its prediction and make more informed decisions.

Second, our solution design can involve a human-in-the-loop to review and override model predictions when necessary. This can help to reduce the cost of a wrong prediction by allowing a human to intervene and make a more informed judgment. This could also include creating a channel for redress (*https://oreil.ly/MFoZj*) to allow consumers to dispute and provide feedback on a model's decisions.

Finally, we can implement guardrails, like defining policies or constraints on the output of the model in certain critical scenarios. For example, if we were developing a chatbot, any references to inflammatory rhetoric (e.g., racial hatred) or self-harm (e.g., suicide) should be handled by our software accordingly (e.g., gracefully decline the request, or trigger an alert).

Let's now look at the final complementary practice—monitoring in production.

Monitoring in Production

Production monitoring is an established practice in software engineering. If done well, monitoring (metrics, logs, and alerts) gives us useful feedback on how our product is behaving in the wild, and alerts us when there are any unexpected errors, performance degradation, or unusual activity.

This gives us insight into scenarios that we haven't considered before in our tests. As Edsger W. Dijkstra once said, "testing may convincingly demonstrate the presence of bugs, but can never demonstrate their absence." That's why monitoring in production is an essential complementary practice to testing.

There are three aspects to monitoring ML models:

Application monitoring
    Metrics such as throughput, latency, and error rates give you feedback on how your application is behaving in production. Is everything going well? Is it crawling to a near-stop? Is everything in flames?

Any errors you observe, complemented with useful application logs, provide you with the prompt and the information needed to reproduce the error and roll out bug fixes. Application monitoring and alerting allows teams to release products with data-informed confidence and respond more quickly in the event of any issues.

Data monitoring

By observing and collecting every data point that your model sees in production, you can detect any data distribution shifts over time. Not only can you visualize the distribution of data over time, you can also run skew tests on the data to detect outliers and drifts (*https://oreil.ly/_f9-C*).

The changes in data distribution over time can signal a need for retraining or fine-tuning the model. This can help ensure that the model remains accurate and reliable for the current domain of the data in production.

Model metrics monitoring

Finally, you typically want to know the correctness or quality of the model's predictions. For this, you can depend on newly labeled data that can be used for evaluation. When you have closed the data collection loop (practice 2) and designed open-closed tests (practice 3), rerunning the model tests using regularly updated evaluation data enables you to continuously measure and visualize the correctness of your model over time.

You can also design model tests to run against not just the model in production, but also candidate or challenger models and observe which model is most suitable for the data that you currently see in production.

While application monitoring and data monitoring aspects can be real-time, the cadence of model monitoring will depend on the rate at which you have freshly labeled data. In many cases, this will be batch due to the time needed for labeling, even in semi-supervised labeling scenarios as we have discussed earlier. All three aspects of monitoring are essential for giving you feedback on the quality of your models in the wild.

Bringing It All Together

From a systems thinking perspective, we can see that model testing is not a stand-alone capability and requires complementary capabilities. Let's put the pieces of the puzzle together by going through Figure 6-8. Each numbered item is a complementary practice described, in order of presentation, in this section.

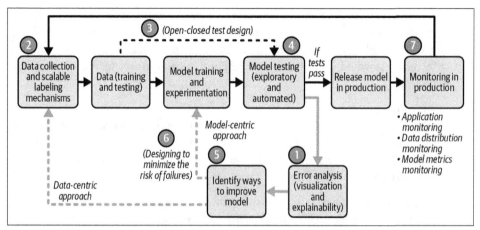

Figure 6-8. Model testing can benefit from other enabling capabilities, such as error analysis, data collection loops, open-closed test design, and more

In the case of a performance degradation or model test failure, we trigger another model improvement cycle by first undertaking *error analysis* (practice 1). We can see the true performance of our model in the wild only when we *close the data collection loop* (practice 2) with regularly updated labels and rerun *open-closed model tests* as regularly as we have updated evaluation data (practice 3).

When we find ourselves stuck in articulating automated tests and spending time on manual testing and troubleshooting of our models, it is an indication that a piece of the feedback mechanism is missing. We can use *exploratory tests* (practice 4) to discover the shape of this missing piece, and eventually automate it to maintain the feedback while reducing the cost and information loss in getting this feedback.

It's not enough for tests to fail, and we need to identify data-centric, model-centric, or UX-centric *means of improving the model* (practice 5).

At the end of the day, we acknowledge that ML is probabilistic and will never be right 100% of the time, especially under conditions of nonstationary data, and we *design to reduce the cost of failures* (practice 6) in way that mitigates the risk (i.e., impact x likelihood) of failures to downstream consumers and users who depend on our ML product.

When we have released a model of a satisfactory quality to production, we *monitor it in production* (practice 7) at three levels: application monitoring, data distribution monitoring, and model metrics monitoring. Monitoring gives us feedback about whether our product is operating smoothly in production, lets us observe our model's true performance in the wild, and provides valuable information on when and how to improve the model.

Well done! At this point of the chapter, we've covered several testing techniques and complementary capabilities that will help you test, understand and improve the quality of your models. And we've talked about how to write these verifications as automated tests so that you can reduce the toil and improve the flow of your team.

With this map in your hand, let's wrap up and discuss how you can embark on—or continue—this journey incrementally and reap the benefits as you go.

On Data Tests

Needless to say, data is the lifeblood of ML systems. The adage of "garbage in, garbage out" rings true. If the data has issues with quality or bias, these issues will be embedded in the model and in its predictions.

In the context of ML, it can be hard to know how a change in the data—e.g., a 10% reduction in the number of samples in one segment of the population—will impact an ML model's performance *a priori*. More often, we observe an unexpected model behavior (e.g., a failed stratified metrics test), and work backward to debug and analyze possible contributing reasons, such as class imbalance in the training data.

However, there is still a place for data tests in ML systems. There are scenarios where it's far better to explicitly capture assumptions about our data in the form of an automated test rather than make implicit assumptions, which can lead to silent failures.

Here are some examples of data tests in an ML system:

Data pipeline tests
> ML systems will invariably have components that ingest and transform data before, during, or after training and inference. There's extensive literature—articles (*https://oreil.ly/mIC3i*), tutorials (*https://oreil.ly/9Iqqs*), book chapters, (*https://oreil.ly/JpS9Z*) and even books—on how to test data processing pipelines to ensure various aspects of data quality including accuracy, completeness, consistency, representativeness, and timeliness.

Data contract tests
> Data contract tests (*https://oreil.ly/PwTl0*) verify that the data being passed between components of an ML solution—e.g., the output of a data pipeline into a training pipeline—match the expected schema in terms of attribute names, value types, and value constraints. Instead of waiting for an ML training cycle to blow up midway—or worse, fail silently—due to an unexpected data schema, we verify that the training and inference data matches the contract of our ML pipeline, before letting the data in.
>
> Failing fast and failing loudly saves us from spending time and effort descending into the depths of logs and troubleshooting subtle errors. Explicit data contracts

---

will make it easier to detect and debug issues rather than having implicit assumptions about data schema littered across the codebase.

Data privacy tests

Data privacy tests verify that the data we provide to our models does not contain any personal identifiable information (PII) such as names, identification numbers, or addresses. These tests verify that we have removed or anonymized PII before the data is consumed in downstream systems such as in model training. PII data is sensitive information and mishandling it can lead to serious privacy breaches and can have legal and compliance repercussions.

Presidio (*https://oreil.ly/0U8j_*) is a Python package that can help to detect PII in a given dataset. In our experience, it does a good job with most PII entities, except for rare names and addresses.

This is not an exhaustive list. In your ML solutions, use manual troubleshooting and manual quality testing to sniff out opportunities to write automated data tests.

Next Steps: Applying What You've Learned

If you always do what you've always done, you always get what you've always gotten.

—Jessie Potter, Director of the National Institute for Human Relationships in Oak Lawn, Illinois

Whether you're a testing expert who wants to encourage your team to do more testing, or you're new to testing and are not sure where to start, here are some practical steps that you can take to apply these testing practices.

Make Incremental Improvements

If you find yourself in a codebase with little to no tests, it's never too late to start improving and enjoying the benefits of test automation. If you or your teammates need a little motivation, just think about the hours you'll save from manual testing in each user story. While it might be daunting, the techniques covered in this chapter can guide you in taking incremental steps toward improvement. Instead of attempting a massive overhaul, focus on making small, incremental changes that can gradually enhance the robustness and clarity of your ML codebase.

At the microlevel, an incremental improvement could be to write one automated test as part of your next commit. You'll be surprised at the mileage you might get even with just basic practices, such as writing unit tests for data transformations, or encoding model quality as stratified metrics tests that you run in your pipeline, rather than manual checks that every ML practitioner on the team has to do with every change set! You can use this chapter's code-along repository (*https://oreil.ly/8UO2v*)

as a reference for how to set up the plumbing—how to define and invoke tests locally and on your CI pipeline.

At a higher level, an incremental improvement could be to outline a test strategy for your ML product with a view toward taking incremental steps every sprint. You can assess the current state of your team with the help of Table 6-1. If you're an engineering leader, this checklist can help your teams to measure current gaps and improvements over time, and it can help to incentivize your teams to improve the reliability of the ML systems they're creating.

Draw from this chapter as you would a recipe book. When you buy a recipe book, you don't feel pressured to cook everything that's in the book—tempting as that may be! Pick a recipe that will meet a need or deliver the most value or happiness in your context and keep on iterating.

Table 6-1. Test checklist for ML systems

Tests	No tests	Tests are manual	Automated tests exist, but coverage is low or patchy	Automated tests are comprehensive, cover majority of lines of code and data scenarios
Software tests				
Unit tests		Example: ✔		
Training smoke tests	Example: ✔			
API tests				
Post-deployment tests				
Model tests				
Metric tests (global and stratified)				
Behavioral tests				
LLM tests (for LLM applications)				
Example-based tests				
Benchmark tests				
Property-based tests				
LLM-based tests				

Demonstrate Value

If your team is regularly encountering defects, or slow feedback points in your development cycle, consider how the tests outlined in this chapter can help. When you add tests, demonstrate the time saved from manual testing and resolving defects. Count how many hours you saved on manual testing in a story. Celebrate the number of times that the tests caught an error on the CI/CD pipeline, thereby preventing an error in production.

Over time, as your test coverage gets increasingly comprehensive, you will see less tedious manual testing, fewer red builds on CI, fewer production incidents, and happier team members.

In some cases, it may be easier to do than to convince. Write some tests, demonstrate the difference that good, readable tests make in terms of the speed of feedback, testing effort, cognitive load, and so on.

Conclusion

> It's only through safety that experimentation can happen.
>
> —Gene Kim (*https://oreil.ly/9e3Yz*), coauthor of *Accelerate*

A colleague of ours once quipped that a litmus test of continuous delivery (CD) is the ability to deploy changes to production when you're on a beach, sipping a choice beverage. When you have a test strategy—and CI/CD pipeline—that comprehensively and automatically validates all changes to the software, data, and model components of your ML system, you can confidently deploy green builds to production at any time. You can do so without anxiety and fear, but only if you have comprehensive tests and production monitoring.

As we have mentioned a few times in the book, comprehensive automated tests lead to shortened feedback cycles, reduced burden, reduced cognitive load, and reduced defect rates, and these further improve your team's experimentation cycles, delivery flow, and satisfaction.

This is not just anecdotal. The book *Accelerate* (*https://oreil.ly/AKkDo*) details a scientific study on performance and effectiveness of technical businesses involving more than 2,800 organizations—the authors found that organizations that adopt continuous delivery practices (of which test automation is a key pillar) and other Lean delivery processes exhibit higher levels of performance, such as faster delivery of features, lower failure rates, and higher levels of employee satisfaction. Our experience in various ML projects corroborate this finding as well.

That concludes our chapters on automated testing. See you next in Chapter 7, where we will harvest a low-hanging fruit that can help ML practitioners write code better: effective code editor practices. The shortcuts that we cover in the next chapter will help us refactor at speed in Chapter 8.

## CHAPTER 7

Supercharging Your Code Editor with Simple Techniques

There are no shortcuts in life, but there are many in coding.

—Juntao Qiu, developer and author (*https://oreil.ly/ZABr2*)

Most ML practitioners that we know love to code. Code is our vehicle for transporting ideas in our head ("will this feature engineering technique improve the model's performance?") into reality. In fact, many bemoan the fact that there are too many distractions, too many meetings, and not enough time to write code. However, when we do get time to code, it's common to find ourselves wasting valuable time on tedious tasks such as manual testing (the focus of Chapters 4 and 5), reading convoluted code (the focus of the next chapter), and unproductive coding practices (the focus of this chapter).

In this chapter, we will detail how you and your team can spend less time getting stuck or even lost in the weeds with unproductive coding practices. We'll demonstrate how your integrated development environment (IDE) can help you to read and write code more effectively. An IDE is an application designed to aid developers, data scientists, and engineers to write, run, test, and debug code productively. It provides development tools such as a source code editor, integrated terminal, version control support, virtual environment management, and code suggestions. It can also assist you with refactoring toward a better designed and more readable codebase (see Figure 7-1).

To that end, this chapter will cover:

- How to configure your IDE in a few steps
- Useful IDE features such as code completion, suggested fixes, effortless navigation, autoformatting, and refactoring
- Keyboard shortcuts for IDE features to help you code at the speed of thought

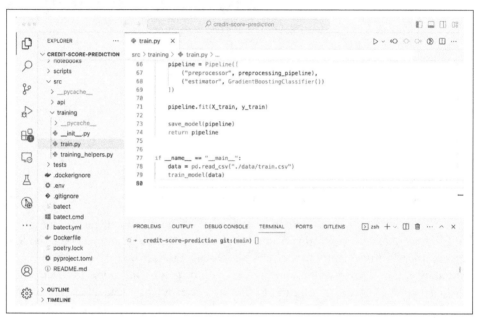

Figure 7-1. An example IDE

If code is like ocean waves, the techniques covered in this chapter will help you ride the waves and get to where you want to go without getting lost in the rip tides. Complemented with the refactoring techniques covered in the next chapter, you'll be able to better understand, tame, and improve a complex codebase into something that helps, rather than hinders, your team.

With the advent of generative AI and the rise of AI-assisted coding, tools such as GitHub Copilot (*https://oreil.ly/NZnKK*) and Blackbox AI (*https://oreil.ly/zMpkt*) are an increasingly important part of a developer's toolkit. However, we've decided to exclude such tools from the exercises in this chapter for two reasons. First, there are already plenty of tutorials (*https://oreil.ly/MOq4r*) demonstrating how you can use tools like GitHub Copilot in Python projects. Second, at the time of writing, the creators of GitHub Copilot are facing a class action lawsuit (*https://oreil.ly/XmRcE*) for training its code-generation model on open source code, many of which are under open source licenses (*https://oreil.ly/QUnsy*)—e.g., MIT license, Apache license, among others—that require attribution of the author's name and copyright. Because the outcome of this lawsuit will affect an organization's decision to use tools such as GitHub Copilot, we didn't want to couple our book to this factor. Furthermore, our experience tells us that even without AI-assisted coding, we can still get plenty of mileage from the fundamental IDE techniques that we'll cover in this chapter.

With that, let's dive into our first section—the benefits and surprising simplicity of knowing our IDE.

The Benefits (and Surprising Simplicity) of Knowing Our IDE

In this section, we'll explore three pitfalls that ML practitioners often experience if they don't properly utilize their IDE while coding. We'll also highlight four ways in which your IDE can help you reason and code better. Finally, we'll explore the barriers and apprehensions that some ML practitioners have regarding this practice, and make a case for embracing the full potential of our IDEs to enhance productivity and improve flow when building ML solutions.

Why Should We Care About IDEs?

We often see ML practitioners using a powerful IDE such as Visual Studio Code (VS Code) or PyCharm but using it as if it were Notepad—just for manually typing code without using the IDE's capabilities for suggested fixes, assisted refactoring, auto imports, and autoformatting, among others. As a result, their flow is often impeded by the following factors:

Excessive cognitive load
> They'll see a screen with many red and amber squiggly lines (or worse, no squiggly lines at all, even when there are errors!) because the code editor wasn't configured with the right virtual environment. The IDE is trying to tell them that there is an error (e.g., a missing import) on an exact line of code, but they choose to ignore it. As a result, they often detect errors much later during runtime—i.e., when they run the code—instead of detecting them while they are coding and accidentally introducing errors.
>
> This adds to their cognitive load because they now need to spend time—amidst dashes of warnings—figuring out exactly where things went wrong and why. In addition, the delayed detection and resolution of errors leads to defects and rework later on.

Tedious and error-prone refactoring
> When they want to refactor—even for something as simple as a poorly named variable—they manually find and replace the variable references, often across

multiple files, and sometimes accidentally introduce errors because they missed a reference.

Context switching

They often jump between their code editor and web browser, gingerly hopping between countless open tabs, to look up documentation and references. For example, they might do this to find out how to import a specific function (e.g., what's the syntax for importing `cross_val_score`?), or to know the parameters of a function (e.g., what arguments does `cross_val_score()` accept?). The constant screen-toggling exposes them to other distractions and further adds to their cognitive load.

All of these distractions take up valuable cognitive resources and time and slow us down in solving the problems that we want to solve. Thankfully, it doesn't have to be this way. Instead, we can make use of the following IDE features to help us code effectively:

Code suggestions

IDEs can provide context-aware code completion suggestions, real-time error highlighting, and on-the-fly code fixes.

Refactoring capabilities

IDEs can help you execute your ideas for refactoring, such as rename variable, extract variable, extract method, among many others, without requiring you to get into the weeds of manipulating characters across multiple files, and potentially making a mistake along the way.

Code navigation

You can directly "teleport" to any file, class, function, or variable that you have in mind, without needing to traverse files one click at a time. You can also zoom in and out of layers of the call stack without getting overwhelmed by countless open tabs.

Keyboard shortcuts

With keyboard shortcuts, the IDE becomes an extension of your mind and helps you execute ideas at the speed of thought, without the friction of multiple mouse clicks and constant scrolling through visual distractions.

The best part is: These are learnable and accessible skills that we can all pick up. We learned these powerful IDE features incrementally through our delivery work, pair programming, and reading documentation. It's a low-cost investment of a few hours with high returns in the form of reduced cognitive load, greater effectiveness, and improved satisfaction.

In addition, these skills are portable across various development tools, such as local or remote Jupyter Notebook servers, and this is possible for both VS Code (*https://oreil.ly/5Gsi3*) and PyCharm (*https://oreil.ly/YtjB3*). As long as IDE integrations for the compute runtime exist, you can apply the practices in this chapter regardless of whether you're developing on your local machine, a remote compute instance, GitHub codespaces (both for VS Code [*https://oreil.ly/8NXzC*] and PyCharm [*https://oreil.ly/BQw7z*]), or managed notebook services such as AWS SageMaker Studio (*https://oreil.ly/0kXHk*).

There are two things to take note of. First, not all cloud providers offer ways to integrate their service with these IDEs. For example, you can connect PyCharm to Google Compute Engine instances (*https://oreil.ly/zx3I8*), but not to Google Colab notebooks (at least not at the time of writing). Second, PyCharm's Jupyter Notebook integration will require a Professional Edition license (we'll discuss this topic in further detail at the end of this chapter).

If IDEs Are So Important, Why Haven't I Learned About Them Yet?

"Know Your IDE" is a principle from the software engineering world that can help ML practitioners be more effective. In fact, it's so useful that it even made it onto the list of *97 Things Every Programmer Should Know* (*https://oreil.ly/ObcVZ*). However, many ML practitioners neglect this practice for three reasons:

- They feel it's not important ("I want to do ML and solve hard problems, not pore over details of IDE configuration and shortcuts").

- All these IDE features can seem overwhelming and scary, and reasonably so since this topic is not usually taught in academic programs.

- Some may not even know that the IDE can be configured to be a powerful and helpful coding assistant!

In the following sections, we'll demonstrate that knowing your IDE will *speed you up, not slow you down*. Imagine you're heading toward a destination that's 20 km away, and you're given a tool: a bicycle, but it's not yet properly set up. Would you just start walking because assembling the bike is a waste of time, or would you invest a few hours assembling the bike and enjoy the velocity and the wind in your hair as you ride toward your destination?

We'll also demonstrate that it's simpler than it looks. A new terrain and situation can be daunting, but a seasoned guide can help make it less so. We'll share day-to-day IDE practices that we use in our projects—practices that *you* can apply to leverage your IDE to achieve more with less effort.

In the past few years, we have paired with many data scientists and ML engineers. One bit of feedback that we often receive is that these IDE productivity practices helped them reduce the cognitive overhead and allowed them to focus on solving the problems they want to solve.

With that, let's dive in!

The Plan: Getting Productive in Two Stages

In this section, we'll walk through how you can fully leverage your IDE for any Python project in two stages:

1. Configure the IDE for a given project by: (i) creating a virtual environment, and (ii) telling the IDE where to find the Python interpreter in the virtual environment.

2. Use the IDE and shortcuts (i.e., profit!). Because you've told your IDE to use the virtual environment you created, it can now make helpful suggestions and execute context-aware tasks (e.g., refactoring).

This pattern will work regardless of which dependency management tool you use (e.g., Poetry, conda, venv). As long as you create a virtual environment for your project and tell your IDE where to find the virtual environment, you can benefit from these IDE features.

We recommend that you code along using the exercise prepared for this chapter (*https://oreil.ly/z1XxU*). As Peter M. Senge once said, "It would be nonsensical to say, 'I just read a great book about bicycle riding—I've now learned that.'" Experiential knowledge is more fun than conceptual knowledge, and it'll help you apply what you learn to your projects right away.

> This exercise has been tested on Python 3.10 and 3.11. If you're on later versions of Python (e.g., Python 3.12) and encounter issues when running `poetry install`, please use Python 3.10 or 3.11 instead.
>
> To install and use a specific version of Python, you can refer to pyenv's documentation (*https://oreil.ly/jtNdz*).
>
> Note that for Poetry, you'd need to tell Poetry to use the active version of Python that you've selected using pyenv by running: `poetry config virtualenvs.prefer-active-python true`. For more information, see issue on Poetry (*https://oreil.ly/3ac00*).

Stage 1: Configuring Your IDE

In this section, we'll describe how you can configure your IDE with the virtual environment for this project.

Install IDE and basic navigation shortcuts

If you haven't already done so, you can download PyCharm (*https://oreil.ly/wFMf_*) (either Professional Edition or Community Edition[1]) or VS Code (*https://oreil.ly/n89Xw*) and follow the installation instructions. If you have doubts about any of the installation prompts, following the default options would be a good start. You may be prompted to restart your computer if you're installing it for the first time.

Below are some important notation conventions used in this chapter.

Mac:

- ⇧ Shift
- ⌘ Command
- ⌥ Option
- Ctrl

Windows/Linux:

- ⇧ Shift
- Ctrl
- Alt

If a command has the same shortcuts for all operating systems (OS), we will omit the OS in our table. Otherwise, we will indicate the OS.

---

1 For PyCharm, you can either download the Professional Edition (30-day free trial) or the Community Edition, both of which you can find on the "Download PyCharm" page (*https://oreil.ly/wgbFd*). You can refer to the feature comparison page (*https://oreil.ly/HytJm*) to see the differences between the Professional Edition and Community Edition. The main advantage of Professional Edition for ML workflows is Jupyter Notebooks and virtual environment integration for Docker or Windows WSL. We recommend using PyCharm Professional Edition as it'll make it easier for you to configure a virtual environment that's inside a Docker container (which is the case for Chapters 3 to 6). Having said that, we didn't want the license cost to be a barrier, so we've written this book to work with either version of PyCharm.

When it's done installing, open the IDE of your choice. For Windows users, launch the IDE as administrator (right-click the IDE icon, run as administrator) because you will need admin privileges to install dependencies in the next step.

In the IDE, warm up with the IDE navigation shortcuts shown in Table 7-1, which we'll use frequently in this chapter.

Table 7-1. Basic navigation shortcuts

Task	PyCharm	VS Code
Quickly find any file, action, command, class, symbol, setting, etc.	*Search everywhere* ⇧ ⇧	*Open command palette* F1
Toggle open/close terminal	*View: Terminal* Mac: ⌥ F12 Windows/Linux: Alt F12	*View: Toggle Terminal* Ctrl `
Toggle open/close file explorer sidebar	*View: Project* Mac: ⌘ 1 Windows/Linux: Alt 1	*View: Toggle Primary Sidebar Visibility* Mac: ⌘ B Windows/Linux: Ctrl B

Clone code repository

To follow along, clone this chapter's code repository (*https://oreil.ly/hcioz*) using the following command:

```
git clone https://github.com/davified/ide-productivity
cd ide-productivity
```

Create a virtual environment

Open the code repository in an IDE of your choice—either PyCharm or VS Code. When prompted about setting up the Poetry environment, you can ignore or cancel it because we will install it using our go script in the next step.

Next, readers working on a Mac or Linux machine can open the IDE's terminal (see shortcut in Table 7-1) and run the following command to create the virtual environment for this project. This step will install the virtual environment on the host—i.e., outside of the Docker container (we'll explain why we do this in a sidebar just before this chapter's conclusion):

```
# Mac
./scripts/go/go-mac.sh

# Linux
./scripts/go/go-linux-ubuntu.sh
```

Windows users should follow these steps:

1. Download and install Python3 (*https://oreil.ly/U9ML-*) if not already installed. During installation, when prompted, select Add Python to PATH.

2. In Windows explorer/search, go to Manage App Execution Aliases and turn off App Installer for Python. This resolves the issue where the `python` executable is not found in the PATH.

3. Run the following go script in the PowerShell or command prompt terminal:

   `.\scripts\go\go-windows.bat`

   If you see an HTTPSConnectionPool `read timed out` error, just run this command a few more times until `poetry install` succeeds.

 For Windows users, this exercise has been tested on Windows 10. If you encounter any issues running the commands on Windows Powershell or Command Prompt, please install the Windows Subsystem for Linux (WSL) (see installation steps [*https://oreil.ly/wHrmJ*]) and use the Linux go script to follow along in this chapter.

This should take a few minutes to complete if you're running it for the first time. When the go script completes successfully, it will print the path to the Python interpreter, which we will use in the next step.

Configure virtual environment: PyCharm

PyCharm's official documentation on how to configure a virtual environment (*https://oreil.ly/M67G9*) is brief and easy to follow:

1. On the bottom right of the screen, click the Python Interpreter tab (*https://oreil.ly/fyYpR*) and choose Add Interpreter (see Figure 7-2).

2. In the left-hand pane of the Add Python Interpreter pop-up dialog, select Virtualenv Environment, and select Existing environment since you have already created your virtual environment when running the go script.

3. Choose the desired interpreter from the list. If the desired interpreter is not on the list, click on the ellipsis (...), and paste the path printed at the end of the go script (see Figure 7-3). You can also obtain this interpreter path by running `echo "$(poetry env info -p)/bin/python"`.

4. Click OK to complete the setup.

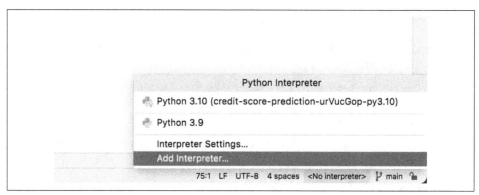

Figure 7-2. On the bottom right of PyCharm, click on the interpreter tab and select Python Interpreter

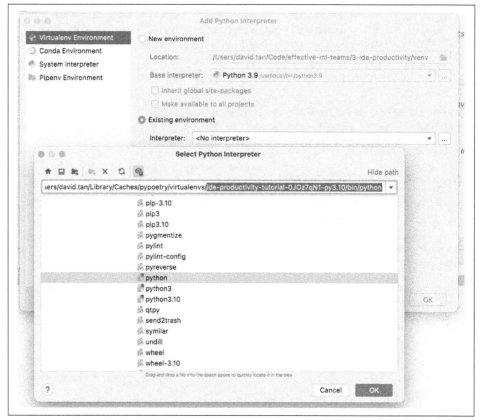

Figure 7-3. How to configure PyCharm to use the virtual environment for this project

For PyCharm users, there is a final step to mark our *./src* directory as the Sources Root directory, so that we can use all of the IDE features (e.g., auto import, get parameter information) on our own source code (see Figure 7-4). To do that, right-click the src directory, click on Mark Directory As, and select Sources Root. (We don't recommend it, but if you want to get into the rabbit hole of why PyCharm doesn't support editable packages, you can see this open issue [*https://oreil.ly/HuaEo*].)

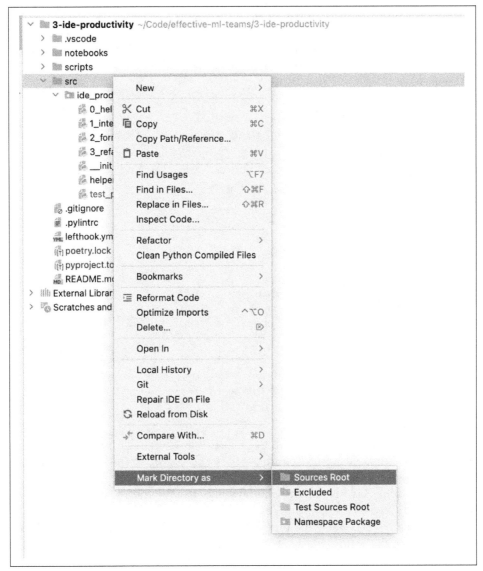

Figure 7-4. Steps to mark ./src directory as Sources Root in PyCharm

Configure virtual environment: VS Code

If you haven't already done so, install the official VS Code Python extension (ms-python.python [*https://oreil.ly/sIyf2*]):

1. Open the command palette (F1).
2. Search for "Install extensions".
3. On the left pane, search for "ms-python.python" and install it.

VS Code's official documentation on how to configure a virtual environment (*https://oreil.ly/ens06*) is also brief and easy to follow:

1. Select and activate the virtual environment. Open command palette (F1), type "Python: Select Interpreter".
2. The *Python: Select Interpreter* command displays a list of available Python environments. You can select the one for this project (`ide-productivity-tutorial-xxx`). If you don't see that option, you can also copy and paste the full path printed at the end of the go script (see Figure 7-5).

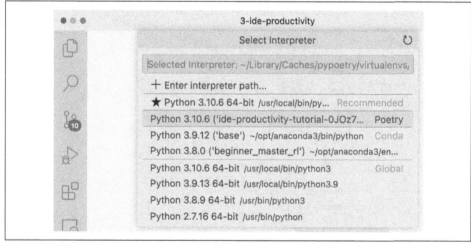

Figure 7-5. How to configure VS Code to use the virtual environment for this project

After you've done this, the editor will know about the Python virtual environment and all the dependencies you've installed in your project, and it can become your helpful assistant. Open any Python file in this project and you should see your virtual environment in the bottom right of your screen (see Figure 7-6). Depending on when you are reading this book and what version of the IDE you're using, the preceding list of instructions may differ slightly. If ever you get stuck, the official documentation—referenced earlier—is always a trusty friend with up-to-date information.

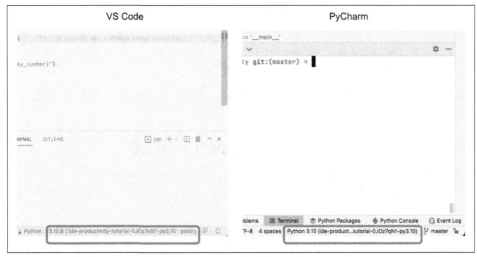

Figure 7-6. The bottom right of your IDE will indicate the virtual environment it has been configured to use

Testing that we've configured everything correctly

As a smoke test to check if we've configured the Python interpreter correctly, let's do our first warm-up exercise:

1. Navigate to *src/ide_productivity/0_hello_ide.py*. Notice the squiggly warning line below the reference to np (numpy)? Hover over it and the IDE will tell us the issue: We have a missing import!

2. Resolve this by placing your cursor on np and hitting the auto-fix shortcut.

   For PyCharm:
   - Mac: ⌥ Enter
   - Windows/Linux: Alt Enter

   For VS Code:
   - Mac: ⌘ .
   - Windows/Linux: Ctrl .

3. You'll see a suggestion to fix this by importing numpy. If you don't see the suggestion, wait a few moments and try again (the virtual environment is a big directory!). Hit Enter to accept the suggestion, and you'll see the issue is fixed. Thanks IDE!

4. Finally, you can test that the issue has been fixed by running the script in the project's virtual environment:

```
# activate virtual environment
poetry shell

# in the container, run the script:
python src/ide_productivity/0_hello_ide.py
```

And that's it! Now the IDE can help you with many tasks, which we'll explore in the following section.

Stage 2: The Star of the Show—Keyboard Shortcuts

This is the best part of the chapter. You've spent a few minutes doing some fairly mundane work to configure your IDE properly and now it's time to get a return on your investment.

For the exercises in this section, we encourage you to read the code sample, try each shortcut, run the code in the terminal (*python src/ide_productivity/name_of_file.py*), and verify that you've completed the exercise. You can subsequently apply these skills in your own projects. Have fun!

Coding

Let's see how the IDE can help you with code completion suggestions, inline documentation, suggested fixes, and linting, among other tasks. Code along in *src/ide _productivity/1_intellisense.py* for this section.

Code completion suggestions. PyCharm calls this code completion (*https://oreil.ly/ Uaam0*) and VS Code calls it IntelliSense (*https://oreil.ly/0Oc2g*). They both refer to the IDE's ability to make code suggestions (e.g., methods that you can call, parameters that you can pass in) that are reachable from the current caret position (see Table 7-2).

 Remember, we'll only note each shortcut once if it's the same for both PyCharm and VS Code.

Table 7-2. Code completion shortcut

Task	PyCharm	VS Code
Code completion / IntelliSense		Ctrl Space

Try it out in Exercise 7-1.

Exercise 7-1. Calculate the mean age of passengers

Task: Put a dot (.) after the series, and you can browse through a list of Series methods that you could use to calculate the mean for the series. If you miss the suggestion, you can trigger the suggestions again using the shortcut (Ctrl Space).

```
mean_age = passengers["age"]
print(mean_age)
```

Inline documentation / parameter information. When we're coding, we often wonder things like: What arguments or keyword arguments does this function (e.g., df.astype()) accept? The shortcuts in Table 7-3 help you get answers to those questions right in your IDE, so that you don't have to toggle between windows and get lost in open browser tabs.

Table 7-3. Inline documentation / parameter information

Task	PyCharm	VS Code
Load documentation for a function	*Quick documentation* Mac: F1 Windows/Linux: Ctrl Q	*Definition preview hover* Hover mouse over any method name. If you don't see any helpful suggestions, add a type hint (e.g., df: pd.DataFrame).
Get information on parameters of a function	*Parameter information* Mac: ⌘ P Windows/Linux: Ctrl P	*Trigger parameter hints* Mac: ⇧ ⌘ Space Windows/Linux: ⇧ Ctrl Space

Try it out in Exercise 7-2.

Exercise 7-2. Convert the age column to integers

Task 1: Place your cursor on the function astype() and hit the shortcut for Quick Documentation. Can you scroll through and see documentation and examples on how you can convert data types?

Task 2: Place your cursor on the parenthesis of astype() and hit the shortcut for Parameter Hints. Can you identify the first parameter that this function accepts?

```
ages = passengers["age"].astype()
print(ages)
```

Auto-fix suggestions. One of the most powerful and useful shortcuts is for auto-fixing warnings and errors.

For example, perhaps we're following a tutorial or documentation and the authors have neglected to include the import statement for a function (e.g., cross_val_score()). The IDE will flag a missing import as an error and, as the next exercise will demonstrate, the shortcut shown in Table 7-4 can help you fix such errors—and other errors—easily.

Table 7-4. Auto-fix suggestions

Task	PyCharm	VS Code
Get suggestions for auto-fixing warnings and errors	*Show intention actions* Mac: ⌥ Enter Windows/Linux: Alt Enter	*Quick fix* Mac: ⌘ . Windows/Linux: Ctrl .

Try it out in Exercise 7-3.

Exercise 7-3. Auto-fix (missing import)

> Task: Hover over the squiggly line to see the error (undefined variable) and use the auto-fix shortcut to fix the error.
>
> ```
> directory_name = path.dirname("/the/path/to/somewhere")
> print(directory_name)
> ```

While this auto-fix feature is useful, it goes without saying that we shouldn't accept the IDE's suggestions thoughtlessly. Always double-check auto-fix updates before accepting them and—as with all code changes—run automated tests to validate the code change.

Linting. Linters help you check for errors, enforce a coding standard, identify problematic code smells (*https://oreil.ly/Xu_Rh*), and even make refactoring suggestions.[2] Linters analyze your code without actually running it—that's why linting is also referred to as "static analysis"—and can help you detect issues and errors, even while you are coding.

When you and your teammates are coding, the linter can tell you, "There's an error here! You've passed the wrong type of arguments to this function"—helping you catch bugs even as you are coding.

For this exercise to make sense, try the task both before *and* after enabling linting (see Table 7-5), and you'll notice how the linter helps you detect an error in greet().

---

2 This definition of a linter is paraphrased from pylint's official documentation (*https://oreil.ly/oRPGL*).

Table 7-5. Linting

Task	PyCharm	VS Code
Enable linting You can see the linter's warnings by either: • Clicking on the "Problems" tab near the IDE's terminal • Hovering over code with amber/red highlights	No action needed. PyCharm's default linter is automatically enabled when you configure the virtual environment.	At the time of writing, VS Code recommends configuring via VS Code extensions. To install the linter extension, which we specified in *.vscode/extensions.json*, open your command palette (F1) and search for "Extensions: Configure Recommended Extensions". Install the recommended extensions (in this case, pylint [*https://oreil.ly/SGToK*]) if it's not yet installed.
Go to next error	F2	F8

Try it out in Exercise 7-4.

Exercise 7-4. Linting

> Task: Uncomment the last line. Notice the linter's warning for greet()? Can you read the error by hovering the warning line and find a fix?

```
def greet(name: str):
        print(f"Howdy {name}!")

# greet()
```

Move/copy lines. The shortcuts in Table 7-6 are helpful when you need to move or copy lines or blocks of code.

Table 7-6. Move/copy lines

Task	PyCharm	VS Code
Move selection up/down	Mac: ⇧ ⌥ up/down Windows/Linux: ⇧ Alt up/down	Mac: ⌥ up/down Windows/Linux: Alt up/down
Duplicate selection up/down	Mac: ⌘ D Windows/Linux: Ctrl D	Mac: ⇧ ⌥ up/down Windows/Linux: ⇧ Alt up/down
Select next occurrence	Mac: Ctrl G Windows/Linux: Alt J	Mac: ⌘ D Windows/Linux: Ctrl D

Now that we've covered the basics of how your IDE can help you with coding (e.g., code completion suggestions, inline documentation, suggested fixes, linting), let's look at how it can help you with formatting.

Formatting

In this section, we will go through IDE features that help team members maintain a consistent code formatting. You can code along in *src/ide_productivity/2_formatting.py*.

Reformat code.   Have you ever had to manually fix the formatting (e.g., indentation, or extra/missing spaces) for 10 lines of code? Was it tedious? How about 200 lines of code? Or have you ever bit your lip during a pull request review even though the code was very hard to read due to inconsistent formatting?

Implementing consistent and automated formatting from the get-go prevents git commits or pull requests from being polluted by irrelevant formatting changes. Here are some real-world scenarios that you may have encountered:

- One teammate, who has properly set up a formatter, just wants to change one line of code but ends up creating a pull request that has 10s or 100s of lines of unrelated formatting changes.

- Two teammates, who had set up different formatters (e.g., black and autopep8), and their commits keep undoing what the other person did. This leads to frequent merge conflicts that take time to fix.

Formatting configuration and shortcuts can help you avoid such annoyances and distractions by enabling your team to apply consistent formatting with just one shortcut.

To further verify your team is using the same formatter and configuration, the pre-commit hooks (*https://oreil.ly/-sIkl*) and CI pipeline can include a step—e.g., `black --check .`—to check if the code is properly formatted. In this project, we've set up git hooks using lefthook (*https://oreil.ly/-sIkl*). We installed lefthook and the git hooks in the go script, and specified what hooks to run in *lefthook.yml*. We've specified two pre-commit hooks: one for linting and one for checking formatting. You can see them in action by making a commit—you'd see the git hook checking if all local files (both committed and uncommitted changes) are consistent with linting and formatting rules.

Configuring the Formatter in VS Code and PyCharm

To configure the formatter in VS Code, open your command palette (F1) and search for "Extensions: Configure Recommended Extensions." You'll see black (*https://oreil.ly/j4Rgg*) as a recommended extension because that's what we've specified in *.vscode/extensions.json*. Install the recommended extension (in this case, black) if it's not yet installed.

To configure the formatter in PyCharm, you'd need to complete two steps: (i) Add black as an IDE "external tool," and (ii) override the default formatting shortcut to use black. For the first step (see Figure 7-7), hit Shift Shift, search for "External Tools Settings," and in the pop-up dialog, click + to add a new tool and enter the following:

- Name: black (you can name this anything)
- Program: $PyInterpreterDirectory$/black
- Arguments: $FilePath$
- Working directory: $ProjectFileDir$

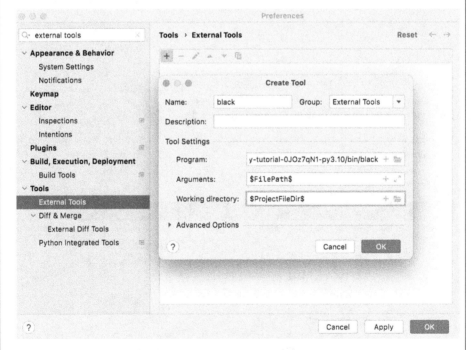

Figure 7-7. How to configure formatter (black) in PyCharm

For the second step to configure the formatting shortcut, hit Shift Shift, search "Keymap," and search for "black" (the name we gave this external command in the previous step). As illustrated in Figure 7-8, right-click "black," click Add Keyboard Shortcut, type a new shortcut (e.g., we use Shift + Alt + F, the same shortcut for formatting code in VS Code; see Table 7-7).

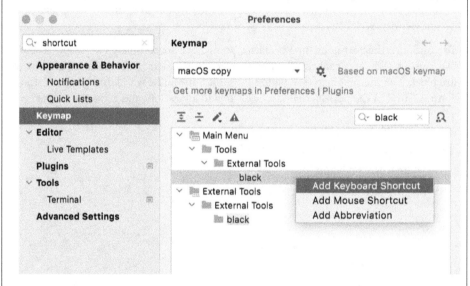

Figure 7-8. How to add a shortcut to trigger formatting with black

Now, you can use the formatting shortcut in Exercise 7-5!

We wish it were less painful, but it only takes a minute to complete these steps and it will save your team hours down the road.

Table 7-7. Autoformat

Task	PyCharm	VS Code
Fix code formatting	*Reformat code (using default formatter)* Mac: ⌘ ⌥ L Windows/Linux: Ctrl Alt L *Reformat code (using black and custom shortcut)* Mac: ⌘ ⌥ F Windows/Linux: Ctrl Alt F	*Format document* Mac: Shift ⌥ F Windows/Linux: Shift Alt F
Organize imports	*Optimize imports* Mac: Ctrl ⌥ O Windows/Linux: Ctrl Alt O	*Organize imports* Mac: Shift ⌥ O Windows/Linux: Shift Alt O

Exercise 7-5. Fix code formatting and organize imports

Task 1: Notice the formatting inconsistencies (e.g., mixed single and double quotes, mixed indentation)? Hit the shortcut to format the code. Notice how the code style is now consistent (e.g., no more mix of single quotes and double quotes)?

Task 2: Notice the unused imports at the top? Hit the shortcut to organize imports, and notice the imports are now tidy.

For VS Code users, after you've gone through the steps to select a linter, you'll see changes like this in *.vscode/settings.json:*

```
# ./.vscode/settings.json
{
  "python.linting.pylintEnabled": true,
  "python.linting.enabled": true,
  # ...
}
```

It's a good habit to commit and check in this setting so that the team shares the same configuration for linting, formatting, and so on. Checking in a shared configuration is better than manual configuration using click-ops (*https://oreil.ly/f9FDF*)—an operations task that is accomplished by clicking on a GUI instead of reproducible, "as-code" automation. That is because while things may work on your machine now, it will be tedious to replicate what you've got working for your teammates and it will be hard to create team alignment. Doing this helps to prevent these minor differences from becoming major distractions during code reviews.

Next, let's look at how the IDE can help us develop an essential habit that every team needs in order to maintain a readable and healthy codebase: refactoring!

Refactoring

In this section, we'll go through the IDE features that help you refactor effortlessly. Refactoring is the act of restructuring code in a way that improves readability, clarity, and maintainability without altering its functionality. It's important to note that refactoring without tests is a very risky undertaking, and in the next chapter we'll describe how you can use characterization tests to create a safety harness before refactoring.

You can code along in *src/ide_productivity/3_refactoring.py.*

Rename variable. The "rename variable" shortcut (see Table 7-8) allows you to easily rename poorly named variables (e.g., _new_df). The IDE will automatically rename all references to the variable, even across multiple files. In Chapter 8, we will illustrate the cumulative benefit of something as simple as a sensible variable name.

When refactoring becomes hard and error-prone, the result is that team members fear refactoring, leading to an accumulating complexity in the codebase. Thankfully, this shortcut makes it easy for you to rename variables, functions, methods, and classes. In PyCharm, you can even rename files and modules and PyCharm will automatically update all references to the module name (e.g., in import statements).

Table 7-8. Rename variable

Task	PyCharm	VS Code
Rename variable	⇧ F6	F2

Try it out in Exercise 7-6.

Exercise 7-6. Rename variable

> Task 1: Rename df to something more meaningful (e.g., passengers).
>
> Task 2: Rename do_something() to something else (e.g., greet()). Notice how all references to that method have been renamed (see src/helpers.py)?

Extract variable/method/function. These shortcuts (see Table 7-9) help you to easily execute common refactoring techniques that will make your code more readable and maintainable.

"Extract method" (*https://oreil.ly/vNCGG*) sounds like a complicated phrase, but it's actually a simple practice of, well, extracting a code fragment (it can be a line or a block) into a function or method with a sensible name that describes the purpose of the method. It can be used to hide complex implementation details (10 lines of long complex code) into a single readable method name (e.g., train_model()).

Table 7-9. Extract variable/method/function

Task	PyCharm	VS Code
Extract variable	Mac: ⌘ ⌥ V Windows/Linux: Ctrl Alt V	Mac: ⌘ . Windows/Linux: Ctrl .
Extract method/function	Mac: ⌘ ⌥ M Windows/Linux: Ctrl Alt M	Same as above
Inline variable	Mac: ⌘ ⌥ N Windows/Linux: Ctrl Alt N	(not supported at the time of writing)

Try it out in Exercise 7-7.

Exercise 7-7. Extract method

> Task: Select the next three lines of code in this exercise, hit the shortcut for extract method, and give the function a name (e.g., `add_prettified_ticket_column`).
>
> ```
> prettified_name = "Passenger: " + df["name"]
> prettified_seat_number = "Seat Number: " + df["seat_number"]
> df["prettified_ticket"] = prettified_name + ", " + prettified_seat_number
>
> print(df)
> ```

Now that we've seen how the IDE simplifies refactoring, let's look at how it can help us to navigate and make sense of a large codebase.

Navigating code without getting lost

In this section, we'll cover shortcuts that can help you effectively navigate code and avoid getting overwhelmed by too many open tabs in your IDE or getting lost in the countless lines of code.

Opening things (files, classes, methods, functions) by name. We often see ML practitioners navigating code on the web browser (e.g., GitHub or GitLab). While that works when you're just reading a small amount of code, it becomes cognitively demanding when you need to navigate in and out of functions, as we often do. The result is an overwhelming number of open tabs. The IDE shortcuts in Table 7-10 help you to navigate in and out of layers of abstraction, seeing valuable git information (who committed the code change, when, and why) and getting the information you want without the many open tabs and disruption to your flow.

Table 7-10. Navigating by name

Task	PyCharm	VS Code
Open file by name	Mac: ⌘ ⇧ O Windows/Linux: Ctrl ⇧ O	Mac: ⌘ P Windows/Linux: Ctrl P
Go to symbol (e.g. variables, functions, methods, classes)	Mac: ⌘ ⌥ O Windows/Linux: Ctrl Alt O	Mac: ⌘ ⇧ O Windows/Linux: Ctrl ⇧ O

Navigating the flow of code. When working in a large codebase, we're often wading through large bodies of text and it's easy to get lost or overwhelmed. Sometimes we end up in an open file after hopping through multiple functions, and we forget what we were trying to do in the first place.

The shortcuts in Table 7-11 will help you easily zoom in and out of layers of abstractions, reduce cognitive load, and allow you to focus on the task at hand.

Table 7-11. Code navigation

Task	PyCharm	VS Code
Go to function definition	Mac: ⌘ B Windows/Linux: Ctrl B	F12
View function definition	Mac: ⌥ Space Windows/Linux: Ctrl Shift I	Mac: ⌥ F12 Windows/Linux: Alt F12
Navigating backward/forward in the sequence of files and code that you've visited	Mac: ⌘ [or] Windows/Linux: Ctrl Alt ← or →	Mac: Ctrl - or Ctrl Shift - Windows/Linux: Alt ← or →
Find usages	Mac: ⌥ F7 Windows/Linux: Alt F7	⇧ F12
Collapse code region in scope (see benefits in the following sidebar)	Mac: ⌘ - Windows/Linux: Ctrl -	Mac: ⌘ ⌥ [Windows/Linux: Ctrl ⇧ [
Expand code region in scope (see the following sidebar)	Mac: ⌘ + Windows/Linux: Ctrl +	Mac: ⌘ ⌥] Windows/Linux: Ctrl ⇧]
Collapse code all regions in file	Mac: ⌘ ⇧ - Windows/Linux: Ctrl ⇧ -	Mac: ⌘ K ⌘ 0 Windows/Linux: Ctrl K Ctrl 0
Expand code all regions in file	Mac: ⌘ ⇧ + Windows/Linux: Ctrl ⇧ +	Mac: ⌘ K ⌘ J Windows/Linux: Ctrl K Ctrl J
Search files	Mac: ⌘ ⇧ F Windows/Linux: Ctrl ⇧ F	Mac: ⌘ ⇧ F Windows/Linux: Ctrl ⇧ F
Navigate tabs	Mac: ⇧ ⌘] or [Windows/Linux: Alt ← or →	Mac: Ctrl [number] Windows/Linux: Ctrl Tab

Try out each shortcut and notice how it can help you reduce visual clutter and cognitive load.

Using the Newspaper Metaphor to Write Readable Code

The Newspaper Metaphor (*https://oreil.ly/0YlkK*) states that we naturally read—and hence should write—our code like we would a newspaper article. We start by reading the headline. If the headline is of interest to us, we may read a summary paragraph and skim through section headers. Where we need to go into details, we can dive into the paragraphs.

Likewise in our code, the names of our files and classes are the headlines, and function names are section headers. As you can see below, organizing code in this manner helps us understand "what" is going on simply by reading the function names. We read the title and very quickly know that this is a metrics test. We then read the section headers and know that we have two tests for the model's global and stratified recall score, respectively. We avoid the need to figure out "how" things are implemented—unless we need to—thereby reducing our cognitive load and making our code easier to read and understand:

```
import...

class TestMetrics:
  recall_threshold = 0.65

  def test_global_recall_score_should_be_above_threshold(self):...

  def test_stratified_recall_score_should_be_above_threshold(self):...
```

Screen real estate management. The shortcuts in Table 7-12 can help you to reduce screen toggling, so that you can clear your headspace and attain focus. Reducing unnecessary visual distractions and cognitive load gives us more clarity for solving the problem at hand.

For example, splitting the screen on the left and right is useful for putting test and code side by side, and saves you from having to overload your working memory ("What was I looking at just now?").

Table 7-12. Screen real estate management

Task	PyCharm	VS Code
Close all other tabs	(No default shortcut, but you can configure a custom shortcut [*https://oreil.ly/12IQL*])	Mac: ⌘ ⌥ T Windows/Linux: Ctrl Alt T
Split screen	Search everywhere (⇧ ⇧) and search for "Split Right"	Mac: ⌘ \ Windows/Linux: Ctrl \

And with that, we've covered the IDE shortcuts for this chapter. The next time you need to wade through large amounts of code to do something, try out these navigational shortcuts to get to your destination without getting lost in the weeds.

You Did It!

By this point in the chapter, you've learned several new techniques that will help you and your team to reduce cognitive load and improve your flow while coding. In the remainder of this chapter, we will go through some guidelines we employ to create team alignment and bring everyone up to a consistent baseline level in a project. We will also touch on some other useful IDE features that you can look further into.

Guidelines for setting up a code repository for your team

Here are some guidelines that can help you bootstrap a new project—or improve an existing project—with the good habits we've been discussing baked in:

Configuration-as-code

All team members should be able to load project-level configurations and have the IDE respect those rules. As much as possible, avoid installing and configuring anything that's needed by the team using graphical user interfaces (GUI) and click-ops. If there's anything you want to do (e.g., set up linting for your project), ensure that it's done as code, that the code is checked in, and that your teammates are able to load the configuration and run the exact same task as you.

For example, in this chapter's *.vscode/settings.json*, we've configured the following for the project:

- A default linter
- A default formatter
- Auto save
- Toggle word wrap (so that you don't have to scroll left and right)

There's certainly room for personal preferences. Think of these as a default to get everyone up to a baseline level of hygiene, rather than squashing everyone down to the lowest common denominator. And while we're on the topic of personal preference, Figure 7-9 shows a funny little comic on over-customization.

Figure 7-9. "Borrow Your Laptop" (source: xkcd [https://oreil.ly/TW4IR], used under CC BY-NC 2.5 [https://oreil.ly/dw8XI])

Team-level consistency

Whichever tool you choose—e.g., a specific linting or formatting library—aim to create consistency and alignment within the team. Where there are disagreements, have a conversation and work out which tool is most suitable for the team. Otherwise, this unresolved conflict will manifest itself as chaos in the code that you produce and annoying disruptions in the team's workflow.

As detailed earlier, you can enforce your agreed practices by committing your configuration in your codebase, and automatically enforce checks using precommit hooks (*https://oreil.ly/-sIkl*) and on the project's CI pipeline.

Keep the scroll bar region clean

If you look closely at the scroll bar in your IDE, you may notice some amber or red lines. (PyCharm calls this the Error Stripe and VS Code the Overview Ruler). When this is littered with amber and red warnings, it makes it very easy for you to miss or misattribute actual errors and issues that your IDE is trying to warn you about. The converse is true, and you can think more clearly and detect issues more quickly when you're coding.

You don't have to memorize the shortcuts

When in doubt, you can find the shortcut by opening the command palette (VS Code: F1) or Search Everywhere (PyCharm: Shift Shift) and type in the command you're looking for (e.g., "Refactor"). If a shortcut exists for it, it will show up next to the command. These basic navigation shortcuts are listed in Table 7-1.

Remember, the internet and IDE documentation are your friends. There are many helpful tutorials and documentation on the internet. For example, here's a PyCharm IDE shortcuts tutorial (*https://oreil.ly/KDJRb*) and a VS Code IDE shortcuts tutorial (*https://oreil.ly/5K1mK*). In addition, these official references are useful:

- VS Code shortcut references (Documentation [*https://oreil.ly/X1Tvi*], Mac [*https://oreil.ly/QEs2Z*], Windows [*https://oreil.ly/ofQp-*], Linux [*https://oreil.ly/SDxct*])

- PyCharm shortcut references (Documentation [*https://oreil.ly/tbd_a*], Mac [*https://oreil.ly/RPbYd*], Windows and Linux [*https://oreil.ly/3pslk*])

Extending This Chapter's Learnings When Working with Containers

In this chapter's exercises, we opted to install Python dependencies on the host instead of using containers. This is simply to keep things simple and let readers focus on configuring and using the IDE's features.

Everything that you've learned in this chapter is still useful when working with containers and will just require a few additional steps in configuring your IDE with a Python interpreter and virtual environment in a container.

For PyCharm users, the easiest option is to get a PyCharm Professional Edition license, which costs about US$10/month (*https://oreil.ly/aOevg*). Your organization may have enterprise JetBrains licenses, which you might be able to use.[3] If that's you, you can follow PyCharm's documentation (*https://oreil.ly/iy2Cy*) to configure your

---

3 From our experience, the benefits—through the time and effort saved as the team becomes enabled to code more effectively with the right tools—justify the relatively small costs of licenses for an organization.

IDE to use the virtual environment in the container in a few steps. The steps are very similar to what you've done to configure your virtual environment in this chapter.

For VS Code users, the Dev Containers (*https://oreil.ly/vkVC_*) feature is free but involves a few more somewhat convoluted steps.

An alternative workaround is to create a second virtual environment on the host—primarily for the IDE. That allows us to use the virtual environment setup on the host (what we did in this chapter) in conjunction and in parallel with the Dockerized virtual environment (which we covered in Chapters 4 and 5). While this workaround makes it easier for us to configure our IDE's virtual environment in a few minutes, it does come with two main drawbacks:

- We will be maintaining two virtual environments (on host and in container) for one project. Every time we change a dependency, we need to run `poetry install` or the scripted equivalent on the host and in the container.

- This workaround is unusable if our Dockerfile starts with a base image that includes other dependencies not specified in *pyproject.toml*.

Hence, we recommend using PyCharm Professional Edition to avoid workarounds and hacks, and to keep our developer setup simple and easy to follow.

Additional tools and techniques

Both PyCharm and VS Code have introduced many useful features in recent years. In this section, we'll spotlight three of them. These are the tools we most often use (and see others use) in our line of work. There are certainly other tools and plug-ins that are useful for solving specific problems or in specific languages, and you can explore those other tools easily in the respective IDE's marketplaces or in developer blogs.

Remote code collaboration tools
> VS Code LiveShare (*https://oreil.ly/V7lZw*) and PyCharm CodeWithMe (*https://oreil.ly/JLQdH*) are both great for remote pair programming. We've used both tools and are happy with how they allow us to collaborate and pair program remotely. There's not much we have to say beyond the official documentation!

Using the IDE's debugger
> The IDE's debugger is a useful tool that allows you to pause and step through your code and inspect its state at each step. This can sometimes be quicker than visually parsing print statements and rerunning code again and again. It won't take long to learn how to use it, and in our experience it's well worth the investment. You can refer to VS Code's documentation (*https://oreil.ly/eli3P*) and PyCharm's documentation (*https://oreil.ly/XHq9g*) on debuggers.

GitHub Copilot

As we discussed earlier, GitHub Copilot is an AI assistant that can—based on all the open source code that it's been trained on—provide you with suggestions for whole lines or entire functions. It works with both VS Code (*https://oreil.ly/9rS8j*) and PyCharm (*https://oreil.ly/N2lhV*).

Conclusion

In a team, we feel most accomplished when we solve problems and make progress, not when we're bikeshedding (*https://oreil.ly/rkETt*)—wasting time and energy in discussion of marginal technical issues.

Here lies the paradox—when we neglect these seemingly inconsequential things (e.g., linting, formatting, IDE shortcuts), things keep getting in our way and hamper our ability to read, write, and review code. It's quite common to see teams waste precious energy on minutiae such as proper indentation during code reviews, instead of addressing larger and more important solution design considerations.

In contrast, knowing the tools of our trade and learning how to leverage them effectively will help you and your team stay in the flow when you're solving problems, designing solutions, and reviewing code.

As a challenge to you, see if you can complete the following tasks in your personal or work project:

- Can you configure your IDE (PyCharm or VS Code) to the virtual environment for one of your projects?
- Can you try something fun (e.g., rename a variable, refactor a block of code into a function)?

Equipped with these techniques, let's now dive deeper into an exciting topic that will help you write code that is more readable, maintainable, and evolvable: refactoring!

## CHAPTER 8

Refactoring and Technical Debt Management

Programs must be written for people to read, and only incidentally for machines to execute.

> —Harold Abelson, *Structure and Interpretation of Computer Programs* (MIT Press)

Without refactoring, the internal design—the architecture—of software tends to decay. As people change code to achieve short-term goals, often without a full comprehension of the architecture, the code loses its structure [...]. Loss of the structure of code has a cumulative effect. The harder it is to see the design in the code, the harder it is for me to preserve it, and the more rapidly it decays. Regular refactoring helps keep the code in shape.

> —Martin Fowler, *Refactoring: Improving the Design of Existing Code*
> (Addison-Wesley Professional)

As ML practitioners, we know that code can get messy, and usually much more quickly than we expect. Typically, code to train ML models comprises semi-boilerplate code glued together in a long notebook or script, generously peppered with side effects—e.g., print statements, pretty-printed dataframes, data visualizations—and usually without any automated tests.

While this may be fine for notebooks targeted at teaching people about the ML process, in real projects it's a recipe for unmaintainable mess, cognitive overload, and friction to the point of halting progress. Poor coding habits and the lack of design makes code hard to understand and, consequently, very hard to change. This makes feature development and model improvements increasingly difficult, error-prone, and slow.

Thankfully, there is a better way. In this chapter, we'll share techniques to help you refactor a problematic, messy, and brittle codebase into a readable, testable, maintainable, and evolvable solution. In the spirit of "learning by doing," we will drive this chapter with a hands-on example, starting with an ML training pipeline that's full of code smells and ending with a better solution. Finally, we'll share practices to help you and your team balance effective technical debt management and product delivery.

The goal of this chapter is not to teach you design patterns so that you can write perfectly designed code without any issues. That is physically and empirically impossible. Rather, the goal is to equip you and your team with skills to incrementally and regularly improve your solutions, so that you can keep technical debt in check and execute ideas at a sustainable pace.

We'll start by discussing the costs of technical debt and how teams can pay down technical debt incrementally and regularly with tests, design, and refactoring techniques.

Technical Debt: The Sand in Our Gears

If you've been an ML practitioner for a while now, you would have no doubt picked up a coding task that seemed straightforward at first, but ended up taking much longer because of reasons such as:

- Code quality issues (e.g., poorly named variables, long functions spanning 100 lines of code or more), which made it hard to understand the code
- Poor design (e.g., a function that conflates multiple responsibilities), which made it hard to implement the code changes
- Accidental errors—often discovered several steps too late—that forced you to drop what you were doing to debug and troubleshoot issues

These three reasons (code quality issues, poor design, and lack of automated tests) are all examples of *technical debt*. Like financial debt, if we don't regularly pay down our technical debt, we will end up wasting valuable resources on paying interest. For example, we may think we have four hours in a particular day to work on a feature, but we might waste three hours getting stuck trying to understand spaghetti code or debugging accidental errors. That's 75% of your time wasted on paying interest.

As the comic in Figure 8-1 illustrates, unrestrained technical debt can make a seemingly simple feature much harder to implement. A codebase with high technical debt tends to attract even more technical debt—because the state and structure of the codebase creates a path of least resistance that makes it easier to put in a quick hack than to "do it right." This further entrenches the vicious cycle for the next time you need to implement a new feature in the same area of the codebase.

Figure 8-1. Technical debt (source: Vincent Deniél [https://oreil.ly/i3gFH], used under CC BY-NC 4.0 [https://oreil.ly/-jzOM])

In the paper "Technical Debt Cripples Software Developer Productivity" (*https://oreil.ly/rWYlk*), researchers found that developers (in their study) waste an average of 23% of their working time due to technical debt. In another paper, "The Influence of Technical Debt on Software Developer Morale" (*https://oreil.ly/0STM1*), researchers found that technical debt negatively impacts developers' morale, confidence, and rate of progress. Developers feel frustrated or fearful when working in areas with large amounts of technical debt.

To extend the financial debt analogy further, there can be conditions under which it's reasonable to take on some debt, so long as we do so prudently (*https://oreil.ly/jBdAl*). Being prudent—acting with care and thought for the future—in this context means that we make and act on plans to pay off our debt. The goal is not to be completely free of technical debt. As Martin Fowler puts it, "crufty but stable areas of code can be left alone. In contrast, areas of high activity need a *zero-tolerance attitude* to cruft, because the interest payments are cripplingly high"[1] (emphasis ours; cruft [*https://oreil.ly/JQDN0*] refers to anything that is left over, redundant, and getting in one's way).

Thankfully, there is a practice from the software engineering world that can help us keep our technical debt at a healthy level: refactoring. In the next section, we'll share practical guidelines and techniques for refactoring (along with tests and good design)

---

1 Martin Fowler, *Refactoring: Improving the Design of Existing Code*, 2nd edition (Addison-Wesley Professional, 2018).

that can help you reduce technical debt and sustain your pace of experimentation and delivery.

Getting to a Healthy Level of Debt Through Tests, Design, and Refactoring

In this section, we'll share useful guiding principles when refactoring, but before you can even refactor, you must understand two things. First, refactoring without automated tests is highly risky, and we wouldn't recommend it. In the hands-on exercise (*https://oreil.ly/-vHKb*), we will demonstrate how you can define characterization tests to first create a safety harness before refactoring.

Second, software design matters. Good design saves time and reduces effort. We know this to be true when we walk into a store room or a kitchen that is well categorized and free of dangling cruft. Because ML systems design is complex, we want to box up these complexities and categorize them well so we don't have to deal with everything all at once, which is overwhelming and sometimes plain impossible. And good design helps us do that.

While we can certainly make low-level tactical refactorings without considering design (e.g., renaming a poorly named variable), we need a *high-level picture* of a *desirable* design to create a *readable and maintainable solution*. There's a couple of loaded concepts in that final sentence, so let's unpack them:

A high-level picture
> This refers to a tangible understanding of the components and modules of our codebase (a physical visualization can often help, even with just pen and paper or virtual stickies). What is in each module, in terms of data (object properties) and behavior (object methods)?
>
> How can we design our solution such that our components (e.g., data store, data processing pipeline, ML model training pipeline, model inference API) can collaborate to achieve the desired functionality? With a clear picture, we can identify and eventually avoid architectural smells (e.g., duplication, tight coupling) so that our solution isn't an entangled mess.
>
> The C4 model (*https://oreil.ly/1KlSE*) for visualizing software architecture is a useful tool for gaining clarity in this regard.

Desirable design
> In the real world, you don't need to hot-wire your kettle to put a brew on (thanks electrical sockets). Similarly, creating software with the right abstractions—functions and classes with clear interfaces—can help us design composable and extensible systems (the sidebar "Software Design Building Blocks" on page 235 will

---

demystify what we mean by abstractions and interfaces). This helps us minimize such "hot-wiring," which is a brittle way of adding functionality.

If you imagine a codebase as a kitchen, are things (e.g., spoons and forks) cohesively grouped or are there spare packets of sauce lurking in the utensil drawer? When you need an oven tray, is it easily found next to other baking-related objects?

Taking the kitchen analogy further, while there is no single way of organizing all kitchens, there are unifying design principles that can help us create reasonable and ergonomic kitchens and codebases (we'll share some helpful design principles as they occur in this chapter). In contrast, without design, chaos is guaranteed.

Software Design Building Blocks

Let's look at two conceptual building blocks that can help everyone design better software: abstraction and interfaces.

Abstraction

Abstraction may seem like a fuzzy and scary concept but, once you get to know it, it will become your best friend. Abstraction is the act of compartmentalizing complicated implementation details and replacing them with a simpler representation, such as *a name* of a function, or a class and its methods.

Imagine you're in a restaurant. You're given a menu. Instead of telling you the name of the dishes, this menu spells out the recipe for each dish. For example, one such dish is:

1. In a large pot, heat up the oil. Add carrots, onions, and celery; stir until onion is soft. Stir in garlic, bay leaf, oregano, and basil; cook for 2 minutes.

2. Add lentils, tomatoes, and water. Bring soup to a boil and then reduce heat to let simmer for 30 minutes. Add spinach and cook until spinach is soft. Finally, season with vinegar, salt, and pepper.

It would have been easier for us if the menu hid all the steps in the recipe (i.e., the implementation details) and instead told us that it was lentil soup (*https://oreil.ly/V64Lw*). The dish's name (i.e., an abstract representation of the dish) helps us understand what we need to know without spending precious cognitive resources in poring through unnecessary implementation details in the recipe.

As Edsger W. Dijkstra famously said, "The purpose of abstraction is not to be vague, but to create a new semantic level in which one can be absolutely precise."

Interfaces

In the real world, an interface provides a user-friendly way to interact with a complex device (e.g., a microwave oven) without the need to know any implementation details of electromagnetic radiation.

Similarly, in the software world, an interface (*https://oreil.ly/oJmKP*) refers to a set of related properties and callable methods that we use to interact with a class. For example, a pandas `DataFrame` interface includes methods such as `.head()` and `.sort _values(by=...)`. You can interact with a dataframe through its interface without needing to know implementation details of sorting algorithms.

As a rule of thumb, components of our ML solution (e.g., training pipeline, data store, various classes in our solution) should interact through each other's interfaces (via callable methods) and should not know about or depend on another component's internal implementation details. Otherwise, we will end up with tightly coupled systems that are brittle and hard to change. We'll explain more about coupling and the appropriate level of coupling in the final section of this chapter.

A Readable and Maintainable Solution

When I (David Tan) started my career, I remember a colleague raving on about why a certain software design practice improved the "maintainability" of a solution. I also remember having no idea why that mattered at all. What's maintainability? It sounds boring—I want to create cool things, not maintain code! I want to write code, not read code!

You are probably wiser than young David and need no convincing on the importance of readable code. But one StackExchange user put it eloquently (*https://oreil.ly/ adPPq*): "Writing code is an iterative process, with each iteration building on the code produced from the last, adding features, fixing bugs etc. In order to do that, you need to be able to *read* the existing code to know how and where to modify it, how to write code that uses the existing code."

Readability matters. Maintainability matters. Without them, we are slowed to a halt when executing our ideas and experiments due to overwhelming complexity and cognitive effort.

We're about to get a messy virtual "kitchen" (codebase) into shape, and by this point you know that you need two essential toolboxes (tests and software design principles). Now let's look at the third and final toolbox of techniques (refactoring), and then we'll roll up our sleeves and get this cleaning party started.

Refactoring 101

In this section, we'll cover principles to guide our micro-decisions when we are refactoring.

Before we begin, let's revisit our definition of refactoring. Refactoring (*https://oreil.ly/UHb_t*) is the act of restructuring existing code without changing its observable behavior. Martin Fowler describes it well: "Refactoring is all about applying small behavior-preserving steps and making a big change by stringing together a sequence of these behavior-preserving steps. Each individual refactoring is either pretty small itself or a combination of small steps. As a result, when I'm refactoring, my code doesn't spend much time in a broken state, allowing me to stop at any moment even if I haven't finished. [...] If someone says their code was broken for a couple of days while they are refactoring, you can be pretty sure they were not refactoring."[2]

If we imagine our codebase or solution as a physical workshop, refactoring helps us sort, systematize, and standardize our workshop so that it's free of dangling cruft, allowing us to work effectively instead of tripping over stuff all the time.

There are plenty of talks, books, and articles on refactoring (we'll reference some really great ones in this chapter) and we've distilled from them these four heuristics that can help guide your decisions when refactoring:

The two hats

When refactoring (one hat), don't add functionality (a second hat), and vice versa. During programming, you may swap frequently between the two hats (*https://oreil.ly/ytTc2*) but wearing two hats at the same time is a recipe for excessive cognitive load and a broken codebase.

Scout rule

Leave the codebase a touch cleaner than when you found it. If you see a bit of "litter" on the road, pick it up as part of your task if it doesn't cost you too much time to do so.

If it's a pothole that requires more time and could potentially blow out the scope of your task, make it visible on your team's technical debt radar so that the team remembers to come back to fix it (more on technical debt radar in the final section). Until it's fixed, the pothole will keep tripping people up and perhaps even damage vehicles.

The goal is not a gold-plated road. The goal is to maintain a functional and reasonable codebase that allows everyone to write code without unnecessary accidents or time-consuming detours.

---

2 Fowler, *Refactoring*.

Assisted refactoring with your IDE

As we covered in the preceding chapter, a properly configured code editor is a powerful tool that can help you with many refactoring tasks. Want to rename a variable or method that's referenced 20 or 100 times in your codebase? Want to extract 20 lines of code as a function? Want to change the signature of a function that's referenced 20 times? You can execute each of these with a single IDE shortcut.

Avoid premature abstraction

In my (David Tan's) career, I've probably watched more than 100 conference talks, but probably only five have stayed etched in my mind. One of them is Sandi Metz' talk (*https://oreil.ly/3s6kY*) where she demonstrates the pitfalls of premature abstraction. She articulates this well in her article "The Wrong Abstraction" (*https://oreil.ly/8b4vT*) when she writes: "Existing code exerts a powerful influence. Its very presence argues that it is both correct and necessary. [T]he sad truth is that the more complicated and incomprehensible the code, i.e. the deeper the investment in creating it, the more we feel pressure to retain it (the 'sunk cost fallacy')."[3]

Sometimes when we're coding, the suitable code design is just lurking beyond the reaches of the team's mind. In such cases, we should prefer doing the simplest possible thing (even if it means having no abstraction) over creating a wrong abstraction. It's far cheaper—mechanically and sentimentally—to create the right abstraction when we see a suitable one than to pick apart an existing, but wrong, design and redo it.

However, remember to come back to create the right design. Otherwise, the design you'll end up with is the Big Ball of Mud (*https://oreil.ly/o8g6_*), which Brian Foote and Joseph Yoder define as "a haphazardly structured, sprawling, sloppy, duct-tape-and-baling-wire, spaghetti-code jungle."

Equipped with these refactoring heuristics and guidelines, we are now ready to start refactoring a problematic codebase!

How to Refactor a Notebook (or a Problematic Codebase)

If we think of our codebase as a physical workshop, we know we have a problem when we struggle to find the right tools or materials when we need them, or even trip over things. The equivalent in our code could be needing to tease apart a 200-line function and tripping over messy and unreadable code in order to understand the logic or behavior that we're trying to update.

---

3 Sandi Metz, "The Wrong Abstraction" (*https://oreil.ly/8b4vT*), Sandi Metz's blog, posted January 20, 2016.

In this section, let's bring together the three toolboxes (tests, design principles, refactoring techniques) to refactor a problematic codebase into a readable, maintainable, and evolvable solution.

To follow along, start by forking and cloning this chapter's exercise (*https://oreil.ly/-vHKb*).

This exercise has been tested on Python 3.10 and 3.11. If you're on later versions of Python (e.g., Python 3.12) and encounter issues when running `poetry install`, please use Python 3.10 or 3.11 instead.

To install and use a specific version of Python, you can refer to pyenv's documentation (*https://oreil.ly/jtNdz*).

Note that for Poetry, you'd need to tell Poetry to use the active version of Python that you've selected using pyenv by running: `poetry config virtualenvs.prefer-active-python true`. For more information, see issue on Poetry (*https://oreil.ly/3ac00*).

The Map: Planning Your Journey

To guide your refactoring journey, use the refactoring cycle as your map (see Figure 8-2). The refactoring cycle includes *both* the preparatory steps (illustrated as the horizontal list of steps along the top) and the iterative refactoring steps (illustrated as the circular list of steps).

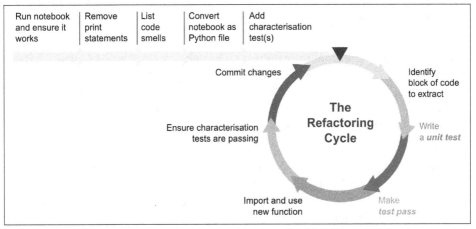

Figure 8-2. The refactoring cycle is a useful process for safely refactoring problematic notebooks and codebases (source: adapted from an image in "Coding Habits for Data Scientists" [https://oreil.ly/j7xdh])

Let's introduce each step in the refactoring cycle:

1. Run the notebook or code and ensure it works as expected.

This step helps identify any errors that could derail your refactoring before you start. This will save you the needless pain of having to figure out whether you broke something while refactoring or whether the code was already broken. For notebooks, always restart the kernel before running all cells to avoid the traps of hidden state in notebooks (*https://oreil.ly/q-L6L*).

2. Remove print statements.

This step removes noise and visual clutter and makes the next step—listing code smells—exponentially easier. If you see a print statement—or a variable left in the last line of the cell, which is displayed in the notebook output—consider whether it's still serving a valid purpose. If it was added once upon a time to help with debugging and is now adding noise to both the code and the runtime logs, remove it.

There may be some exceptions where print statements are performing a critical function (e.g., reporting model quality scores). You can keep such statements for now, but they should eventually be replaced with actual function return values and automated tests, instead of a printed side effect.

It's also crucial to review print statements for any potential logging of personally identifiable information (PII). Removing such print statements not only enhances code cleanliness but also helps safeguard sensitive data from being persisted in logs, reducing the risk of data breaches and ensuring compliance with privacy regulations.

3. List code smells.

If you open a box of leftover dinner and something assails your sense of smell, it's an indication that something has probably gone bad. Similarly, code smells are useful signals that point to deeper problems in the codebase. For example, a function with five lines of explanatory comments is a smell that suggests that the function could be convoluted, obscure (i.e., not obvious), and possibly doing too many things.

There are tools that can assist you with this as well—such as pylint (*https://oreil.ly/ia1Bm*) and SonarQube (*https://oreil.ly/AFc3d*). You can refer to Chapter 7 for simple instructions for installing and configuring pylint. This will help you identify lower level code smells and allow you to focus on design issues and other code smells. For a full list of code smells and best practices, see the clean-code-ml repo (*https://oreil.ly/FCY_q*) and refactoring.guru's "Code Smells" (*https://oreil.ly/anSAQ*). We have also included a handful of common code smells in the sidebar "Code Smells" on page 242.

The adage "a problem well stated is half solved" rings true. By going through the codebase and listing the code smells, we are essentially creating a todo list and a plan of attack for improving the codebase.

4. Convert the notebook as a Python file.

When working with Python files rather than notebooks, it'll be easier for you to decompose your spaghetti code into importable Python modules. As an added benefit, it'll enable you to use your IDE to execute refactorings (e.g., slide lines up or down, extract method, move function to another module). This is where the shortcuts that we covered in Chapter 7 really shine.

5. Add characterization tests.

This is the most critical step in enabling refactoring. A characterization test (*https://oreil.ly/mfIex*) is an automated test that describes the actual behavior of an existing piece of software, and therefore protects existing behavior of legacy code against unintended changes.

A characterization test treats your program as a black box and characterizes its behavior—e.g., my notebook creates a model that has an accuracy score of 90%—and asserts on that characteristic (i.e., the test fails if we run our code and get a model with an accuracy score less than 90%). For reference on what such a test would look like, you can use metrics tests and training smoke tests (detailed in Chapter 6) as characterization tests.

Characterization tests allow you to boldly and safely refactor because any and every code change can be quickly tested against the specified expectations.

6. Refactor iteratively.

This is where you iteratively decompose a problematic codebase into modular, reasonable, tested components.

In the refactoring cycle, you:

- Identify a block of code to extract
- Write a unit test and watch it fail (the test will be red)
- Make the test pass (the test goes green)
- Import and use a new function
- Ensure characterization tests are passing
- Commit changes

It's important that we make small and frequent commits when tests pass after a reasonable chunk of code changes. When we make small and frequent commits, we get the following benefits:

- Reduced visual distractions and lessened cognitive load.

- No worries about accidentally breaking working code changes that have already been committed.

- Beyond red-green-refactor (*https://oreil.ly/kelfI*), you can also red-red-red-revert (*https://oreil.ly/gmvbq*). If you were to inadvertently break something, you can easily fall back by checking out to the latest commit and try again. This saves you from wasting time undoing problems that you accidentally created when trying to solve the essential problem.

Code Smells

Here are some common code smells that we often see in ML codebases.

1. Variable Names That Don't Reveal Intent

Poorly named variables force us to waste mental effort to figure out puzzles. One common culprit in ML code is dataframes—every dataframe is named as df. To find a better name for dataframes, a useful rule of thumb is to think about what is in each row. For instance, if each row in my dataframe is a loan, then the dataframe is a collection of loans. Hence, we could call the dataframe "loans."

Let's illustrate the value of well-named variables with two contrasting examples.

Bad example:

```
df = pd.read_csv('loans.csv')
_df = df.groupby(['month']).sum()
__df = filter_loans(_df, month=12)
# let's try to calculate total loan amount for december
total_loan_amount = __df... # wait, should I use df, _df or __df?
```

Good example:

```
loans = pd.read_csv('loans.csv')
monthly_loans = loans.groupby(['month']).sum()
monthly_loans_in_december = filter_loans(monthly_loans, month=12)
# let's try to calculate total loan amount for december
total_loan_amount = monthly_loans_in_december.sum()
```

2. Comments

Comments can become problematic in a few ways:

- If some code needs comments, it's a smell for deeper issues (e.g., bad variable naming, violation of single responsibility principle, poor abstraction).
- Comments can grow stale and they can lie.
- Comments can make code even harder to understand when there's too many of them.

We can avoid these problems by using sensible variable names, proper abstraction of our code into functions with single responsibility, and unit tests, as illustrated in the following examples.

Bad example:

```
# Check to see if employee is eligible for full benefits
if (employee.flags and HOURLY_FLAG) and (employee.age > 65):
    … do something
```

Good example:

```
if employee.is_eligible_for_benefits():
    … do something
```

3. Dead Code

Dead code is code that is executed but its result is never used in any other computation. Dead code is yet another unrelated thing that developers have to hold in their heads when coding. It adds unnecessary cognitive burden. If there's code that does not change the result of the program, whether it runs or not, then it's not required for the code to run. Remove it to keep the codebase clean.

Bad example:

```
df = get_data()
print(df)
# do_other_stuff()
df.head()
print(df.columns)
# do_so_much_stuff()
model = train_model(df)
```

Good example:

```
loans = get_data()
model = train_model(loans)
```

Now that you've charted your path, it's time to hit the road and refactor this problematic notebook.

There are more than 60 refactoring techniques, which you can refer to in Martin Fowler's "Refactoring Catalog" (*https://oreil.ly/mGfkc*) and refactoring.guru's "Refactoring Techniques" (*https://oreil.ly/UdtiV*).

In this chapter, we will introduce you to just a handful of refactoring techniques (e.g., extract function [*https://oreil.ly/zVZAc*], and slide lines [*https://oreil.ly/cXUeO*]) that help with code smells that we commonly face in typical ML codebases. We hope you will check out these two great resources though, as you might find other techniques relevant to code smells in your projects.

The Journey: Hitting the Road

In this section, we'll cover each step of the refactoring cycle to clean up this problematic codebase! The notebook performs feature engineering on the Titanic dataset (*https://oreil.ly/JHbjZ*) and trains a simple classification model to predict passengers' likelihood of survival. We'll go from this long, messy, and brittle notebook (*https://oreil.ly/MXR3T*) (see Figure 8-3) to a modular, readable, and tested solution (*https://oreil.ly/oCdUy*), as shown in the code that follows, in which complexity is compartmentalized into functions with clear responsibilities and understandable names. We can read the code like a story, and we know where to go to understand or update a piece of logic.

The Titanic dataset contains PII such as passenger names. In a real-world model training dataset, we will likely remove such features before it's even made available as training data.

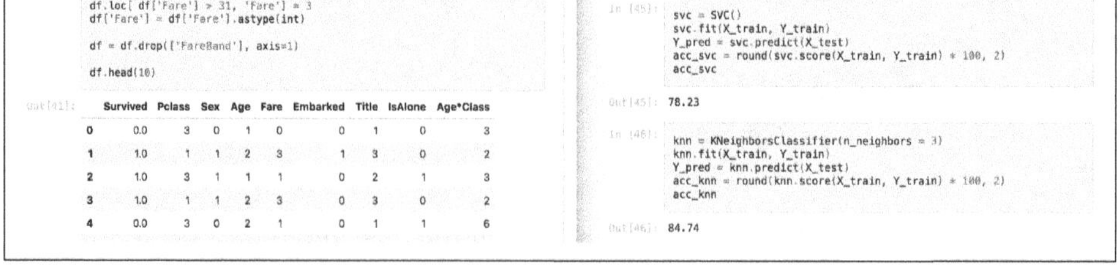

Figure 8-3. A small snippet of our starting point—a long, messy, and brittle notebook

```
def prepare_data_and_train_model():
    passengers = pd.read_csv("./input/train.csv")

    passengers = impute_nans(passengers,
                            categorical_columns=["Embarked"],
                            continuous_columns=["Fare", "Age"])
    passengers = add_derived_title(passengers)
    passengers = add_is_alone_column(passengers)
    passengers = add_categorical_columns(passengers)
    passengers = passengers.drop(["Parch", "SibSp", "Name", "Passengerid",
                                "Ticket", "Cabin"], axis=1)

    y = passengers["Survived"]
    X = passengers.drop("Survived", axis=1)
    X_train, X_test, y_train, y_test = train_test_split(X, y)

    model = train_model(RandomForestClassifier, X_train, y_train,
                        n_estimators=100)

    return model, X_test, y_test

model, X_test, y_test = prepare_data_and_train_model()
```

Step 1. Run the notebook or code and ensure it works as expected

The first step is self-explanatory: Run the notebook or code and ensure it works as expected. When you've cloned the repo, start the Jupyter server:

```
# Clone repo
git clone https://github.com/davified/refactoring-exercise

# Run the respective go script for your OS, e.g.
scripts/go/go-mac.sh

# Start jupyter notebook
jupyter notebook
```

Open *titanic-notebook-0.ipynb* and run the entire notebook. The entire notebook runs successfully, trains several models, and prints each model's metrics.

Step 2. Remove print statements

In this step, you want to remove print statements and plots that are obscuring your vision. As demonstrated in the resulting notebook (*https://oreil.ly/w37x1*), we have much less visual clutter and the next step of listing code smells will be much easier. In this step, we shortened the notebook from 37 pages to 10 pages.

To illustrate the benefit of doing this, compare the difference between Figures 8-4 and 8-5. The two lines of data transformations are no longer buried in noise.

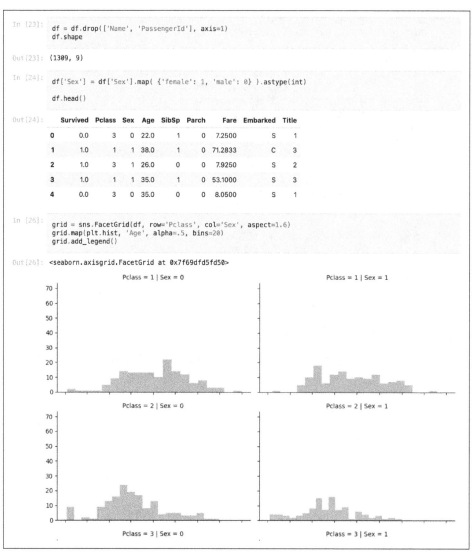

```
In [23]:  df = df.drop(['Name', 'PassengerId'], axis=1)
          df.shape

Out[23]:  (1309, 9)

In [24]:  df['Sex'] = df['Sex'].map( {'female': 1, 'male': 0} ).astype(int)

          df.head()
```

Out[24]:

	Survived	Pclass	Sex	Age	SibSp	Parch	Fare	Embarked	Title
0	0.0	3	0	22.0	1	0	7.2500	S	1
1	1.0	1	1	38.0	1	0	71.2833	C	3
2	1.0	3	1	26.0	0	0	7.9250	S	2
3	1.0	1	1	35.0	1	0	53.1000	S	3
4	0.0	3	0	35.0	0	0	8.0500	S	1

```
In [26]:  grid = sns.FacetGrid(df, row='Pclass', col='Sex', aspect=1.6)
          grid.map(plt.hist, 'Age', alpha=.5, bins=20)
          grid.add_legend()

Out[26]:  <seaborn.axisgrid.FacetGrid at 0x7f69dfd5fd50>
```

Figure 8-4. Before removing the print statements (visual clutter and noise obscures our vision of the essential logic in our codebase)

```
In [7]:  df = df.drop(['Name', 'PassengerId'], axis=1)

In [8]:  df['Sex'] = df['Sex'].map( {'female': 1, 'male': 0} ).astype(int)
```

Figure 8-5. After removing the print statements (essential logic and data transformations required for training our model become much more obvious)

Step 3. List code smells

In this step, we go through the notebook and leave a comment for each code smell we notice. As depicted in Figure 8-6, we've spotted quite a few! For example, the first code smell is *exposed internals*—remember our analogy earlier about reading the whole lentil soup recipe? It would be far better if such complex implementation was hidden (i.e., abstracted) in a well-named function (e.g., `derive_title_from_name()`).

```
In [4]:   df = df.drop(['Ticket', 'Cabin'], axis=1)

In [5]:   # [code smell] - Exposed Internals

          df['Title'] = df['Name'].str.extract(' ([A-Za-z]+)\.', expand=False)

          df['Title'] = df['Title'].replace(['Lady', 'Countess', 'Capt', 'Col',
                                    'Don', 'Dr', 'Major', 'Rev', 'Sir', 'Jonkheer', 'Dona'], 'Rare')
          df['Title'] = df['Title'].replace(['Ms', 'Mlle'], 'Miss')
          df['Title'] = df['Title'].replace(['Mme'], 'Mrs')

In [6]:   title_mapping = {"Mr": 1, "Miss": 2, "Mrs": 3, "Master": 4, "Rare": 5}

          df['Title'] = df['Title'].map(title_mapping)
          df['Title'] = df['Title'].fillna(0)

In [7]:   # [code smell] Duplicate Responsibility - df.drop() happens at multiple places.
          # it would be better if they were consolidated
          df = df.drop(['Name', 'PassengerId'], axis=1)

In [8]:   # [code smell] Duplicate Responsibility again - encoding of string variables into integers
          # should be consolidated into one place
          df['Sex'] = df['Sex'].map( {'female': 1, 'male': 0} ).astype(int)

In [9]:   # [code smell] Dead Code - 'AgeBand' column is defined but never used
          df['AgeBand'] = pd.cut(df['Age'], 5)

In [10]:  # [code smell] - magic numbers: 16, 32, 48
          df.loc[ df['Age'] <= 16, 'Age'] = 0
          df.loc[(df['Age'] > 16) & (df['Age'] <= 32), 'Age'] = 1
          df.loc[(df['Age'] > 32) & (df['Age'] <= 48), 'Age'] = 2
          df.loc[(df['Age'] > 48) & (df['Age'] <= 64), 'Age'] = 3
```

Figure 8-6. The list of code smells becomes our todo list for refactoring the notebook

The second code smell is *duplicate responsibility.* The logic of dropping columns happens in five different places in the notebook. It would be easier to reason about the code if we dropped all the unnecessary columns in one place.

As shown in Figure 8-6, naming these latent problems one by one eventually creates a todo list and a plan of attack for our refactoring. To make it easier to work through this list, we prefix each comment with a searchable "[code smell]." We'll remove these comments one-by-one as we refactor and resolve the code smell. You can refer to this notebook (*https://oreil.ly/KpQBi*) to see the resulting list of code smells, and at the end of this chapter you'll see it in a better state after refactoring.

Step 4. Convert the notebook to a Python file

To convert the notebook to a Python file, run the following commands:

```
jupyter nbconvert --output-dir=./src \
    --to=script ./notebooks/titanic-notebook-refactoring-starter.ipynb
```

Now that you have converted your notebook to a Python script, you'll use the following command to ensure that it runs to completion without errors. In this example, we see that there were errors due to two lines of code that only work in the IPython kernel (e.g., cd ..). Read the error messages and delete the two problematic lines of code. Run the following command again and this time the script will run successfully:

```
python src/titanic-notebook-refactoring-starter.py

echo $? ❶
```

❶ This checks the exit status code of the preceding bash command. In our case, it will return 0 when the preceding Python script runs successfully without errors.

You may also remove the comments that were introduced in the notebook conversion process (e.g., # In[1]: ...). Two IDE shortcuts that we learned in the preceding chapter can make this quick and easy: "Select next occurrence" and "Fix code formatting." Refer to Chapter 7 if you need to look up keyboard shortcuts.

Finally, you can rename the Python file to match snake_case convention:

```
mv src/titanic-notebook-refactoring-starter.py src/train.py
```

Step 5. Adding characterization tests

To add a characterization test, we'll treat the code (now a Python script) as a black box and characterize its behavior.

In this case, the code trains seven classification models with accuracy scores ranging between 71% and 86% (see Figure 8-7).

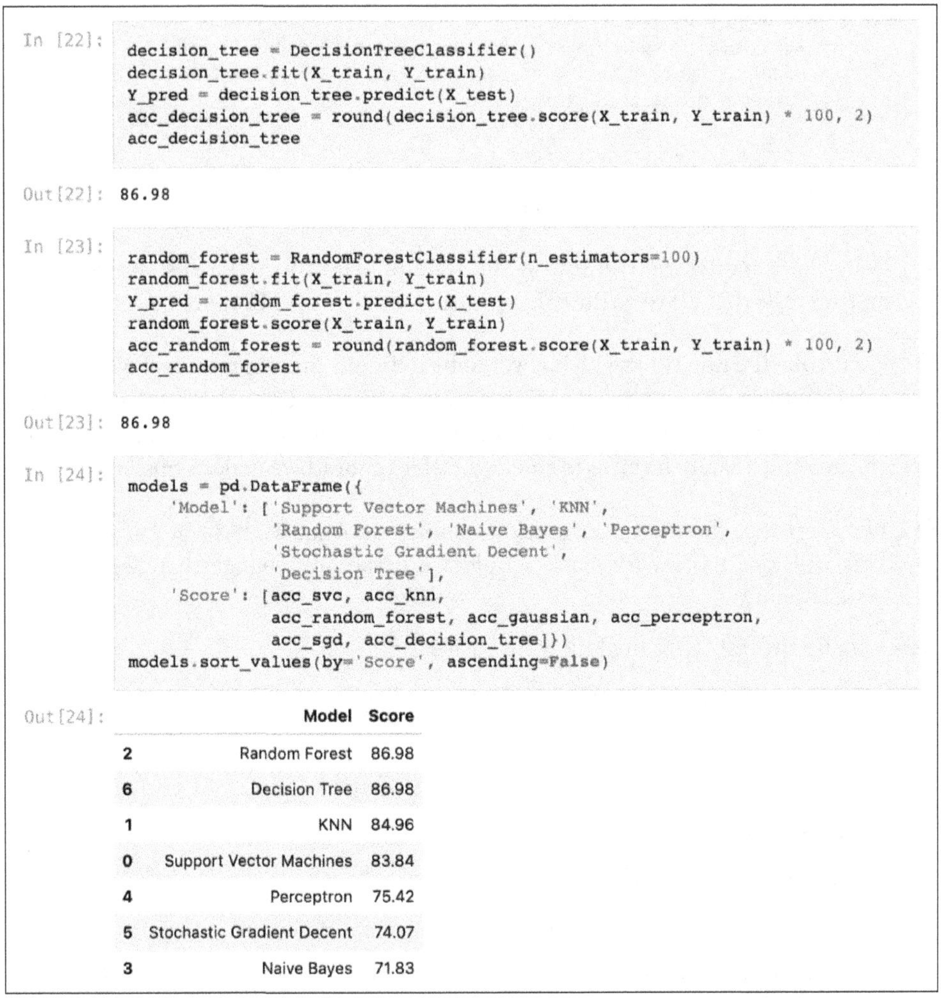

```
In [22]:  decision_tree = DecisionTreeClassifier()
          decision_tree.fit(X_train, Y_train)
          Y_pred = decision_tree.predict(X_test)
          acc_decision_tree = round(decision_tree.score(X_train, Y_train) * 100, 2)
          acc_decision_tree

Out[22]:  86.98

In [23]:  random_forest = RandomForestClassifier(n_estimators=100)
          random_forest.fit(X_train, Y_train)
          Y_pred = random_forest.predict(X_test)
          random_forest.score(X_train, Y_train)
          acc_random_forest = round(random_forest.score(X_train, Y_train) * 100, 2)
          acc_random_forest

Out[23]:  86.98

In [24]:  models = pd.DataFrame({
              'Model': ['Support Vector Machines', 'KNN',
                        'Random Forest', 'Naive Bayes', 'Perceptron',
                        'Stochastic Gradient Decent',
                        'Decision Tree'],
              'Score': [acc_svc, acc_knn,
                        acc_random_forest, acc_gaussian, acc_perceptron,
                        acc_sgd, acc_decision_tree]})
          models.sort_values(by='Score', ascending=False)
```

Out[24]:

	Model	Score
2	Random Forest	86.98
6	Decision Tree	86.98
1	KNN	84.96
0	Support Vector Machines	83.84
4	Perceptron	75.42
5	Stochastic Gradient Decent	74.07
3	Naive Bayes	71.83

Figure 8-7. At the end of this notebook, we see that the code trains seven classification models with a range of accuracy scores

The training of seven models looks like something we'd do in exploratory data analysis, and in our case, we may determine that our training pipeline needs to produce just one model—the one with the best performance. As such, we can characterize our program with the following test (in *tests/test_model_metrics.py*):

```
import unittest
from sklearn.metrics import accuracy_score

from train import prepare_data_and_train_model
```

```
class TestModelMetrics:
    def test_model_accuracy_score_should_be_above_threshold(): ❶
        model, X_test, Y_test = prepare_data_and_train_model() ❷
        Y_pred = model.predict(X_test)

        accuracy = accuracy_score(Y_test, Y_pred)

        assert accuracy > 0.869 ❸
```

❶ We write a model metrics test in the style of a unit test. This is similar to the metrics tests that we've written in the earlier chapter on ML model tests.

❷ We invoke the function (which is yet to be defined) that represents the "seams" of our refactoring boundary. This function (prepare_data_and_train_model()) is the box within which we will refactor, and by writing a test on this function, we are creating a safety harness to catch ourselves should we make a mistake.

❸ We assert that the model accuracy is as good as what we have in our notebook. This will give us fast feedback should we make any change that degrades the model quality.

Let's wire up the tests with the following bash script:

```
# ./scripts/tests/model-metrics-test.sh
#!/bin/sh

set -e

python -m pytest -rA tests/test_model_metrics.py
```

Run the test by running this bash script:

```
./scripts/tests/model-metrics-test.sh
```

You'll see this test fail because prepare_data_and_train_model() is not defined yet. Your first task is to do the simplest possible thing to get this test to pass, and you do so by leveraging your IDE to "extract method":

1. In your IDE, select all the lines of code in the script after the import statements.

2. Hit the IDE shortcut for "extract method." Use the handy shortcut for PyCharm (Mac: ⌘ ⌥ M, Windows/Linux: Ctrl Alt M) or VS Code (Ctrl .). You can name the function whatever we specified in our test (i.e. prepare _data_and_train_model()).

3. Run the test and see it fail because the function does not return the values that we expected it to in the model metrics test.

---

4. In the final line of `prepare_data_and_train_model()`, make the function return an instance of a model, the validation set (`X_test`), and validation set labels (`y_test`).

5. The test should now pass. Woohoo—feel the dopamine!

In your context, you're free to finesse this characterization test(s) further to create the right safety harness around the existing behavior. For example, you could choose a better metric than accuracy or you could write a stratified metrics test. For our exercise, this is sufficient as a safety harness to give us fast feedback on whether we're going in the right direction or whether we've made a misstep during refactoring.

Step 6. Refactor iteratively

This is where you reap the returns on your investments and rapidly work through the list of code smells to improve your codebase. We'll demonstrate the refactoring cycle (see Figure 8-8) three times and leave the remaining code smells as an exercise for you to practice and gain confidence.

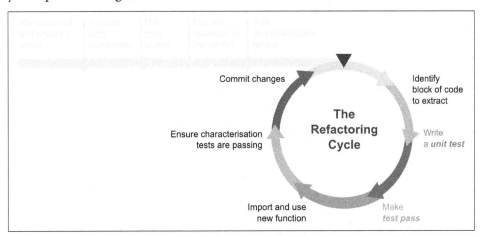

Figure 8-8. Six steps for iteratively refactoring problematic parts of the codebase (source: adapted from an image in "Coding Habits for Data Scientists" [https://oreil.ly/j7xdh])

The first refactoring: Remove dead code.   Let's start with a fun and easy one. Now that we expect our model training code to only return the best performing model, the lines of code for training the six other candidate models are essentially dead. This means that the program will function according to our expectations (i.e., our tests will still pass) with or without these lines of code (highlighted in Figure 8-9).

```
train.py ×
107
108        perceptron = Perceptron()
109        perceptron.fit(X_train, Y_train)
110        Y_pred = perceptron.predict(X_test)
111        acc_perceptron = round(perceptron.score(X_train, Y_train) * 100, 2)
112        acc_perceptron
113
114        sgd = SGDClassifier()
115        sgd.fit(X_train, Y_train)
116        Y_pred = sgd.predict(X_test)
117        acc_sgd = round(sgd.score(X_train, Y_train) * 100, 2)
118        acc_sgd
119
120        decision_tree = DecisionTreeClassifier()
121        decision_tree.fit(X_train, Y_train)
122        Y_pred = decision_tree.predict(X_test)
123        acc_decision_tree = round(decision_tree.score(X_train, Y_train) * 100, 2)
124        acc_decision_tree
125
126        random_forest = RandomForestClassifier(n_estimators=100)
127        random_forest.fit(X_train, Y_train)
128        Y_pred = random_forest.predict(X_test)
129        random_forest.score(X_train, Y_train)
130        acc_random_forest = round(random_forest.score(X_train, Y_train) * 100, 2)
131        acc_random_forest
132        models = pd.DataFrame({
133            'Model': ['Support Vector Machines', 'KNN',
134                      'Random Forest', 'Naive Bayes', 'Perceptron',
135                      'Stochastic Gradient Decent',
136                      'Decision Tree'],
137            'Score': [acc_svc, acc_knn,
138                      acc_random_forest, acc_gaussian, acc_perceptron,
139                      acc_sgd, acc_decision_tree]})
140        models.sort_values(by='Score', ascending=False)
141
142        return random_forest, X_train, Y_train
```

Figure 8-9. The highlighted lines represent dead code

For your first refactoring, remove these lines of dead code, run the test, see the tests pass, and make a commit. By our count, we'd have removed 44 lines of code (out of a total of 146 lines of code), making our problem 30% smaller. Hooray!

We're taking a shortcut in our refactoring cycle and skipping steps 2–4 (writing a test, getting it to pass, and extracting a function) because we're just removing dead code and we're not creating any new abstractions.

The second refactoring: Abstract away implementation details. Following the steps in our refactoring cycle, we first identify a block of code to extract. The following code section contains complex implementation details to derive a set of titles (Mr, Miss, Mrs, Master, Rare) from a regex-matched prefix in the Name column (e.g., Mr, Ms, Mlle, Mme, Lady, Countess, Sir):

```
# [code smell] - Exposed Internals
df['Title'] = df['Name'].str.extract(' ([A-Za-z]+)\.', expand=False)
df['Title'] = df['Title'].replace(['Lady', 'Countess', 'Capt', 'Col',
                                    'Don', 'Dr', 'Major', 'Rev', 'Sir',
                                    'Jonkheer', 'Dona'], 'Rare')
df['Title'] = df['Title'].replace(['Ms', 'Mlle'], 'Miss')
df['Title'] = df['Title'].replace(['Mme'], 'Mrs')
```

The code smell of *exposed internals* suggests that a well-named function could help to hide the complex implementation details and make the code more readable at the call site (i.e., where the new function will be invoked). In addition, by abstracting these data transformations into a callable function, it then becomes unit-testable.

Next, in the second step of our refactoring cycle, we write a failing unit test:

```
from pandas.testing import assert_frame_equal


def test_extract_honorifics_from_name_column_as_standardised_titles(): ❶
    df = pd.DataFrame({
        'Name': ['Smith, Mr. Owen Harris   ',
                 'Heikkinen, Miss. Laina ',
                 'Allen, Mlle. Maisie',
                 'Allen, Ms. Maisie',
                 'Allen, Mme. Maisie',
                 'Smith, Lady. Owen Harris '],
    }) ❷

    expected = pd.DataFrame({
        'Name': ['Smith, Mr. Owen Harris   ',
                 'Heikkinen, Miss. Laina ',
                 'Allen, Mlle. Maisie',
                 'Allen, Ms. Maisie',
                 'Allen, Mme. Maisie',
                 'Smith, Lady. Owen Harris '],
```

```
        'Title': ['Mr',
                  'Miss',
                  'Miss',
                  'Miss',
                  'Mrs',
                  'Rare'] ❸
    })

    assert_frame_equal(expected, add_derived_title(df)) ❹
```

❶ Remember, with a sensible test name, the test virtually writes itself.

❷ We specify the input dataframe with production-like values based on what we observed in our training dataset.

❸ In the expected output dataframe, we add a Title column with the expected values, based on the existing logic.

❹ Using pandas' handy `assert_frame_equal()` test utility, we assert that the actual dataframe returned by our function matches our expected dataframe. This assertion will fail because we have yet to define `add_derived_title(df)`.

Coming back to *src/train.py*, we select the code block that we wish to refactor, and again we apply the *extract method* IDE shortcut, and name it as `add_derived_title()`. We can now import this function in our test. Now that the function is defined, the IDE's auto fix shortcuts (PyCharm: Alt/Option Enter, VS Code: Ctrl .) can help us import this function automatically in our test.

Run the test again and it'll pass. Run all the tests (including the characterization test) and if they're all passing, we can commit our changes in git. We've completed one full round of the refactoring cycle, and our codebase is several steps toward a better state!

The third refactoring: Abstract away implementation details (again).   Let's go through another round of the refactoring cycle. For step 1, we've identified a code block with several code smells:

```
df['FamilySize'] = df['SibSp'] + df['Parch'] + 1 ❶
df['IsAlone'] = 0
df.loc[df['FamilySize'] == 1, 'IsAlone'] = 1 ❷
df = df.drop(['Parch', 'SibSp', 'FamilySize'], axis=1)
```

❶ `SibSp` and `Parch` are poor column names (they stand for number of Siblings and Spouses, and Parents and Children, respectively).

❷ This line, along with the entire code block, exposes too many implementation details, and makes the code hard to read and understand.

Let's write a unit test and watch it fail:

```
def test_add_is_alone_column():
    df = pd.DataFrame({
        'SibSp': [0, 1, 2, 0, 0],
        'Parch': [0, 0, 5, 0, 1]
    })

    expected = pd.DataFrame({
        'SibSp':   [0, 1, 2, 0, 0],
        'Parch':   [0, 0, 5, 0, 1],
        'IsAlone': [1, 0, 0, 1, 0]
    })

    assert_frame_equal(expected, add_is_alone_column(df))
```

As usual, this new test fails (as it should). In the next step, we apply the *extract method* refactoring shortcut to extract this logic to a new function: add_is_alone_column(). We import this new function, ensure all tests are passing, and commit our changes. Hooray again!

Looking Back at What We've Achieved

After a few more iterations on the refactoring cycle, we got our codebase to a modular, readable, tested state. What was originally a 37-page Jupyter Notebook is now a fluent, well-abstracted, 30-line Python script composed of smaller, tested modules and functions:

```
def prepare_data_and_train_model():
passengers = pd.read_csv("./input/train.csv")

passengers = impute_nans(passengers,
categorical_columns=["Embarked"],
continuous_columns=["Fare", "Age"])
passengers = add_derived_title(passengers)
passengers = add_is_alone_column(passengers)
passengers = add_categorical_columns(passengers)
passengers = passengers.drop(["Parch", "SibSp", "Name",
"PassengerId", "Ticket", "Cabin"], axis=1)

y = passengers["Survived"]
X = passengers.drop("Survived", axis=1)
X_train, X_test, y_train, y_test = train_test_split(X, y)

model = train_model(RandomForestClassifier, X_train, y_train,
n_estimators=100)

return model, X_test, y_test

model, X_test, y_test = prepare_data_and_train_model()
```

You can read the training pipeline almost like a piece of English text. Let's have a go: In `prepare_data_and_train_model()`, we impute NaN values, add a "derived title" column, add an "is alone" column, add categorical columns, and we drop six columns that we don't need. We then split the data into a training set and test set, and train a model. That's it! Unlike the original notebook, this all fits in our head—thanks abstractions!

Along the way, we've improved our test coverage from 0% to ~90%. For any future changes or refactorings, we can run a single command and get feedback on the quality of our changes within a few seconds. Any accidental errors will be caught by tests during development, even before we commit our changes. By paying down our technical debt and doing some refactoring and testing, we've enabled ourselves to move faster.

Design principles that helped guide us

We've kept software design principles to the end of this section because they're more tangible when discussed in the context of the design improvements we've made to the problematic codebase in this chapter.

Perhaps unbeknownst to you, in performing the refactorings in this chapter, you've been applying several design principles! Let's go through each of them.

Separation of concerns.   Separation of concerns is a design principle that states that different aspects of a system should be separated and handled by different modules. Instead of creating a large system, we could break it down into smaller, independent modules. This can help us separate data preprocessing, feature extraction, model training, and inference into different modules, making it easier to understand, test, and add features to parts of the system.

In our refactoring, our preprocessing module is solely concerned with data transformations before model training. If we needed to add another type of behavior—such as saving or loading the model to disk—we could define it in another Python module concerned with persistence or disk I/O.

Open-closed design.   The open-closed principle (*https://oreil.ly/55S3c*) states that software entities should be open for extension but closed for modification. This means that a system's behavior can be extended without modifying its existing code.

In our refactoring, when we created `categorize_column()` to replace the following complex implementation detail of converting Age from a continuous variable (0 to 100) to a binned ordinal variable (0, 1, 2, 3, and 4), we later realized that this function could be easily extended (without modification) for a similar data transformation on the Fare column. `categorize_column()` was extensible—we can specify how many bins we want using the `num_bins` argument—without the need to modify the function's implementation:

```
# before refactoring
df.loc[ df['Age'] <= 16, 'Age'] = 0
df.loc[(df['Age'] > 16) & (df['Age'] <= 32), 'Age'] = 1
df.loc[(df['Age'] > 32) & (df['Age'] <= 48), 'Age'] = 2
df.loc[(df['Age'] > 48) & (df['Age'] <= 64), 'Age'] = 3
df.loc[(df['Age'] > 64, 'Age'] = 4


df.loc[ df['Fare'] <= 7.91, 'Fare'] = 0
df.loc[(df['Fare'] > 7.91) & (df['Fare'] <= 14.454), 'Fare'] = 1
df.loc[(df['Fare'] > 14.454) & (df['Fare'] <= 31), 'Fare']   = 2
df.loc[ df['Fare'] > 31, 'Fare'] = 3

# after refactoring.
df['AgeGroup'] = categorize_column(df['Age'], num_bins=5)
df['FareBand'] = categorize_column(df['Fare'], num_bins=4)
```

We extended the functionality we created for `Age` to also work with `Fare`, without needing to modify the function's implementation. That's the beauty of code that's designed to be open for extension and closed for modification (i.e., "open-closed").

Prefer obvious over obscure code (or explicit over implicit). John Ousterhout puts it well in his book *A Philosophy of Software Design* (Yaknyam Press): "In an obvious system, a developer can quickly understand how the existing code works and what is required to make a change. [...] The second cause of complexity is obscurity. Obscurity occurs when important information is not obvious."

We started this chapter with heaps of obscure code—e.g., nameless data transformations—that forced us to spend cognitive resources to understand the "how" to know "what" the code is doing. After refactoring, the well-named abstractions made the code's behavior much more obvious. For example, if ever we have a new requirement to handle a new honorific title (e.g., Reverend), we can easily find out where to implement the changes.

Code smells are symptoms of obscurity. Refactoring techniques (e.g., extract method, extract variable, move method, type hints) are tools to help improve clarity.

Reduce tight coupling (or couple to interfaces, not to implementation). Coupling refers to the degree to which different components within a system depend on each other. High coupling means that the components are tightly connected and changes in one component can have a significant impact on other components.

In ML systems, high coupling can lead to complex dependencies between the data preprocessing, feature extraction, model training, and inference modules, making the system difficult to maintain and scale.

Another closely related concept is cohesion. Cohesion refers to the degree to which the elements *within* a module or component are related to each other. High cohesion means that the elements within a module work together toward a common goal or purpose. In ML systems, high cohesion can be achieved by grouping related functionality, such as feature extraction and model training, into separate modules that work together toward a common goal.

Designing ML systems with low coupling and high cohesion can lead to a more modular and maintainable system. This can be achieved by breaking down the system into smaller, more manageable components, each with a well-defined purpose.

For example, let's say a column name (e.g., Name) was changed in our data store. In a tightly coupled solution, the coupling to the Name column (an *implementation* detail) will be littered all over our codebase and we would need to make the change all over the codebase (aka shotgun surgery [*https://oreil.ly/xnuQ0*]).

A better design would be to create an abstraction (e.g., PassengersDataFrame) around the dataset that, among other things, would encapsulate this implementation detail (["Name"]). The rest of our code would program to passengers_df.name (an *interface*). To handle this column name change, we would simply need to update it in one place—in the definition of PassengersDataFrame.

This design pattern—the Anti-corruption Layer (*https://oreil.ly/yiiAT*)—helps us contain all of the logic necessary to translate between the two components (our model training pipeline and the data store) in one place, and reduce coupling between our training pipeline and data store.

Simple design.   In a universe (and codebase) that tends toward chaos, simple design helps us keep complexity at a manageable level. When designing new logic to implement some new functionality, Kent Beck's four rules of software design (*https:// oreil.ly/6rqS3*) can help ensure a functional and simple design:

- Passes all the tests (existing and new)
- Reveals intention (states every intention important to the programmer)
- Has no duplicated logic
- Has the fewest possible classes and methods (removes anything that doesn't serve the three previous rules)

If anything gets in the way of these rules (e.g., premature abstraction, unnecessary design patterns, no design), consider whether there is a simpler and more suitable design. It always helps to have a chat with a teammate, someone from your community of practice, or with the internet (*https://oreil.ly/4IWbe*).

Extending Codebase Design Principles to System Design

So far in this chapter, we've discussed design principles, smells, and refactorings in the context of a single codebase, but what we've learned in this chapter is also applicable to system-level interactions between components of an ML solution, such as its upstream feature store, ML training pipeline, inference service, and data product.

In "Machine Learning: The High-Interest Credit Card of Technical Debt" (*https://oreil.ly/MrcRx*), the authors enumerate 14 examples of system-level technical debt, such as boundary erosion, entanglement, undeclared consumers, bloated data dependencies, dead experimental code paths, and pipeline jungles.

The design principles in this section can help us design better ML systems as well. For example, one common system-level smell is a tight coupling (or entanglement) between a model training pipeline and upstream data. If an upstream data producer changes a column name one day, our ML system could go down in production.

If we notice this smell, we can resolve it by *coupling to interfaces instead of implementations* (as described earlier). We can also avoid boundary erosion by having both producers and consumers define contract tests (*https://oreil.ly/wGyk4*) to detect breaking changes before they are rolled out into production.

As a takeaway exercise, can you identify one or more system-level smells in your project, sketch out what the issue is and why, and sketch a design improvement using one of these principles?

By this point in this chapter, you've learned to see alternate possibilities for messy codebases. They don't always have to be a "big ball of mud," but can be readable, maintainable, and even elegant solutions that are a joy to read and maintain. Now, let's turn to how you can create space in your day-to-day work to continuously and iteratively improve your team's solution design.

Technical Debt Management in the Real World

Work is like air—it fills up any vacuum faster than you can say "should we refactor that?" Delivery "pressure" (real or manufactured) and the social pressures to be a high-performing teammate that's always "getting things done" and "shipping stuff" divert time and energy from paying down technical debt.

In projects, we've seen two reactions to such pressures. In one extreme, there can be ML practitioners that focus on feature delivery without caring about anything else. Not only do they forgo any improvement opportunity, they'll likely take on more debt to move fast. On the other extreme, we may have zealots who digress too much on refactoring when working on a card, causing the scope to blow up and introducing significant delays to the cards they are working on.

The truth is that coding and refactoring are inherently social activities, and depend on sociostructural forces. ML practitioners who wish to manage technical debt effectively need to establish a social contract of desirable behavior within their team and create a shared understanding of problems and how to resolve them together.

In the next section, we'll look at techniques that we use to keep technical debt in check in our projects.

Technical Debt Management Techniques

Here are some techniques that we apply in our real-world projects to ensure that we balance effective technical debt management with product delivery.

Make debt visible

Making debt visible is a great first step for paying down the debt. A useful information radiator is a technical debt "wall." Having it all in one place allows us to cluster and order each debt along two axes: value and effort. As Figure 8-10 illustrates, this helps us to see the zones of *low-hanging fruits* (high value, low effort), *quick wins* (low value, low effort), *worthy investments* (high value, high effort), and no-go (low value, high effort). Shared visibility also nudges the team toward shared ownership in technical debt management.

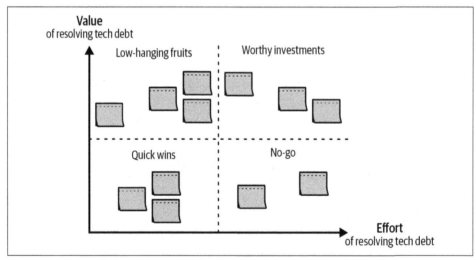

Figure 8-10. A technical debt wall helps to make debt visible and helps the team pay down the most important debt as part of ongoing delivery

In our experience, you can easily bootstrap a new technical debt wall by asking teammates to jot down any issues that they've observed in the course of their work over a few days, and then collectively put them on the technical debt wall in a short

20-minute team huddle. Thereafter, anyone who notices or creates new technical debt can add it to the wall asynchronously for the team's awareness.

In terms of execution, low-effort debt can be subsumed into an upcoming related story card. High-effort debt could have its own story card, like any other feature development cards, that is prioritized accordingly and added to upcoming sprints (see the next point on the 80/20 rule).

Over time, this practice helps the team identify waste—i.e., time wasted on paying interest—and eliminate waste by paying down technical debt incrementally and regularly.

The 80/20 rule

We have seen many teams squabble over whether to spend time refactoring or paying down technical debt. In our experience, an approximate 80/20 rule can help. For each story card, focus 80% of the time on delivering features and completing the story, and spend 20% of the time paying off some technical debt, so that the team can continue to deliver features at a sustainable and predictable pace.

If a particular technical debt task is high-effort and high-value, teams can consider applying the 80/20 rule at the sprint level. Focus 80% of the sprint's allocated effort on the sprint goal and delivering new features, and 20% (typically 1 or 2 cards) on paying down technical debt.

Both of these are practices that have worked well for us in the past to improve the quality of our solution. In our experience, frequent and iterative improvements yield better results than a "big bang refactoring" over many days or weeks.

Make it cheap and safe

We often find ourselves in one of two scenarios when dealing with technical debt. In the first, paying down technical debt is time-consuming (due to a lack of automated tests) and overwhelming (because the solution is too convoluted). In this scenario, teams want to do the right thing (they create "technical debt cards"), but these cards are often relegated deep in the graveyard of low-priority backlog cards never to be seen again, thereby reinforcing the vicious cycle of technical debt.

In the second scenario, refactoring is quick, low-cost, and safe—high test coverage tells us a refactoring worked as expected. In this scenario, it's easy to practice the scout rule and pay off debt as we go. Even if a technical debt requires a card of its own, a pair can tackle it in steady steps without getting mired in errors and troubleshooting.

For example, in a past project, we had an attribute in our codebase that was Title-Cased instead of a Pythonic snake_case. This attribute was referenced in multiple places in our solution, including the data ingestion pipeline, feature engineering, ML model training, ML model API, and in a few test cases. However, we could make this seemingly drastic change *in an hour's work* because our entire ML system had high test coverage (unit tests, integration tests, model quality tests) and we could use IDE shortcuts to help with renaming. When the refactoring was done, all the tests passed, we committed our changes, all the tests on the CI pipeline passed, and the change was deployed to production with no drama.

Demonstrate value of paying off technical debt

In a situation where technical debt work is repeatedly deprioritized, we can motivate the team or decision makers toward action by quantifying and demonstrating the value of reducing technical debt. For example, say we have an API endpoint that is untested. We can quantify the hours we spend on manually testing that endpoint during development and testing, for each pull request before they can be merged. Or we could do a daily or weekly count of the number of production alerts relating to that endpoint and the corollary time spent on resolving said alerts!

And when that technical debt is paid off, we can showcase what we gained as a team—e.g., hours saved from manual testing, reduction in production alerts, faster delivery cadence. This efficiency gain can be quantified and used to showcase how spending some time reducing technical debt (recall the 80/20 rule) directly contributes to more productive development cycles.

A Positive Lens on Debt: Systems Health Ratings

To scale these technical debt management practices above the level of an individual team and to the level of an organization or an enterprise, we need to somewhat formalize how teams regularly track their current state across key dimensions and make regular progress in suboptimal areas.

One useful technique in this regard is a regular (e.g., quarterly) Systems Health Rating (*https://oreil.ly/3qImZ*) exercise that all teams do to rate the health of the systems they own using simple and well-defined RAG (red, amber, green) classifications. This is a practice pioneered by REA Group (*https://oreil.ly/rTwMq*) and has been useful in governing and steering dozens of product engineering squads toward good practices.

As detailed in REA Group's article on Systems Health Rating (*https://oreil.ly/j3P0E*), evaluation dimensions are grouped into three categories: development, operations, and architecture. Each category contains several dimensions that can be summarized into three central questions:

Development

Can I set up the codebase, understand it, and confidently make changes?

Operations

Can I deploy the system, understand it and its dependencies, handle disaster recovery, and know if it's performing in line with established service-level agreements (SLAs)?

Architecture

Does the system encapsulate a single responsibility with a clearly defined interface within understood realms?

Taking the development category as an example, evaluation dimensions relate to the changeability of the system because easily changeable software enables a rapid pace of feature delivery and quick response to defects or vulnerabilities. Teams would rate each system they own along the following dimensions (RAG definitions excluded here for brevity):

- Code readability or quality score
- Development environment setup automation
- Presence and coverage of automated tests
- Presence and coverage of continuous integration (CI) pipelines
- Appropriate measures to protect customers, consumers, and data
- Design documentation and decision history documents

The "ML Test Score" paper (*https://oreil.ly/hGTTh*) describes a similar approach at Google, where teams use the ML Test Score rubric to measure and improve their systems over time. This was inspired by Google's Test Certified program (*https://oreil.ly/nR324*), which provided a scoring ladder for overall test robustness, and which was highly successful in incentivizing teams to adopt best practices.

As a takeaway exercise, consider creating a rubric for teams in your organization that are working on ML products. You could distill the practices in this book into a one-pager to cover key categories (e.g., ML, engineering, product, delivery, data) and for each category (e.g., engineering) enumerate the dimensions of a healthy system (e.g., automated test coverage, development environment setup automation). We've provided an example rubric in Table 8-1 as a starting point.

Define your rubric collectively with the relevant stakeholders (e.g., technical leads, architects, product managers), and give teams clear targets and paths for improvement. Start simple and evolve it over time.

Table 8-1. Example Systems Health Rating scorecard for a given ML system

	Definitions		
	Red *Falls significantly short of our expectations*	**Amber** *Partially meets our expectations*	**Green** *Meets our expectations*
Development			
Automated tests	No automated tests.	Some automated tests, but gaps in coverage necessitate nontrivial manual testing effort before production deployments.	Comprehensive automated tests with high coverage; minimal or no manual testing needed to release changes to production.
Dev setup automation	Limited automation and time-consuming manual dev environment setup. "Lead time to first push" on a new machine is more than one week.	Partial automation; setup process still involves several manual steps. "Lead time to first push" on a new machine is between one day and one week.	Automated, quick, and consistent dev environment setup. "Lead time to first push" on a new machine is less than one day.
CI/CD pipeline	CI/CD pipeline may exist, but lacks tests. Untested bugs and errors are hidden beneath illusory green builds.	CI/CD pipeline exists with some tests, but still require manual quality gates due to lack of comprehensive tests before and after deployments.	CI/CD pipeline contains comprehensive automated tests before and after automated deployments. Team can deploy any candidate green build to production on demand.
Code quality	No automated code quality checks.	Automated code quality checks exist, but major issues have been identified and are not resolved; code quality scores are low.	Automated code quality checks exist, and major code quality issues are resolved; code quality scores are high.
Operations			
Documentation	Insufficient or no documentation.	Documentation exists but is incomplete or outdated.	Documentation exists and is discoverable from organization's service catalog.
Monitoring: Service health and alerts	No monitoring; no visibility on any potential service errors or health issues.	Service health monitoring and alerts in place but alerts are frequent and dismissed without resolving root cause, leading to "alert fatigue."	Comprehensive monitoring in place; proactive issue detection and resolution, resulting in minimal alerts over time.
Logging	Inadequate or no logging; difficult to troubleshoot.	Some level of logging, but lacks essential details for troubleshooting issues. For distributed systems, lack of a correlation ID means logs need to be manually retrieved from multiple disparate sources.	Use of structured log formats and persistence in organization's centralized logging service; easy to inspect logs and troubleshoot issues. For distributed systems, easy to retrieve logs with a correlation ID.

	Definitions		
	Red *Falls significantly short of our expectations*	**Amber** *Partially meets our expectations*	**Green** *Meets our expectations*
Disaster recovery	No disaster recovery plan or data replication; data lost in the event of a disaster is irrecoverable.	Recovery time objective (RTO) and recovery point objective (RPO) (*https://oreil.ly/DO6rg*) defined. Disaster recovery approach identified but not implemented.	Disaster recovery plan and backups exist; team can follow steps to restore systems and data in line with RTO and RPO; quick recovery assured.
Secure delivery	Security not considered; vulnerabilities in delivery process.	System has been assessed based on secure delivery and secure architecture practices in the organization; key security issues identified but not resolved.	System is in line with secure delivery and secure architecture practices in the organization; key security issues are resolved.
Vulnerability scanning and dependency updates	No vulnerability scanning; software dependency risk profile is unknown.	Vulnerability scanning exists but significant vulnerabilities not resolved.	Regular and automated vulnerability scanning; tools exist to automatically create pull requests for dependency updates.
Data privacy	Inadequate or unclear data privacy measures; sensitive data at risk of exposure, noncompliance with regulations.	Clarity on relevant data privacy requirements; measures are partially implemented.	Robust data privacy measures in place; PII is masked in source systems so they're not propagated and persisted in other systems and environments (e.g., in logs).
FinOps	No visibility on the total cost (including cloud hosting, headcount, licensing costs) of systems or products owned by a team.	Team can manually find out the total cost of building and operating their tech estate.	Team follows organizational FinOps policies and tags cloud resources consistently. The total cost of a team's tech estate can be automatically attributed to the team and can be analyzed.
Architecture			
Well-encapsulated interfaces	System violates the principle of encapsulation and depends too much on internal implementation details of other systems, or reveals too much about its internal implementation.	Well-defined interfaces exist, but still tightly coupled to upstream and downstream systems.	System is well encapsulated with a well-defined interface; system is concerned with a single responsibility or business operation.
Loosely coupled architecture	No clear view on a system's architecture and responsibilities, and how it interacts with upstream and downstream dependencies.	Too many dependencies on other systems; unnecessary runtime coupling. Cannot release a change to production without depending on or being blocked by one or more teams.	Components are loosely coupled. A team owning a system can release an interface change without depending on other teams; downstream consumers can update to use new interface on their own cadence.

	Definitions		
	Red *Falls significantly short of our expectations*	**Amber** *Partially meets our expectations*	**Green** *Meets our expectations*
Error handling	System handles only "happy path" scenarios and fails at runtime when given unexpected data or scenarios.	Some error handling exists, but error messages are not clear or obvious for the intended downstream consumer.	Functionality gracefully degrades in the face of failure with clear and understandable messages.

With that, let's wrap up this chapter!

Conclusion: Make Good Easy

Many teams make the mistake of accumulating and neglecting a crushing amount of technical debt and production defects that eventually slow the production line to a virtual halt. Refactoring then becomes so daunting and risky that refactoring tasks always end up in the backlog graveyard, reinforcing the vicious cycle of pressure-haste-debt.

In response, it's common to see teams get trapped in analysis paralysis when it comes to technical debt. Add in our human propensity to status quo bias (*https://oreil.ly/KHOmh*), and we often end up doing nothing about technical debt. And ironically, doing nothing *is* doing something—the result being the ever-growing burden of technical debt.

To break this vicious cycle, you can employ the techniques and principles that we covered in this chapter in real-world projects to help to make good easy.

The second law of thermodynamics states that the universe tends toward disorder. Our codebases are no exception. We believe that the techniques you've learned in this chapter will help you, just as they've helped us, to effectively manage technical debt and continuously improve your codebases and systems. This will allow you and your team to get into the rhythm and culture of developing healthy systems, and to sustain your pace in delivering value.

In the next chapter, we'll turn our attention to MLOps and continuous delivery for ML (CD4ML).

## CHAPTER 9

MLOps and Continuous Delivery for ML (CD4ML)

That anxiety makes its appearance is the pivot upon which everything turns.

—Søren Kierkegaard, *The Concept of Anxiety*

It's 10:36 a.m. Dana is pairing with Ted, an infrastructure engineer, to deploy the new model her team has been working on for several months. The energy in the room is mixed with determination and anxiety—it's a new model for a high-profile release. They've been testing the model for three weeks, but the next hurdle—deployment to production—has typically been fraught with issues and numerous retries.

As they navigate the labyrinthine web of deployment scripts, configuration files, and infrastructure components, Dana couldn't help but feel that something was amiss. She wasn't confident that their test dataset was representative of what the model would be seeing in production. It didn't help that the complexity of the system was so overwhelming—the sheer number of moving parts made it difficult to get a sense of where things might go wrong.

It's 12:45 p.m. Dana and Ted completed the last of their deployment procedures 10 minutes ago, but the trickling stream of alerts is a cruel reminder that something has gone awry.

It's 7:10 p.m. After hours of troubleshooting, a fix has finally been deployed. Dana and Ted exhale relief and finally go home, exhausted.

A week has passed, and one Tuesday morning Dana hears a scrape-triple-knock on her Slack. A message at 8:45 a.m.—it is Sarah from product analytics. She informs Dana that online loan applications have dropped by 44% since last Thursday's release. Dana pings Ted right away and they dive into the logs, desperate to understand what is causing the sudden downturn.

After a thorough investigation, they realize that a key feature that the model depends on—loan type—is set as an optional field in the UI. Many users omitted this detail, which caused the new model to return unreasonable results, leading users to give up on their application midway.

Dana's heart sank as she realized the gravity of the situation—the months of work that her team put into this high-profile release had gone down the drain.

The emotions we feel when delivering ML solutions are useful signals that we should pay attention to. For example, we may feel tedium and general "ugh" when doing repetitive manual testing for every pull request or production deployment. We may experience anxiety when deploying a large set of changes in code and data to production once every two months—so much has changed; who knows what could go wrong in this production deployment?

In this chapter, we'll describe two complementary schools of thought that help teams reliably and iteratively develop, test, deploy, monitor, and improve ML models. The first—MLOps—you have probably heard of. The second—CD4ML—may be new to you. By the end of the chapter, however, you should understand the role of both. Practiced together, MLOps and CD4ML reduce risks of failures during deployment and in production, time-to-feedback, cognitive load, and general stress around operating models in production.

MLOps is a fast-advancing field. At the time of writing, there were more than 20 books (*https://oreil.ly/NSYF4*) and even more libraries and platforms in the MLOps space. These advances in MLOps tooling and practices are great, yet in our experience, they are also insufficient. MLOps literature and practitioners tend to focus on "ops-y" components (e.g., infrastructure, model deployment, monitoring, tools, platforms), while neglecting the equally important aspects of software engineering and sociocultural practices (e.g., test automation, deploying early and often, trunk-based development, continuous improvement).

CD4ML practices address these latter aspects and help teams ensure that changes to their software and ML models are continuously tested and monitored for quality. Any changes in code, data, or ML models that satisfy comprehensive quality checks can be confidently deployed to production at any time. In our experience, CD4ML is an effective risk-control mechanism to detect issues and failures in an ML system before production deployments (through tests) and after production deployments (through monitoring).

Research from the book *Accelerate* (IT Revolution Press) shows that continuous delivery practices enable organizations to achieve better technical and business performance by helping teams deliver value reliably and respond to changes in market demands more nimbly. In our experience practicing CD4ML when working with ML teams, we've seen great results[1] in velocity, responsiveness, cognitive load, satisfaction, and product quality.

To that end, this chapter will:

- Establish the basic building blocks of MLOps
- Outline traps that teams often encounter when implementing MLOps
- Complement existing MLOps literature with CD4ML principles and practices
- Explore how CD4ML supports ML governance and Responsible AI

If you're already familiar with MLOps techniques, feel free to skip the "MLOps 101" section and jump straight into MLOps smells and how CD4ML helps teams address these issues. Now that we've set the scene, let's jump into the fundamentals of MLOps and common MLOps traps that teams encounter.

MLOps: Strengths and Missing Puzzle Pieces

In our experience, CD4ML complements MLOps well by adding a set of principles and practices that help ML practitioners shorten feedback loops and improve reliability of ML systems (see Figure 9-1). In this section, we'll deliver a quick overview of MLOps, and look at some common smells that suggest gaps in feedback mechanisms on a model's path to production. In the next section, we'll look at how CD4ML addresses these gaps.

---

1 CD4ML has helped us accelerate the delivery of ML products. The following case studies provide more detail: "Staying Nimble, Delivering Transformative Fintech at Speed" (*https://oreil.ly/PC7os*), "The Journey to Build Australia's Most Accurate Property Valuation Tool" (*https://oreil.ly/MsnVj*), and "Getting Smart: Applying Continuous Delivery to Data Science to Drive Car Sales" (*https://oreil.ly/2ZF4-*).

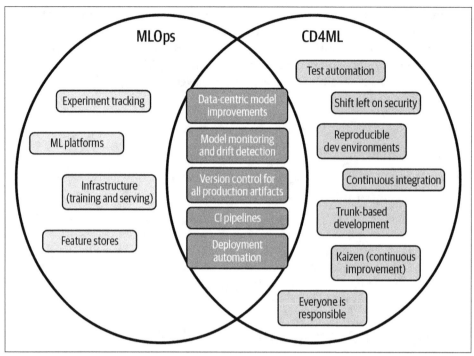

Figure 9-1. CD4ML complements MLOps well by adding a set of principles and practices that help ML practitioners shorten feedback loops and improve reliability of ML systems

MLOps 101

MLOps is an ML engineering culture and practice aimed at streamlining the development, deployment, and management of ML models. Practicing MLOps means that you automate and monitor key components used in the training and deployment of an ML system, including the model, data, and software. It is an interdisciplinary field that combines elements of ML, infrastructure engineering, software engineering, and data engineering to create a more efficient and robust workflow for ML projects.

There are many articles enumerating the technical building blocks of MLOps (e.g., Google's "MLOps: Continuous Delivery and Automation Pipelines in Machine Learning" [*https://oreil.ly/Z31qn*], Thoughtworks' "CD4ML Framework" [*https://oreil.ly/3t0Vh*], INNOQ's "MLOps Principles" [*https://oreil.ly/HuxKJ*]), and they generally converge on a canonical architecture for supervised learning models, as depicted in Figure 9-2.

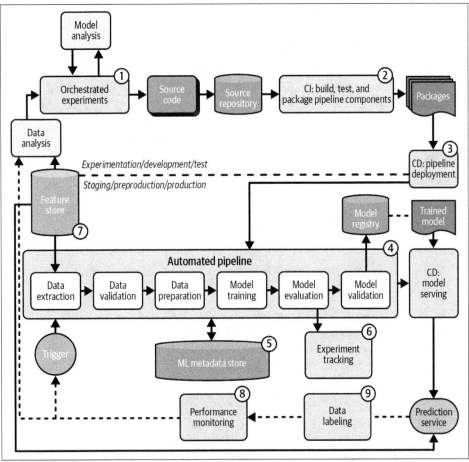

Figure 9-2. A typical MLOps architecture, including technical components and flow of tasks and actions (source: adapted from an image in "MLOps: Continuous Delivery and Automation Pipelines in Machine Learning" [https://oreil.ly/Z31qn] by Google Cloud, used under CC BY 4.0 [https://oreil.ly/x-mKJ])

Let's go through the key components of an MLOps architecture:

1. Scalable training infrastructure

A scalable training infrastructure refers to large-scale and ephemeral compute resources that are right-sized for an ML model's training workload. While this could involve complex implementation details and many hundreds of lines of YAML or IaC (infrastructure-as-code) configuration, a good ML platform or tool will abstract away this complexity and provide a simple way for ML practitioners to provision large-scale compute resources on-demand without needing to tinker with training infrastructure.

An important characteristic to call out here is experimental-operational symmetry of training infrastructure. This means ensuring that the development environment is consistent and production-like. This symmetry ensures that what works during experimentation will work during large-scale training in production, and simplifies troubleshooting and development in general.

Tools include: Metaflow, Ray, Databricks, and various cloud services (e.g., AWS SageMaker, Azure ML, Google Vertex AI).

2. CI/CD pipelines (with tests, of course!)

Continuous integration and continuous delivery (CI/CD) pipelines are essential for automating the process of testing and deploying ML models. When done properly, they help to verify the quality of every code push and automate the deployment of code changes if all prior tests pass. They enable teams to iterate rapidly while maintaining confidence in the system's stability and performance.

Most ML teams that we've seen don't practice CI, even though they have a CI pipeline (the following Note defines exactly what qualifies as CI and CD). As we explained in Chapter 5, CI/CD without tests is a contradiction in terms. For a CI/CD pipeline to provide useful and fast feedback to ML practitioners, it must perform automated tests—such as the metrics tests and behavioral tests that we detailed in Chapter 6—and automated deployment, minimally to a preproduction environment, on every code push.

Tools include: GitHub Actions, BuildKite, CircleCI, TeamCity, Jenkins, and various cloud resources.

Let's define exactly what qualifies as continuous integration (CI), continuous delivery (CD), and continuous deployment:

Continuous integration (CI)
This is a practice that encourages developers to frequently *merge their code changes onto the main branch* (aka trunk-based development [*https://oreil.ly/949Mn*]), ideally multiple times a day. Every code commit is then automatically built and tested to catch and report any errors quickly. Nothing is deployed.

Continuous delivery (CD)
This extends CI by ensuring that the code changes are not only tested but also prepared for release to production. Deployables (e.g., an ML model service) are deployed to a preproduction environment, with post-deployment tests. If all tests pass up till this last stage, we're confident that this release candidate can be deployed to production at any time.

Continuous deployment
This practice goes one step further than continuous delivery—if post-deployment tests after deployment to a preproduction environment pass, the deployable is automatically deployed to production, without human intervention. This requires a mature testing and monitoring setup to ensure that any issue or failure in the production environment is caught and fixed quickly.

3. *Deployment automation*
In MLOps, automated deployments help reduce manual intervention, human errors, and inconsistencies, while also accelerating the development and deployment process. It enables teams to streamline their workflows, making them more efficient and reliable.

Tools include: Seldon, TensorFlow Serving, TorchServe, and various cloud providers.

4. *"As code" everything*
Adopting an "as code" approach in MLOps involves treating all aspects of the infrastructure, configuration, deployments, and monitoring as code. This practice allows for better version control, reproducibility, automation, and collaboration among team members.

5. Artifact stores

Artifact stores such as model registries, container registries, and metadata stores persist various artifacts generated during the ML lifecycle. These stores enable easy tracking, versioning, and retrieval of artifacts such as models, data, and metadata. This helps to facilitate collaboration, traceability, reproducibility, and auditability across projects.

Tools include: Metaflow, Zen ML, and various cloud providers.

6. Experiment tracking

Experiment tracking tools help ML practitioners manage and compare the numerous experiments that teams invariably run when iterating on ML models. They enable ML practitioners to track model performance metrics, hyperparameters, and other relevant information, which gives them valuable feedback on the effect of their changes. This feedback helps them identify the most promising models and, when organized well, can accelerate the development process.

Tools include: Weights and biases, MLFlow, and AWS SageMaker Experiments.

7. Feature stores or feature platforms (with data versioning)

Feature stores serve as a centralized repository for feature engineering, storing preprocessed features used in training and inference stages. Data versioning in feature stores enables the tracking and management of different data versions, ensuring reproducibility and consistency in ML models. By using feature stores, teams can share and reuse features across projects without needing to duplicate feature processing logic in multiple places wherever features are consumed.

Tools include: AWS SageMaker Feature Store, Feast, Tecton, and Feathr.

8. Monitoring in production

As we discussed in Chapter 6, monitoring in production can and should happen at multiple levels. The first level (service health) applies to ML models that are deployed as a web API and involves monitoring service-level health metrics that matter to the team (e.g., HTTP status codes, errors, latency). The model service should also produce well-structured logs to provide teams with valuable insights into system behavior.

The next level of monitoring (model health) involves tracking and evaluating key performance metrics, data drift, and model degradation over time. (Refer to the section "Learn from Production by Closing the Data Collection Loop" on page 187 for a definition of types of model drift.) This enables teams to assess their real-world performance and identify potential issues with the deployed model. To monitor the model's real-world performance, we need to add new labels to the new predictions that the model is making in production (more on this in the next point).

The final level of monitoring (business health) involves tracking business metrics relevant to our ML model. This varies according to the specific outcome that the ML model is intended to influence, but could involve metrics such as user engagement, sales, conversions, and number of subscribers.

Tools include: Alibi Detect, Evidently, Giskard, NannyML, New Relic, Splunk and various cloud providers.

9. *Scalable data-labeling mechanisms*

The final and arguably most important component of any MLOps stack is a scalable data-labeling mechanism. By *scalable*, we mean techniques where user interaction signals, expert judgments, natural labels, etc., can be applied to many data points, or to just the most important data points for model performance, rather than labeling every point individually and indiscriminately. This enables data-centric model improvements and enables teams to retrain their model regularly with better data, to keep up with a nonstationary world.

The key challenge is that teams often face a bottleneck in labeling large volumes of data, which is a tedious, time-consuming and labor-intensive task. In addition to active learning and representation learning, one technique that we've found to be effective in addressing this challenge is weak supervision (*https://oreil.ly/yNoND*), which can reduce annotation time by 10x to 100x compared to unassisted hand labeling, allowing teams to create large labeled datasets quickly.

Tools include: Snorkel, Cleanlab, and various cloud providers.

Guide to Evaluating ML Platforms

The MLOps landscape has been changing rapidly in the past few years, with an overwhelming variety of tools emerging. Some tools specialize in one (or more) areas in model training, deployment, monitoring, and data management, while other ML platforms (e.g., AWS SageMaker, Google Vertex AI, and Azure ML) are all-in-one.

Naturally, ML practitioners often grapple with questions like: How can I choose the best platform among so many? Which one(s) are suitable for the problems that I'm solving? Do I need an ML platform? What costs are my teams paying when we do *not* have the right ML platform for our needs?

There are some great resources that lay out considerations and parameters to help teams identify a suitable ML platform for their needs. One such vendor-agnostic resource is the *Guide to Evaluating ML Platforms* (*https://oreil.ly/6nov4*), which we have used in various teams.

And while we're on the topic of platforms, we find that "platform" is one of those fuzzy words that can mean different things to different people. We find that having a clear definition helps teams differentiate between good and not-so-good platforms,

---

and identify which ones suit their needs in the next stage of their ML maturity journey.

So here's a practical definition of platforms from Evan Bottcher (*https://oreil.ly/MhC3P*): A digital platform is a foundation of self-service APIs, tools, services, knowledge, and support, arranged as a compelling product. The purpose of platforms is to *enable multiple autonomous delivery teams* to *deliver product features at a higher pace*, with reduced dependency and coordination among teams.

If you find that your teams are repeatedly reinventing tools (e.g., to train, deploy, monitor models; or to manage and label data) or doing repetitive undifferentiated labor (e.g., ad hoc provisioning and deprovisioning of large-scale training infrastructure), it's probably time to find a suitable ML platform. Or perhaps you already have an ML platform but it's not helping your teams deliver product features at a higher pace. If that's the case, then perhaps it's worth reassessing your ML platform. We'll further explore the organizational role of ML platforms and key implementation considerations in Chapter 11.

Now that we've covered the basic building blocks of MLOps, let's look at some common mistakes that teams make when implementing MLOps tools and practices.

Smells: Hints That We Missed Something

While the lay of the MLOps land from 10,000 feet looks logical and straightforward, teams building ML systems on the ground often find themselves getting ensnared in a complex terrain with many moving parts.

If each MLOps component is a waypoint in a journey, teams either completely miss out on a critical waypoint (e.g., they don't have a scalable data-labeling mechanism), or they stop at the right waypoint but miss what they were meant to do there (e.g., implementing CI/CD pipelines without automated tests). This oversight can lead to detrimental consequences, including model quality issues in production and unwarranted friction that slows down experimentation and model improvements.

In this section, we'll use the concept of "smells" (i.e., signals that suggest deeper problems) that we introduced in Chapter 7 to illustrate some common mistakes that we've seen in how teams apply MLOps practices. This sets the stage for the next section, where we explore how CD4ML complements MLOps and helps teams overcome these challenges.

MLOps smell 1: CI/CD pipelines with no tests

As we mentioned in Chapter 6, CI/CD pipelines without tests is a contradiction in terms—how can we continuously integrate (CI) code to the main branch if we don't have automated tests to check for errors? Yet it's common to see teams with this smell—possibly because ML engineers know how to set up CI pipelines and data scientists know how to train and evaluate models, but not all teams have worked out how to bridge both practices to automate model-evaluation procedures.

The consequences are manifold. First, bugs and errors easily slip into the codebase and even into production. Second, we end up wasting significant amounts of time testing for or fixing errors. Third, even if we've optimized other parts of our CI/CD pipeline (e.g., model deployment in 30 seconds), the testing and quality assurance step will remain a bottleneck (e.g., manual testing takes a few hours, or whenever we have time to do it, which then stretches the bottleneck out to days or weeks).

Fourth and finally, the lack of automated quality checks nudges us out of the main branch and into feature branches, because no one wants to: (i) accidentally commit defects or issues into the main branch, or (ii) manually and comprehensively test every commit. In our experience, this deferred integration (as opposed to continuous integration to the main branch we defined earlier) often causes merge conflicts when team members finally merge their branch after days or weeks of work. We have never met a single person who likes merge conflicts and unnecessarily wasting time and cognitive effort resolving merge conflicts.

MLOps smell 2: Infrequent model deployments to production or preproduction environments

Infrequent deployments to production and preproduction environments suggest that a team is not confident in the reliability and quality of changes (in code, data, and model).

Infrequent deployments increase the likelihood of deployment failures. For example, deploying 100 commits (e.g., to a preproduction environment) every four weeks is very different from deploying five commits every day, even though the net number of commits is the same. In the first scenario, if a deployment fails, you have 100 potential suspects and 4,950 pairwise interactions between suspects, which is far more difficult to debug than five (and 10 pairwise interactions). This is true for both production and preproduction environments.

That's the value of having small batch sizes. David Farley and Jez Humble put it well in *Continuous Delivery* (Addison-Wesley Professional): "The earlier you catch defects, the cheaper they are to fix." Smaller batch sizes allow you to catch defects earlier. In addition, infrequent deployments can hinder the team's ability to respond to user feedback, fix issues, or introduce new features, ultimately impacting the overall responsiveness of the team and ML product.

MLOps smell 3: Data in production goes to waste

Teams often throw away the data that a model generates in production (e.g., requests and predictions)—data that could be used to improve their ML models. This can occur due to lack of proper data collection, processing, and labeling mechanisms. As a result, teams throw away a valuable feedback mechanism that can enhance the performance of the ML system.

Failing to process and leverage this new data from production for subsequent training can lead to models becoming outdated or less accurate over time, as they may not account for shifts in user behavior, changes in the environment, or emerging trends. Moreover, it can hinder the team's ability to identify and address potential issues or biases in the models, which negatively impacts the ML product's user experience in the real world.

In contrast, when teams design their ML system to close the data collection loop, they create a flywheel effect (*https://oreil.ly/h-h6l*), where more usage of the model results in more data, which in turn leads to further refinements and improvements in the model.

MLOps smell 4: X is another team's responsibility

When you hear the phrase, "X (e.g., deployment, integration, customer experience, security) is another team's responsibility" in one form or another, it's usually a smell that suggests a number of deeper underlying problems. The first issue relates to team structure: The team wasn't set up correctly and is lacking some key competency (e.g., deployment, integration, customer experience, security). To move fast, a team should have these core competencies, or be supported by enabling teams for cross-cutting competencies such as security, as we will explore in Chapter 11. This will allow the team to operate autonomously without depending on (and risk being blocked by) other teams.

The second issue relates to culture: X is someone else's problem. We often detect the "someone else's problem" mindset at the boundaries between teams, which indicates that both issues—structure and culture—are often mutually reinforcing. This mindset hinders collaboration and creates an environment where issues are left unaddressed, resulting in a suboptimal MLOps process and potentially compromising the quality and reliability of the ML models. This runs contrary to the DevOps mindset, which is focused on breaking down the wall between Dev and Ops (see Figure 9-3) and now ML and Ops, so that ML folk (e.g., data scientists) and operations folk (e.g., ML engineers) pair to solve difficult challenges (e.g., automated quality assurance for ML models) and productionize reliable ML systems.

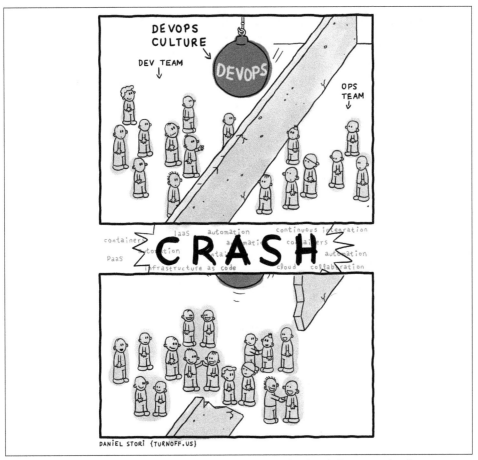

Figure 9-3. The DevOps culture seeks to break down the divide between development teams and operations teams (source: "DevOps Is Not a Role" by Daniel Stori [https:// oreil.ly/CH_Q8], used under CC BY-NC-SA 4.0 [https://oreil.ly/-MSwI])

By this point, you understand the fundamentals of MLOps and have seen, and perhaps identified with, these four gaps of MLOps—lack of automated tests, infrequent deployments, wasted production data, and "someone else's problems." Let's now look at how the principles and practices of continuous delivery (CD) complement MLOps and mitigate these issues to help teams deliver reliably.

Continuous Delivery for Machine Learning

What if we told you that there was a way to get changes of all types—including new models, new features, and bug fixes—to production and into the hands of users, safely, quickly, and reliably? Well, that is exactly what continuous delivery (CD) helps us achieve.

In this section, we will go through:

- Benefits of CD4ML (the "why")
- Principles of CD (the "what")
- Practices and building blocks of CD4ML (the "how")

Let's begin by digging into the "why."

Benefits of CD4ML

Fully practicing CD4ML yields outcomes that virtually all ML teams desire. Let's look at three key benefits:

Shorter cycle times (between an idea and shipping it to customers in production)
CD4ML enables faster development and deployment cycles. By automating the processes involved in building, testing, and deploying ML models, teams can reduce the time and effort required in tedious, undifferentiated labor, such as repetitive manual testing. In our experience, this has helped us accelerate the time-to-market for changes of any kind, allowing teams to quickly respond to evolving business needs or market conditions.

Lower defect rates
Another advantage of CD4ML is improved model quality and performance. With comprehensive automated tests (as described in Chapters 5 and 6) at each stage in the path to production, ML teams can quickly detect and fix any issues or bugs in their models before deployment. This enables them to ensure quality and reliability in their ML applications. The practice of monitoring model performance in production also allows teams to detect any degradation in model quality as it happens and make necessary updates or retrain models as needed.

CD4ML enables teams to "fail fast and fail loudly." This ability to detect issues—through tests or monitoring—is especially important in ML systems because, unlike typical software applications, ML models are prone to silent errors. Such errors might not immediately crash the system or cause noticeable failures, but they can cause mispredictions that adversely affect the user experience. The result is that *users* will be the ones detecting and experiencing quality issues in production for an extended period of time until the issues are detected and resolved by the team.

Faster recovery times (should something go wrong in production)
By embracing the practice of small, frequent deployments, teams can more easily triage and resolve problems. With an automated and streamlined deployment process, it becomes easier to roll back to a previous stable version or deploy fixes, minimizing downtime and potential damage to the user experience or the organization's reputation.

In *Accelerate*, the authors present the findings of four years of research on software development practices to answer the question: What factors and practices set high-performing technology organizations apart from organizations with poorer business and financial performance?

They present insights based on data collected from thousands of organizations and highlight the key practices that drive excellence in software delivery. One of the key findings is a set of 24 key capabilities (*https://oreil.ly/BJhd7*) that drive improvements in software delivery performance in a statistically significant way. These 24 capabilities can be grouped into five categories:

- Continuous delivery (the focus of this chapter)
- Architecture
- Product and process (see Chapter 2)
- Lean management and monitoring (see Chapter 11)
- Culture (see Chapters 10 and 11)

While this empirical study hasn't been replicated for ML teams yet at the time of writing, our experience working with teams to deliver ML solutions corroborate the authors' conclusions.

A Crash Course on Continuous Delivery Principles

Now that we've seen the benefits of CD4ML, let's delve into the core principles that guide CD practices. There are five principles at the heart of CD (*https://oreil.ly/W-AXL*):

Principle 1: Build quality into the product
It's much more cost-effective to address issues and defects if they are detected as soon as they are introduced. Identifying defects later in the process through inspection methods (e.g., manual testing) is time-intensive and demands significant triage efforts. As stated in "14 Points for Management" (*https://oreil.ly/JsKu9*) by Lean pioneer Edward Deming, we should "cease dependence on

inspection to achieve quality. Eliminate the need for inspection on a mass basis *by building quality into the product in the first place."*

Preferably, we want to detect defects before they are even committed, by running automated tests. For ML, this can be achieved by writing automated tests for software, ML models, and data. Having an ML platform that enables ML practitioners to train models on-demand on scalable ephemeral infrastructure and run tests thereafter can help to obviate the need to commit and push code to know if something works.

By creating mechanisms to detect and resolve issues as soon as they appear, teams save effort and reduce context-switching between creating solutions and fixing broken stuff. Recall that in Chapter 2, we go even further upstream, introducing methods to catching defects in *requirements* before we even write a line of code.

Principle 2: Work in small batches

In the 1990s and even into the 2010s, it was common for software to be handed off between multiple teams (from a team of business analysts to architects to developers to testers to operations) so that it could be deployed to production. In these cases, batch sizes were incredibly large—this is typically weeks and months of work before anything is deployed to production. (We still see this happening in some ML teams today!)

When continuous delivery was introduced circa 2010, it enabled teams to ship work in smaller batch sizes. Working in smaller batches offers numerous advantages, such as reduced time-to-feedback, reduced cognitive load, easier problem triage and remediation, and improved efficiency and sense of progress.

Along the path to production, we instrument multiple quality gates to give us rapid and comprehensive feedback on the quality of our changes. In the ML context, quality gates include automated tests (for software, data, and model), deployments to preproduction environments, post-deployment tests, and other fitness functions that we described in Chapter 6. When the quality gates are comprehensive, we can confidently deploy any green build (triggered by code changes or scheduled training runs) to production.

Principle 3: Automation—computers perform repetitive tasks, people solve problems

Automation is a critical component for streamlining and optimizing the process of delivering ML solutions. By automating repetitive tasks such as linting, testing, and deploying code, teams reduce the amount of manual intervention needed and consequently the amount of human error. This significantly improves efficiency and reliability.

Automated processes can also shorten feedback loops, enabling developers to identify and fix issues more quickly. This allows teams to focus on higher-level problem solving and innovation, rather than being bogged down by tedious tasks.

Principle 4: Relentlessly pursue continuous improvement

As you may recall from Chapter 1, continuous improvement (or *Kaizen* in Japanese) is one of the five principles of Lean. The goal of Kaizen is to help organizations and teams identify and eliminate waste, thereby improving the flow of value.

In our experience, the team's mindset and actions—to pragmatically pursue collective continuous improvement—are more important than the forum (e.g., retrospectives, tech debt huddles, standups). Without the Kaizen mindset, suggestions for improvement are almost always procrastinated to accommodate other priorities, and team members can often give up trying.

Principle 5: Everyone is responsible

In high-performing ML teams, nothing is "somebody else's problem." In contrast, low-performing teams often exude behavior that implies beliefs such as "deployability is not my concern," or "we don't have to worry about these vulnerable dependencies warnings because security is not an area of focus for our team."

While the will and desire to do the right thing is important, individuals and teams can quickly run out of steam and lose hope when they're not supported with the right capabilities. Remember our earlier point on how structure and culture are mutually reinforcing? We can use the appropriate team structure (e.g., a cross-functional team) to build a practice and culture of developing and deploying reliable ML solutions. Everyone—data scientists, ML engineers, data engineers, platform engineers, product owners, security specialists, domain experts, etc.—works together to deliver reliable ML solutions, rather than optimizing for what's best for their team or department.[2]

Now that we've established the five principles of CD, let's now delve into the supporting practices for each principle. Together, these practices help ML teams ship reliable ML solutions to production early and often and enjoy their benefits.

---

2 While some roles (e.g., data scientists, ML engineers, product owners) can often be in a vertical cross-functional team, some other roles (e.g., security specialists) tend to be situated in a horizontal enabling team. We will discuss these nuances and team shape options in Chapter 11 when we cover ML team topologies.

Building Blocks of CD4ML: Creating a Production-Ready ML System

In this section, we will describe the CD practices that help teams reduce waste and improve flow when delivering ML models. For the impatient, Table 9-1 provides an overview of these practices.

Table 9-1. Mapping practices for ML teams to CD principles

CD principle	Supporting practices in ML teams
1. Build quality into the product	1.1 Test automation 1.2 Shift left on security
2. Work in small batches	2.1 Use version control for all production artifacts 2.2 Practice pair programming 2.3 Implement continuous integration (CI) 2.4 Apply trunk-based development
3. Automation: Computers perform repetitive tasks, people solve problems	3.1 Create reproducible development environments for developing models 3.2 Automate deployments (minimally to a preproduction environment) 3.3 Monitor in production
4. Relentlessly pursue continuous improvement	4.1 Practice Kaizen (identify and act on opportunities for improvement)
5. Everyone is responsible	5.1 Adopt the appropriate team topologies for your organization

Build quality into the product

Let's look at the practices that help teams build quality into their ML solutions.

Test automation. We've covered the why, what, and how of testing ML systems extensively in Chapters 5 and 6. A key point we made is that without comprehensive automated tests, teams *cannot* practice CI and CD. (We elaborate on why in the section "Implement continuous integration (CI)" on page 288.)

Without tests that run automatically on every code push or every model training run, ML practitioners are forced to take on the burden of regression testing, which then diverts energy from other higher-value work, before any code change can be merged to the main branch (or model deployed to production). If they don't, teams roll the dice and run the risk of introducing defects into the codebase and into production, which they then have to fix later whenever the defect is detected. As we've discussed before, it's much more cost-effective to detect such issues early through comprehensive automated tests.

Shift left on security. Shifting left on security means incorporating security measures early and throughout the ML development process, rather than considering them as an afterthought or a final checkpoint before deployment. This proactive approach helps teams preempt and defend against vulnerabilities and security issues before they become deeply embedded in the system, making them more costly and difficult to address later.

This practice can include:

- Conducting security reviews and threat modeling (*https://oreil.ly/0p1V_*) of ML solutions including involving the information security (InfoSec) team early on in the process of design and delivery
- Reviewing, identifying, and mitigating failure modes of an ML model (*https://oreil.ly/gFDG1*) (e.g., adversarial attacks, data poisoning)
- Establishing access controls to prevent unauthorized use
- Automating the detection and updating of vulnerable dependencies (see Chapter 4)
- Including automated security tests (*https://oreil.ly/TK7xZ*) as part of the automated testing suite on the CI pipeline
- Supporting your organization's security function, for example by having security champions (*https://oreil.ly/BX9Ry*)

Beyond ML, there are also critical security practices for data:

- In terms of data privacy, teams must anonymize personal identifiable information (PII) so that they are not at risk of accessing it.
- In terms of data security, teams must encrypt and establish access control on production data.

Implementing security measures early can prevent costly and damaging security breaches down the line. Securing ML systems is also not a static destination. As malicious actors find new ways to compromise ML (*https://oreil.ly/Edc3M*), teams need to stay updated with ongoing recommendations from the cybersecurity (*https://oreil.ly/eRHR1*), MLSecOps (*https://oreil.ly/oofV4*), and DevSecOps (*https://oreil.ly/w6Exh*) communities.

Work in small batches

As we established in the previous section, working in smaller batches brings numerous benefits: reduced time-to-feedback, reduced cognitive load, easier problem triage and remediation, and improved efficiency and sense of progress.

Beyond just appropriate task sizing and scoping—which is important—the following practices help ML practitioners ship value in small batches.

Practice pair programming.   Pair programming involves two people writing code together to complete a user story or task. When we pair program, instead of working solo and having code reviews via pull requests, we shorten the feedback cycle from days (waiting and back-and-forth on pull request reviews) to minutes (feedback from your teammate as you are pairing).

Pair programming is also more than just writing code—it involves collaboration, planning, problem-solving, discussions, and knowledge sharing. The result is the cocreation of better solutions and socialization of preferred practices within the team.

Pair programming is a common practice in the software engineering world and is also practiced—albeit to a lesser extent—in ML teams. It's not uncommon to see data scientists go off on their own to work on something for a period of time. During that time, there are probably many assumptions that they make alone, questions that they didn't ask, things that they weren't aware of. In one anecdote, we worked with a data scientist who was working on a user story for three weeks, and finally the PR was rejected because the code was too messy, had no tests, and slowed down the training pipeline too much. What a frustrating waste of time that was for the data scientist!

Pair programming has many well-documented benefits:

Knowledge sharing

As two individuals work together on a problem, they share and learn from each other's approaches and techniques, which spreads local pockets of knowledge and best practices across the team. This is especially beneficial in ML teams where data scientists, ML engineers, and data engineers can learn from each other's expertise, leading to more learning and higher-quality solutions.

This also helps to increase the team's bus factor (*https://oreil.ly/pB9mS*)—the number of team members that, if they get "hit by a bus" (or win the lottery), will cause a project to slow to a stall due to lack of contextual knowledge. Pair programming increases the bus factor above one—thereby allowing team members to go on holidays without needing to stress about working on vacation or blocking the team's work.

Fast feedback

When we pair—and have intentional pairing—we get feedback on our code in minutes. This immediate feedback can help catch potential issues or bugs early, leading to higher-quality code and reduced debugging time. This is in contrast to getting feedback via pull requests—which, as an aside, is arguably a reliance on inspection rather than automated quality assurance. Pull requests tend to take days or even weeks before they're ready for review, and another few hours or days of low-context back-and-forth between teammates before it can be merged.

Best of both worlds: high-level and detailed thinking

When pairing, the navigator focuses more on high-level problem solving and design, while the driver focuses on low-level implementation details and execution. By combining two minds, teams can leverage the strengths of both individuals and reduce blind spots.

Fast onboarding of new team members

New team members can quickly learn the codebase, the team's working practices, and tools by pairing with more experienced team members. This accelerates the onboarding process and helps new members to contribute effectively more quickly. This is much better than reading reams of documentation or watching recordings as a mode of onboarding.

Staying focused

With pair programming, it's harder for individuals to get distracted or go off track. The social nature of the activity keeps both programmers engaged, ensuring more focused and efficient work.

There are several techniques that help teams pair program effectively, such as driver-navigator, ping-pong, and "Dreyfus squared." We encourage you to read about the benefits and mechanics of pair programming for you and your team in the brief article "On Pair Programming" (*https://oreil.ly/VIoSD*).

Use version control for all production artifacts. Version control of code, data, and artifacts (e.g., configuration, intermediate data, trained models) helps teams with reproducibility, traceability, auditability, and debugging. In our experience, when we can access these intermediate and final artifacts, we can reproduce past results and perform various tasks, such as understanding the impact of changes in data on model performance. We can "summon" (or technically speaking, deserialize) models and data to re-create scenarios (bugs or otherwise) without needing to wait for long and potentially nondeterministic training runs.

Version control is indispensable for ensuring the reproducibility in ML systems. This is not just a matter of tracking changes in code but also involves versioning the datasets, model parameters, configuration settings, and even the random number generator seeds used during training. By seeding all random number generators (RNGs) used in the process, we can ensure that the stochastic elements of ML workflows—e.g., data shuffling and initialization of model weights—are consistent across runs. This helps us better correlate changes in model quality to specific changes in the model's inputs (e.g., code, data) and save time from debugging quality changes due to randomness.

In the context of version control of source code, it's also important to make small and frequent code commits (*https://oreil.ly/T1ip7*). We often see ML practitioners lumping multiple unrelated changes (even across 10–20 files) into a single commit. If that commit breaks the build on CI (i.e., tests fail), which logical set of changes caused the error? It's hard to tell when change sets are large. So, in addition to using version control, we should also use it *well* by making changes in logically segregated and ideally small changes.

Implement continuous integration (CI). Continuous integration (CI) actually has a strict definition that is often watered down to the point of losing its actual meaning (see the note earlier in this chapter on the definitions of CI/CD). This is especially true among ML practitioners. CI refers to the practice of committing all code changes onto the main branch (aka trunk-based development [*https://oreil.ly/949Mn*]—more on this in the next point), ideally several times a day.

Each code push is then automatically tested and verified on the CI pipeline. This approach helps to spot and address quality and integration issues as early as possible, enhancing the overall software quality and reducing the time it takes to validate and deploy new features.

Often, ML practitioners hesitate to practice CI because they don't want long training runs (sometimes taking several hours or even days to complete) to block their ability to make a code commit. Hence, they carve out their own "workspace" in the form of a feature branch, and whenever they're satisfied with the quality of their changes, they create a pull request to merge the changes to the main branch.

This concern is valid, but teams should consider two factors that can help them avoid the costs and pitfalls of feature branching. First, don't let ML be a "get out of jail free" card. If a component's path to production doesn't require time-consuming training runs (e.g., solutions with small models, LLM applications that don't require fine-tuning, or supporting packages and libraries), then teams should practice CI, test automation, and trunk-based development to reap the benefits of flow, velocity, and quality.

Second, in cases where the path to production of a code change *does* require time-consuming training runs, feature branching and pull requests (i.e., not doing trunk-based development and CI) may be an acceptable trade-off. But ML practitioners must still execute fast-running tests (e.g., training smoke tests as described in Chapter 6) locally and on the CI pipeline, before long and costly training runs. This affords ML practitioners fast feedback on the quality of their changes as they make small and frequent commits (*https://oreil.ly/T1ip7*) on feature branches.

This was true for us in one particular project (*https://oreil.ly/oHIJT*). We had CI pipelines with high test coverage, but we worked on feature branches (i.e., we didn't do trunk-based development and CI). However, we ensured that branches were short-lived (two to three weeks max). We pair-programmed, wrote tests, advocated for nonblocking code reviews (*https://oreil.ly/pcz3m*), and ensured all branches underwent the same comprehensive tests on our CI pipelines. Now, when a code change is committed and pushed, the CI pipeline:

- Runs a series of automated tests
- Triggers large-scale training

- Runs model quality tests
- Builds and publishes our model image to a container registry
- Automatically deploys the image to the preproduction environment
- Runs post-deployment tests in the preproduction environment

When the entire CI pipeline is green, it means the trained model has passed all the fitness functions (*https://oreil.ly/hv_5B*) we defined, and we can confidently merge the branch and deploy changes to production.

Apply trunk-based development. As detailed in Table 9-2, trunk-based development is the practice of committing code changes to the main branch. This contrasts with feature branching, where developers create a separate branch and pull requests for each feature or bug fix. Trunk-based development benefits ML practitioners in myriad ways and helps address common challenges that ML teams grapple with long feedback cycles, broken builds, code quality issues, tech debt, blocked work, and inter-team and intra-team silos, among others.

Table 9-2. Benefits of trunk-based development versus feature branching (source: adapted from Mattia Battiston's work on trunk-based development [https://oreil.ly/OeGHI])

Feature branching *Work in isolated branches; raise pull request (PR); merge to main branch when PR is approved*	Trunk-based development *Push straight to main branch; pair program; run comprehensive tests on CI; enjoy reliable builds; branch by abstraction/feature flags*
Feedback comes late: Too late to change anything substantial	*Fast feedback:* As you're writing code or even before
Low-quality feedback: Through comments, lacking context and nuance; feedback sometimes withheld or not actioned due to friction of PR review process	*Better-quality feedback:* Through in-context discussion and demonstrating suggestions in action
Large refactorings are dreaded and deferred: Because they are likely to cause merge conflicts and slow down PR review process	*Large refactorings are easier to tackle:* The rest of the team is always up-to-date and immediately benefits from any refactoring
Easy to ignore a failing build: Because it runs on an isolated branch	*We get used to not breaking things:* Team makes a habit of keeping main branch green
Individual coding styles: Tendency for fragmentation of styles, designs, and approaches even within a single codebase	*Team coding style:* Preferred styles, designs, and approaches are socialized and spread through pairing
People work in isolation: Harder to spot if someone needs help	*Visibility of what everyone is doing:* Easier to spot if someone needs support

Trunk-based development is the icing on the cake of the CD practices we've detailed so far. It's a practice that can and should only be done when you have implemented the safety prerequisites of test automation, pair programming, and CI/CD pipelines.

The reverse is also true: without these safety prerequisites, trunk-based development is risky and often leads to broken builds and defects.

Automation: Computers perform repetitive tasks, people solve problems

Algorithmia's "2021 Enterprise Trends in Machine Learning" report (*https://oreil.ly/ 9FAXH*) found that 38% of organizations surveyed are spending *more than 50% of* their data scientists' time on model deployment. And deployment is not the only undifferentiated tedium that ML practitioners are often tasked with—there's also the grunt work of configuring development environments, troubleshooting and debugging in production, among others.

The following practices help ML practitioners reduce such manual toil so that they can focus on solving important problems and delivering value.

Automate development environment setup. We discussed in Chapters 3 and 4 the challenges that ML practitioners often face in creating reproducible and consistent development environments, and practical techniques to overcome these challenges. We mention this here again for completeness—automation is useful not just for testing and deploying models, but also for creating development environments.

To achieve this, teams can leverage container technologies and infrastructure-as-code (IaC) tools, enabling the creation of consistent, production-like compute environments locally or in the cloud for both development and production environments (i.e., experimental-operational symmetry [*https://oreil.ly/Z31qn*]).

This frees up ML practitioners to focus on higher-order problem solving and innovation, leaving the repetitive tasks of environment setup and configuration to the computers.

Automate deployments (minimally to a preproduction environment). As mentioned earlier, deployment automation is typically well-covered in MLOps literature and tooling. Specific techniques, such as canary deployments and A/B testing, are also explained comprehensively in Chip Huyen's *Designing Machine Learning Systems* (O'Reilly), so we won't reiterate those points here but we will highlight the delta that CD4ML adds to the practice.

CD4ML takes the *ability* to automate model deployments further by recommending teams: (i) *trigger* automated deployments—minimally to preproduction environment(s)—on every code push, and (ii) run post-deployment tests to verify that the deployment succeeded and is ready for production at any time.

In traditional software development, separate environments such as development, testing, user acceptance testing, and production are commonly used to ensure that changes are thoroughly vetted before they are deployed to end users. However, in ML systems, this approach usually doesn't make sense because model training requires access to the most relevant, comprehensive, and up-to-date data, which often resides only in the production environment.

As such, run full model training in only one environment where you have access to the best data—in most cases, it's production. You can still run training smoke tests on a small sample of data (as described in Chapter 6) in the other lower environments before running full training in production.

Monitoring in production. Production monitoring is an established practice in software engineering. If done well, monitoring (metrics, logs, and alerts) gives us useful feedback on how our product is behaving in the wild, and alerts us when there are any unexpected errors, model drift, performance degradation, or unusual activity.

Monitoring gives us insight into scenarios that we haven't considered before in our tests. As Edsger W. Dijkstra once said: "Testing may convincingly demonstrate the presence of bugs but can never demonstrate their absence." That's why monitoring in production is an essential complementary practice to testing.

We've written about the three levels of monitoring in the first section of this chapter, so we won't reiterate the details, except to call out the components of monitoring that are useful in ML systems:

- Service monitoring (e.g., HTTP status codes, errors, latency)
- Model monitoring (e.g., key performance metrics, model drift over time) (Refer to the section "Learn from Production by Closing the Data Collection Loop" on page 187 for a definition of types of model drift.)
- Data monitoring (e.g., data quality monitoring, anomaly detection, adherence to expected schemas)
- Business-level outcomes (e.g., user engagement, sales, conversions, number of subscribers)
- Structured logs that are informative and readable and don't contain confidential or sensitive data (e.g., PII); they should have correlation IDs if production requests go through multiple services to facilitate debugging in distributed systems
- Alerts for undesirable scenarios in production (e.g., API errors, requests that go beyond latency budget; alerts should be informative and actionable, and be careful to avoid alert fatigue [*https://oreil.ly/CAh0D*] and broken windows [*https://oreil.ly/hpXp2*]!)

Kaizen: Relentlessly pursue continuous improvement

No system will ever be perfect, and there will always be issues and opportunities for improvement. Effective teams are those that can acknowledge their imperfect knowledge and set aside sufficient time and energy to identify and act on improvements.

Continuous improvement (or Kaizen) is especially relevant to ML teams because of the sheer heterogeneity and novelty of teams, tools, platforms, processes, and problems in ML. As a community of practitioners, we're constantly finding out new ways to solve problems, and the goal is not to get it right the first time (an impossible task!), but to make it easy and safe to iteratively change and improve how things are done.

It's important to call out that we can practice point Kaizen and system Kaizen. Point Kaizen can happen quickly during the course of work. For example, team members can simply call out issues that repeatedly add friction (e.g., too many meetings, or manual deployment procedures), and identify follow-up actions to resolve these issues.

For addressing system-level problems (e.g., team shapes that lead to too many handoffs and blockages, lack of platform capabilities), system Kaizen techniques such as value stream mapping (*https://oreil.ly/k_kn7*) and 5 whys (*https://oreil.ly/lh5ES*) can help teams identify the problems and find ways to improve.

Everyone is responsible: Rationalizing and cultivating ownership by adopting the appropriate team topologies

While the CD principle, "everyone is responsible," is a useful belief that guides the decisions of individuals, we often find that things that are everyone's responsibility often end up being no one's responsibility.

To realize this cultural aspiration, teams need to be supported by the right structure and systems of work that incentivize individuals and teams to fulfill their respective responsibilities, be it in ML, operations, customer experience, or security. Let's look at how the principles and practices of Team Topologies (*https://oreil.ly/DWhOY*) can help us in this regard.

As many of you know, before the DevOps movement, developers would write code and throw it over the wall for operations engineers to package and deploy. We still see this happening in some ML teams, albeit not always to such drastic extents, where teams are sliced by function (i.e., a data science team, an ML engineering team, an API team). Such a structure nudges individuals to think of responsibilities (e.g., production monitoring or testing ML models) as belonging to other teams, even though this mindset can make or break the ML product they're contributing to.

In addition, this structure increases handoffs and backlog coupling between teams, which then increases wait time and friction. For example, in an informal study (*https://oreil.ly/MhC3P*) of hundreds of tasks passing through a delivery center, tasks that had to wait for another team took *10–12 times longer* than tasks that could be completed by a single empowered team without dependency.

We also see Conway's Law—organizations produce designs that are copies of their communication structures—take effect, and each team undertakes some level of rework as opposed to coordinating to create a shared capability. In one instance, we worked with an organization that had two data science teams. Both teams independently solved the same problems repeatedly, such as tooling for large-scale model training, experiment tracking, and model explainability.

To address these challenges and to promote collaboration and collective ownership, consider the appropriate team structures and team topologies for your organization's level of maturity and scale. We'll discuss this in greater detail in Chapter 11, but here's a brief overview of the four types of teams in the Team Topologies model and how organizations can leverage them to scale the practice and delivery of ML in an organization:

Stream-aligned teams
Cross-functional teams are organized around a product or set of products. The team should be empowered with the required capabilities and context to develop, test, and deploy ML model enhancements to production, without the need to wait on (and be blocked by) another team. Typically, this is a "two-pizza team" with competencies such as data science, ML engineering, software engineering, quality assurance, and product.

Platform teams
These teams (e.g., data platform team, ML platform team) build and maintain platform capabilities that stream-aligned teams can use on a self-service basis. They also support stream-aligned teams where necessary to guide or trouble-shoot existing platform capabilities or develop new platform capabilities.

Enabling teams
These teams offer expertise (e.g., security consulting, ML governance, architecture) that equips and supports stream-aligned teams on an as-needed basis. Their role is to accelerate the stream-aligned teams by providing the necessary support, rather than owning a product or service themselves.

Complicated subsystem teams
These teams handle parts of the system that require specialized technical expertise (e.g., legacy platforms, search, personalization).

In the ML context, where there are multiple ML product use cases, we often see ML practitioners embedded in *stream-aligned teams* or *complicated subsystem teams* (e.g., a data science team building and supporting personalization in an organization). These teams are also enabled by a self-service ML platform and data platform capabilities, and supported by ML/data *platform teams* where necessary. They are also supported by *enabling teams* such as governance and architecture teams that can consult and support the stream-aligned teams where necessary.

Establishing the right team structures help organizations improve the flow of information and, more importantly, keep cognitive load at a manageable level. Matthew Skelton, coauthor of *Team Topologies* (IT Revolution Press) puts it well:

> If we stress the team by giving it responsibility for part of the system that is beyond its cognitive load capacity, it ceases to act like a high-performing unit and starts to behave like a loosely associated group of individuals, each trying to accomplish their individual tasks without the space to consider if those are in the team's best interest. [...] When cognitive load isn't considered, teams are spread thin trying to cover an excessive amount of responsibilities and domains. Such a team lacks bandwidth to pursue mastery of their trade and struggles with the costs of switching contexts.

With the principles and practices of CD4ML under our belt, let's turn to the final section of this chapter and look at how CD4ML supports teams in practicing ML governance and responsible AI.

How CD4ML Supports ML Governance and Responsible AI

With increasing ML capabilities, and reliance on those capabilities, comes increasing potential for harm, such as the amplification of biases and unforeseen use cases with detrimental societal impacts. For some examples of such harm, refer to the AIAAIC (AI, Algorithmic, and Automation Incidents and Controversies) repository (*https://oreil.ly/h1-FN*), which contains over 1,000 incidents and controversies including examples such as deepfakes, false claims, embedded racism, and privacy breaches.

If ML teams don't proactively identify potential failure modes and sources of harm, and implement risk controls accordingly, they are essentially building a house of cards that is not only vulnerable to functional failures, but that also risks causing harm to users and public reputational damage to the business. That's why ML governance, which intersects with Responsible AI, is critical for any team building ML systems.

In Chapter 1, we referred to MIT Sloan's definition of Responsible AI:[3]

> A framework with principles, policies, tools, and processes to ensure that AI systems are developed and operated in the service of good for individuals and society while still achieving transformative business impact.

---

3 Elizabeth M. Renieris, David Kiron, and Steven Mills, "To Be a Responsible AI Leader, Focus on Being Responsible" (*https://oreil.ly/XbPUv*), *MIT Sloan Management Review*, accessed November 8, 2023.

A Responsible AI framework should provide teams with practical tools to guide their decisions in the design, development, and deployment of ML systems. Responsible AI is an important component of ML governance. Effective ML governance ensures that we deliver value from ML systems, while adhering to ethical and regulatory standards, quality controls, risk management protocols, and engineering best practices.

There is little existing literature on these topics but what there is includes some good references. For ML governance, see the reports "AI Governance: A Lean Approach" (*https://oreil.ly/l67w_*) and "The Framework for ML Governance" (*https://oreil.ly/5RYHG*). For Responsible AI, see Google's "Responsible AI Practices" (*https://oreil.ly/d6lT0*) and *Responsible AI: Best Practices for Creating Trustworthy Systems* (Addison-Wesley Professional). We won't go into these two topics in detail, but we'd like to describe four ways in which CD4ML can help teams operationalize ML governance principles into their daily workflows and decisions:

Enabling iterative improvements

CD4ML—the ability to make small changes to ML systems with a specific intent, evaluate and monitor if those changes had the desired result, and roll them back if not—is a powerful enabler for Responsible AI in multiple ways.

First, it enables an iterative, human-centered approach to solution development, where we can research and test solutions with people in a series of small steps, allowing the early discovery and resolution of issues to reduce the likelihood of releasing anything harmful to users in production.

Second, if a harm—or indeed any other issue—is later detected, we can respond nimbly and deploy resolutions with confidence and within a short period of time, minimizing the impact of the harm.

Maximizing model lifetime value

Ad hoc development and deployment of models is typically the first stage of ML adoption in organizations, and indeed it may be difficult to justify investment in sophisticated MLOps or CD4ML at this stage, before the value is empirically established. Once the value of ML—or its potential to cause harm—is clear, then the lack of MLOps and CD4ML actually slows teams down in their efforts to improve model quality from their initial baseline performance.

MLOps and CD4ML—and the ethos and practices of automation and building quality in—help teams evaluate, monitor, and improve model quality in a timely manner, minimizing any cost of delay (*https://oreil.ly/z3ypM*). This allows teams to quickly reclaim value left on the table, understand and responsively manage their risk exposure, and hence maximize a model's value over its lifetime.

Defining and enforcing policy-as-code

MLOps and CD4ML enable the automated application of Responsible AI policies at various points in the software development lifecycle. For instance, we may validate that training data has been obtained with consent for a particular purpose, and produce documentation and a journal of experiments. Bias tests or data privacy tests may be defined as a fitness function that is part of a model validation and assurance suite, and model drift may be monitored in production. The same approaches can help maximize lifetime value of models.

Automating policy enforcement and value accounting in this way reduces manual effort, improves compliance, and provides an audit trail. Like automation of testing, policy-as-code allows people to focus on defining Responsible AI policies, while machines do the repetitive, tedious work of evaluating compliance.

Asking tough questions (a key aspect of Kaizen)

As mentioned earlier, CI (or Kaizen) is a core practice in CD4ML. Kaizen requires us to prioritize quality outcomes over discomfort, and collective success over groupthink. Organizationally, it's important to nurture a culture—through values, policies, and behavior—where it's acceptable and even encouraged to highlight and explore potential issues, failure modes, and sources of harm. It can be as simple as any team member asking a question or making an observation when they notice practices that aren't aligned with their values and principles, and exploring the implications and any necessary mitigations as a team.

To implement any Responsible AI framework, team members need to know it's OK to ask tough questions about what should be done with AI and how it should be done. (For more on this topic, see the story of Andon Cord and NUMMI in Chapter 10, which talks about the importance of essence over form.)

Our experience has taught us that ML governance is not a hindrance to innovation but a guiding framework that ensures faster and safer delivery of ML applications. CD4ML actually *enables* innovation by facilitating ML governance and encouraging teams to embed quality assurance, monitoring, and compliance as part of the ongoing delivery cycle, rather than being one-off checkpoints.

Too frequently we encounter ML teams that are constrained by an inability to assess or see the risk of a particular application, because the elements described in this chapter are not in place. When good ML governance is in place, it sets safe boundaries for teams to experiment and build great solutions.

To close, if your team or organization doesn't have an ML governance framework in place, this would be a great opportunity to define one. The ML governance references mentioned earlier in this chapter offer a good starting point for you to adapt to your context.

It also helps to embed Responsible AI as an integral part of the development process, rather than an afterthought. You could consider starting with a statement of values regarding how the good of AI will be realized and how harms will be mitigated. The values statement establishes the purpose and guidance for the next element, which is a framework for designing and implementing AI solutions. That framework should accommodate external obligations, such as government regulations and third-party contracts, and also be aligned with internal policies and procedures. This can then cascade into a set of principles for the use of AI, of which there are many great examples from governments and NGOs, as well as books like Cathy O'Neil's *Weapons of Math Destruction* (Crown Books) or Ellen Broad's *Made by Humans* (Melbourne University Press). For anyone wanting to educate themselves further about potential harms from ML and proposed mitigations, explore and follow the work of leading researchers such as Dr. Joy Buolamwini, Dr. Timnit Gebru, Prof. Emily M. Bender, and Dr. Abeba Birhane.

Now, let's wrap up this massive chapter with a brief recap.

Conclusion

Coming back to our opening story, if Dana and Ted had these MLOps and CD4ML practices in place, the production deployment would have been a no-drama, no-nerves, click-of-a-button affair. This is not an aspiration, but a reality, based on our experience practicing CD4ML in real-world projects.

Wherever you are on your organization's ML maturity journey, we hope that these practices will help you scale and improve your organization's ML practice. As MLOps tooling and techniques continue to grow, we find that these CD4ML principles and practices are enduring and provide a useful framework for identifying a set of quality gates and processes to help teams deliver ML models rapidly and reliably.

To recap, in this chapter, we've:

- Established the basic building blocks of MLOps, and outlined common pitfalls that teams experience when practicing MLOps
- Described how ML teams can benefit from CD principles of building quality into the product, working in small batches, automation, continuous improvement (Kaizen), and shared ownership
- Delved into why and how CD4ML is a great complement to MLOps, and the CD4ML practices that can help ML teams ship reliable ML solutions to production early and often
- Explored how CD4ML supports ML governance and Responsible AI

Well done on completing this chapter! See you in the next chapter, where we'll kick off Part III, "Teams".

## PART III

Teams

## CHAPTER 10

Building Blocks of Effective ML Teams

All happy families are alike; each unhappy family is unhappy in its own way.

—Leo Tolstoy, *Anna Karenina*

The Anna Karenina principle (*https://oreil.ly/gUUdq*) contends that many factors must be in alignment for success, and that issues with any one of those many factors could lead to failure. The same may be said of effective ML teams, which must contend with all the complexities of teamwork in organizations, in addition to the complexities of ML product development.

But this principle needn't doom our endeavors. On the contrary, as every environment in which teams operate—market, business, organizational structure, technology, data—is unique and dynamic, it stands that there is no cookie-cutter approach to success, and that every effective team must discover, and rediscover, its own unique path to success. In this chapter, we share some of the many tools we have at our disposal to move us closer to success, step by step.

As the Dalai Lama said: "Happiness is not something ready-made, it comes from your own actions." So, it is crucial for individuals, teams, and whole organizations to experiment, reflect and adapt, and to have leadership guidance and support to do so. The building blocks of effective teams we present here help us work toward those ends at the level of individuals, teams, and organizations. In fact, we can think about the building blocks like the Swiss cheese model (introduced in Chapter 5): The more blocks we have in place, the less likely our teams are to suffer major issues, and the more resilient they will be if they do.

Throughout this book, you've seen how neglecting some building blocks can result in not building the right thing (Chapter 2), not building the thing right (Chapters 3–9), or not building the thing in a way that is right for people, which is what we'll explore in this chapter. In that respect, the Anna Karenina principle should still ground our thinking through this last mile (or two) of the book, in a form that empowers us and directs us to action.

In this chapter, we'll start by exploring common challenges facing ML teams to illustrate the lived experience of many of us—you might call these the unhappy families, but only temporarily so! Then, we'll look at techniques for improving team effectiveness by addressing issues with various building blocks. While the theories and techniques that we cover will benefit any team, not just ML teams, we have noticed that some ML teams tend to overlook them, to their detriment. If you're in a team that is not as effective as it could be, consider the improvement potential of each of these blocks.

Organizational psychology professor Steve Kozlowski recognizes that "at a minimum, three levels of the system need to be conceptually embraced to understand team effectiveness...within person over time, individuals within team, and between team or contextual effects."[1] In this chapter, we'll consider effective team internals: individual and intra-team dynamics (Kozlowski's first two levels). We'll wrap up this chapter with the topic of engineering effectiveness and DevEx. This will position us well to explore in Chapter 11 wider inter-team dynamics across an organization— Kozlowski's third level—which we will do through the lens of the Team Topologies model (*https://teamtopologies.com*). We'll close Chapter 11 and the book by looking at how leaders and leadership throughout the organization create environments that cultivate effective teams. This roadmap, and the building blocks for each level, is summarized in Figure 10-1.

Many brilliant authors have written on these recurring topics, and we'll reference key resources throughout the chapter. Each section of this chapter is worth a book (or many) in its own right. We hope the breadth of this chapter helps you identify where you might go deep and explore more resources to improve the effectiveness of your teams.

If you've followed us this far, we presume it's because you recognize there's still more you could do to make your teams even more effective. Our hope is that you'll find what you're looking for in these two final chapters.

---

1 Steve W.J. Kozlowski, "Groups and Teams in Organizations: Studying the Multilevel Dynamics of Emergence," in *Research Methods for Studying Groups and Teams: A Guide to Approaches, Tools, and Technologies*, edited by Andrea Hollingshead and Marshall Scott Poole (New York: Routledge; 2012), 260–283.

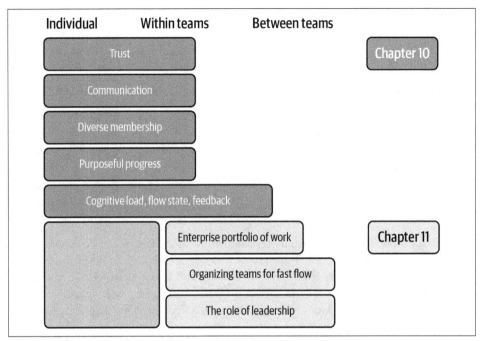

Individual   Within teams   Between teams

Trust

Communication

Diverse membership

Purposeful progress

Cognitive load, flow state, feedback

Enterprise portfolio of work

Organizing teams for fast flow

The role of leadership

Chapter 10

Chapter 11

Figure 10-1. Building blocks of effective ML teams and effective ML organizations discussed in Chapters 10 and 11

Common Challenges Faced by ML Teams

In this section, we'll look at common challenges that ML teams face, through the lens of some fictional but relatable scenarios.

Earlier in this book, we covered technical and product challenges that ML practitioners face when working in teams. These challenges could apply equally to isolated individual roles—e.g., long feedback cycles during development, wasting effort in building a product that users didn't want. When we put individuals with the potential to be effective together in teams, a whole new class of challenges arises. These challenges are driven by how teams are organized and how individuals interact with one another as teammates and as human beings.

In larger organizations, even if individual teams have all the right building blocks, how teams interact with each other and how work flows to each team can also render them more or less effective. We'll introduce some more scenarios relevant to organizations in the next chapter.

For now, let's look at a few scenarios illustrating the common challenges that individual ML teams face:

Unsurfaced conflicting approaches

Dana and Ted are on the same team. Dana is a fervent supporter of TensorFlow for deep learning, praising its flexibility and extensive toolset. Ted, on the other hand, is a staunch advocate for PyTorch, valuing its intuitive design and dynamic computation graph. They've never openly discussed the pros and cons of each tool, or which is suitable for the team's needs.

This unstated disagreement has resulted in a fragmented set of codebases, with some projects developed in TensorFlow and others in PyTorch. Andy, a new team member, needs to learn two ways of training and serving models, compounded by the number of models and repositories using different deep learning frameworks. Oh, and also two sets of anything else that the team hadn't agreed and aligned on.

Intra-team silos of specialization

Tanvi built a simple hand-rolled feature store to address a critical need, and now every time a feature is added or changed, the work comes to Tanvi. Meanwhile, since Daksha spent a week trialing and tuning varied classification techniques to boost model performance, he is now responsible for model development.

No one thinks to challenge this arrangement. It's accepted by the team and all their external stakeholders, and that acceptance perpetuates the status quo. When Daksha is on holiday, the team has to wait for his return to explain why a model started failing a stratified test. When Tanvi gets a new job offer, feature changes are blocked for a month while a replacement is found and comes up to speed. All this time, Charli really wants to learn about both feature stores and model development but is limited to working on pipeline orchestration. And finally, Daksha isn't aware that Lani, the new graduate, just completed a PhD addressing some of the issues he's wrestling with, because Lani is always doing data cleaning.

Each team member, engrossed in their specific area, lacks awareness of their colleagues' challenges, intentions, and progress. The segregation in responsibilities leads to multiple divergent goals, and the team can't help one another achieve those goals or respond to incidents. As a result, work is less rewarding for team members, teams are less responsive, less connected, less innovative, deliver lower quality, and are less resilient.

Lack of shared purpose

Mitsuko's data science team has been studying an analytics problem for some time with existing data. The team has defined an exhaustive set of specifications for a solution, which it provides to Naomi's data engineering team for implementation.

Naomi's data engineering team doesn't understand the problem Mitsuko's team is trying to solve and it has found some new data that it thinks invalidates some of the solution assumptions (e.g., data drift). But Mitsuko's team isn't interested in engaging since it thinks it's just a matter of implementing the provided specifications.

Meanwhile, Nadine's platform team is working on functionality for a business unit that is due to be restructured in the near future and it doesn't know whether its work will ever see the light of day.

Both Naomi's and Nadine's teams will struggle to find purpose or a goal that they can buy into. Some issues are generic and some—like data drift—are specific to ML teams. Without purpose and autonomy to solve problems, it is unlikely that these teams will be high-performing and morale will fizzle out over time.

No sense of progress

Piotr's team is working on a new ML platform. There is a long backlog of items for the first release. Every iteration, new items are added to this backlog through discovery of scope. It's not clear whether these items are critical for the first release because they are described in technical terms and no users are involved in their prioritization.

The team delivers working code every iteration, but a burndown chart shows no appreciable progress toward the first release. The team doesn't know which items are high-priority so it chooses which items to work on based on what's most interesting—from autoscaling to z-test support—which also leads the team to deciding the scope of each item. Week to week, the team loses any sense of accomplishment and has no incentive to coordinate activities because it has no mechanism for determining which tasks will move it closer to its goal. Stakeholders can't see any progress either. This is not a high-performing team.

Lack of diversity

Melanie's team of data scientists can't source the data they need because it has a narrow skill set that doesn't extend to data pipelines. Takeshi's team just released a model that discriminates against women because it didn't have many women in its training and validation dataset, and no one in Takeshi's all-male team thought this might be an issue for a consumer product.

Diverse teams (*https://oreil.ly/qvSqk*) are better problem solvers, process facts more carefully, produce more innovative solutions, and produce better financial results. If you don't prioritize diversity in your teams, not only are they likely to be less effective, they are also more likely to fail in preventable ways.

No common ground

Chin Sun's team is a brand new global remote team. Previously, some were developers, some data engineers, some ML engineers. Everyone has a different way of doing things, different names for processes and artifacts.

Like a Pictionary game where your partner just can't guess what the spiral and intersecting lines represent, this team has trouble communicating and building shared understanding of the work, leading to delays and quality issues.

This is, however, one of the easiest challenges to address if other issues are not present. Building shared experience and finding common interests through well-considered social activities, and aligning on ways of working by delivering value to production early and often in a safe-to-fail environment will rapidly unlock the effectiveness of a diverse team.

Unsafe to fail, or even to ask

In Hugh's team, there are some outspoken data scientists, and Hugh likes them to maintain a high profile internally as he believes it reflects well on him and his team with stakeholders. He therefore tolerates them dictating to the team how to do things and constantly showing off their mathematical prowess. Jack, a business analyst studying Python and ML in his spare time, has spotted what he thinks is a bug in the model training code. It seems that some training data is included in the validation set. The data scientists recently gave a big presentation on changes they made to dramatically improve the model, with lots of impressive equations. The bug was introduced at the same time the performance increased. Their company will make a big announcement to the market about this soon.

Jack thinks he must be in the wrong, that it's some failing of his to understand what the data scientists have done. He fears ridicule and a lecture if he raises his concerns. Even if Jack was right, he is scared that Hugh is so committed to the announcement that he would find a way to make it Jack's fault rather than acknowledge the team's mistake, so what's the point of raising it?

This is purely fictional, but it's what an unsafe-to-fail, or even to ask, environment might look like. When people are afraid of negative consequences for raising concerns, or admitting they lack knowledge (maybe the suspected bug was introduced because one of the data scientists didn't want to diminish their reputation by asking how to use a feature of scikit-learn they hadn't used before), they will keep their thoughts to themselves. This causes stress and inhibits growth of team members, and causes errors and knowledge gaps to remain hidden and to compound over time with magnified consequences. Not an effective team at all!

If you've done ML for a while now, or if you're new, or even if you've worked in any sort of team, you'd have likely encountered some of these challenges. Thankfully, there's rich existing literature and wisdom on how teams can understand and address these challenges and make internal adaptations, and that's the focus of the next section.

Effective Team Internals

In this section, we'll consider the internal building blocks that teams can use to address issues and improve their effectiveness. Throughout this book, we've been exploring systems, practices and processes for team effectiveness. We consider these elements important building blocks, too, and here we'll extend from the more mechanistic considerations to the more humanistic considerations of effective teams.

Specifically, in this section we'll address the following building blocks:

- Trust
- Communication
- Diverse membership
- Purposeful, shared progress

We'll refer to some core, established models and literature for each building block, and we'll present advice targeted at the central concepts. You'll also notice that these models and building blocks have overlapping elements; you'll start to see how building blocks can be interlocking and mutually reinforcing. Keep an eye out for the connections.

While these building blocks are common to any team engaged in complex and ambiguous work, we will also highlight specifically why they might be relevant and how they apply to ML teams.

There are more perspectives you might take and models you might use on teamwork, but in our work, we've found these building blocks to be a great starting point. The good news is that every team member can influence these dimensions, especially organically developed or formally designated leaders.

Trust as the Foundational Building Block

> Purposefulness and intentionality must combine with courage to act if anything mean-
> ingful is going to be achieved.
>
> —Patrick Lencioni, *The Five Dysfunctions of a Team*

Patrick Lencioni's *The Five Dysfunctions of a Team* (Jossey-Bass) is a leadership book
that explores team dynamics by first showing us how to spot team failures, or team
dysfunctions. Let's be honest, who hasn't experienced team dynamics that had either
distrust, tension, or even frustration? Lencioni describes a pyramid mental model,
summarized in Figure 10-2. The foundational building block of this mental model
is *trust* within the team. In the absence of trust, we cannot truly foster healthy and
respectful conflict around ideas, build collective commitment to decisions and plans
of action, or develop a culture of accountability. Without any of this support, a team
will not achieve results.

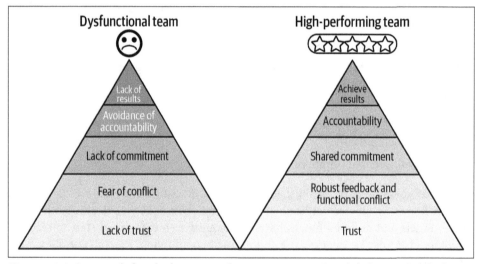

*Figure 10-2. Lencioni's five dysfunctions of a team, presented with behaviors of dysfunc-
tional teams contrasted with behaviors of high-performing teams (source: adapted from
Patrick Lencioni's Five Dysfunctions of a Team, used with permission)*

You might be thinking: "OK, so team trust is important. Let's organize a one-off
team-bonding activity and call it done!" Not quite. Fostering and cultivating team
trust isn't a one-and-done activity; building trust takes time. It takes advocacy from
leadership and it requires us to have a certain level of self-awareness, and awareness
of the group dynamics at play.

You may have experienced some of these challenges in building trust in an ML team.
Individuals come to the team with different academic and professional backgrounds,
perspectives and skills, that collectively require some assembly into a team. Maybe

some ML practitioners don't have prior experience working in a product delivery setting with intense cross-functional collaboration. Products and projects are high stakes, results are expected quickly, and mistakes can be highly consequential. Execution is challenging, however, and it's easy to point the finger somewhere else when many complex activities must be lined up within a team and many more factors—like data quality—are out of the team's control. People may suffer from "imposter syndrome" or feel there's an expectation to be the smartest person in the room.

Let's look at how we can address these challenges through vulnerability.

Daring Greatly

Lencioni's model focuses on trust between team members. It doesn't explore the trust we have to have in *ourselves* in order to partake in those behaviors described in Figure 10-1: the ability to ask for help, share weaknesses, help each other, and believe that everyone is trying their best. (Lencioni's model further doesn't focus on trust between teams. We'll tackle this when we look at teams of teams in Chapter 11.)

Brené Brown's book *Daring Greatly* (Gotham Books) explores how the need to feel invulnerable to avoid the feeling of shame prevents us from being comfortable with our vulnerability. And the root of shame is fear and the sense of scarcity. Scarcity refers to the sense of "Never [*fill in the blanks*] enough," which can be emotional, physical, financial, and social. In ML teams, it's easy to fill in the blank with "smart."

Time is a common example of a perceived scarcity, and thus many of us fear, "I never have enough *time*." For example, there's never enough time to do pair programming and to finish our work, to have feedback and retrospectives, or 1:1 conversations. As a result, when we start believing we never have enough time, our interactions with the rest of the team are influenced. One way this might manifest is that we might be impatient in a standup, as we perceive it to be running "over time." When our actions and behaviors become more and more influenced by feelings of fear and a sense of scarcity, we end up perpetuating the five dysfunctions as described by Lencioni.

Lencioni describes vulnerability as a means for building trust, a complementary perspective to Brown's identification of the need to feel invulnerable as problematic. *Vulnerability*, in Lencioni's context, means that teammates should be prepared to share some of their weaknesses, failings, and fears with one another. This is part of building connections with one another as fellow human beings, as well as teammates.

It's hard for many of us to just flick a vulnerability switch with a group of new people, though. While we were a little flippant about the team-building activity mentioned earlier, when done thoughtfully—recognizing each individual's social preferences and interests—team-building activities *can* lay foundations of shared experience, interest, and empathy that can lower barriers to being vulnerable. Vulnerability is also something leaders can model, for instance, by simply saying, "I don't know," and followed constructively by, "How might we find out?"

We can further build self-awareness and empathy for our teammates through understanding various models of team dynamics. Luckily for us, many who came before us have done the hard work of collecting and distilling varied team experiences for us.

In the sections that follow, we'll share a selection of management theories and frameworks. This is far from a comprehensive set, but we've found this selection useful in broadening our awareness. These models of team behavior enable us to view individual and team dynamics from different and more objective perspectives. This lets us build awareness of the experience of others, while also better understanding our own contribution to certain dynamics. These frameworks also equip us with the shared language and a suite of potential strategies for collectively addressing team dysfunctions. ML teams may dial these frameworks up to 11 with complex work, diverse specializations, and high expectations.

We've designed a simple exercise to help you remember these frameworks: For each theory that we introduce, consider how it explains or relates to one experience in your current or most recent job.

As a warm-up exercise, consider the role of trust in Theory X and Theory Y (*https://oreil.ly/2NcCc*)—also known as directive and permissive management (see Figure 10-3). Theory X contends that workers are inherently lazy and management's role is to dictate tasks and provide extrinsic motivation, while Theory Y contends that workers are intrinsically capable and motivated and management's role is to remove blockers to their work.

And here's your first exercise: *Has management in the ML space acted differently from management in other roles and functions, like your first job in (possibly) hospitality or retail?*

Figure 10-3. Mnemonic device for Theory X and Theory Y—a person refusing to work ("X") and a person cheering the opportunity to work ("Y") (source: adapted from an image by Martin Adámek [https://oreil.ly/2NcCc], used under CC BY-SA 3.0 [https://oreil.ly/tOJq1])

Tuckman's stages of group development

Would you consider a team that's been newly formed more effective than a team that has been working together for at least a year, and that hasn't experienced any turnovers? Why?

Tuckman's stages of group development (*https://oreil.ly/M1YyB*) presents the theory that a team's effectiveness can be correlated to phases, or stages, of a team's development (see Figure 10-4). Bruce Tuckman describes these five stages as:

Stage 1: Forming
> A new team has just been formed, or a new team member has just joined. Team members first meet, learn their roles and responsibilities, and are cautious with their behavior as they try to assimilate with the group.

Stage 2: Storming
> Tensions rise as team members start to speak their minds and solidify their places within the group, and latent conflicts surface.

Stage 3: Norming
> Conflicts start to resolve, team members appreciate each other's strengths, and respect for authority grows.

Stage 4: Performing
> The group functions together as a cohesive unit and without as much direction from the team leader.

Stage 5: Adjourning
> The original goals of the team have been completed, and everyone can move on to new projects or teams.

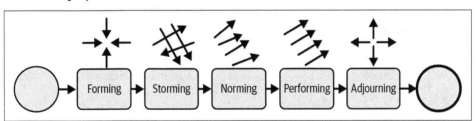

Figure 10-4. Tuckman's stages of group development (source: adapted from an image by Diogo Nicoleti [https://oreil.ly/f9pXC], used under CC BY-SA 4.0 [https://oreil.ly/ JlwN5])

Tuckman's theory posits that, together as a team, we move through these stages. With intentional and situational leadership (covered in Chapter 11), we can rationalize intense, emotional reactions in these stages. Being aware of these typical stages, we are more likely to consider team issues at a systemic level than allow them to degrade trust between individuals in the team. Note that, as Tuckman's model has been applied and reviewed, it has been proposed that many events (such as new team members joining) may cause even long-lived teams to revert to earlier stages.

Forming and adjourning may be less frequent in a long-lived team environment, such as an ML product team, than a project-driven environment. However, even where long-lived teams are an objective, the very dynamic nature of digital businesses means that teams pragmatically (and sometimes frequently) may need to re-form. The process of team formation shouldn't be seen as a barrier to effectiveness; rather, deliberate attention to this process may even be seen as a competitive advantage (*https://oreil.ly/Q-dBf*).

Which stage do you think best describes your team? Why?

Belbin's Team Roles

> The types of behavior in which people engage are infinite. But the range of useful behaviors, which make an effective contribution to team performance, is finite. These behaviors are grouped into a set number of related clusters, to which the term 'Team Role' is applied.
>
> —Dr. Meredith Belbin

Belbin's Team Roles framework (*https://oreil.ly/L4ULT*) defines nine archetypes for team roles (see Figure 10-5). The archetypes, categorized by behavioral attributes, are:

- People/social roles:
  - Resource Investigator
  - Teamworker
  - Coordinator
- Thinking roles:
  - Plant
  - Monitor Evaluator
  - Specialist

- Action roles:
  - Shaper
  - Implementer
  - Completer Finisher

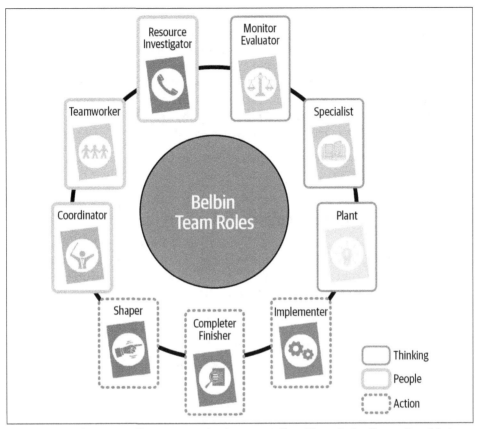

Figure 10-5. The nine Belbin Team Roles (source: Belbin Team Roles [https://oreil.ly/ L4ULT], used with permission)

Roles such as resource investigator search for and incorporate new ideas. Plant roles creatively solve problems. And completer finisher roles polish work and scrutinize it for errors. No role is better or worse; all contribute to effective teams.

Individuals default to certain archetypes that can be determined through a questionnaire that surfaces behaviors. However, in a given team, individuals are able to play multiple roles at any time or different times.

In an ML team, a resource investigator might be happy to propose novel techniques, such as reinforcement learning, with no regard for the state of the project, always considering it better to have another option available even if the technical direction is more or less set. This might bring them into conflict with a completer finisher, who is focused on steering the team to the next release on their current supervised ML trajectory. With sufficient self-awareness, however, this conflict is easily reconciled, and even a source of gentle amusement for the team.

Knowing your default role can be very helpful for you to recognize when this behavior would not help the team. It's also helpful to be able to identify roles that aren't being played, such as being a teamworker, and suggesting everyone grab a coffee and come back fresh at times when teamwork starts stalling. While writing this book, the Belbin Team Roles framework helped us remember to channel our inner completer finisher at key junctures, even when our natural inclination was to continually plant new ideas! Actively monitoring and moderating the roles you are all playing—or failing to play—leads to much more effective teams.

Identifying your default roles in the Belbin Team Roles framework (*https://oreil.ly/L4ULT*) is a great exercise to do as a team.

Hofstede's Cultural Dimensions Theory

Hofstede's Cultural Dimensions Theory (*https://oreil.ly/AnOv3*) presents a cross-cultural, psychological framework that describes how our behavior is influenced by the values and culture of the society we live in. The theory describes six key dimensions that exist among cultural groups:

- Individualism (*https://oreil.ly/teuTC*)-collectivism (*https://oreil.ly/gtb81*)
- Uncertainty avoidance (*https://oreil.ly/qtIRk*)
- Power distance (strength of social hierarchy) (*https://oreil.ly/TAv6l*)
- Task-orientation versus person-orientation
- Long-term orientation (*https://oreil.ly/YuvUI*)
- Self-restraint

The theory posits that behaviors will vary in these important dimensions between cultural groups. It's widely used in management and research across cultures to account for variations, and it can help raise awareness of potential differences in teams.

This theory has its limitations, including the fact that it was originally based on a population predominantly of privileged white males and that nation-states are treated as homogeneous. Nonetheless, it raises awareness of varied cultural experiences, and is simple to understand and apply. This theory can also help us be better at communicating with one another, understanding better each other's behaviors, and can be particularly helpful in global remote teams.

You've seen how trust is a foundational building block for high-performing teams and the challenges ML teams present, and you've explored a range of personal and team models for building trust in the presence of systemic team issues. Let's explore the next building block of effective teams: communication.

Communication

Communication is a key building block in teams, and something that challenges us all at times. In ML teams, where there are many different specializations, communication can be particularly hard. Are you referring to a product "feature" or a data "feature?" Although the average Joe says "average" did you mean "mean?" And recall, precision in ML may be more important than accuracy! (We hope the puns in this introduction aided rather than hindered our communication; the last one refers to the problem of class imbalance.)

Communication is another skill we can improve with deliberate attention, guided by frameworks. A typical team in the tech industry has many noisy communication channels to choose from, raising the question of which channel(s) to use for communications. A typical team also has its ups and downs, and trivial and critical matters to raise and resolve, and it's important that communication works well in all of these scenarios—especially the difficult conversations. Let's dive deeper into some key frameworks.

Models of communication

Technically minded readers may appreciate models of interpersonal communication that reflect the elements we might see in digital communication. Figure 10-6 illustrates this idea from Randy Fujishin's book *Creating Communication* (Rowman & Littlefield Publishers), though it may well have come from the work of "the father of information theory" Claude Shannon! Many models of communication include the idea that a sender encodes a message and uses a channel to transmit it to a receiver. Noise may distort the message along the way. The receiver then decodes the message and gives some form of feedback, which the sender must in turn decode.

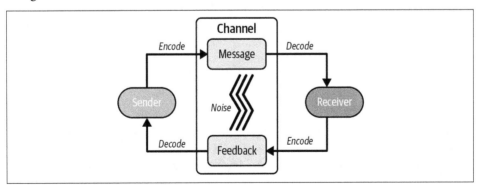

Figure 10-6. Many models of interpersonal communication can map to the process of digital communication (source: adapted from an image by Phlsph7 for Wikipedia [https://oreil.ly/1Cgu8], used under CC BY-SA 4.0 [https://oreil.ly/Hq5C_])

When communication in a team isn't working, you can do worse than treat it as a technical debugging problem! Let's take a simple scenario: Imagine you didn't get a response to what you thought was an important email. First, attempt to identify the source of the problem. Is it the assumptions you made about shared context with the receiver when you phrased (*encoded*) your email (*message*)? Is the encoded message unclear, contradictory, or incomplete? Is it the *noise* in the email *channel* that leads people to ignore emails? Is it that the receiver was missing some important context when they read (*decoded*) your email? Or is it that the *feedback* got filtered out by one of your many inbox rules? With a hypothesis about the source of the problem, you can isolate the potential issue and try again (and again) with an alternative approach.

One of the key decisions you can make in this framework is which channel, or channels, to use when communicating. For complex, nuanced messages that may be misunderstood, face-to-face conversation (where possible) is far preferable to email. However, these conversations don't leave a record[2] that can be easily shared with other teammates for direction, so you may want to follow up with actions in an email rather than have multiple 1:1 interactions. Both of these channels may sound hopelessly antiquated to a fully remote team working asynchronously through a messaging platform, which includes various bots and systems integrations. However, Fujishin's model can still help us analyze communications on any channel.

We understand individuals may have their own preferences for channels and forums, depending on factors such as work location, time of day, introversion or extroversion, and so on, and establishing this up front as a team is helpful. Stakeholders and external parties may also have particular channel requirements that your team needs to adhere to, so the reality of team communications will always be multichannel.

We also saw in Chapter 6 the value of data visualization. In ML projects, we frequently need to communicate about data. When communicating about data to any audience with any intent through any channel, considered data visualization (*https://oreil.ly/vetxm*) can greatly enhance the decodable signal in your message. Creating and consuming data visualizations are skills the team should develop to aid communication.

Crucial Conversations framework

Communication will be improved even further—especially at critical junctures—if treated fully as an interpersonal endeavor. The Crucial Conversations framework (*https://oreil.ly/5uy90*) provides great tools for teams to improve communication,

---

2 As a counterpoint, videoconferencing AI transcripts now read more like "recognizing speech" than "wrecking a nice beach." If you're prepared for the occasional gaffe, they can offer multichannel communication time savings.

highlighting that some uncomfortable but important conversations, if done well, can have outsized impact on your work together.

There are three key points from the Crucial Conversations framework that we'd like to highlight:

Neither violence nor silence is beneficial

Avoiding communication can be as bad as communicating poorly. In *Crucial Conversations* (McGraw-Hill), the authors place *silence* and *violence* on opposite ends of a spectrum with good communication in the middle. When it comes to effective teams, the old adage that "If you don't have anything nice to say, you shouldn't say anything at all" is not the final word on communication. When and how to raise difficult issues needs critical reevaluation, and Crucial Conversations provides the framework for this.

Recognize when conversations become crucial

Conversations turn into "crucial conversations" when the stakes are high, when opinions differ, and when emotions are strong. Our lizard brains just aren't wired for these situations. Awash with hormones evolved for wild environments, we enter fight or flight mode instead of responding with intellect and empathy. If we recognize these moments, however, we can quell our instinctive response, and use the framework to hold an effective conversation.

How to have a crucial conversation

We encourage you to refer to the book *Crucial Conversations* for the full picture on how to hold a crucial conversation. We summarize the key elements of the approach as follows:

- Remain focused on the outcome you're collectively trying to achieve, and maintain a safe space by watching for signs of withdrawal or sabotage.

- Know your own motivations, and be prepared to *explore your own path* by sharing stories to which others will be receptive.

- Explore others' paths with genuine empathy and compassion.

- See this process of communication as contributing to a *pool of shared meaning*.

- Be prepared and able to move from shared understanding to shared action.

The Crucial Conversations framework provides more detailed guidance and learning resources. ML product development environments are fertile ground for crucial conversations, with high stakes, different opinions, and more emotion than most technologists would like to admit. If you think you could have better handled the last conversation you had that qualified as crucial, then this framework is worth exploring further.

Candor in feedback

Even when conversations aren't crucial, we need to understand and appreciate the concept of *candor* as described in *Creativity, Inc.* by Ed Catmull (Transworld Publishers Limited) or *Radical Candor* by Kim Scott (St. Martin's Press)—where discussions are robust, respectful, and focused objectively on ideas and products rather than personalities. We find the concept of candor to be a helpful framing for communicating feedback about a team's deliverables.

Note the similarity between candor and productive conflict in Lencioni's model. Through candid feedback, a team can continuously reshape its product from very rudimentary beginnings to progressively more and more valuable stages of completion. As Ed Catmull of Pixar says:[3]

> Candor could not be more crucial to our creative process. Why? Because early on, all of our movies suck....And this is how it should be. Creativity has to start somewhere, and we are true believers in the power of bracing, candid feedback and the iterative process—reworking, reworking and reworking again until a flawed story finds its throughline or a hollow character finds its soul.

The first versions of ML models and products are similarly rudimentary, and benefit similarly from candid feedback and revision.

So, we see that communication and trust are building blocks that reinforce one another. Communication is also the glue that binds *diverse teams* together and is the basis for collaboration in teams that are able to make *shared progress*.

Diverse Membership

Diversity has many dimensions, as illustrated by the Diversity Wheel (*https://oreil.ly/ G_MRQ*) (see Figure 10-7) developed by Marilyn Loden and Judy Rosener in the early 1990s. Beyond personality dimensions, other primary (or internal) dimensions of individual diversity include age, ethnic heritage, race, gender, sexual orientation, and mental and physical capabilities. Secondary (or external) dimensions relate to an individual's societal relationships and include geography, work experience, and education. Tertiary (or organizational) dimensions describe individuals' relationships to an organization and include role, department, and seniority.

---

3 Ed Catmull with Amy Wallace, *Creativity, Inc.: Overcoming the Unseen Forces That Stand in the Way of True Inspiration* (Random House, 2014).

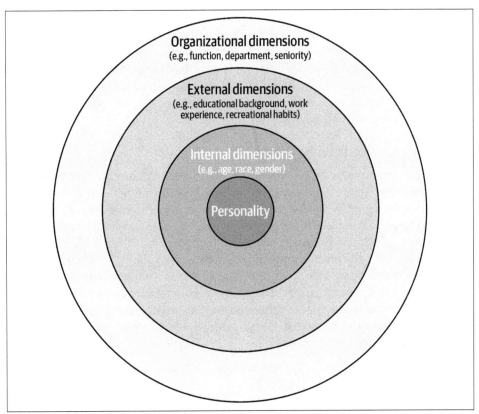

Figure 10-7. The Diversity Wheel enumerates the many dimensions that constitute diversity (source: adapted from Diversity Wheel, Loden et al. 1991 [https://oreil.ly/ G_MRQ])

Primary and secondary dimensions: Sociodemographic diversity

Diverse teams have been shown to be better at solving problems and processing facts and to more carefully produce more innovative solutions and better financial results (*https://oreil.ly/TKFWn*). If you don't prioritize diversity in your teams, not only are they likely to be less effective, they are also more likely to fail in preventable ways.

In short, diverse teams perform better at building ML products and effective ML teams should therefore prioritize diversity, and not just deep individual technical skills. In our experience, diverse membership typically leads teams to consider problems from more angles—and, as a result, identify better solutions—versus the echo chambers of a uniform team.

As a member or leader of ML teams, you will need to collaborate with many organizational functions, including Talent or Recruitment, People or HR, Learning and Development and of course Diversity, Equity, and Inclusion to shape and execute your diversity objectives. While this may sound daunting, the rewards are great and worth the effort, and you'll find many willing collaborators if you start the conversation. We hope we've made a brief case for why you should prioritize diversity and provided some initial direction.

Tertiary dimensions: Functional and role diversity

We've already examined Belbin's nine team roles, which are the *emergent* patterns of individuals' behaviors in teams, and why we should be intentional about diversifying these roles. In Chapter 1, we also introduced the concept of vertically sliced, cross-functional teams that include many diverse *functional roles* (which also correspond to the tertiary dimensions of diversity identified by Loden and Rosener). The required functional roles for any given team will be determined by the type of work the team does and its interactions with other teams in the organization, which we will cover in more detail in the next chapter. For now, we will consider the diverse roles of a team that is delivering a product feature end-to-end, leveraging internal and external platforms where required, so that it is capable of eliciting customer feedback and delivering on customer expectations.

In the Preface, we identified key personas this book is designed to help:

- Data scientists and ML engineers
- Software engineers, infrastructure engineers, architects
- Product managers, delivery managers, engineering managers

In addition, a cross-functional team may include many other functional roles so it's capable of delivering end-to-end value. For the benefit of the key personas this book is designed for, we provide some more examples in Table 10-1.

Table 10-1. Further cross-functional roles in ML teams

Cross-functional role	Objective of role	Symptoms when absent
UX research, UX design	Understand user needs and validate that solution designs will satisfy these needs	Unknown or poor product-market fit
Product manager	Shape and define the product vision, strategy, and roadmap; prioritize features to align with business objectives	Lack of compelling product direction, misalignment between customer needs, business goals and development efforts
Business analyst	Facilitate conversations between business stakeholders and delivery teams	Ambiguity about requirements or their priority
Domain subject matter expert (SME)	Share deep expertise about a particular business or knowledge domain	Lots of guesses, assumptions, and opinions; possible rework due to wrong assumptions

Cross-functional role	Objective of role	Symptoms when absent
Data engineer	Get data from A to B with appropriate governance	Hard or slow to access data or understand its suitability
Quality analyst	Help the team understand and assure quality in its deliverables	Unclear testing strategy, defects, and incidents; resultant rework

Your ML team probably doesn't have individuals in each of these roles, because if it did it would likely exceed the target size of five to nine members, which we'll discuss in Chapter 11, and it would be very unwieldy as a result. If your teammates have T-shaped skills (*https://oreil.ly/IJfGf*) (e.g., a data scientist who can also wear the hat of a data engineer or a business analyst), then these individuals might be able to play multiple roles, in which case you get both benefits of small teams and cross-functional role coverage.

Given these roles are part of delivering end-to-end value, if they are not permanently in your ML team, you will likely interact with them either through temporarily borrowing people or because these roles are being played by someone in another team upstream or downstream in the delivery process. It's worth thinking about how to make this work effectively, and we provide patterns for this in the Team Topologies section in Chapter 11.

ML teams also often require specialized *activity* focus for individuals—ongoing or for discrete periods—such as research into ML techniques to determine feasibility and viability of a proposed solution, the outcome of the research being hard to predict in advance. This type of research would contrast with more predictable product development activities (e.g., for a typical web application), which have a much lower risk of being infeasible, a wider variety of viable solutions, and a faster cadence of delivery. It's much easier to share these activities amongst the team as they require less specialization. While necessary in ML, specialized research shouldn't become siloed; we should seek to maintain communication and alignment on progress around these activities through established team practices like pairing, reviews, and showcases.

The point is not to collect an exhaustive set of roles here, but to highlight diverse functional roles—in addition to diverse individuals in the primary and secondary dimensions of diversity—as a building block of effective teams. In our experience, diverse teams deliver more effectively in dynamic environments because they can identify and resolve more issues that would otherwise create risk or block progress.

When team members appreciate the need for other roles, it helps build empathy and improves the flow of work through the team. In this respect, a diverse team will catalyze and nourish one another. We'll learn more about this in the next section, which shows how this final internal building block reinforces the others.

Purposeful, Shared Progress

> Knowing what serves to catalyze and nourish progress—and what does the opposite—
> turns out to be the key to effectively managing people and their work.
>
> —Teresa M. Amabile and Steven J. Kramer, "The Power of Small Wins" (*https://oreil.ly/-N2Sg*)

In their book *The Progress Principle* (Harvard Business Review Press), authors Teresa M. Amabile and Steven J. Kramer demonstrate the power of small wins (*https://oreil.ly/-N2Sg*) to improve the inner life of each of us at work. By studying nearly 12,000 diary entries from 238 participants drawn from 26 project teams at seven companies, the researchers were able to correlate various factors to improved or reduced quality of inner work life—feelings of satisfaction and achievement or of frustration and sadness.

The single most important factor in how participants felt each day was whether they made progress in meaningful work. The second most important factor was whether workers felt they were supported by catalysts (enabling systems and processes) or held back by inhibitors (lack of support or active blockers to completing work).

Throughout this book, we've studied how good team processes, practices, and tools act as catalysts to great work, while poor processes, practices, and tools act as inhibitors. A catalyst could be access to an awesome module like `scipy.spatial.KDTree`; an inhibitor could be waiting days or weeks for access to data. The Progress Principle provides another perspective on the importance of effective work systems to effective ML teams.

This research from over a decade ago is consistent with the most recent research into engineering effectiveness and developer experience, which we discuss later in this chapter. These two sets of research found that flow state, feedback loops and cognitive load are all factors that impact a positive work experience.

Work should be meaningful, or done with purpose, Amabile and Kramer recognize. Complex knowledge work like ML has the prerequisites for meaningful work, but this can be amplified by how ML objectives are connected to a wider organizational purpose. If an organization's purpose doesn't resonate with employees, or ML objectives are irrelevant or counter to that purpose, then doing ML for the intellectual exercise will quickly lose meaning. On the other hand, defining unique constraints based on the organization's purpose creates engaging challenges that lead teams to innovative ML solutions.

Indeed, where solving complex problems is aligned to an engaging organizational purpose, leadership of effective teams is about getting out of the way. This is demonstrated by Daniel Pink in his book *Drive* (Riverhead Books). Pink identified three key factors that motivate workers engaged in complex tasks: autonomy, mastery, and purpose. Extrinsic rewards may be irrelevant or even counterproductive in these scenarios. Autonomy is the freedom to self-direct, mastery is the cumulative effect of progress on personal skills, and purpose is the desire to contribute to something greater. Amabile and Kramer acknowledge: "For the progress principle to operate, the work must be meaningful to the person doing it."

Progress and purpose are key motivators for individuals. But if individuals are working to many different ends, to many different purposes, then it can be hard to see progress as a team, because *progress is a vector*, as illustrated in Figure 10-8 (note the similarity to Figure 10-4). By that, we mean that if everyone is progressing in the same direction, the progress adds up in that direction to greater than any individual contribution. But if everyone is progressing in different directions, the net result is no substantial change, and indeed some efforts undoing others. When individuals are working to different ends, it becomes apparent that we no longer have a team. When efforts are aligned, the results are much greater than when efforts of similar magnitude are misaligned.

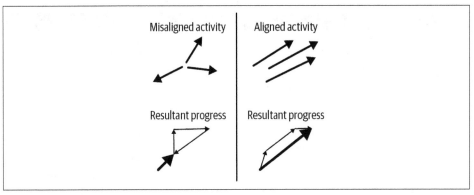

Figure 10-8. Progress as a vector

In ML teams, this misalignment may manifest in different tech stacks, different weighting of errors, or different product priorities between members of the team. There are some circumstances where we'll want to trial multiple approaches in parallel (aka a "bake off"), but these should be deliberately designed and timeboxed rather than linger indefinitely.

When individuals work together as team members, they become each other's *catalysts*. But when individuals work only to their own ends, their impact on each other is at best neutral— more likely, they *inhibit* one another. So, when progress is aligned between members of a team, we see more progress and more catalysts. When progress is misaligned, we see less progress and possibly inhibitors. This demonstrates why shared progress with purpose is a key building block of effective teams.

You've seen a set of building blocks and some detailed research behind them, leading to multifaceted frameworks for action. These are worth studying and will help you be a better team member or team leader, as they have helped us. But the good news is that you don't need to study this information exhaustively before acting. There are very simple tactics that address many of these building blocks at the same time, and that you can put into action right away!

Let's take a look at some of those tactics.

Internal Tactics to Build Effective Teams

This section isn't intended to deliver a prescriptive, theoretical approach to addressing team dysfunctions. Instead, Table 10-2 presents tactics that have been shown to work *in practice*. We have introduced many of these in earlier chapters. The frameworks and theories we've covered so far provide helpful mental models and some basis for why these tactics work.

Table 10-2. Internal tactics to build effective ML teams

Tactic	Description	Key targets	What good looks like
Team charter (*https://oreil.ly/FAWjC*)	Description of values and commitments the team makes to each other	• Trust • Diversity	Genuine, achievable, and relevant commitments
Personal canvas (*https://oreil.ly/HUw0q*)	A3 management (*https://oreil.ly/VVUzF*) technique for capturing personal objectives	• Purposeful, shared progress • Diversity	Goals related to immediate work, interests, and long-term career
Visual management of work (*https://oreil.ly/Oai1L*)	Use of a Kanban board or wall to track stage of completion and collaboration on tasks	• Communication • Purposeful, shared progress	Board is source of truth for progress and coordination, further active information radiators (*https://oreil.ly/mg8gg*) as required
Iteration planning (*https://oreil.ly/AvPX4*)	Alignment on work over the next cycle	• Communication • Purposeful, shared progress • Trust	Clarity on objectives within team and with stakeholders, retaining flexibility in plan
Showcase (*https://oreil.ly/pDhnr*)	Regular demonstration of solution to stakeholders	• Communication • Purposeful, shared progress • Trust	Working software that stakeholders can interact with; feedback rapidly incorporated into product requirements
Speedback (*https://oreil.ly/Q1z76*)	Feedback sharing between pairs of team members in rapid rotation	• Communication • Trust	Team members (while possibly apprehensive prior) emerge energized by recognition and growth opportunities
Retrospectives (*https://oreil.ly/I9YFX*)	Regular review of what's working and what's not	• Trust • Purposeful, shared progress	Safe environment, actionable changes to system of work

Form Versus Essence: The Story of NUMMI

In their book *Lean Enterprise* (O'Reilly), the authors recounted a story about the success of NUMMI (New United Motor Manufacturing, Inc.). Before it became NUMMI, it was a Fremont assembly plant operated by General Motors between 1962 and 1982, and employees at the Fremont plant were considered the worst workforce in the US automobile industry (*https://oreil.ly/fnv2m*). Following Toyota's takeover, the plant adopted Toyota Production System (TPS) practices. Within two years, the NUMMI factory was producing cars at the same speed as the Japanese factories, and Corollas produced at NUMMI were judged to be equal in quality to those produced in Japan with a similar number of defects per 100 vehicles.

A salient feature of the TPS was the importance placed on building quality into products. The TPS emphasizes embedding quality within products as its utmost priority; hence, when an issue arises, it's addressed immediately and the system is then refined to prevent such issues in the future. When an issue arose, workers could pull the Andon Cord (*https://oreil.ly/hEbcb*) to flag any concerns. Managers were then expected to attend to the issue, collaboratively working with the employee to find a resolution. If the problem persisted, the production line could be halted, ensuring quality was prioritized. Post-incident, the team would collaboratively brainstorm and implement strategies to prevent similar issues in the future.

While Toyota was transparent about its operational practices, even offering plant tours to competitors, the real magic lay not in the tools and processes like Andon Cords but in the ingrained organizational culture. An anecdotal instance reflects this, when a GM vice president aimed to emulate NUMMI's success by documenting every aspect of the plant. The superficial replication resulted in a factory equipped with Andon Cords, but with nobody pulling them. The core reason was that the managerial incentives were misaligned—managers and their reports were driven by the number of cars produced, irrespective of quality, rather than the collaborative ethos central to NUMMI's success.

The takeaway is clear: While practices are essential, the underlying culture and values are what truly drive success.

We mentioned in Chapter 1 common traps relating to Ways of Working: going through the motions of team ceremonies, without substance, without understanding the *why*. Now that you've finished reading this section, which ceremonies are your team currently doing that contribute to its building blocks, and which are empty theater?

Now, let's complement these theories and techniques for building effective ML teams with techniques on how to improve engineering effectiveness.

Improving Flow with Engineering Effectiveness

While the techniques we've discussed thus far are applicable to any team, we've also highlighted particular considerations for *machine learning* teams. As we've discussed, ML teams share many of the same characteristics as software engineering teams (with some additions), and hence approaches to engineering effectiveness are generally applicable to ML teams.

Where ML product development differs from software engineering is in the extent of discovery activities (which result in applicable knowledge) and delivery activities (which result in maintainable working software). Of course, discovery is an integral part of software delivery because not all the answers are known *a priori*, but ML products are distinguished by the extent of discovery required to determine if a product is feasible and viable, based on data that might be curated.

The curation of this data also requires complex data supply chains that introduce additional dependencies, effort, and failure modes, in both discovery and delivery. In contrast, software systems that deal primarily or exclusively with operational data minimize or avoid this complexity of analytic data supply chains. To the further applicability of software engineering, however, we note that modern data engineering practice aims to make these data supply chains "software-defined" as much as possible. So we find software engineering remains a useful framing for ML product development, with these caveats.

In recent years, research on developer experience (or DevEx) and engineering effectiveness has yielded some insights about the factors that improve or hinder the flow of value. In a research paper, "An Actionable Framework for Understanding and Improving Developer Experience" (*https://oreil.ly/9r4aA*), the authors identified more than 25 sociotechnical factors that affect DevEx. For example, interruptions, unrealistic deadlines, and friction in development tools negatively affect DevEx, while having clear tasks, well-organized code, and pain-free releases improve it. (High-five your book if you can relate with the sentence you just read.) A common misconception is that DevEx is primarily affected by technology and tools. This paper, however, similar to "The Power of Small Wins," shows that human factors such as having clear goals for projects and feeling psychologically safe on a team have a substantial impact on developers' performance.[4]

---

[4] A special thanks to this paper's coauthor Abi Noda (*https://oreil.ly/CFuTr*) for his thought leadership and curation in the space of developer experience.

In another paper, "DevEx: What Actually Drives Productivity" (*https://oreil.ly/yLDNq*), the same authors along with Nicole Forsgren further distill these factors into three core dimensions: feedback loops, flow state, and cognitive load (see Figure 10-9).[5]

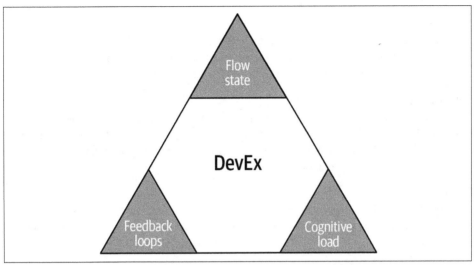

Figure 10-9. Three dimensions of developer experience (source: adapted from an image in "DevEx: What Actually Drives Productivity" [https://oreil.ly/yLDNq] by Abi Noda, Margaret-Anne Storey, Nicole Forsgren, and Michaela Greiler)

Let's go through the three core dimensions of DevEx.

Feedback Loops

A typical developer or ML practitioner's day consists of numerous tasks relying on feedback from tools and people. For example, ML practitioners may spend significant time waiting for model training runs to complete. Later, they may wait for approval from code reviewers, and later still, wait for an ops team to deploy a model. All of this waiting blocks their ability to make progress.

Slow feedback loops interrupt the development process, leading to frustration and delays as developers wait or decide to switch contexts. Slow feedback loops cause additional interruptions when feedback from systems (e.g., production alerts) or people (e.g., code review comments) is returned at some unpredictable time and

---

5 Another interesting result in distilling the dimensions of developer productivity comes from Ciera Jaspan and Collin Green (*https://oreil.ly/QSdez*), who lead the Engineering Productivity Research team at Google. They find the following three key dimensions: speed (how fast work gets done), ease (how easy the work gets done), and quality (how well work gets done). Each dimension entails a set of measurable factors and metrics.

requires immediate attention. In contrast, fast feedback loops allow developers to complete their work and test their ideas quickly with minimal friction.

In our book, we've expounded on many techniques for shortening feedback loops across disciplines:

Product

Practices such as prototype testing, customer research, and data product canvases help teams discover customer's pains and needs in a much more cost-effective way than building actual software and ML solutions (see Chapters 1 and 2).

Engineering and ML

Practices such as automated testing, pair programming, and CD4ML give ML practitioners fast feedback on code changes. Proof-of-concepts also help to validate the feasibility of ML solutions before investing in engineering effort (see Chapter 1 and Chapters 3 to 9).

Delivery

Practices such as user stories with clear acceptance criteria, regular showcases, and pair programming shorten ML practitioners' feedback cycle by orders of magnitude—from days to minutes, from weeks to days (see Chapters 1 and 2).

As products mature, datasets grow in size and improvements become more marginal. Training runs may require lots of computation. Short of large capital investments, there may not be much you can do to reduce cycle time for any one job. The next best thing you can do is to reduce your *duty cycle* so that long-running jobs are mainly hands-off, and easy to context-switch in and out of. This allows you to run multiple jobs—from one product or multiple products—in parallel. The same techniques that rapidly brought you to this stage of product development—such as clear definitions of done and heavy automation of processes—will help you shift smoothly from minimizing feedback cycle time to minimizing the feedback duty cycle. However, when stuffing your off-cycles with more jobs, keep in mind that chasing high utilization is like kryptonite to fast feedback. You should periodically review whether there's anything you can do to reduce cycle time, and you might even set hard limits on cycle time (*https://oreil.ly/vK80R*) as a fitness function of your development process.

Cognitive Load

Building ML systems is a complex undertaking, with many moving parts, and the fast-evolving toolchain further adds to an ML practitioner's cognitive load.

Cognitive load comprises all the mental processing required for a developer to perform a task. Factors that contribute to total cognitive load can include *essential* complexity (e.g., understanding an unfamiliar ML technique or problem space) but a big part of the cognitive load can arise from *incidental* complexity (e.g., messy codebases, interruptions from accidental mistakes, too much mental work in progress, context switching, and lack of clear documentation).

To make the concept of cognitive load more tangible for management in your organization, you may determine your own specific definition and measures of cognitive load, or you may use the upcoming cognitive load assessment tool (*https://oreil.ly/xflKg*) from Team Topologies.

To improve team effectiveness, organizations and teams should focus on reducing cognitive load by removing avoidable obstacles in the development journey. This helps to minimize context switching and creates bandwidth for teams to focus on producing good and maintainable solutions. Platform teams can help by providing user-friendly, self-service tools to help ML practitioners with undifferentiated, repetitive labor (e.g., manual model deployments) and help the team streamline the steps for model development and release.

Flow State

Flow, a term coined in 1990 by Mihaly Csikszentmihalyi, refers to a mental state in which a person performing an activity is fully immersed in a feeling of energized focus, full involvement, and enjoyment.

Csikszentmihalyi's research (*https://oreil.ly/TmuNq*) found that being in a state of flow at work leads to higher productivity, innovation, and employee development. Similarly, studies have shown that developers who enjoy their work perform better (*https://oreil.ly/5dGGO*) and produce higher-quality products.

Interruptions and delays—which relate to the feedback loops dimension—hinder a developer's ability to experience flow state. Other factors that contribute to a state of flow include having autonomy at work, having clear goals, and engaging in stimulating and challenging tasks.

To protect a team's flow state, teams can minimize disruptions by having well-run meetings (e.g., the 7P framework [*https://oreil.ly/2i2w1*]), developing appropriate etiquette for messaging channels (e.g., Slack's guidelines [*https://oreil.ly/8DqGL*]), leveraging asynchronous modes of feedback where appropriate, and reducing unplanned work. Team leaders, even as they steer the team toward a common goal, should foster a flow state by giving team members autonomy and opportunities to work on fulfilling challenges.

Note that when we describe protecting flow state, we're not advocating for developers to behave antisocially, avoid communicating with the rest of the team, and measure themselves purely on individual output. Flow state only delivers outcomes if aligned to the team's collective purpose, which must be established and refreshed by ongoing communication as the team's understanding of the problem and solution evolves.

Throughout this book, we've shared many techniques that help teams shorten feedback loops (e.g., prototype testing, customer research, automated tests), manage cognitive load (e.g., refactoring, tech debt management, reduce WIP) and maximize flow state (e.g., avoid context switching, prefer pair programming over code reviews, writing clear user stories). These specific practices will help you improve the set of overarching DevEx metrics proposed by Forsgren et al. (see Table 10-3). This provides a set of measures for any interventions you might make across these three core dimensions.

Table 10-3. Example DevEx metrics (source: "DevEx: What Actually Drives Productivity" [https://oreil.ly/yLDNq])

	Feedback loops	Cognitive load	Flow state
Perceptions *Human attitudes and opinions*	• Satisfaction with automated test speed and output • Satisfaction with time it takes to validate a local change • Satisfaction with time it takes to deploy a change to production	• Perceived complexity of codebase • Ease of debugging production systems • Ease of understanding documentation	• Perceived ability to focus and avoid interruptions • Satisfaction with clarity of task or project goals • Perceived disruptiveness of being on-call
Workflows *System and process behaviors*	• Time it takes to generate CI results • Code review turnaround time • Deployment lead time (time it takes to get a change released to production)	• Time it takes to get answers to technical questions • Manual steps required to deploy a change • Frequency of documentation improvements	• Number of blocks of time without meetings or interruptions • Frequency of unplanned tasks or requests • Frequency of incidents requiring team attention
KPIs *North star metrics*	• Overall perceived ease of delivering software • Employee engagement or satisfaction • Perceived productivity		

As you can see, these metrics are further grouped into three categories:

Perceptions

Metrics in the Perceptions category are intended to measure the three dimensions of DevEx based on human opinions and sentiment. Example metrics here include satisfaction with test speed, perceived code complexity, and clarity of tasks and goals.

Workflows

Metrics in the Workflows category evaluate the effectiveness of system and process behaviors in development. Example metrics here include the turnaround time for code reviews, steps or time required to deploy a change, and frequency of unplanned work and incidents.

KPIs

Metrics in the KPIs category focus on overarching indicators that gauge the overall success and health of the developer experience. Example metrics here include employee engagement and satisfaction, perceived productivity, and perceived ease of delivering software.

To reiterate, these are example metrics and meant to be a starting point. You should adapt them to your team's specific contexts and needs. Select metrics that accurately pinpoint bottlenecks and inefficiencies so that your teams can refine and optimize the flow of value as you build out ML systems.

Pitfalls of Measuring Productivity, and How to Avoid Them

A hot topic of debate in 2023 is whether we can (and should) measure developer productivity. McKinsey's article "Yes, You Can Measure Software Developer Productivity" (*https://oreil.ly/r8ENB*) will have caught the attention of many in management and leadership positions. It also caught the eye of many software engineering leaders, who penned responses based on their own experience and research, which refute many of McKinsey's contentions.

Kent Beck offers cautionary tales (*https://oreil.ly/uCKvk*) from his time at Facebook, revealing the downsides of overemphasizing such metrics. Initially, surveys at Facebook provided valuable insights into developer sentiments. However, people who wanted to track trends translated surveys into numerical scores, then people conducting performance reviews started referring to the scores, and then people set targets on these scores derived from surveys, divorced from their original meaning. What followed was a cascade of unintended behaviors: managers negotiated scores with their teams and directors made cuts based solely on scores. Rather than empowering managers and teams to understand their performance, management's incorrect application of metrics led to people gaming the system, reducing actual productivity while negating any insight that could have been gained.

Peter Gillard-Moss, in his article "Beyond Metrics: Creating Cultures of Engineering Excellence" (*https://oreil.ly/Me0DU*), notes the measurement motivation of many C-suites, who have "discover[ed] they are blind now [that] engineering has replaced business operations as their strategic execution engine". Gillard-Moss talks about the correct use of metrics for teams and leaders. Metrics help to set direction, visualize progress, spot opportunities, and so on. All the things your car measures—speed, fuel, oil, temperature—are indicators that your car is working correctly. And you want to keep them within reasonable boundaries and act on them when they move outside. The problem is when metrics are used as targets, rather than as indicators—you drive to get to a destination, not to maintain a certain engine temperature.

Dan North addresses the content of the 2023 McKinsey article in an imagined technical review (*https://oreil.ly/PFmwd*). He raises numerous issues but summarizes them as the fallacies that: (i) software development is a reducible activity (and should be measured as such) and (ii) software development is primarily about coding (and should be measured as such). North raises issues with individual contributor metrics, and other reductionist approaches, which align with our contention of effective *teams* and reinforcing practices. North also highlights the value-add activities in development beyond writing application code, such as testing and infrastructure automation, which we also cover in detail earlier in this book. North makes the point that software engineering is not under-measured, rather frequently mismeasured.

We described in Chapter 2 the extent of discovery activity in ML product development. This might be described as the "data science" part. We note that the McKinsey authors didn't contend that you can measure data scientist productivity, but similar measurement pressures may exist. A key indicator that the data science doohickey in your product development vehicle is working correctly is that you have a portfolio of experiments that can be conducted in reasonable timeboxes. With this in place, you might then equally apply the flow state, feedback loops, and cognitive load triad to data science activity to give you confidence that you're within reasonable boundaries of productivity, without resorting to counterproductive measurements.

Hence, these critics agree it's imperative to treat productivity metrics as tools to facilitate understanding rather than absolute objectives. They collectively reiterate Goodhart's law (*https://oreil.ly/ab0hg*): When a measure becomes a target, it ceases to be a good measure. As ML practitioners, we are well aware that when systems are naively optimized to an objective function, they ignore any common sense we might expect, and this may produce wildly unexpected effects. The more productive (pun intended) approach to more effective development is to address the issues that are known to reduce developer and team productivity, as DevEx research demonstrates.

Thanks for sticking with us through a wide-ranging chapter. We're ready to wrap things up now and hope you are ready for the next stage of your ML journey with a vastly more effective team.

Conclusion

Let's recap the tremendous ground that we've covered in this chapter:

- We outlined the common challenges that we've seen ML teams face—such as trust, communication, purposeful progress, and diversity—that if not managed properly reduce a team's effectiveness.

- We summarized some key research and frameworks that help us understand what enables and inhibits behaviors that improve a team's effectiveness.

- We shared a set of tactics and techniques that you can apply in your teams to cultivate trust, alignment, diversity, and shared purpose.
- Finally, we discussed engineering effectiveness, developer experience, and pitfalls to avoid when measuring productivity.

These theories and frameworks are valuable tools for understanding and improving factors that hinder teams, but despite this they are all limited models of real human behavior, each with its nuances and shortcomings. They don't tell us what to do in every situation, and we've already contended that every team is unique. To bridge the *knowing-doing gap* and convert understanding to practical action, we highlighted the common ground and many connections between these tools and we provided some simple tactics that are widely used. These tactics are also incomplete, however, in that they will require repeated practice and adaptation. Despite these challenges, we've used these building blocks time and again to help build high-performing ML teams. When you notice any of the challenges we described in your team, consider which building block you could use to create the conditions that help your team members be their best and do their best work.

Ultimately, we see that building effective ML teams is a challenging journey, but the learning, shared achievement and growth opportunities on offer make the journey worthwhile. We share some final words of encouragement for the doers of deeds, from former President Theodore Roosevelt's speech "Citizen in a Republic":

> It is not the critic who counts; not the [person] who points out how the strong [person] stumbles, or where the doer of deeds could have done them better. The credit belongs to the [person] who is actually in the arena, whose face is marred by dust and sweat and blood; who strives valiantly; who errs, who comes short again and again, because there is no effort without error and shortcoming; but who does actually strive to do the deeds; who knows great enthusiasms, the great devotions; who spends himself in a worthy cause; who at the best knows in the end the triumph of high achievement, and who at the worst, if [they fail], at least [fail] while daring greatly...

Join us in the next chapter, where we'll look beyond the effectiveness of one team to consider the challenges that teams face when the organization scales to multiple teams working on ML, delving into the complexities of inter-team dynamics, coordination, and the broader organizational challenges that arise with growth.

## CHAPTER 11

Effective ML Organizations

I've given all I can,

It's not enough

—"Karma Police" by Radiohead

Have you ever worked on a great team that nonetheless struggled to have an impact because it was being asked to do the wrong sort of work, or focus on too many things at once, or was constantly waiting on other teams to get things done?

On our journey so far, we've looked long and hard at what happens inside ML teams, including the complementary mechanics of work practices, how we configure our technology, and the humanistic elements of teamwork. We've also looked at the interplay between product and ML delivery in teams. This chapter takes us a step further, examining how team effectiveness is moderated by organizational factors and, in turn, how effective organizations are built from effective teams.

This organizational perspective is critical to building effective ML teams, because even the best team—a team with finely tuned dependency management, continuous delivery, automated testing, supercharged IDEs, trust, communication, diversity, and purpose—will be beaten by a bad system of poorly shaped work or excessive organizational dependencies.

From a systems perspective, a team transforms work into outputs. The work may come directly from interactions with a customer (*https://oreil.ly/fruBw*) or it may be defined by another dependent team in the organization. The team's outputs either directly serve the customer or serve dependent teams. Poorly designed work and output dependencies between teams are the external causes of ineffective teams, as visualized in Figure 11-1.

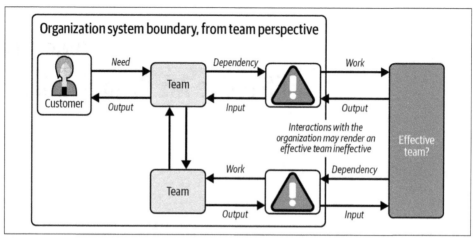

Figure 11-1. A systems perspective of team and organizational interactions

Poorly designed interactions between teams result in a poor fit of work for teams. Both of these issues—poorly designed work and output dependencies—cause technology, process, or knowledge dependencies. Dependencies result in waiting, defects, and other wastes due to backlog coupling, interruptions to flow, and increased cognitive load. All these things impact team performance and satisfaction. When multiplied across many teams, these things severely impact organization performance. But they can't be solved within any individual team alone.

> Everything,
>
> Everything,
>
> Everything,
>
> Everything in its right place
>
> —"Everything in its Right Place" by Radiohead

We can address these two issues and improve team effectiveness by considering the design of team shapes and interaction modes in organizations, as demonstrated in *Team Topologies* (IT Revolution Press) by Matthew Skelton and Manuel Pais.

To conclude our journey, we'll explore in this chapter the symptoms of poorly coordinated teams and introduce a framework based on *Team Topologies* to help scale effective ML teams across the organization. In this chapter, we will:

- Describe the challenges that organizations face as they scale and have more teams involved in the delivery of ML solutions

- Introduce the Team Topologies model, its concepts and principles for reducing coupling between teams and improving the flow of value

- Apply the Team Topologies lens on ML teams, by describing the pros and cons of various team shapes, their associated interaction modes, and how to pick the suitable team shape based on your current objectives
- Explore how ML teams may be combined in team topologies and how topologies may evolve over time with increasing scale
- Outline the principles of intentional leadership that help to cultivate high-performing teams and organizations

Figure 11-2 shows the building blocks we cover in Chapters 10 and 11. Organizing for fast flow is the objective of the Team Topologies model. We'll also discuss how an organization can shape its portfolio of work to improve the effectiveness of multiple teams. Finally, we conclude with the role of intentional leadership and practices that leaders can adopt to build high-performing teams.

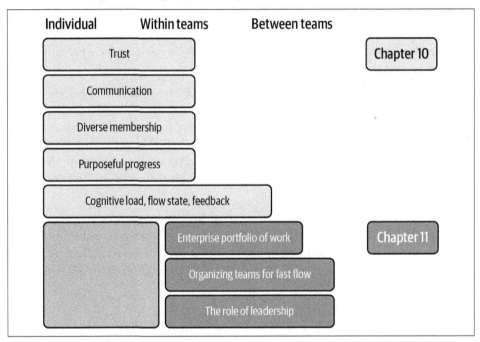

Figure 11-2. Building blocks of effective ML teams and effective ML organizations covered in Chapters 10 and 11

Because each organization has unique factors in terms of market, product, technology, and Ways of Working, some thought is required to adapt these building blocks but they are nonetheless generally applicable. Through these building blocks, we'll explore what might be the right place for every type of ML team in an organization to enhance the effectiveness of *all* teams—let's get started.

Common Challenges Faced by ML Organizations

In this section, like in Chapter 10, we'll look at common challenges that organizations with multiple ML teams (hereafter referred to as "ML organizations") face, through the lens of some fictional, but relatable scenarios. While Chapter 10 considered problems faced by individuals and teams, in this section we introduce scenarios related to how teams interact with each other and how work flows to each team, which can also render teams more or less effective.

Let's look at a few scenarios illustrating some common challenges that ML organizations face:

Centralized team has too many responsibilities
> Dana, Ted, and all the other ML practitioners in the organization are rolled up into a centralized Data Science team to consolidate expertise and to service all the ML needs of multiple cross-functional product engineering teams across the organization. All things ML gravitate toward the centralized Data Science team, leading to a long queue and varied backlog of projects and operational ML systems owned by Dana's team.
>
> All stakeholders claim their work is urgent, while not always responding with urgency to Dana's team's asks of them. Without an enterprise prioritization mechanism, Dana feels compelled to run many projects and operational ML models simultaneously. This means her team is highly utilized, but also frequently context switching (and perhaps also divided by intra-team silos). As a result, projects begin to lag and operational performance and robustness of systems suffers.
>
> The team members feel dispirited by this lack of progress, while also feeling overworked and unable to deliver their best work. Meanwhile, stakeholders and other teams are also frustrated by the lack of progress toward current goals and put their future ML ambitions on hold, making the organization as a whole less responsive and competitive.

Inter-team dependencies: handoffs and waiting
> Dana's Data Science team is responsible for training ML models. Anaya leads the team that owns the frontend and API that will serve the model.
>
> Dana just finished a story that improved the model performance by 5%, by including a new feature. However, before she can release the model to production, she needs to wait on Anaya's team to pick up a story to update the frontend and API to include the new feature when sending requests to a model.
>
> This mode of dependency is also known as backlog coupling (*https://oreil.ly/ 6vz_r*).

After a few weeks, when Anaya's team has capacity to pick up the story, Dana has to drop whatever she is working on, context switch back to this story, and coordinate with Anaya's team to implement the change on the backend and frontend. In between these bursts of activity, this story card, along with other similar cards, sits in the "Waiting" column. In addition to the delays, quality issues are easily introduced in this mode of working.

Duplication of effort in multiple cross-functional teams

Ellie and Eduardo are both team leads in two different cross-functional teams. Each of them owns an end-to-end vertical slice of the product experience, including data engineering, model training, API, and UI deployments. Neither team needs to wait on or depend on another team to deliver a feature to customers.

However, both teams have independently spent significant effort in solving similar problems. For example, to solve the problem of provisioning scalable ML training infrastructure, Eduardo's team wrote some intricate DevOps scripts to provision and tear down GPU instances. Unknown to Eduardo, Ellie's team has integrated a GPU-as-a-service offering.

This cost both teams additional weeks and months in their respective release timelines, as well as the ongoing maintenance cost of each solution.

Effective Organizations as Teams of Teams

In the previous chapter, we primarily considered effectiveness at the level of individuals combined into teams—an inside view of a team. In this chapter, we'll take an outside view, and look at the roles of whole teams and the interactions between teams. While it's helpful to take both views, it's also not possible in general to cleanly decouple one view from the other.

The work and systems in organizations require heterogeneous skills to deliver and maintain, and the people who work in an organization have heterogeneous skills, too. Finding the best match is not always straightforward. In working with one delivery center of approximately 100 people, we found that nearly 150 distinct technology and business skills were required to manage the systems and deliver the work for which they were responsible.

Historically, the teams at this delivery center were organized by function and used waterfall delivery. The flow of work was slow and unpredictable. To address this, the center organized around cross-functional teams using agile delivery, and the flow of work became visible and improved somewhat, but it was still complex and slow due to inter-team dependencies. In a third iteration, the cross-functional teams were clustered in complementary groups of three with an explicit collaboration mechanism coordinating the work between the units of each "superteam." This enabled faster flow of work, improved capacity to do work, and greater delivery of value.

Also contributing to improved flow during this period was the improved ability of the delivery center and its constituent teams to slice their work vertically, which allowed regular realization of value (as described in Chapters 1 and 2). This was in contrast to the historical alternative of delivering one "horizontal" solution component at a time and waiting for its later integration to realize value, which would be in far less frequent and less predictable lumps.

The lesson here is that the work, technology systems, team member skills, and team interactions are interdependent. The Team Topologies model—while advocating for long-lived teams—doesn't assume static work, static systems, static team membership, or static interactions. Rather, it allows give and take in each element to find an optimal configuration that may evolve over time.

The Role of Value-Driven Portfolio Management

> Team Topologies stresses that teams should be cross-functional with a strong purpose aligned to the flow of value. EDGE stresses that portfolios should be managed by value and delivered by self-sufficient cross functional teams, again aligned to value.
>
> —Peter Gillard-Moss, "Beyond Team Topologies with Team Portfolios" (*https://oreil.ly/Ip_M5*)

You've seen in previous chapters how the shape of the work that feeds into a single team can impact its effectiveness. As you saw in this chapter's earlier examples, the same is true at the team-of-teams level—the shape of an organization's entire portfolio of work can impact the effectiveness of multiple teams. If the collective teams are expected to execute a portfolio of work that is not clearly aligned to customer or business value, or that is to be delivered in large batches over long time horizons, it will be much harder or even impossible to organize effective teams around its delivery.

The book *EDGE: Value-Driven Digital Transformation* (Addison-Wesley Professional) by Jim Highsmith, Linda Luu, and David Robinson shows how to build an enterprise portfolio of work that is aligned to business vision and strategy, and reflects an evolving plan of execution for autonomous cross-functional teams. The authors describe this as *value-driven portfolio management*, and the primary representation of the portfolio of work is the *Lean Value Tree*, as shown in Figure 11-3.

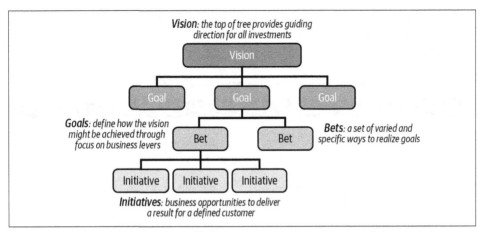

Figure 11-3. The Lean Value Tree allows an enterprise to capture and share its vision and strategy

These concepts, it hardly needs stating, are further topics about which an entire book has been written, and we encourage you to read it if you are curious. The key takeaway for us is that a portfolio organized into dynamic bets and initiatives, each aligned to strategic goals, shapes the work in a way that effective ML teams can reasonably deliver it.

Conversely, if the enterprise portfolio is characterized by large and inflexible programs, designed for teams with limited autonomy and infrequent feedback, this arguably violates the core assumption that we are organizing for fast flow. For the purposes of this chapter, we'll assume the portfolio of work is sympathetic to the Team Topologies model we explore. Let's now see how the different team shapes and their interaction modes form the building blocks of the Team Topologies model.

Team Topologies Model

Team Topologies (https://oreil.ly/yPzsl) offers a structured approach for optimizing how teams should be organized and how they should interact to improve delivery flow and feedback in a software delivery context.

One of its central tenets is that by having the appropriate team structures and establishing a limited set of well-defined interaction modes (between teams and the systems they own), we can *reduce coupling* between teams, keep *cognitive load* at a manageable level, and thereby *improve delivery flow* among autonomous and aligned teams.

As we introduced in Chapter 9, Team Topologies emphasizes teams as the primary mechanism of software delivery and introduces four fundamental team types and three interaction modes (see Table 11-1).

Table 11-1. Fundamental team types and interaction modes in Team Topologies

Term	Definition	Examples (nonexhaustive)
Team types		
Stream-aligned teams	Teams aligned to a flow of work from a segment of the business domain, focusing on delivering end-to-end value.	• Product checkout page • Product details page
Platform teams	They offer services, tools, and platforms to other teams, allowing them to work more effectively.	• Data platform • ML platform
Enabling teams	These teams assist stream-aligned teams in overcoming obstacles, typically by helping them through internal consulting and advisory.	• Security • Architecture
Complicated subsystem teams	Teams that focus on parts of the system that require deep, specific expertise and can't be simplified.	• Search and ranking • Recommender systems • The "Data Science team"
Team interaction modes		
Collaboration	Teams work closely together for a defined period to discover new solutions.	A stream-aligned team (e.g., home page) works with a complicated subsystem team (e.g., recommender systems) to work out how to provide users with personalized recommendations when they visit the homepage.
X-as-a-service	One team provides something as a service to another team, with a clear contract.	A complicated subsystem team (e.g., recommender systems) creates a data product or service that provides a list of product recommendations for any given user. Teams owning other parts of the product (e.g., web home page, mobile home page, checkout, marketing) can consume this product-recommendations capability on a self-service basis.
Facilitating	One team helps another team achieve its goals by fast-tracking its learning.	The security team (an enabling team) helps a stream-aligned team by running security threat modeling workshops to help the team identify security failure modes and design recommendations for building security in.

Figure 11-4 shows the visual nomenclature for these four team types and three interaction modes. Each team type has a distinct geometric shape and color in this guide, and each interaction mode also has a specific representation. The more intensive interactions—*collaboration* and *facilitating*—are shown as geometric intersections between the interacting teams, with a distinct pattern for each, while the mode of *x-as-a-service* indicates a mediated interaction (e.g. with technology) with a back-to-back brackets symbol. We use a pragmatic variant of this visual nomenclature in diagrams in this chapter.[1]

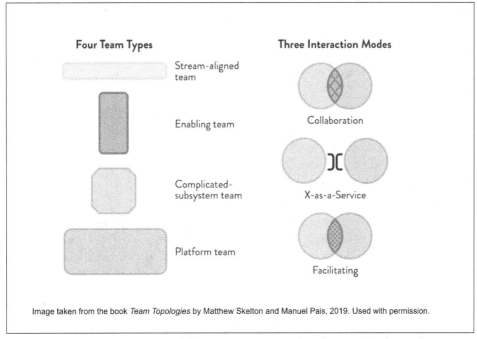

Image taken from the book *Team Topologies* by Matthew Skelton and Manuel Pais, 2019. Used with permission.

Figure 11-4. Four team types and three interaction modes of Team Topologies (source: Team Topologies by Matthew Skelton and Manuel Pais [IT Revolution Press, 2019], used with permission)

---

1 The visual guide to Team Topologies in Figure 11-4 is visually pleasing to your authors, but we note some practical shortcomings for diagramming, primarily: three rounded rectangles only varying in aspect ratio, interaction modes as shape intersections with patterned fills, and the use of back-to-back-brackets for an as-a-service glyph. These issues challenge some drawing tools, and accessibility in some media, in addition to making some custom topologies difficult to draw (though maybe that's a deliberate decision to encourage simplicity!). We only raise these issues because we find Team Topologies so useful and hence, we frequently find ourselves drawing them. A better visual nomenclature is provided in "Team Interaction Modeling with Team Topologies" (*https://oreil.ly/vg_3n*), and we will use this treatment going forward for diagrams in this chapter.

Now that you're equipped with the basic concepts of Team Topologies, let's look at the core principles of this model and how they help to reduce coupling between teams and improve flow:

Conway's Law

Conway's Law states that a system's design will often mirror the organization's communication structure. Team structures should, therefore, be consciously designed to produce the desired system architecture.

Cognitive load

Each team should only have as much work as they can handle while fully understanding the system they're responsible for. Overloading teams harms productivity. Note that we provide a definition for *cognitive load* in Chapter 10 in the section on engineering effectiveness.

Team-first thinking

Team-first thinking prioritizes the collective intelligence and capability of a team over individual capacities, recognizing that long-standing teams develop deeper synergies and collaborations. The idea is to maintain stable, long-lived teams that evolve, learn, and grow together, as opposed to frequently disbanded and reformed teams for different projects.

It is worth noting here that the term "team" has a very specific meaning in Team Topologies. As Skelton and Pais note: "The team is the smallest entity of delivery within an organization and should be a stable group of five to nine people working towards *a shared goal* as a unit." In Chapter 10, we also highlighted the importance of working toward a shared goal.

Fracture planes

Fracture planes (or software responsibility boundaries) refer to the divisions or boundaries within a system where subsystems and their supporting teams can—with the help of clear and well-defined interfaces—be separated to work independently.

Fracture planes may be:

- Business "domain" (*https://oreil.ly/96uoY*) boundaries—a distinct area of business capability (e.g., for an online travel booking platform, some domains might include holiday experiences, booking, payment)

- Regulatory compliance—make compliance easier where required but don't require it everywhere

- Other discontinuities in risk profile (e.g., acquiring versus retaining customers)

- Change in cadence—avoid coupling fast-changing areas to slow-changing areas

- Performance isolation—decouple bursty from predictable workloads
- Technology—assuming you have already tried to bring the more constraining technology up to the level of the less constraining technology
- Team location—aim for either colocation or remote-first and be aware of the impact of major time zone differences on communication
- User personas—where different user groups have sufficiently different needs
- Any other "natural" fracture planes at your organization

By identifying and organizing teams around these fracture planes, organizations can ensure that teams have a clear, cohesive domain of responsibility, enabling them to operate with greater autonomy and reducing the need for frequent coordination with other teams. Fracture planes guide the formation of decoupled, self-sufficient teams that can deliver value more rapidly.

Team encapsulation

Teams should maintain a certain level of encapsulation, where they expose well-defined interfaces or APIs that can be consumed and depended upon by teams while keeping their internal workings and details hidden.

Team interactions

Organizations should use defined team interaction modes (Collaboration, X-as-a-service, and Facilitating) to reduce miscommunications, misalignments, and unnecessary dependencies between teams. The number of interaction modes for any one team should also be limited to avoid coordination overhead and cognitive overload.

Handoffs

Handoffs between teams introduce delays and potential misunderstandings, leading to quality issues and rework. Reducing handoffs streamlines delivery.

Evolvable team structures

Team shapes are not one and done and set in stone forever. As technology and the organization mature, the team structures and interactions should adapt accordingly.

These core elements and principles of application are relevant to many organizational settings, especially in technology delivery. Reflect for a moment on the team shape that best reflects your current team, your interaction modes with other teams, and how well this organizational design aligns with the core principles. Do you see opportunities for improvement?

These elements and principles are the basis of Team Topologies for ML teams, too. Many of them apply directly to ML teams, and we'll explore the nuances specific to ML next.

Team Topologies for ML Teams

In this section, we'll share the various topologies we've identified for ML teams in the wild, along with their strengths and weaknesses, and interaction modes with other teams.

You can consider these team shapes as suitable building blocks for building effective ML organizations. These aren't the only building blocks and they can be misapplied (see weaknesses) but we think they are sensible defaults for a small set of reference topologies given the many possible arrangements of teams. The scale of ML applications and number of people in an organization help to identify whether simple topologies will be sufficient, or more complex topologies are required.

If you're experiencing organizational ineffectiveness with ML, and your team topologies deviate from the sensible defaults below, we recommend exploring what you can do to move closer to these defaults.

Stream-aligned team: ML product team

A stream-aligned ML team has a mix of digital, data, and ML capabilities, and delivers user-facing ML features, such as content recommendations. Presuming its interactions and dependencies can be limited, this is the default unit of scaling your organization's ML capability—either from 0 to 1, or from N to N + 1 products or features at any stage. Ask first if an ML product team will address your business needs, and then explore other options if not.

To strike the appropriate balance of the many digital and data capabilities required within a reasonably-sized team, however, the stream-aligned team cannot support many ML specialists. In scaling from 0 to 1, the aim should be for the team to have minimal dependencies on other teams. The first applications of ML in an organization will probably use tried-and-tested techniques, meaning deep, specialized ML knowledge is not required and a cross-functional team can be self-sufficient. In scaling from N to N + 1 for large N, we anticipate the product team can consume the specialized services of data and ML platforms as-a-service and has access to specialized enabling teams such as privacy. These dependencies are appropriate for fast flow at this scale. (Of course, it can also be self-sufficient.) Table 11-2 summarizes the strengths, weaknesses, and interaction modes of an ML product team.

Table 11-2. Strengths, weaknesses, and interaction modes of an ML product team

Strengths	Weaknesses	Interaction modes
End-to-end value delivery flow due to minimal intensive dependencies on other teams.	May lack deep expertise in ML techniques deployed. Multiple ML product teams are prone to operate in silos if they're not intentional about knowledge sharing.	Aim to minimize required interactions for the first product team, while new team typically consumes data or ML platform as-a-service and collaborates with established specialist enabling teams.

Figure 11-5 visualizes the typical topologies of an ML product team. ML product teams are shown as stream-aligned teams that directly serve an end-user or customer. The first instantiated product team will be largely autonomous, consuming only well-defined digital services (e.g., application hosting, observability), represented for simplicity as a *digital services* platform team. Beyond a certain scale, multiple ML product teams may also consume ML platform or data platform services designed to improve the flow of product development. The interaction with platform teams is as-a-service (as-a-service denoted as a dashed-line triangle).

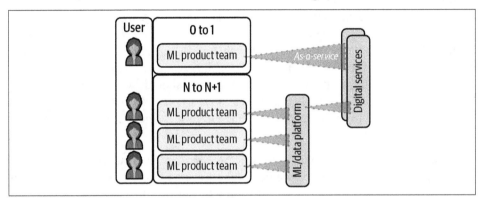

Figure 11-5. Visualization of typical topologies for ML product team

From the starting point of an ML product team, we now work inwards from the user to topologies that help ML organizations to scale.

Complicated subsystem team: ML domain team

Some ML applications are sufficiently complex, or the business advantage from superior ML performance is sufficiently great, that there is a justification for building a team of experts around the application of ML, such as retail forecasts or content recommendations. This is essentially an example of using the business domain fracture plane, though things like user personas, risk, and compliance are also valid and may be synonymous with domain in some cases. In this case, we consider a complicated subsystem team, comprising primarily domain, data science, ML, and data experts. The ML domain team makes its products (e.g., ML model, model predictions) available as-a-service to multiple stream-aligned product teams and other consuming teams in the business. In this respect, a product management capability is also highly desirable in the ML domain team.

This team type is one possible next stop on an organization's scaling journey, provided that the team (and supporting teams) can make these ML products available to internal consumers as a service, and they are not expected to serve consumers from many diverse areas of the business, as otherwise it is very easy for this team to become overwhelmed by context switching between the requirements of different domains, or the toil of manual maintenance of solutions, or both. If a complicated subsystem team is servicing a wide range of business domains, we would instead call it a centralized data science or ML team.

The reality of many so-called "centralized" data science or ML teams is that they are in fact domain teams—primarily servicing a single domain such as personalization—but have also attracted a long tail of additional use cases that make this topology less effective because the demands and interactions with other teams proliferate beyond what is manageable. Sometimes, centralized teams don't have much diversity in functional roles (e.g., they comprise only data scientists), which means that they have little hope of supporting other teams through as-a-service interactions (e.g., they cannot deploy a model as a reliable service that meets enterprise SLAs). In this case, these teams should arguably be considered enabling teams (more on that below) that will act in facilitation mode, or the team topology should be redesigned to make the team more cross-functional so that it can better enhance flow. We see that when organizations fail to properly manage interaction modes, they limit the effectiveness of "centralized" teams.

To address the toil of manual solutions, the ML domain team should focus on tooling or platforms that automate much of the serving of inference and retraining or maintenance of models "in the wild," providing these capabilities as-a-service to consumers. This creates capacity for the high-quality development of new models, which requires intensive collaboration. Table 11-3 summarizes the strengths, weaknesses, and interaction modes of an ML domain team.

Table 11-3. Strengths, weaknesses and interaction modes of an ML domain team

Strengths	Weaknesses	Interaction modes
Provides deep expertise in related ML disciplines and business domains, offering differentiated organizational capabilities.	Can be overwhelmed by the variety of requirements due to consumers from diverse business domains, or too heavy reliance on manual processes. Without cross-functional roles, may be a blocker.	Progress from collaboration to as-a-service delivery of models to consuming domain teams (see Figure 11-6). May consume data and ML platforms where there are multiple domain teams.

Figure 11-6 visualizes the typical topologies of an ML domain team. Here, an ML domain team is shown as a complicated subsystem team. The visualization shows one ML domain team supporting many product teams in multiple, evolving interaction modes, starting with collaboration and transitioning to as-a-service. This is to represent the maturity of the particular services provided. Another ML domain team is shown supporting further product teams as-a-service, presumably because its services are more mature. The ML domain teams also consume ML and data platforms to provide their more domain-specific services to product teams. The visualization also shows that the aim is for the ML domain team to eventually consume platforms as-a-service but that they will also need to collaborate with platform teams as the platform services are evolved (see also the section "Platform team: ML and data platform team" on page 350).

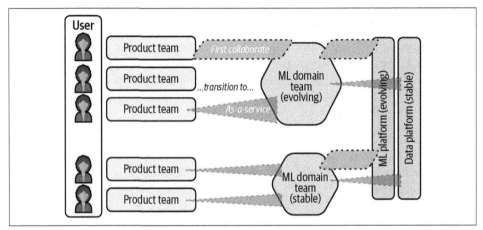

Figure 11-6. Visualization of typical topologies for ML domain team

At this point, we'd like to note the connection between Team Topologies and data mesh (*https://oreil.ly/f5lDN*). In general, where data mesh defines a logical data model for (part of) an enterprise in terms of data products and their connections, Team Topologies defines a corresponding operating model in terms of teams and their connections. Conway's Law shows that it's natural and most productive for the two models (data and operating) to be aligned.

In this respect, the ML domain team can be seen as owners of *aggregate data products*. Aggregate data products are defined, in the context of data mesh, as those data products that are combined from multiple sources, and that may be used by multiple consumers, so they are neither strictly source-aligned nor consumer-aligned. An example we have seen in the wild is matched customer records across multiple sources (or "single view of customer," but we're specifically talking about the data product that identifies unique and potentially duplicated records). If ML domain teams are seen as owners of aggregate data products, then conversely, we may propose that sufficiently complex aggregate data products should be owned by complicated subsystem teams. Data mesh data product concepts (*https://oreil.ly/wYTCw*) such as discoverability and trustworthiness then provide additional guidance in reducing the toil of manually serving many consumers.

We'd also like to note that in this section we've intentionally used the term "product team" to differentiate from "ML product team" in the stream-aligned team example. This is to highlight—when delivering a product or feature leveraging ML—that ML experience is necessarily embedded in a stream-aligned team with no dependencies, whereas it's optional in a product team that can interact with an ML domain team. Treat "ML product team" as a specialization of the generic "product team" type.

So far, we've seen platform teams supporting both ML product teams and ML domain teams, so let's see next what platform teams look like.

Platform team: ML and data platform team

At some scale of product teams and domain teams, introducing common ML and data platform capabilities will greatly reduce the duplication of effort and accumulation of complex tech and data estates for teams building ML solutions. Common capabilities might include scalable infrastructure, feature stores, production monitoring, and data-labeling tools.

For example, we have seen the lack of a shared ML platform lead two different ML teams to spend several months of effort to independently roll their own feature store. If they had a shared ML platform at their disposal, both teams could have delivered outcomes several months sooner and reduced the size of the tech estate (i.e., infrastructure, pipelines, systems, and digital products) that both teams now have to maintain.

The fracture plane for a platform team may be thought of as a change in cadence, but with related associations. Multiple stream-aligned teams must adapt fast to their evolving understanding of customer preferences, whereas the underlying technology capabilities they draw on evolve more slowly. These underlying capabilities may also have different risk and performance profiles, and so on.

ML platform teams may deliver "sensible defaults" (aka best practices), accelerator tooling, or digital services backed by service-level agreements (SLAs). What they deliver is in support of consumers building ML solutions and depends on the extent of the need and the maturity of the organization. Platform teams will typically interact with their consumers in as-a-service mode, with targeted facilitation support. However, when they interact with "exemplar" early adopters of services, this may be primarily through collaboration, so that the platform team develops their understanding of the requirements of new services. The platform team will likely use these stages of sensible defaults, accelerators, and services to manage the lifecycle of the services they provide.

Picking the right time to build platforms is always fraught, as platforms can represent a sizable investment. Too early, and platform teams won't have a good understanding of their consumers' requirements, leading to low platform uptake (which in turn leads to the problems of too late). Too late, and you leave a lot of value on the table as teams are slower to market and the technology estate becomes more complex with many custom solutions. We propose the rule of three (*https://oreil.ly/zBQPR*) applied to ML product teams or domain teams, and we propose delivering platform features in thin slices through the platform services lifecycle, described in the preceding paragraph, to further manage risk. Spotify, for example, describes (*https://oreil.ly/Wplij*)

keeping the product vision broad and future-looking, and the product strategy concrete and iterative.

ML platforms and data platforms offer similar but distinct capabilities. ML product teams or domain teams may consume both. Organizations should use data platforms to make well-governed organizational data available for appropriate uses, and to support teams transforming and serving derived data products. An ML platform requires access to data and will be required to serve data, but organizations should focus ML platform teams on supporting the transformation of data and features using ML techniques and models, as well as specialized serving of derived data products, such as feature stores or model serving. ML platforms support ML models ultimately at inference time, but also leading up to that—at training time and even further back to exploratory analysis, experimentation with ML models, and data labeling.

A platform team is typically composed of infrastructure engineers, data engineers, ML engineers, and developers. Platform teams should include—as per ML domain teams—product management capability (*https://oreil.ly/1QnMH*) where there are many internal consumers and the goal is to design services that effectively and efficiently meet their needs. Table 11-4 summarizes the strengths, weaknesses, and interaction modes of an ML platform team.

Table 11-4. Strengths, weaknesses, and interaction modes of an ML platform team

Strengths	Weaknesses	Interaction modes
Provides efficiency at scale, improves speed to market and reduces cognitive load for product teams or domain teams	Benefits may not be realized if the timing of introduction is too early or too late, or if features are not consumer-centric	Progress from collaboration to as-a-service delivery of services, supported by facilitation

Platform teams are required at some scale to support many internal customers. They aim to interact as-a-service, which allows them to support many teams simultaneously on an ongoing basis. The final typical ML team shape we'll cover also serves many internal customers, but their interaction mode is more intensive, and so they tend to work with only one or two teams at any time to uplift their capability, and they timebox their interactions to scale their reach.

We'll look next at enabling teams in ML.

Enabling team: Specialists in some aspect of ML product development

Enabling ML teams evolve in similar patterns to ML platform teams, but with a focus on solving novel problems with their expertise, rather than automating rote work. Some digital enabling teams, such as architecture or security, may already exist in your organization. These enabling teams facilitate or collaborate on the work of other teams. ML product teams, ML domain teams, and ML platform teams will likely work with these existing enabling digital teams at some point in their journeys.

Again, at some scale, an organization will require more specialized enabling teams for deeper cross-functional ML concerns—concerns that are repeated across applications and products, and that benefit from shared experience rather than repeated point solutions—and this is where enabling ML teams come in. The fracture plane for an enabling team may be any of those identified earlier, any dimension where deeper expertise is needed case-by-case, but only temporarily or periodically.

Areas of ML specialization that enabling teams might support include privacy, ethics, and compute performance optimization. Enabling teams typically consist of subject matter experts, analysts, and functional peers of the roles in the teams to which they consult. In this way, they bring unique knowledge, problem-solving capabilities, and empathy and understanding of the work of other teams to the support they provide. These roles are likely supported by other roles that aid the team to interact effectively with the enabling teams' clients ("client teams" for short), such as project management, communications, and learning and development experts.

If there is not enough demand to sustain an entire enabling team, then it is likely these roles will either be embedded in the most appropriate ML product team or ML domain team, or in the most appropriate enabling digital team for technology across the organization. In this case, individuals embedded in varied teams may form a "guild" or Community of Practice (CoP), as illustrated in Figure 11-7.

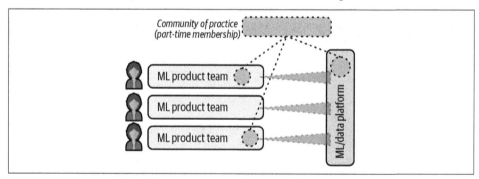

Figure 11-7. Community of Practice drawn from multiple teams

The ability of a CoP to do substantial work toward the flow of organizational value is limited, however, as the capacity of individuals involved is stretched across multiple objectives and their cognitive load is increased. CoPs are not an explicit construct in Team Topologies, but they are compared to enabling teams. CoPs nonetheless play valuable roles for organizations: as a key organizational "sensing" mechanism to detect where change might be required, and as a forum (*https://oreil.ly/osh1-*) that allows individuals to make productive connections—socially and for capability development—that benefit the organization. So typically, CoPs focus on building informal networks, and raising awareness, literacy, and capability around a topic. When instead, it's time to get something new done that is beyond the capability of a typical team, an enabling team is the right topology.

The aim of the enabling team should be in simple terms to "make themselves redundant" for a particular class of problem. A particular class of problem might move through phases, which will determine the enabling team's interaction mode. For novel problems, or "unknown unknowns," it's likely that intensive collaboration between the enabling team and a client team will be required to understand the problem and develop a custom solution. For familiar problems that don't have a common solution, or "known unknowns," the enabling team will facilitate a client team by sharing their knowledge of the problem space and similar solutions.

For common problems with common solutions, or "known knowns," the enabling team should systematize their knowledge (into a platform) to be provided as-a-service, which would involve collaboration with a platform team. Making themselves redundant for a class of problems allows the enabling team to continue to provide outsized value by solving novel problems in their area of expertise. Table 11-5 summarizes the strengths, weaknesses, and interaction modes of an enabling ML team.

Table 11-5. Strengths, weaknesses, and interaction modes of an enabling ML team

Strengths	Weaknesses	Interaction modes
A means for upskilling multiple teams and solving repeated but idiosyncratic problems in certain facets of ML product delivery.	Can only serve a small number of teams at any time due to intense interaction in collaboration.	Facilitation or collaboration.
	Requires a certain scale to be economical.	May also broadcast communications.
	Not to be confused with Community of Practice.	

Figure 11-8 shows a typical topology for an enabling ML team. The example used is an enabling team focused on helping teams adopt privacy best practices. This privacy-enabling team interacts with a number of ML product teams, in collaboration mode or facilitation mode. The enabling team may also collaborate with the platform team to systematize its knowledge and promote its capabilities to as-a-service interactions.

Now that you have seen some typical patterns, let's look at how these, in conjunction with the internal team considerations from earlier in the chapter, can be put to use for building effective teams at an organizational level.

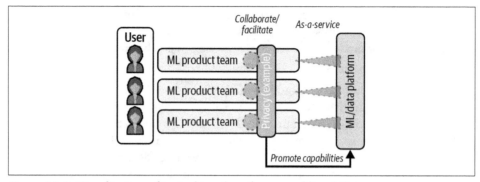

Figure 11-8. Visualization of typical topology for an enabling ML team

Combining and evolving topologies

While an objective of Team Topologies is to support long-lived teams to build effective teamwork over a period of time, an organization's Team Topologies are not static. In particular, as we saw earlier, the path to implementing an internal platform in some form is a key example of evolving services and interaction modes at the very least, and likely team shapes and overall topology, too.

There are many possible evolutionary pathways for ML team topologies. In Figure 11-9 we show, based on our experience, two pathways that might diverge and then converge again.

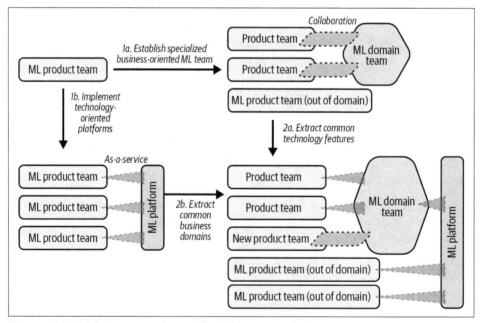

Figure 11-9. Evolutionary pathways for ML team topologies

Figure 11-9 shows path A as steps 1a and 2a and path B as steps 1b and 2b. Note that at step 1, both paths A and B intentionally show a similar scale of product teams. The choice of direction for step 1 depends on whether there is more leverage in standardizing technology components for many different business domains, or in building deep expertise in a business domain and related set of data science and ML techniques.

Beyond this scale, there is likely a need to provide both types of assistance to product teams, and it's also likely that these areas of commonality emerge (with the rule of three). Hence, in step 2, paths A and B converge again, to fill in the missing business or technology support.

On path A, where we've extracted a business domain first, we are likely to find that the domain team is suffering the toil of collaborating with and facilitating many product teams. In this case, the ML domain team needs assistance to automate the consumption of data and ML services, as well as to leverage platform services in the automated service of its own internal consumers (the product teams), and introducing ML platform features via a platform team supports this.

On path B, where we've extracted platform components first, we are likely to find that a one-size-fits-all solution doesn't reduce aggregate cognitive load as the number of teams increases, either because services are too low-level across different applications or because high-level abstractions don't apply to all applications. In this case, some cluster(s) of product teams will benefit from the higher-level business-oriented abstractions that can be provided by an ML domain team.

Note also that we might add enabling teams in what would typically be a similar pattern to platform teams, on the assumption of homogeneous needs across business domains. However, if the subject matter expertise is specific to certain areas of the business (e.g., if an organization has a regulated and an unregulated business), then an enabling team's interactions might look more like the complicated subsystem team example.

Changes like this might be driven by organic business growth or they might be due to merger and acquisition activity. Both cases present complex organizational change challenges in addition to the product delivery and technology challenges the evolving topologies aim to solve. While it's always an option to add an independent ML product team where there's no strong affinity to any existing platform or domain capability, the unbounded proliferation of disconnected ML product teams is also problematic. Just like the notion of technical debt (*https://oreil.ly/fnh8q*), we may make short-term trade-offs but we should be cognizant that these may become unsustainable if not actively managed. Wherever we decide to refactor multiple ML product teams, we can also keep in mind the two key dimensions for scaling:

a. Is there more benefit in providing deeper business-oriented solutions to multiple product teams with common needs?

b. Is there more benefit in consolidating technology support for reducing cognitive load and automating multiple ML workflows?

We've seen a range of canonical ML team topologies and how they have evolved over time. A recurring theme has been choosing interaction modes compatible with team shapes. This is where we can come back to the issue of trust between teams raised in Chapter 10. The best strategy for building and maintaining trust between teams depends on their interaction mode. For collaborating teams, which work like one big team, we should primarily consider the internal team factors of Chapter 10. For facilitating teams, which typically involve a transfer of expertise, in a consulting relationship, we might look to share prior experience in the field, clearly set expectations with client teams, and demonstrate the impact of the enabling team's work. As-as-service interactions are similarly based on setting clear expectations and demonstrating an ability to meet them, and in this case we should aim to precisely define and publish service levels, and monitor the satisfaction of those service levels, in order to maintain trust.

An example topology

Here we provide an example based on a hypothetical scenario where multiple product teams are adopting Generative AI solutions, which requires making some specialized knowledge available to teams that are responsible for elements of the user experience. This example is meant to illustrate how Team Topologies constructs can help us organize teams optimally. Figure 11-10 illustrates this scenario.

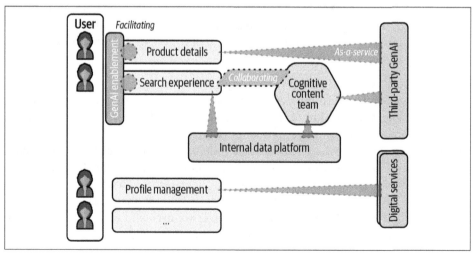

Figure 11-10. Multiple product teams adopting Generative AI solutions

Figure 11-10 shows two product teams that are currently adopting Generative AI solutions—Product Details and Search Experience—and further teams for which this isn't a current priority, including Profile Management. Product Details have only superficial Generative AI requirements (to summarize some structured product data), and they are able to use a third-party platform as-a-service to provide the required functionality. However, they must still adhere to the organization's Generative AI guardrails, and to this end, the enabling team facilitates their work, providing support and guidance. The enabling team is also facilitating the Search Experience team, but it limits its facilitation interactions to these two stream-aligned teams.

The Search Experience team has more demanding Generative AI requirements (including matching structured intents from unstructured search queries and supporting embedding-based vector search). To realize this functionality, this team is collaborating with the Cognitive Content Team, which help product teams develop custom solutions based on unstructured data (the Cognitive Content Team use embeddings as-a-service from the third-party Generative AI platform and support traditional NLP slot-filling techniques, among other things). Due to the complex nature of the work for Search Experience, they collaborate with Cognitive Content but this is the only collaboration either team is engaged in. Both Cognitive Content and Search Experience consume data as-a-service from the internal data platform. In general, while interactions in the other modes are tightly constrained, it's possible for teams to support many as-a-service interactions.

Phew! As we can see, different team shapes and different interaction modes are appropriate for different elements of the product development and organizational problems for which we are solving. Team Topologies provides a simple but rich language for describing a system in which each team can do good work aligned to their capabilities, and the teams collectively can achieve the desired outcomes.

Team Topologies is a great model for effective organizations that are able to flow value to their customers. However, like all useful models, it is also "wrong" (*https://oreil.ly/R11E6*). We think its issues are minor compared to its amazing utility and are easily remedied—such as the Community of Practice augmentation to enabling teams—but let's quickly review some shortcomings that we have experienced in applying Team Topologies (and that others have noted, too).

Limitations of Team Topologies

While Team Topologies is our go-to model for effectively scaling ML teams across an organization, we have experienced some limitations in applying the standard model. In this section, we'll describe one primary limitation that we haven't addressed and some further limitations that we've partially addressed.

Management team structures and reporting lines can cut across the teams that are designed for fast flow, especially as coordination between disparate parts of an organization may be required to deliver data for ML models and to integrate ML models into products, and especially as Team Topologies evolve. This is the primary limitation. Management incentives can also sometimes work counter to the flow of value. We don't present a single solution here, as organizations vary significantly in this dimension, but we encourage each organization to ensure that management understands and can contribute productively to a Team Topologies implementation, and that this is a first-class concern for an effective ML organization.

Jurgen Appelo has noted this and a number of minor differences, easily reconciled (*https://oreil.ly/osh1-*), between his *unFIX* model and Team Topologies. In the context of ML teams and organizations, we will also highlight the important focus on *purpose* and pragmatically being able to accommodate *reteaming*, both of which we discussed in Chapter 10. This chapter also looked at one type of *forum*—the Community of Practice—that can augment the standard Team Topologies model but we also extol the virtues of striving for a simple model, uncluttered by many similar concerns, to simplify decision-making. The product practices discussed in Chapter 2, scaled here to *EDGE*, address further concerns. We think the other concerns are less relevant to ML organizations. We also think interaction modes remain a key concept for managing cognitive load and fast flow, particularly in the specialized environment of ML, which is overlooked in *unFIX*.

We hope that you also find the utility of Team Topologies far outweighs any shortcomings, and that you recognize some effective elements in practice within your organization. Additionally, we hope you recognize how you might evolve your topology to become yet more effective. In the following section, we'll share some tactics for doing this.

Organizational Tactics to Build Effective Teams

Now that you're equipped with principles and techniques from both our team-level building blocks and the broader building blocks of value-driven portfolio management and Team Topologies, let's revisit the challenging scenarios we covered at the start of this chapter and look at how we'd address them with what we've just learned regarding Team Topologies. Table 11-6 lists some tactics to address a selection of challenges.

Table 11-6. How to address team-related challenges using what we've learned so far

Challenge	Example	How to address this challenge
Inter-team dependencies: handoffs and waiting	Dana is in the data science team and her team is responsible for training ML models. Anaya is the team lead that owns the frontend and API that will serve the model.	Dana's team (a complicated subsystem team) is tightly coupled to Anaya's team (a stream-aligned team) and the two teams can't deliver value independently of each other.
	Dana just finished a story that improved the model performance by 5%, by including a new feature. However, before she could release the model to production, she needed to wait on Anaya's team to update the frontend and API to include the new feature when sending requests to a model.	We should identify a *fracture plane* around the capability that this model provides and support it with a *well-defined interface* that other teams (e.g., Anaya's team, and any other teams that wish to use this model) can consume on a *self-service basis*. This is typically a data product (*https://oreil.ly/mTEOK*), which can be consumed in real-time (e.g., via an API) or in batch (e.g., via a data warehouse query).
	Dana's story was sitting in the "waiting" column for weeks before it could be moved to "Done" (i.e., deployed to production).	When we do that, Dana's team can then deploy changes and model improvements to production on their own cadence. As the producer, Dana's team owns and is responsible for the quality of this software interface. It should have contract tests and use techniques such as expand-contract (*https://oreil.ly/qduqi*) to ensure that any breaking interface changes (e.g., adding a new input feature) are detected and managed properly.
Duplication of effort in multiple cross-functional teams	Ellie and Eduardo are both team leads in two different cross-functional teams—i.e., each of them owns a vertical slice of the product experience, including data engineering, model training, API, and UI deployments. Neither team needs to wait on or depend on anybody to deliver a feature to customers.	This is a classic case of Conway's Law—two tech stacks and architecture, reflecting the two distinct teams.
		This challenge is common in organizations where:
		• There isn't an ML platform.
		• The ML platform team isn't providing sufficient tooling, or the right tooling, or documentation and socialization of the platform tooling.
	However, both teams have independently spent significant effort in solving similar problems. For example, to solve the problem of provisioning scalable ML training infrastructure, Eduardo's team wrote some intricate DevOps scripts to provision and tear down GPU instances. Unknown to Eduardo, Ellie's team has integrated a GPU-as-a-service offering.	• There's no enabling team performing a similar role.
		This is where management and Communities of Practice have a role to play in fostering Aligned Autonomy (*https://oreil.ly/lnrsR*)—i.e., teams are autonomous, but are also aligned on goals and the methods they use to achieve their goals.
		This can then be a precursor for establishing enabling teams or engineering capacity to provide *ML platform capabilities* within the organization.

Challenge	Example	How to address this challenge
Centralized team has too many responsibilities	Dana and Ted, along with all the other ML practitioners in the organization, are rolled up into a central "data science team" to service all the ML needs of multiple cross-functional product engineering teams across the organization. Different projects and teams frequently depend on their team's expertise. One day, while Dana was deeply engrossed in refining a neural network's hyperparameters, the team was suddenly summoned to address deployment concerns for another model. Once that was settled and they returned to their original task, the team struggled to regain momentum. Projects begin to lag as they frequently hinge on the team's collective input, leading it to be perpetually spread thin, resulting in constant context switching, not being able to focus, and suffering a diminished capacity to excel in any single endeavor.	It's evident that this central "data science team" has exceeded a reasonable *cognitive load* for a team. We can consider dividing the team along any relevant *fracture planes* (such as domain boundaries) and *adding capacity* where needed, so that each team has the resources to create, maintain, and improve the respective ML capabilities within an organization (e.g. product recommendations, pricing). As before, each team will work toward quickly progressing from initial *collaborations* to well-defined *as-a-service interfaces* through which other parts of the organization can consume a particular ML capability (e.g., product recommendations) in a self-service manner, without the need for additional effort for each new consumer.

This has been a quick crash course of how Team Topologies concepts address common challenges that ML teams face. You will get a lot more out of this chapter if you read it in conjunction with the Team Topologies book, which gives more context for the model, more detailed guidance, and more comprehensive strategies. Think of this chapter as the ML "expansion pack" for *Team Topologies*!

Throughout the book, you've seen a lot of opportunities to change teams for the better. The final topic we cover explores the role leadership plays in making change happen.

Intentional Leadership

We couldn't conclude a chapter on effective teams without talking about the role of intentional leadership. Many of the practices in this chapter can be advocated by anyone on the team. However, some interventions, such as setting an organizational mission or reconfiguring team shapes, depend on the influence and resources commanded by formally appointed leaders. These may be leaders at various levels and with various functional specializations—tech lead, engineering manager, product or analytics manager, or executive leader. Whichever leadership role we consider, they have at least one thing in common: They lead a team.

In all instances, a leader should model the values and behaviors they expect from their team. For instance, a leader won't be the most knowledgeable person in the team in every dimension of their work, and they can use this to demonstrate vulnerability, model curiosity, instill a learning culture, productively resolve ambiguity, and respond practically to failures in ways that are positive for the team.

Leaders also have a role to play outside the team, in engaging stakeholders and coordinating organizational resources for the team. ML teams present particular challenges in this regard. Their work is sometimes unpredictable, with many dependencies, and their solutions are often complex and full of trade-offs. Leaders' outward engagement with the rest of the organization should create the space for their teams to do great work.

The following sections describe some key things leaders can do to enable effective ML teams.

Create Structures and Systems for Effective Teams

Since Chapter 1, we've established that the delivery of ML solutions requires a system of capabilities. At a high-level, any team that wants to deliver successful products needs to consider three subsystems (*https://oreil.ly/eJNiL*):

- From a *product* point of view, a team needs to produce something worthwhile for customers and for the business. That is the team's primary purpose of existence—to create something valuable for customers.

- From a *technical* standpoint, the team also needs to be able to deliver fit-for-purpose, high-quality products and services without accumulating overwhelming and crushing complexity.

- From a *people* perspective, team members need to be equipped with clear objectives, tools, knowledge, supporting processes, safety, autonomy, and purpose. Where entropy sets in, we need to foster alignment to ensure the team is steering in the same direction.

These three subsystems correspond to building the right thing, building the thing right, and building it in a way that is right for people.

Throughout this book, we've laid out principles and practices that help teams create structures and systems of work. It's a leader's role to help their team succeed by ensuring that these systems are in place, continually improving them, and that team members understand why and how these systems help them build great products. This means leaders need to be able to adopt directive and coordinating styles in some instances, coaching and enabling styles in other instances ("situational leadership"). In further instances, it's a leader's role to boldly challenge the status quo where there might be a better path.

Engage Stakeholders and Coordinate Organizational Resources

ML leaders need a specific set of skills (or be able to collaborate with teammates with the skills) to communicate ML models to stakeholders. ML models are often opaque boxes that are not inherently explainable. Models are never 100% correct, so there are always some failures, the cost of which needs to be understood. Leaders need to care about developing the right measures, and allowing stakeholders to develop trust in those measures and what they reveal about the model's performance.

ML leaders also need to be adept at communicating ML delivery, which is characterized by unpredictable experimentation and many dependencies on other teams. This requires leaders to bring the rest of the organization on a journey with them, clearly articulating what's required to get started (end-to-end ML infrastructure), what progress looks like (probably a collection of incremental gains made by experimenting with a range of different model-centric and data-centric approaches), and what role other teams (such as data providers) play in making the endeavor a success.

Cultivate Psychological Safety

If trust can be described as "how much I believe my team members will do what they say they'll do," psychological safety (*https://oreil.ly/gkD6z*) is "the belief that I will not be punished or humiliated for speaking up with ideas, questions, concerns, or mistakes." The absence of psychological safety and trust can negatively impact our ability to do effective ML delivery, handle ambiguity, share new ideas, and even find innovative solutions to business problems. It's amazing how many breakthroughs are made and problems avoided by the simple question, "Why?" But it goes unasked without psychological safety.

Psychological safety can be described in four stages, as defined by Timothy Clark in his book *The 4 Stages of Psychological Safety* (ReadHowYouWant):

- Inclusion safety: "I am worthy, I belong and I feel safe to be here."
- Learner safety: "I'm growing, it's safe for me to be a learner, I can ask questions and I can show up and not have all the answers."
- Contributor safety: "I am making a difference somewhere, and I feel it's safe to contribute my ideas, vision, hopes and dreams."
- Challenge safety: "It is safe for me to challenge the status quo and help to fix what's not working."

Leaders play a critical role in maintaining psychological safety among their teams, through leading by example, seeking input and expertise from the team, advocating for trying new things, being resilient in the face of failure and embracing it as a learning opportunity, and facilitating the dialogue for us to build the team culture we want to have.

Champion Continuous Improvement

The journey to excellence is unending, marked by a commitment to constant learning. Leaders who prioritize continuous improvement recognize that both successes and failures offer insights that can refine a team's processes, practices, and dynamics.

A leader helps to set the tone and lead by example in modeling desirable behaviors within a team. By demonstrating they care about continuous improvement, leaders ensure improvement actually happens, and teams are not just going through the motions with these ceremonies (recall the story about essence versus form at NUMMI in Chapter 10).

Some techniques that help make continuous improvement real and habitual—not just good intent and ad hoc changes—through following a structured process include the Plan-Do-Check-Act (PDCA) cycle (*https://oreil.ly/F6cOF*) or a version specifically tailored to continuous improvement called the Improvement Kata (*https://oreil.ly/OVpq1*). Both work through regular assessment of the current state, setting a new target state, taking small actions toward the new target state, evaluating their impact, and repeating.

Embrace Failure as a Learning Opportunity

Leaders set the emotional and cultural tone for their teams. When a leader embraces failure as a learning opportunity, it cultivates an environment where innovation and calculated risk-taking is encouraged.

By highlighting the instructive power of setbacks, a leader ensures that the team doesn't become paralyzed by the fear of making mistakes. Instead, failures become springboards for growth, fostering resilience, adaptability, and a solutions-focused mindset. This approach not only accelerates the learning curve but also deepens trust and collaboration within the team, as members feel safe to share their challenges and learn collectively.

In any case, if we've leveraged the product discovery and engineering practices in this book, failures should be low-cost. By lowering the cost of failures, these practices create a safe-to-fail environment where teams can experiment and learn rapidly.

Build the Culture We Wish We Had

Culture isn't an abstract concept but "the way we do things around here." It's a tangible, daily reality that influences team dynamics, decision-making processes, and overall productivity. Leaders play a pivotal role in shaping this culture, not just through policies or mission statements but through their daily actions, reactions, and interactions—how they "do things around here."

Building the culture we wish we had means envisioning the ideal environment that fosters creativity, collaboration, and well-being, and then actively working toward it. This might involve open dialogues about team values, addressing toxic behaviors, or introducing rituals that celebrate team camaraderie and milestones. By embodying the desired cultural traits and actively nurturing them, leaders can transform the abstract vision of an ideal team culture into a lived, shared reality for all members.

Encourage Teams to Play at Work

To pick a final leadership theme to take away, we choose playfulness. Play may sound unserious, but as comedian John Cleese said, "Too many people confuse being serious with being solemn." Teams that are serious about effectiveness need to play. Play engages people more deeply in their work (*https://oreil.ly/BrPJy*) and is in fact essential for learning and creative problem solving. Indeed, what do the ML systems we are building do but play (rather inefficiently compared to humans) with many different parameters for solving a problem, in order to find those that fit best?[2]

The leaders' role is to model and guide playful behavior in teams. While some work-adjacent play, such as ping pong or Mario Kart, provides an important mental break and social activity, too much leaves no capacity for doing meaningful work. This is not the playful behavior a leader needs to model, and they should set appropriate boundaries on this type of play at work. Instead, a leader should find and amplify opportunities for being playful in the course of understanding problems and developing effective and efficient solutions. It's not always an easy line to walk, but such is leadership.

This type of play must remain relevant and meaningful to the team. On hearing Principal Seymour Skinner's suggestion that "Licking envelopes can be fun... All you have to do is make a game of it...for example, you can see how many you can lick in an hour... Then try to break that record," we all, like Bart Simpson, may have thought "Sounds like a pretty crappy game to me." However, later in episode 4 of season 3, "Bart the Murderer" (*https://oreil.ly/PWvIL*), Seymour puts the same principle into action in a way that is highly relevant and meaningful, helping him to survive (the somewhat absurd situation of) being trapped under a pile of newspapers in his garage—"I made a game of [dribbling a nearby basketball with my one free hand], seeing how many times I could bounce the ball in a day, then trying to break that record." This is a great example of situational leadership through play, but hopefully not a situation you will have to deal with in your work!

---

2 In advocating play, we also recognize the seriousness of the consequences of poorly designed ML systems, which can result in exclusion and harm to marginalized and vulnerable people. We're not advocating play in ignorance of consequences. A willingness to play-act undesirable scenarios is one tool to educate technologists and stakeholders alike, and proactively anticipate such unintended consequences (*https://oreil.ly/-4anU*).

So, we see humor is a big part of play, and play is most effective when integrated with the work in a way that is meaningful for the people doing the work. Here are some examples of how we and our colleagues have played at work:

- Presented consulting recommendations like the pitch for a Pixar movie
- Held a showcase for a simulation tool that was run as a game show, where stakeholders tried to devise progressively more optimal solutions, which were then simulated and scored live—the winner took home a "prize pack"
- Shared whimsical side projects (*https://oreil.ly/443Kw*) like rubber duck–shaped gravitational fields, AI wheelie coaches, and predicting a pet cat's location with ML (*https://oreil.ly/KyI8a*)
- Created data visualizations with a serious performance improvement focus, but with fun pop culture themes, such as *Space Invaders* or *The Matrix*
- Devised lightly competitive coding katas based on COVID-19 disruptions, such as path planning in office environments while maintaining social distancing, or optimal allocation of tasks-to-children in remote schooling (or is it still too soon to raise this?)

These are all things your team might do anyway, that can be made far more engaging with a little playfulness. Play can help contribute to improved psychological safety, find improvement opportunities, make sense of failures and aid the consequent learning. It can be integral to team culture—all the other things we've said leaders should drive in teams. We've covered a lot of heavy topics in the last two chapters, but they needn't weigh heavily on teams that can be playful. So, when you've finished this book, take this as encouragement to go forth and play at work!

W. Edwards Deming (*https://oreil.ly/D1r5Q*), a thought leader whose work has transformed modern management and quality control, once said, "The aim of leadership should be to improve the performance of man and machine, to improve quality, to increase output, and simultaneously to bring pride of workmanship to people. Put in a negative way, the aim of leadership is not merely to find and record failures of men, but to remove the causes of failure: *to help people to do a better job with less effort*."

If you're a leader, consider how these techniques can help you create the conditions for your team to amplify their collective expertise and achieve their goals.

With that, let's wrap up the final chapter of this book!

Conclusion

In Chapters 10 and 11, we've explored and expounded on the human and social aspects of inhibitors and enablers toward our ultimate goal: cultivating effective ML teams to iteratively and reliably deliver customer value. We've summarized the goals, tenets, and techniques that we covered in Chapters 10 and 11 in Table 11-7.

Table 11-7. Summary of building blocks, frameworks, and tactics for effective ML teams covered in Chapters 10 and 11, including references to earlier chapters

Building block	Framework(s)	Tactics and references
Trust	• Daring Greatly (vulnerability) • Tuckman's Stages of Group Development • Belbin's Team Roles	• Team Charter • Showcase • Retrospectives • Feedback
Communication	• Models of communication • Crucial Conversations • Candor	• Visual management • Showcase • Feedback culture • Retrospectives
Purposeful, shared progress	• The Progress Principle • Autonomy • Mastery • Purpose	• Visual management • Personal Canvas • Iteration Planning • Shorten feedback loops (→ Chapters 1–9)
Diverse membership	• Diversity Wheel • Belbin's Team Roles • Cross-functional teams	• Team Charter • People team support • Cross-functional roles (→ Chapter 1)
Team flow	• Engineering Effectiveness • Developer Experience	• Manage cognitive loads (→ Chapters 1–9) • Shorten feedback loops (→ Chapters 1–9) • Maintain flow state (→ Chapters 1–9)
Organizational flow	• Team Topologies	• Value-Driven Portfolio Management • Team shapes and interaction modes • ML product teams • ML domain teams • ML platform teams • Enabling ML teams • Evolving topologies
Intentional leadership	• Psychological safety • Continuous improvement • Resilient culture	• Leading by example • Systems Thinking • Improvement Kata • Celebrate learning from failure and celebrate success!

And now, congratulations on finishing *Effective Machine Learning Teams*! As we've mentioned before, this book is informed by our practical experience working with various companies to deliver ML products. We hope you appreciated our journey around the winding contours and many pitfalls of ML, as well as our guidance on paved roads for building teams and delivering ML solutions.

We hope that you'll put these techniques into practice in your ML projects—we know we will continue to do so—to reduce feedback latency, lower the cost of failures, and iteratively deliver…you know the rest of it by now! And we hope that you'll write and speak about your experience and continue to add to our collective wisdom as a global community of ML practitioners.

Epilogue: Dana's Journey

As Dana geared up for the next ML product lined up for her team, she resolved to learn from her past experiences—both highs and lows—and to nurture a high-trust, high-performing team that relishes delivering value early and often and learning continuously.

She knew the importance of cross-functional capabilities—product, engineering, ML, delivery, and data—that it takes to build a great product. She also knew that she couldn't do it alone and that leaders like herself needed to align on principles, practices, and processes to cultivate such teams.

Following a discovery and inception, she and her team had a clear vision of what they were building and why customers would find it valuable. ML practitioners in her team began to deliver value in small batches and build quality in through Lean engineering practices. They took W. Edward Deming's wisdom to heart and eliminated the need for belated inspection in large batch sizes by building quality into the product in the first place. Manual testing and production alerts became lesser over time, and her team began to feel the power, speed, and joy of small wins in delivering value and getting feedback in every iteration. All the time she reclaimed from such tedium meant that after her office hours, she could devote energy to other parts of her life—family, community, personal well-being, and indeed, living life itself.[3]

---

3 Say no to workism! An inspiring read: *The Good Enough Job: Reclaiming Life from Work* by Simone Stolzoff (Portfolio).

Dana and her peers also started small, taking intentional steps and opening channels of communication that encouraged them to share their challenges and successes. They set up regular show-and-tell sessions, not just for triumphs but for failures, too, normalizing the learning process inherent in building ML systems.

It's not a "happily ever after" story, though. There were still legacy systems that created unplanned work, new problems that seemed untestable, challenging individuals, and crucial conversations to be had. But she and her team had a trusted set of tools and techniques to call on, and were adequately resourced to decompose problems and work as a team to find a way forward.

There was always something new to learn, some new challenge to overcome, especially in the fast-moving world of ML and AI. Doing it alone was a solitary slog, but Dana was glad that she was on a team of aligned practitioners that knew where they were going, had the tools and techniques to get them there, and could deliver value rapidly, reliably, and responsibly along the way.

Index

Symbols

80/20 rule, 261

A

A3 management techniques, 324
AAA (arrange, act, assert) structure, 152
abstraction, 235, 238, 253-255, 258
acceptance criteria, 62
Acquisition, Activation, Retention, Referral, Revenue (AARRR), 76
active learning, 29
ADRs (Architecture Decision Records), 72
aggregate data products, 349
agile principles, 75
AI-assisted coding, 202
AIAAIC (AI, Algorithmic, and Automation Incidents and Controversies) repository, 294
alpha releases, 74
AMD64 versus ARM64 instruction sets, 93
Anna Karenina principle, 301
Anti-corruption Layer pattern, 258
API latency tests, 172
API tests, 143, 159-162
application monitoring, 194
application-level dependencies, 87, 95
application-level environment isolation, 89
architectural decisions, 72
Architecture Decision Records (ADRs), 72
arrange, act, assert (AAA) structure, 152
artifact stores, 274
"artificial artificial intelligence", 18
"as code" approach, 273
assertions, piecemeal, 161

assumptions, riskiest, 53
Atlassian's Product Delivery Framework, 39
auto-fix suggestions, 216
automated deployments, 290
automated fitness functions, 146
automated testing
    benefits of, 133, 136-139
    characteristics of good tests, 147-152
    as foundation for iteration, 135
    identifying components for testing, 143-146
    misconceptions concerning, 139-142
    ML model tests (see model tests)
    ML Systems Test Pyramid, 146
    shortening feedback loops with, 23
    software tests, 154-164
    test structure, 152
automation, 282, 290

B

backlog coupling, 20, 338
barriers to success, 3-6
batches, 282, 285
batect, 101-107, 115-118
behavioral tests, 144, 177-179
Belbin's Team Roles framework, 312
benchmark analysis, 92
benchmark tests, 183
beta releases, 74
bias testing, 176
Big Ball of Mud, 238
broad integration tests, 163
build-time caching mechanisms, 105
burn up chart, 74-76

C

D

HELM (Holistic Evaluation of Language Models), 183
hidden state, avoiding traps of, 240
hidden stratification problem, 173
high-effectiveness environments, 7-10
Hofstadter's Law, 76
Hofstede's Cultural Dimensions Theory, 314
Holistic Evaluation of Language Models (HELM), 183
host (Docker), 99
Hypothesis Canvas, 26, 49

I

IaC (infrastructure-as-code) tools, 290
IDE (see integrated development environments)
images (Docker), 98
impediments to success, 6
imperative shell, 155
Improvement Kata, 363
Inception artifacts, 60
Inception phase
   basics of, 56
   planning and running, 58-61
   user stories, 61-69
incidental complexity, 328
infrastructure-as-code (IaC) tools, 290
infrequent deployments, 277
injection attacks, 59
inline documentation, 215
instruction sets, 93-95
integrated development environments (IDEs)
   configuring, 207-214
   definition of term, 201
   effective coding with, 204
   example IDE, 202
   keyboard shortcuts, 214-226
   "Know Your IDE" principle, 205
   navigation shortcuts, 208, 223-226
   refactoring and, 238
   underutilization of, 203
integration test, 158
IntelliSense, 214
intentional leadership
   building culture, 363
   continuous improvement, 363
   embracing failure, 363
   encouraging teams to play at work, 364
   psychological safety, 362

role of formally appointed leaders, 360
stakeholders and resources, 362
structures and systems for effective teams, 361
inter-team dependencies, 338
interactive digital prototypes, 51
interfaces, 236, 258
interpersonal communication, 315
invariance tests, 177
Inverse Conway Maneuver, 20
INVEST principles, 65
iteration planning, 70, 324
iterative improvements, 295
iterative prototyping, 52

K

Kaizen, 283, 292, 296
Kanban boards, 324
keyboard shortcuts, 204, 214-226
knowledge sharing, 286

L

label shift, 187
large language models (LLMs), xiv, 30, 179-184
lead UX specialists, 44
leadership (see intentional leadership)
Lean Canvas, 17
Lean principles, 13-15
Lean Value Tree, 340
least privilege, principle of, 29
LIME (local interpretable model-agnostic explanations), 186
lines, moving and copying, 217
linting, 216
living documentation, 138
LLM-based tests, 184 (see also large language models)
local interpretable model-agnostic explanations (LIME), 186
low-effectiveness environments, 6, 8

M

machine learning (ML)
   continued optimism in, 2
   five disciplines for effective delivery, 13-32
   MLOps practices and, 10
   systems thinking approach for, 11-12
   why projects fail, 2-10

About the Authors

David Tan is a senior ML engineer. He has worked on multiple data and machine learning projects and applied time-tested software engineering practices to help teams iterate more quickly and reliably in the machine learning development lifecycle.

Ada Leung is a senior business analyst and product owner at Thoughtworks. She has delivery and advisory experience across technology, business, and government services. Her experience includes breaking down complex problems in varying domains, including customer-facing applications, scaling of ML solutions, and more recently, data strategy and delivery of data platforms. She has been part of exemplar cross-functional delivery teams, both in-person and remotely, and is an advocate of cultivation as a way to build high-performing teams.

David "Dave" Colls is a technology leader with broad experience helping software and data teams deliver great results. David's technical background is in engineering design, simulation, optimization, and large-scale data-processing software. At Thoughtworks, he has led numerous agile and Lean transformation projects, and most recently he established the Data and AI practice in Australia. In his practice leadership role, he develops new ML services, consults on ML strategy, and provides leadership to the delivery of ML initiatives.

Colophon

The animals on the cover of *Effective Machine Learning Teams* are bishop birds. Bishops constitute several species of small African, passerine birds belonging to the genus *Euplectes* in the weaver family (*Ploceidae*), so named for the intricately woven nests created by its members.

While all bishops are native to Africa south of the Sahara, they are otherwise distributed fairly widely across the continent, with the southern red bishop appearing south of the equator in countries such as Mozambique, Zimbabwe, Eswatini, Lesotho, and South Africa, and the northern red bishop appearing north of the equator in Nigeria, Ethiopia, Ghana, and neighboring countries, to name two examples.

Among bishops, the plumage of breeding males tends to include bright coloration, though the color may vary depending on the species—from the dazzling red or orange of the southern red bishop, to the brilliant yellow of the yellow-crowned bishop. Nonbreeding males and females tend to be more nondescript, often having mostly brown or buff coloration, making it sometimes difficult to distinguish between species.

Bishops and their widowbird relatives in the genus *Euplectes* are believed to be polygynous, with males having more than one female mate at a time. Males are known to perform a display flight to attract a mate. When choosing their mates, females of the genus reportedly tend to choose males with longer tail lengths, even in species with comparatively shorter tails. Two to four eggs per season are ultimately laid in the birds' exquisite nests woven of grasses and other vegetation.

While there are more than 60 species in the genus *Euplectes*, all bishop bird species currently categorized by the IUCN (nine species) are considered of least concern from a conservation standpoint, due to stable populations. Many of the animals on O'Reilly covers are endangered; all of them are important to the world.

The cover illustration is by Karen Montgomery, based on an antique line engraving from Dover. The series design is by Edie Freedman, Ellie Volckhausen, and Karen Montgomery. The cover fonts are Gilroy Semibold and Guardian Sans. The text font is Adobe Minion Pro; the heading font is Adobe Myriad Condensed; and the code font is Dalton Maag's Ubuntu Mono.

O'REILLY®

Learn from experts.
Become one yourself.

Books | Live online courses
Instant answers | Virtual events
Videos | Interactive learning

Get started at oreilly.com.